THE ONE STATE REALITY

THE ONE STATE REALITY

What Is Israel/Palestine?

Edited by Michael Barnett, Nathan J. Brown, Marc Lynch, and Shibley Telhami

CORNELL UNIVERSITY PRESS ITHACA AND LONDON

First published 2023 by Cornell University Press

Library of Congress Cataloging-in-Publication Data

Names: Barnett, Michael N., 1960– editor. | Brown, Nathan J., editor. | Lynch, Marc, 1969– editor. | Telhami, Shibley, editor.
Title: The one state reality : what is Israel/Palestine? / edited by Michael Barnett, Nathan J. Brown, Marc Lynch, and Shibley Telhami.
Description: Ithaca : Cornell University Press, 2023. | Includes bibliographical references and index.
Identifiers: LCCN 2022039679 (print) | LCCN 2022039680 (ebook) | ISBN 9781501768392 (hardcover) | ISBN 9781501768408 (paperback) | ISBN 9781501768415 (pdf) | ISBN 9781501768422 (epub)
Subjects: LCSH: Arab-Israeli conflict. | Palestine—Politics and government—1948– | Israel—Politics and government.
Classification: LCC DS119.7 .O575 2023 (print) | LCC DS119.7 (ebook) | DDC 956.04—dc23/eng/20220823
LC record available at https://lccn.loc.gov/2022039679
LC ebook record available at https://lccn.loc.gov/2022039680

Contents

Preface

This book began with a random encounter in an elevator at the George Washington University's Elliott School of International Affairs. It was the spring of 2019 when GW colleagues Michael Barnett, Nathan Brown, and Marc Lynch began discussing the disconnect between academic and policy discussion about the Israeli-Palestinian peace process. That sounded like a perfect topic for a workshop under the auspices of Lynch's Project on Middle East Political Science (POMEPS), which regularly convenes gatherings of scholars to think collectively about thematic issues of interest to political science and to the broader public.

In October 2019, POMEPS convened a day-long workshop at the Elliott School with a wide range of scholars from diverse national and disciplinary backgrounds under a simple but provocative theme: "What is Israel/Palestine?" As the discussions evolved, it became clear that many—if not all—the participants were converging around a recognition that it was no longer possible to usefully think in terms of two states, incipient or otherwise. Israel and the territories occupied after 1967 were today governed by a single authority that was implemented in profoundly different ways across territory, citizenship, and identity. Most of the short essays produced for that workshop were ultimately published in June 2020 in the open-access journal *POMEPS STUDIES* under the title "Israel/Palestine: Exploring the One State Reality."

We all believed that there was far more to be done with this topic, given the deep disconnect between our conclusions and the still-prevailing views in the policy world. Shibley Telhami of the University of Maryland took the lead on the next step, a conference planned by the Anwar Sadat Chair Program for April 2020 that would bring many of the scholars from the POMEPS workshop together with leading figures in Washington's Middle East policy community. Participants were asked to write short papers that would ultimately be developed into the chapters of this book. Unfortunately, COVID interfered with our plans. We instead convened virtually over two days in August 2020 to discuss the short chapter notes and to develop a shared set of questions, if not answers. This book collects the fully realized chapters from those workshops.

As editors, we neither sought nor achieved consensus on critical policy issues or on controversial theoretical choices. We asked our authors not to offer policy recommendations or to express their normative preferences over what should be done or what should be. Instead, we asked them to describe Israel and Palestine as they are, in reality, from their own theoretical frameworks and research findings. This, we believe, is a vital first step toward developing effective policy interventions and productive research agendas. And we found some vindication as the ideas we had been developing among ourselves began to push forcefully into the public sphere, even sooner than we had anticipated, through the high global visibility of Palestinian struggles to resist the confiscation of their homes in East Jerusalem.

We benefited from the assistance of many people along the way, especially those who participated in our workshops. Jim Lance at Cornell University Press ushered the project into the publication phase, helped by thoughtful and constructive suggestions from outside reviewers and members of the Cornell University Press Faculty Board. In addition, we thank the following for their assistance along the way: Brittany Kyser and Kirsten Langlois at the University of Maryland; and Nora Palandjian, Stephanie Dahle, Prerna BalaEddy and Tessa Talebi at the Project on Middle East Political Science.

This volume represents a beginning, not an end, and it raises questions more than provides answers. We invite you to join those discussions as we collectively seek a path forward.

Michael Barnett, Nathan J. Brown,
Marc Lynch, Shibley Telhami

Introduction

WHAT IS ISRAEL/PALESTINE?

Michael Barnett, Nathan J. Brown, and Shibley Telhami

Israel/Palestine has always seemed to be in a state of becoming something else; for more than a century, the political status of the area has been contested by numerous parties, all working to make their vision a reality.[1] The premise of this volume is that viewing Israel/Palestine as in the process of becoming has obscured understanding it as a state of being. Today, the inhabitants of the territory are living a one state reality. Between the Mediterranean Sea and the Jordan River, there is one state that controls the entry and exit of people and goods, oversees security, and has the capacity to impose its decisions, laws, and policies. Over these decades the parties have spoken and often acted as if this were a temporary state of affairs. But a half-century defies most definitions of temporary: it has a permanence. We recognize that there are many who continue to want an alternative reality. We do not present this book to refute them but to focus on the reality that exists. We do recognize that a one state reality does not presume that it is a "solution" to the often-conflicting demands of Jewish and Palestinian nationalisms; indeed, the fact that the reality is not necessarily a solution allows many to cling to the hope that there will be a two state reality.

This volume is about the one state reality. When we began this project three years ago, we thought we were being bold. At that time much international discussion continued as if the status quo were temporary and headed, inevitably, toward a two state solution. But increasingly, a different tune can be heard: the status quo is being treated not as temporary but as permanent.[2] Our purpose is to aid in the reorientation of conversations—a reorientation already begun in different ways (and to very different degrees) in scholarly circles, in policy discussions, and in broader publics—toward understanding the current situation less as an interim stage and more as a settled reality. We do not deny the likelihood of change, but we gathered a group of specialists to think through the implications—and give more concrete meaning—to a perspective that the one state reality is not a future bogeyman or a fleeting interim step but an accurate description of well-established and even deeply entrenched existing arrangements. Our objectives in this introduction are to (1) explain that this approach, although it is spreading rapidly, is different from earlier ones that often tended to describe where matters were coming from or going to and treated the present implicitly as an interlude; (2) explore some of the reasons why it is more conceptually difficult than it may seem to be to analyze existing arrangements as a one state reality; (3) examine briefly the normative aspects of this kind of analysis; and (4) map out the rest of the volume. We hope that this volume, in its totality, will enable interested readers to better understand the implications of starting with a single state as a departure for analysis and understanding.

Shifting the prism of the two state solution to the one state reality has advantages (and some disadvantages that we consider later). It forces analysts to begin not with what they would like but rather with what is. In doing so, it does not necessarily remove the prescriptive and normative, but it gives greater weight to the descriptive, theoretical, and conceptual. The one state reality in this context forces a reconsideration of foundational concepts such as state, sovereignty, and nation. Moreover, by getting back to conceptual and theoretical basics, it facilitates discussions across political and intellectual divides. The focus on "reality" also encourages a different reading of history. Many of the chapters focus less on diplomatic struggles and so-called missed opportunities and more on the underlying conditions and trends that made some outcomes more likely than others. They are not about using the present to rewrite a deterministic reading of history but rather about becoming more attuned to forces and factors that were overlooked in more conventional interpretations of the conflict. Relatedly, an interesting development that has accompanied the rise of the one state reality is a wider consideration of different solutions, including complex confederations and a rediscovery of proposals, such as a binational state within a British empire, that died along the way.

In addition, asking about the one state reality can facilitate a more useful confrontation with uncomfortable and impolitic questions. For instance, is Israel/Palestine an "apartheid state"? We have more to say about this later, but casting Israel/Palestine as a one state reality raises difficult questions that a view of the situation as temporary allowed many to avoid; in particular, how an Israel with a Jewish identity will rule over a "minority" population that arguably now comprises the majority.

This introduction begins by offering an alternative history of Israel/Palestine that focuses on how the parties debated alternative visions at the time.[3] Most of these alternatives focused on either one or two states for two peoples—with several hybrids (such as confederation) also put forward. However, over the last couple of decades, the international conversation shifted strongly toward a two state solution. That idea remains quite popular in policy circles and still has some strong support in Israeli and Palestinian society in theory—but it is seen as increasingly improbable. A one state reality, viewed by many Israelis and supporters of Zionism—and by some advocates of Palestinian nationalism—as a disaster, is increasingly viewed as fated (or, as we claim, already here).[4]

After our quick historical overview, we offer some observations for why this reality has been so hard to see and what a one state reality means in the current context. The introduction and the entire volume adopt an analytical approach, attempting to be as clear as possible regarding the concepts, theories, and evidence that inform and support our observations. That said, we are writing about an area littered with emotional landmines—and we count ourselves among those who feel deeply about the issues. Accordingly, our third section of this introduction briefly addresses the challenges of making a scholarly contribution in an area where passions run deep and strong and where moral questions force themselves at every stage.

We conclude the introduction with an overview of the book's four parts. Part 1 examines the conceptual, theoretical, and historical bases for recognizing the one state reality; part 2 considers some of the state and nonstate practices that follow from the one state reality; part 3 draws from emerging trends to examine the responses by local, regional, and global actors to the one state reality, regardless of whether they declare its existence; and part 4 shifts attention to how policy makers make sense of and respond to this new reality. The conclusion provides retrospective and prospective analyses of past patterns and future possibilities.

An Alternative History of Alternatives

In the aftermath of World War I, "Palestine" became not merely a geographic, religious, or historical reference but a political unit, acknowledged as such internationally but with a future that was yet to be determined. At that moment it began a journey to becoming something else. This brief alternative history of alternative arrangements to the Israeli-Palestinian conflict considers the powerful political, religious, emotional, and at times messianic impulses that offered different visions of what was to become.

Even as "Palestine" as a political unit came into being, international, regional, and local discussions focused on what should become of that unit after the current interim phase. The League of Nations "awarded" a mandate to the United Kingdom with the instruction to develop "self-governing institutions"—although what the ultimate relationship of any subsequent entity would be with the British Empire was left unsaid. The Palestine Mandate also endorsed the development of a "Jewish national home," provided that "nothing should be done which might prejudice the civil and religious rights of existing non-Jewish communities in Palestine."[5] Zionists—those who advocated for a national home in Palestine—had different and sometimes conflicting ideas about what that home should look like. Zionism, of course, and Jewish settlements in Palestine preceded World War I and had roots in the late nineteenth century, largely driven by growing antisemitism in Europe and elsewhere. The rise of Nazism in Germany increased political demands to open Palestine to Jewish immigration. The Arab majority who inhabited that territory believed instead that Jewish immigration should be ended before it changed the demographic character of the land and that the Mandate should give way to an independent state—and the sooner the better. Palestinian concerns went beyond numbers, because Jewish settlement in Palestine was clearly aimed at establishing autonomous Jewish economic and political structures from the outset. In the broader Middle East, Arabs—having been divided into European spheres of influence by the Sykes-Picot agreements—expected regional independence, including in Palestine, after World War II.

The British Mandatory authorities often found that a step that satisfied one party outraged another. During the mandate period the British did attempt to build central institutions, but Zionist and Palestinian leaders tended to view such moves in part by what they suggested Palestine might become. As political contestation increased, the British established a string of commissions that proposed one alternative and then another; some were accepted as the basis of discussions by one side and not the other, and some were summarily rejected by both sides. The British found themselves forced to suppress direct challenges—a Palestinian rebellion in the late 1930s and a Jewish one in the 1940s—from those willing to push hard for their vision of an alternative future. It was in this period that various ideas, including the introduction of partitioning the territory, were advanced.

In the aftermath of World War II, an exhausted United Kingdom, rapidly losing the ability to retain its imperial presence in the Middle East and elsewhere, returned Palestine to the League of Nations' successor, the United Nations. The UN considered various proposals, many of which had been advanced and then rejected over the previous three decades, before endorsing a resolution to create Jewish and Palestinian states and an internationalized Jerusalem. But the UN

General Assembly resolution was a recommendation and without any enforcement mechanisms. When the mandate ended, Zionist leaders declared the establishment of a Jewish State of Israel. Most matters, including fundamental questions like constitution and borders, were left to be specified later—and have yet to be specified by the State of Israel. The new Israeli state presented its legitimacy as based in part on the UN resolution to partition Palestine. (The partition plan allocated 55% of mandate Palestine for a Jewish state, but at the end of the 1948 war, Israel came to control 78% of Palestine; after the 1967 War, it came to control all of Palestine). Palestinians—a term that came to refer to Arabs in the territory after a distinct Israeli nationality was established—and neighboring Arab states rejected that move and moved militarily against the newly declared state. Israel won the war. Hundreds of thousands of Palestinians fled or were forcibly removed, most as a result of an Israeli strategy to depopulate the Israeli-held territory of Palestinians and to keep them out; unable to return to their homes, the Palestinians became refugees. Jordan and Egypt controlled the remaining parts of mandatory Palestine: the West Bank and Gaza, respectively. Partition, though not the version outlined by the 1947 UN resolution, seemed to be the outcome. Israel and the Arab states agreed to armistice lines.

The war ended with an outcome that was somewhere between interim and permanent. Israel began the process of state-building, which involved critical issues regarding how to govern a society with socialist, religious, secular, and Western and Eastern communities. There were background debates regarding the purpose and identity of the Jewish state, but they always took a backseat to the enormous practical challenges at hand. Israel's population doubled in just a few years with the immigration of hundreds of thousands of Jews, including Holocaust survivors and Jews coming from Arab lands. Even the decision to write a constitution was postponed (permanently, it seems). Other unresolved questions left interim arrangements in place for a long period; for example, Palestinian citizens lived under martial law until 1966. Differences of opinion in Israeli society concerned not only domestic governance but also Israel's borders, with some Zionist and religious leaders believing that Israel remained incomplete without the holy sites in Jerusalem and the West Bank. But the Israeli government and most segments of Israeli society were either too consumed by state-building to care or were reasonably satisfied with the status quo. The Israeli state had an easier time establishing its authority and legitimacy at home than abroad. It did gain admission to the UN, but Arab states refused to recognize Israel. There were considerable international diplomatic efforts to turn the Israeli-Arab negotiations over boundaries into peace treaties and legal borders, but they failed; the most that could be gotten was an agreement on armistice lines, the functional equivalent of borders.

On the other side of the armistice lines, discussion about the relationship between the Arab world and Israel was even more wide-ranging and indeterminate. No Arab state accepted Israel as a sovereign state. Transjordan—the country on the other side of the Jordan River—annexed the West Bank, renamed itself Jordan, and granted West Bankers Jordanian citizenship. Its fellow Arab countries rejected the move. Some Palestinians met in Gaza in 1948 in an abortive effort to establish an "all Palestine government," rejecting partition but also establishing their own state; the statehood initiative received lip service support from some Arab states but soon fizzled. Egypt administered Gaza but made no effort to annex it. Some Palestinians in the diaspora established their own organizations and movements, in part to challenge Israel but also to assert a right for Palestinians to speak and act for themselves. The king of Jordan wanted to speak for Palestinians (at least for those it had granted citizenship), and Egypt's president Gamal Abdel Nasser took up the Palestinian cause during the era of Pan-Arabism, for which Palestine was projected to be a core issue. It was not until 1974, after the 1973 Arab-Israeli war, that the Arab League accepted the Palestinian Liberation Organization as the "sole, legitimate representative of the Palestinian people," giving Palestinians something far less than a state but at least an interim diplomatic presence. Palestinian refugees in other Arab countries were told that their rights could be redeemed in a future state of Palestine; in the meantime, their privileges would vary according to the needs and interests of the home country. It should not be surprising that most Palestinians seem to have combined an individual strategy of making do with a hope that something better would come along—and that something better increasingly took programmatic form as nationalist Palestinian leaders and structures slowly took root and debated concepts like a "secular democratic state in all of Palestine." Conceptual thinking about the future did not seem to shape realities on the ground, however.

In 1967, the ground shifted dramatically—but in a way that only deepened the determination of most actors to think about different futures. Indeed, the war itself was a product of the indeterminacy of the status quo. The idea that existing arrangements were permanent had few adherents on either side of the conflict, although many leaders were too cautious to push boldly for change. But leaders are not always cautious, and in 1967 a cycle of escalating action and rhetoric preceded a short but dramatic war. The Israeli government that initiated hostilities portrayed its actions as stemming from self-defense against hostile actions and threats, but there were certainly voices within Israeli leadership who saw the time as opportune to amend the outcome of 1948 in a decisive manner. In the war itself, Israel took control of the West Bank and Gaza, neither annexing nor withdrawing from the territory as ceasefires replaced the pre-1967 armistice arrangements. Israel also occupied parts of Egypt and Syria. The war was followed by renewed vigor for international diplomacy, resulting in more verbal formulas pointing toward resolution—but not ones that resulted in any immediate change in the situation on the ground. Most notably, Resolution 242 called for Israeli withdrawal from occupied territories while demanding Arab acceptance of Israel's right to live in peace and security.

Internally, Israelis argued with each other about the future of the West Bank and Gaza and the nature and boundaries of the Israeli state. Israel was reserved with words but active on the ground: it annexed those parts of the West Bank that included Jerusalem and its suburbs, removed any barriers at the old armistice lines, set up interim arrangements to govern the West Bank and Gaza, subsidized the construction of towns and cities for Jews in the territory, declared the intent to annex large parts of the West Bank, and ultimately decided to . . .

Up to the present, it has been impossible to complete the previous sentence. The "occupation" of those territories continues to evolve in form without any authoritative statement from Israel about its claims or even wishes. Yet again, it is important to stress that, although Israel as a state did not lay down any borders or make any clear claims asserting or abjuring sovereignty over the West Bank and Gaza, individual Israelis were much more definitive about their preferred outcome. One of the central divisions in Israeli political life centered on whether to come to terms with Palestinians as a nation and, if so, on what conditions: indeed, Israeli leaders accepting some kind of self-rule for Palestinians in a part of mandatory Palestine did appear to be guiding Israel to that outcome for a time, especially in the 1990s.

Arab countries were also divided on how to respond to the changes wrought by the 1967 War. With Israel in possession of territory claimed by Egypt, Jordan, and Syria, the status quo was less tolerable as a modus vivendi. That led to a very slow and uneven process of diplomatic activity: Egypt and Jordan eventually signed bilateral peace treaties with Israel, Jordan abandoned its claims to the West Bank, and Arab states recognized the PLO as "the sole legitimate representative of the Palestinian people" in 1974, as mentioned earlier. The PLO in turn was gradually able to secure acceptance as the international interlocutor for Palestinians, as it became increasingly recognized as a national group (albeit one without a state). But although those long-term trends are clear in retrospect, every step in that direction was bitterly contested, in large part because each one reflected deeply different versions of what Israel/Palestine should be. Egypt was suspended by the Arab League when it signed its bilateral peace with Israel in 1979; some Palestinian groups pushed for revolutionary change in the Arab world (precipitating a civil war in Jordan in 1970) out of fear that what they saw as corrupt Arab regimes were unable to reverse any part of the outcome of their 1967 defeat.

In this post-1967 period, Palestinian society and leadership maintained a collective position of refusing to recognize the State of Israel and, with it, any idea of a territorial compromise based on the pre-armistice lines. Behind the scenes, however, there was considerable division and debate among the Palestinian leadership regarding both the tactics and the goals for the Palestinian national struggle. Although often viewed as trivial and deceptive by Israel and the United States at the time, the PLO signaled its potential willingness to accept the idea of a Palestinian state in part of mandatory Palestine, alongside an Israeli state. Based in exile, the PLO was pulled toward a two state possibility by an emerging Palestinian leadership coming from the Israeli-occupied territories, who were generally loyal in principle to it; however, many felt the daily onus of occupation and were often more willing to compromise on long-standing aspirations. The PLO then smashed all its previous red lines with the Oslo Accords, recognizing Israel—and securing recognition in return as an interlocutor for Israel but involving no move toward a permanent settlement other than the promise of negotiations. By signing the Accords, the PLO decisively shifted its goal toward a two state solution. Israel and the United States were often seen as implicitly making the same shift, but it took them years to say so publicly. Eventually Arab states collectively endorsed such a vision in the Arab Peace Initiative of 2002. These parallel—if fitful and contentious—steps toward partition into two states became the basis for diplomatic efforts.

Although the parties' embrace of an outline of a two state solution seemed to have sprinted ahead of what some of their champions wanted, in many respects they were drawing on international precedents. In addition to the 1947 partition plan, the UN Security Council passed Resolution 242 the month after the 1967 War: it called on Israel to withdraw from territories it occupied in that war, reaffirmed the inadmissibility of territorial acquisition by force, and restated Israel's legitimacy and right to security and peace. Whether Israel was expected to return every inch of captured territory became a matter of dueling interpretations. Importantly, Resolution 242 seemed to implicitly legitimize Israel's 1949 armistice line as Israel's boundary, while also defining the West Bank and Gaza as occupied territories from which Israel was obligated to withdraw. But what would emerge if the Israelis withdrew? It took more than a generation to answer that question, and that answer—a Palestinian state alongside Israel—may have come too late. How did an outcome that so many had rejected for so long become officially embraced? And why did this embrace come too late to be realized?

In the 1960s and 1970s none of the parties accepted the two state solution, although there were those within various camps moving in that direction. A collection of events made the two state advocates gradually bolder in the quarter-century after the 1967 War. Among many Palestinians it was despair over any other possibility, grudging and gradual Arab acceptance of the exit of Egypt as a military challenge to Israel, fear felt by the PLO leadership that Palestinians in the West Bank and Gaza would cut a separate deal, loss of Gulf financial support because of the PLO's perceived tilt toward Iraq in the 1990–1991 war, and the end of the Cold War and thus any hope that Soviet diplomacy would compensate for Arab weakness. Among many Israelis it was the grueling nature of the first Palestinian uprising beginning in 1987, the fear that an ascendant Iran would use the Palestinian issue to pose a security challenge that Arab states no longer seemed able or willing to mount, and the prospect of full international diplomatic acceptance, even in the region.

In the 1980s and early 1990s, Israeli and Palestinian leaders moved increasingly to voice the language of territorial compromise, leaving many with a cautious optimism, despite the tragic and bloody history of the conflict that seemed to be set to an endless cycle of repeats. Perhaps peaceful change ending with two sovereign states was possible. But the formula of a "two state solution" elided many difficult issues: what would be the status of East Jerusalem, which Israel had annexed but which Palestinian leaders insisted would be the capital of their state; what would happen to the large number of Israelis who were moving into territory occupied in 1967; what provisions could be made for Palestinians made stateless by the 1948 outcome, scattered throughout the region and the world; what would be the precise border between Israel and Palestine; and whether Palestine would be a real state or a truncated pretender unable to control its borders and security.

Yet there was sufficient interest to allow diplomacy to begin and, in the early 1990s, to enable direct negotiations between Israel and the PLO. During much of the 1990s, an Israeli-Palestinian peace process—clearly identifiable as such with rounds of negotiations among national leaders from both sides, generally under US auspices—produced a series of interim agreements, under the umbrella of the 1993 Oslo Accords. These Accords sidestepped all these thorny issues, only listing those needing resolution, while holding out the prospect of a "final status agreement." The phrase "peace process" was used to suggest that negotiations would build the trust necessary to snowball into such an agreement. That did not happen. Instead, stalled negotiations, frozen agreements, and then renewed violence in 2000 gave way to deepening mistrust not only at the level of leadership but also deeply penetrating both societies. The negotiations themselves took place not between two equal entities but between two vastly unequal parties: one powerful state and one nonstate actor whose leaders were themselves under occupation.

Oddly, it was only at that point that international diplomacy began openly to embrace the solution that had dared not speak its name: two states for two people. Among diplomats throughout the world, "two states" was suddenly framed as the only rational solution. And once it was rational, it became inevitable, almost to the point that those who were late to the party seemed to suggest that they were supporting it all along. United States and Israeli officials had studiously avoided referring to it until after the second intifada had erupted; indeed, George W. Bush was the first US official to use "Palestine" as a proper noun, and most of his predecessors even had avoided the word "Palestinian." But by the early 2000s, US officials began to speak of the two state solution as if it had obviously been the endpoint of diplomacy for years; informally, many frequently said, "The solution is known; it is just a question of how to get there." But speaking of it did not make it so. Not even a broadly endorsed "road map" led anywhere near a two state solution. Israeli leaders bobbed and weaved around the possibility of a Palestinian state, attaching so many qualifiers and conditions that they seemed to be speaking less of a state and more a series of townships. Palestinian leaders clung to the idea of a Palestinian state but increasingly lost their ability to lead Palestinians in any clear way toward that goal (or toward articulating any alternative). The United Nations and the European Union churned out endorsements; the Arab League rallied behind the idea—but international platitudes rang increasingly hollow.

Today it appears that the two state idea was already dead at the time it was so widely celebrated, as some—though not all—our contributors in this volume argue. Grappling with that reality is what brings us to assemble this book. So here we are, which is where? In the next section, we explore why that simple question can be difficult to answer.

A One State Reality?

There may seem to be an underlying hubris to our claim to be presenting the "reality" in contrast to those who are so fixated on one solution or another that they have difficulty seeing the present as it is. We are indeed suspicious of those arguments that begin with the desired outcome—usually a one or two state solution—and then proceed to write history in a way that leads to its desirability or inevitability. But it is also the confusing nature of the present, its nested ambiguities, and the difficulties of applying broad concepts to complicated situations that steer analysts away from understanding the current (and longstanding) reality as "one state." In this section we explore why ambiguities in the conceptual tools lead so many away from focusing on the reality we now claim should be seen as central. We acknowledge those ambiguities while still insisting on starting from a one state reality. Specifically, the idea of "one state" sounds simple, but it confronts analysts with a set of barriers built by three foundational concepts: state, sovereignty, and nation. Each one raises difficulties in the context of Israel/Palestine.

We start with the state because it is at the core of any consideration of a one state reality. Max Weber's definition of the state is the starting point for most discussions of contemporary political organization and authority: a "human community that (successfully) claims the monopoly of the legitimate use of physical force within a given territory."[6] A state needs to have this monopoly: there should be no rival source of the legitimate use of violence. Other actors may use violence, but it will never be considered legitimate. Legitimacy can have various bases, but in modern society, according to Weber, it is rational-legal authority (often translating into the rule of law) that originates from the state. Within a given territory this means that the community and its use of force are always spatially circumscribed: usually from the capital to the borders and back again. Weber's view that the state has legitimate force is central to the issue of control. Control can derive from the use or threat of force, but it also can exist because the community confers legitimacy and authority on the state; if the state has such attributes, control can be maintained without resorting to force. Control, capacity, and power are often viewed as variables that translate into different kinds of states. Strong states possess a monopoly of the use of force; an extensive and intensive administration and bureaucracy; and the ability to mobilize, direct, and extract from society; conversely, weak states are barely able to hang on. The idea of Israel as a one state reality highlights its control over a given territory.

Sovereignty is central to the modern world order, and states without sovereignty can seem to be an anomaly. It means that the state is the highest authority in international relations and that states profess to recognize the principle of noninterference. When one state recognizes another state's sovereignty, it recognizes that state's right to exist, treats its internal affairs as its own business, and accepts that no international authority trumps that of the state. Sovereignty gives a state various rights and privileges denied to other actors, such as the right to militarize and defend itself, as corollaries of its right to exist and thus foster its own survival. Historians of modern international history quickly interject at this moment that sovereignty has had many meanings over its life, depending on time and place, and point to various moments when the meaning and practice of sovereignty were hotly contested by states and others. For instance, because sovereignty is dependent on recognition by other states, international society has had different legal and political benchmarks for when recognition can be conferred and withheld. Sovereignty has been limited in other ways. Today it is not seen as giving states a license to engage in atrocity crimes and genocide; if they do, then they might forfeit their sovereignty, and other states may feel authorized to intervene to stop the killing.

Understood this way, "state" and "sovereignty" are powerful concepts at their core but often very hazy around their edges—and that haziness is especially intense in Israel/Palestine. It is quite common for scholars of international relations to use the cases of Israel and Palestine to demonstrate how sovereignty works in international society. In its early decades, Israel has struggled to assert its sovereignty precisely because many states, and especially its neighbors, refused to recognize its existence, even though it was admitted as a sovereign state to the United Nations. As of 2019, 162 of 193 states recognize the State of Israel; Arab states comprise the bulk of those who do not, though the 2020 Abraham Accords led the United Arab Emirates, Morocco, Bahrain, and Sudan to switch from nonrecognition to recognition. There are many reasons why more states do not recognize Israel's status as a sovereign state. Some nations, including many Arab states, claim that such recognition is dependent on the end to Israel's occupation and the creation of a Palestinian state. Others point to the ambiguity regarding Israel's borders, a situation that is Israel's own making: it has yet to declare what it believes are its borders, denies that any other sovereign entity exists within the boundaries of mandatory Palestine, and deploys a variety of legal arguments to justify a variety of state-like actions in the territory that it classifies as "disputed." Israel itself does not know—and actually seeks to obscure—where it begins and ends.

If Israel lives in some ambiguity, Palestine is in worse condition. Indeed, Palestine has never met the standards of modern sovereignty. It has declared independence and statehood on several occasions, beginning in 1948; over the past decade, Palestine was admitted into the United Nations (sort of, as a "non-member observer state") and signed on as a state to many international conventions. "Palestine" in some form (Palestinian Authority/State of Palestine/Palestinian Liberation Organization) is recognized by 138 of 193 states as of July 2019. This juridical recognition does not translate into being a state in anything closely resembling Weber's terms. It does not have control over its affairs, it has no authority over who comes and goes, it cannot raise an army to protect its borders, it cannot directly collect most of its own taxes, its people cannot become citizens, and it has an administration only in sharply defined realms and very limited geographic areas. So, it might be a state in terms of diplomatic rituals and declarations but not the sort of state that controls territory.

It should now be clear why our insistence on starting with "one state" as a reality might not have been an obvious choice. Stateness and sovereignty have been precisely at the center of contention, so "reality" might just as much be seen to lie in conflict—and in rival hopes for the future—as in "one state." Starting with Israel as a sovereign state hardly resolves ambiguities. Adding Palestine as a sovereign state does not add as much clarity as Palestinian leaders would like.

Our goal is not to deny these ambiguities but to avoid equating ambiguity with impermanence. Given that abstract concepts almost always fit awkwardly, which one is most revealing in this case? How best to consider the current reality? What is Israel/Palestine? What is that reality we need to face? We know a lot about the facts on the ground but have difficulty putting a name to them. And the difficulty of the naming process is partly conceptual and partly normative. Labeling and naming do important descriptive and analytical work, and these labels and names always contain normative elements and implications. We delve into the normative issues more fully in the next section, but for now we note that description can sound like and have elements of justification or denunciation. This is partly because of ideologies and beliefs that certain groups are entitled to having their own states: indeed, such a claim lies at the heart of almost all nationalisms.

That brings us to the third concept used in our analysis: nation. A nation, generically speaking, is a political community that is bound by a common history, language, religion, spirit, or sense of fate. What give the nation something of a special status in modern politics are the project of nationalism and its goal of statehood. In short, nationalism consists of a claim that a nation, with a collective identity and interests, exists and the belief that the nation's interests and self-determination are advanced by gaining or maintaining sovereignty or authority over a homeland. The concept of nation became attached to the state and sovereignty—so much so that the terms "nation" and "state" can sometimes be elided. The state is supposed to protect and represent the community within its boundaries, a community that is a nation. The nation as political community is also supposed to reside in a territory; therefore, the expectation is that it would fight not only for statehood but also to be recognized as sovereign by other members of international society. Nations without states cannot participate fully in international relations: they are exposed—and indeed it is precisely the fear of exposure to statelessness that has given powerful force to Zionism and Palestinian nationalism.

But again, the clarity of the concept maps onto a messy set of lived experiences. In common parlance, we may often slip between "nationality" and "citizenship" (and the terms can have overlapping meanings[7]), but Israelis and Palestinians can show us how fraught the path can be between nationhood, community, and belonging, on the one hand, and statehood, legal status, and juridical rights, on the other. Israel presents itself as the state of the Jewish nation, but there are non-Israeli Jews and non-Jewish Israelis. There are also non-Jewish non-Israelis who are governed by its laws, procedures, officials, and institutions. For their part, Palestinians comprise citizens of dozens of states (including Israel) and many stateless individuals who travel internationally (when they can) with a bewildering array of travel documents. Palestinian nationality—in the sense of identity—would seem to make a mockery of the idea that nationality and statehood normally (or normatively) coincide.

The ambiguities of nationhood are intense in the case of Israelis and Palestinians and Israel/Palestine, but that is in part because the word "nationalism" comprises some sharply different ideas. An analytical distinction is frequently made between civic and ethnic nationalism.[8] In ethnic nationalism, membership is determined by blood, lineage, kinship, and tribe. As Michael Ignatieff famously described, in this brand of nationalism "an individual's deepest attachments are inherited, not chosen."[9] States that subscribe to this form of nationalism favor one group over another. An alternative form of nationalism is based not on blood or heritage but rather on a shared civic character. "This nationalism," Ignatieff argues, "is called civic because it envisages the nation as a community of equal, rights-bearing citizens, united in patriotic attachment to a shared set of political practices and values."[10] In the early days of nation- and state-building, this meant transforming regional, religious, and ethnic identities into a unifying national identity.

For Zionists and Palestinians, nationalism prevails. But of what kind? That nationalism can take varied forms on each side. It tends toward the ethnic for Zionisms (the plural here is intentional because there has always been a debate about the nature of the nation at issue). Palestinian nationalisms, again in the plural, have not only shown a strong attachment to place—with a geographic component encompassing all residents that thus might bear some resemblance to civic nationalism—but also elements of emphasizing Arabness, indigeneity, and culture as much as shared national values. But for all the differences within and between the various camps, the focus has been on self-determination for a people, however that people is defined. Israeli and Palestinian leaders seek to build a world in which their nationalisms can be expressed by states, and states have nationality and citizenship laws that are based on legal categories, not inner feelings of belonging. The translation can be messy in the easiest of circumstances, and Israeli and Palestinian leaders do not live in the easiest of circumstances. With undetermined borders, dispersed populations, numerous individuals deemed to be members of the nation who value citizenship in another state, Jews who do not regard their Jewishness as national in nature, and Palestinians who cling to whatever kind of citizenship they have been able to obtain outside Palestine, nationalism seems every bit as complicated and contested terrain as state and sovereignty.

So, it is not mere blindness that leads so many analysts to focus on what various actors wish Israel/Palestine to become and to avoid treating entrenched realities as anything more than interim and ultimately untenable arrangements subject to further struggle or negotiation. We therefore do not dismiss their efforts as fundamentally misguided or without value. But we insist that despite the various meanings and practices that have arisen, they still coalesce to produce the reality of a single state and that this outcome has shown remarkable staying power.

Although we have written "Israel/Palestine" repeatedly to signal how these two entities have become intertwined, there is little question which one has the power and control over the other. When we talk about the one state reality, we are talking about an Israeli state that has a monopoly on the "legitimate" use of force in the territory; can mobilize, guide, and extract from society; and has a relatively well-developed administrative apparatus and bureaucracy. Israel has control from the Jordan River to the Mediterranean Sea. There are areas where its internal control is much more attenuated, most especially in Gaza, but even there it controls what (and who) goes in and comes out. A Palestinian state may exist in the minds of many, but it has none of the empirical attributes of a state.

Referring to Israel/Palestine as one state is built on these realities—and these realities are long-standing and have proven difficult, if not impossible, to dislodge. But we should also acknowledge that they are not absolute. The one state idea has considerable legitimacy with a significant percentage of its population, but this legitimacy varies widely among ethnic, national, and religious groups. And when we fold in our second concept, sovereignty, the situation seems even more contested. Israeli sovereignty over the territory it controlled before 1967 is widely (but not universally) accepted internationally: everything else is highly disputed. Also, as several of the chapters note, Israel has slowly extended its military, administrative, and civilian law to parts of the territories, but we doubt that the few who recognize Israeli sovereignty over Jerusalem are prepared to do the same if Israel annexes these additional lands. Palestine's sovereignty is recognized by 138 states, but this has translated into few rights or privileges.

One final point of caution. There are advantages and disadvantages to seeing the current reality in Israel/Palestine as a one state reality. We laid out some of the analytical advantages earlier. There are also ethical advantages. The implicitly temporary idea that it is occupation, not statehood, that is involved suggests that the current severe inequality between Jews and Palestinians under Israeli control is temporary and begs for the patience of international actors until a more equitable final status is attained. The hope that it will end can edge out the realization that this occupation has so far lasted more than a half-century. Seeing the reality as that of one state forces a more urgent attention to this severe inequality, increasingly labeled as apartheid (a term whose implications we explore later). The recognition also forces attention to the arguments of Jewish supremacists, who feel no need to justify forms of unequal control in lands that some see as bestowed to the Jews by God.

But there are also disadvantages. Even though Israel has often violated international law and norms, as well as UN resolutions, such as in building Jewish settlements in the West Bank, its actions have been at least slowed or constrained by the effort not to stray too far from international positions, at least in appearance. The framework of occupation and of two states in the making remains the standards by which the United Nations and international and regional actors judge Israeli and Palestinian behavior. The fact remains that when Israel builds new settlements in the West Bank, they are considered illegal by nearly all international actors. What happens if everyone starts seeing a one state reality? Does that supplant the legal occupation framework that has served as a reference guiding international judgments about Israeli and Palestinian behavior? How would one judge new Jewish settlements built on public West Bank lands, for example?

Acceptance of one state as a reality can create winners and losers in various ways. Theoretically, the very international actors who may find the construction of Israeli settlements in the West Bank more palatable under a one state paradigm would also be demanding full equality for Palestinians at the same time. But given Israeli supremacy on the ground, it is more likely that Israel could pick and choose what it implements; one can imagine the state seeing the new perception reality as license to construct more Jewish settlements while paying only lip service to equality. At a minimum, the international community would have to adopt new terms of reference because the existing ones would not suffice. And there are no guarantees that such terms would lead to an inequitable outcome, as the Middle East Scholar Barometer showed in its September 2021 poll: although 57 percent of Middle East scholars said that two states were no longer possible, 80 percent said they would expect Israel/Palestine to become a one state reality akin to apartheid, if two states were assessed to be no longer possible.[11]

So, if we refer to Israel or Israel/Palestine as a single state, we cannot use it as a device to wave away the struggles, contests, and ambiguities. Israel/Palestine is a one state reality, but what kind of one state? This is the moment when polemics can often start to fly, with many adopting labels not based on their empirical validity but on their political utility. We assembled this volume to add analytical and conceptual alternatives to the polemics.

The critical perspectives raised in this volume are interventions to end one chapter of the Palestinian/Israeli story and to begin another: to move from what Israel/Palestine can or should become to what it has become for some time. But it is not as if we are now in totally unfamiliar territory. Many people have long worried about the end of the possibility of the two state solution and have proposed views of the emerging reality. But the ground has shifted, and it is unclear where it will settle. We therefore did not start from a policy conclusion ("one state is a preferable outcome" or "two states are the only solution") or a knowledge of the future ("two states are inevitable" or "Israel cannot be sustained") and work backward to make sure that participants fell on one side of the divide or were evenly divided between them. Indeed, readers will find a group of scholars who would have likely disagreed sharply a decade or two ago about policy preferences.

Instead, we asked participants to start with the current reality, as they see it, and grapple with what that reality means for politics within that territory, among national communities, and internationally. Did we ask them to write only as cold analysts? Not exactly, but we insisted that they be analytical. And this raises the difficult issue of the relationship between ethics and scholarship.

The Normativity of Reality

We may appear to some readers as if we are claiming to be studying Israel/Palestine as one may approach classifying a tree: armed with a set of fancy names but no vested interests or moral sensibility. Some may suspect we are masking our moral positions, perhaps a bit like the realists of international relations theory who argue that they are analyzing the world as it is, rather than as others would like it to be (but nevertheless at times sliding into suggestions of what policies are best). So, we begin by clarifying our own positions and then explaining what we asked the authors to do.

As editors, our assessment of the reality of a single state is not an endorsement of it. It is possible to desire a two state solution and recognize the one state reality. Indeed, all four editors advocated separately in the past for a two state solution on the grounds that it was the best—or perhaps the least bad—of the alternatives, and we reached this conclusion even while it was still seen as extreme (and sometimes even taboo) in American, Palestinian, and Israeli discussions. We each began to doubt the likelihood of a two state solution on our own and at different times.

But if we traveled separate paths to this realization, we each did so with little joy and much heartache. As much as we tell ourselves that we worried about the consequences of its failure, we still find ourselves in disbelief. Even though we believe that we now live in a one state reality, if Lazarus were to rise, we might feel relieved; some of us might even be elated. We simply stopped using the two state idea as a prism for understanding. And that is still a controversial step. Although we write at a time when a growing number of laypeople and experts are prepared to contemplate the existence of the one state reality, our sense is that most still write as if what we see as permanent is temporary.

The reasons for these differences of opinion are many. There are sincere differences regarding how to interpret historical trends, facts, and the likelihood of contingencies that might move mountains. There are emotional obstacles as well. Giving up on a two state solution means accepting the end of the dream of a Palestinian state that strictly reflects Palestinian nationalism. Israeli Jews whose visions of a Jewish state may have included democracy and human rights will have to adjust to an Israel that is challenged on both fronts, not just as an intermediate step but also as a more enduring reality. A similar barrier exists for all those supporters of Israel who see it as part of the liberal international community. Not all such resistance is based on idealism: clinging to the two state solution can be politically useful. In the US political and elite arenas, sticking with two states is, as one of us has suggested, also "a psychological trick" to avoid having to choose between Israel's Jewishness and Israel's democracy.[12] Others fear that openly abandoning the two state solution will simply strengthen the same forces that killed it. Palestinian leaders have lost nearly all popularity and legitimacy, in part because they staked their reputations to a peace process that showed little progress. To acknowledge defeat would have deep personal and political costs and, given their weakness compared to Israel, generates few real options. Israeli leaders have been quite content to continue the ruse because it creates a buffer from harsh criticism, attacks on its legitimacy, and campaigns to use sticks to force Israel from the territories. But with all these reasons to deny the one state reality, the number of recent converts to the cause—even those who were two state enthusiasts—is striking.

Still, as much as we cite reality as our ally, we are fully aware that any analytical take (including our own) has ethical consequences. We recognize that our focus on describing "what is" could have the unintended consequence of projecting acceptance of a new reality born out of unethical or internationally illegal behavior—a sort of scholarly laundering of the indefensible. And even as we are social scientists committed to the analytical enterprise, our values are constant. We do not wish our description of reality to be mistaken for a refusal to explore the origins of the situation we describe or an endorsement of policies that come close to celebrating that reality. Nor should we use it to avoid questions of responsibility. For instance, the editors—all US citizens—acknowledge that the asymmetry embedded in the one state reality itself is a function of US policy over the decades, particularly in shielding Israel from being sanctioned by the UN through the exercise of its veto power; and in uniquely providing Israel with cutting-edge military technology to maintain a regional upper hand—all in the name of helping Israel compromise in the process of attaining a fair diplomatic settlement.

So as editors we acknowledge that ethical and analytical perspectives cannot be disentangled, not from history itself and not from scholarship or the scholar. But such a recognition does not mean that normative commitments must trump analytical reasoning. We are committed to a broad understanding of social science, the critical role of evidence, the importance of examining alternative claims and theories, and a skeptical attitude toward our own conclusions and beliefs. Social science aims at reasoned dialogue. This dialogue occurs among scholars from different perspectives, disciplines, and epistemes, which puts the onus on self-reflexivity: the constant reassessment of one's views and beliefs.

We imposed no litmus test on our contributors beyond a commitment to the common standards of social science research. We did not ask them whether they think a two state solution remains viable, whether Israel is (or is not) an apartheid state, who is to blame for the current situation, or any of the other hot-button questions (though we hardly barred them from raising such questions if they were germane to their analysis). We understood that this would lead to an unpredictable diversity of thought—and embraced that. Part of the problem with the conversation on Israel and Palestine is the tendency for scholars and practitioners to stick to those with whom they already agree on fundamental issues. At a time when there is such uncertainty about what is and what will be, diversity of thought is not a luxury but a necessity. We know that some readers will be made uncomfortable and even angered by some of the chapters. But part of the point of scholarship is to unsettle how we see the world and our own normative positioning. There are significant moral and empirical and analytical issues at stake: ignoring those issues is not a prerequisite for analysis. Committing to social science research encourages something like a dispassionate tone: not one emptied of normative content but one that attempts to engage with those who may not share the same normative orientation. Writing in a dispassionate tone is not seen as an end in itself—and certainly we do not wish to use it to empty analysis of the passion that can inform it. But such a tone advances clarity of analysis and allows those with different normative orientations (or who do not share the same passionate commitment) to learn from each other's analyses. The authors took up the challenge, presenting analyses that will indeed make various readers uncomfortable at various places as they find their understandings challenged and their own normative commitments questioned—but working to ensure that even uncomfortable readers will find their analyses serious. In short, a dispassionate tone is not about norm-free scholarship. We seek to allow normatively driven questions to guide analysis.

Collectively, this is what we believe that scholars can contribute to a vexatious set of questions. Indeed, collectively we are left with nothing besides questions. But questions are not a bad thing, especially after a period when so many scholars and policymakers thought they had the answers. Indeed, our hope is to allow conversation to begin where it previously ended. We can illustrate that on the very contentious terrain of whether the one state reality constitutes apartheid. Our purpose in this introduction is not to answer that question but to explain why it is asked and why the stakes and emotions surrounding it seem so high; in short, our approach clarifies the question and renders it amenable to dialogue.

Apartheid can have different meanings, but the origin of the term is clear: it began as a system of rule established in South Africa designed to enshrine white supremacy and the permanent subordination of Black (and other) South Africans. But it is not only a historically specific term and one used to describe a policy; it is also a legal one on the international level and has come to be classified as a crime against humanity. Consequently, classifying Israel as an apartheid state not only situates Israel alongside one of the most contemptible and hated regimes of the twentieth century but also possibly holds severe legal and political consequences. Some, but certainly not all, who wield the charge of apartheid may not accept Israel whatever form it takes, and it is for that reason that it can engender a degree of outrage that ends discussion. The legal and moral stakes are high, and so, we must not exclude the question from scholarly inquiry. We will not calm partisans, but we can clarify terms and move from vituperation to analysis.

Putting the term "apartheid" aside for a moment (we return to it later), it is still important to understand what Israel is as a Jewish state and what it is not—even aside from its control of the Palestinians in the West Bank and Gaza. What kind of state is Israel? Let us start with the label that is at the root of many political and scholarly discussions: liberal democracy. Does Israel qualify as a liberal democracy? Israel's relationship to liberal democracy has always been much more problematic than its supporters have wanted to accept. It starts not with its relationship to the territories but rather the very nature of the Israeli state. Israel is a Jewish state or a state for the Jews. These terms are subtly different, but the distinctions should not distract us from an underlying consensus among most Israeli Jews (and also most diaspora Jews who have an opinion) that Israel has a Jewish identity—and it should stay that way. Israeli Jews have heated debates about what a Jewish identity implies; religious Jews will cite Judaism and secular Jews some version of humanity. But there is no disagreement about Israel's Jewish character. Jews around the world have a "right of return" and can become Israeli citizens, but such a "right" is not recognized for Palestinians whose families left or were expelled from what is now Israel before it became an independent state.

Israel's 2018 Nation-State Law has even more boldly emphasized its Jewishness and downgraded the status everyone who is not Jewish.[13] This law defines Israel as "the nation state of the Jewish People" and holds that "the exercise of the right to national self-determination in the State of Israel is unique to the Jewish People"; it makes no mention of democracy or equality for others.[14]

Relatedly, if Israel is to have a Jewish identity, then those who are not classified as Jewish will—and must—have a lesser status. How much lesser is a matter of debate. Some argue that non-Jews should have civil and political rights but should have restrictions on where they can live. The belief that Jews should have different and more rights than non-Jews is so ingrained among Jewish Israelis that a major 2014–2015 Pew Research Center study of 5,601 Israelis showed that 79 percent of Jewish Israelis say Jews deserve preferential treatment in Israel.[15]

This inequality is evident in law and all aspects of life. Certainly, there are Palestinian citizens of Israel—and other non-Jewish Israelis—who have achieved considerable economic, political, and cultural success. Defenders of Israel's liberal and democratic status often point to these exceptions—but exceptions cannot prove rules. Maintaining a liberal democracy under these conditions of systematic discrimination will be challenging, to say the least, and as the Pew poll implies, it is not even clear whether Israeli Jews are desirous of liberalism.

Jews and non-Jews have a different status in Israel, and the status of non-Jews depends on where they reside and when they were brought under the control of Israeli rule. Non-Jews who are citizens of Israel have many of the same political and civil rights as Israeli Jews. However, as many of the chapters note, Arabs did not have freedom of movement from 1948 through 1966; they continue to face restrictions on their ability to buy property and where they can live and confront deeply unequal economic and social rights. Discrimination based on religious and ethnic identity is legal under Israeli law.

Palestinians living in East Jerusalem operate with different rights than do Palestinians residing in other parts of the West Bank. Palestinians in the West Bank have a different set of rights from those residing in Gaza. Following the 1993 Oslo Accords, Palestinians residing in Zone A of the West Bank have different sets of rights in practice from those Palestinians residing in Zone B, and the latter from those in Zone C. Palestinian citizens of Israel have individual rights that approach the rights enjoyed by Israeli Jews, even if not fully equal and lacking the same economic and social rights. Beyond juridical rights, all these various categories differ dramatically in the tools available to them to enforce their rights. The legal and juridical maze can lead to bureaucratic madness and classification confusion disorder. Asking a Palestinian to describe their legal status can provoke an answer that takes several minutes—and one still full of ambiguities.

Despite these variations, one thing is clear: distinctions between Jews and non-Jews with separate and unequal rights are constitutive of modern Israel. This point should not be controversial. Most Israeli Jews would not have it any other way. Said otherwise, this inequality between Israeli Jews and Palestinians is not temporary but rather is intended to be permanent. There are no plans in Israel to rid distinctions between Jews and non-Jews in all aspects of Israeli law. In fact, the Nation-State Basic Law, in the absence of an Israeli constitution, may be further institutionalizing Israeli Arabs and Palestinians as a permanent minority. This permanence is based not on numbers but rather identity. Arabs and Palestinians can outnumber Jews by 2:1, and they will still be a "minority."

The label "apartheid" has partly served as a warning: if current trends continue, apartheid will become a reality. But we seek to analyze the present. And here we note that the warning of impending apartheid has been repeated enough that the term is increasingly being used even by in-house critics to describe what they see today.[16] In fact, what is preventing more people from seeing the reality as one of apartheid or akin to it—at least in the legal sense that has led the top US-based human rights organization, Human Rights Watch, to say that Israeli behavior matches the legal definition of apartheid—is the view of the current reality through the prism of occupation, which entails a temporary state of affairs that is tolerated only because it is intended to be temporary. Once one makes the move to see the reality as that of one state, the (legal) apartheid label becomes harder to resist. An emerging approach is looking less at ideology, intentions, or future trends but simply at the checklist for what constitutes apartheid and then comparing it to the situation in Israel today: some have found Israel checking many of the boxes. In fact, in a poll two of us conducted in September 2021 among scholars of the Middle East, 65 percent described the reality in Israel/Palestine as a "one state reality with inequality akin to apartheid"—a 6 percent increase from a similar poll conducted just seven months before.[17] The diverse contributors to this volume are unlikely to find a way to speak with a collective voice in this regard, although all see stark inequalities, however they may label them. As editors our task is to frame, not preclude, debate—and to ask those who address difficult questions to do so in a way that is reasoned and accessible for those with different orientations.

Organization of the Volume

This volume explores the premise that today there is already a de facto single state with a complex, undertheorized, and variegated form of layered sovereignty. Its focus is to grapple with what that one state is, not what it should be or will become. We do not seek to develop a single answer (and have deliberately referred to that one state as "Israel" and as "Israel/Palestine" out of our own respect for the difficult in naming that reality).

Thus, all chapters in this volume wrestle with "what is Israel/Palestine," but we organize the four parts around where they start their analysis: concepts, practices, attitudes, and policies. Part 1 attempts to transform Israel/Palestine from an enigma to an identifiable category. Ian Lustick starts us off by asking for a shift regarding what we think Israel is and where it is located. The image of Israel as a metropole controlling an entity separate from itself, "the occupied territories," has been the standard model of "what Israel is" (as a state) since 1967. The divisibility—indeed the ontological fact of this division into "Israel" and "not Israel"—has served as the political and conceptual basis for a partitionist solution to the Israeli-Palestinian dispute. The image of a Palestinian Arab state in the West Bank and Gaza existing alongside the Jewish-Zionist State of Israel crystallized as the effective meaning of that type of solution. That formula still exists, though it no longer inspires fresh insights, guides effective political action, or holds out the promise of satisfying change. The September 2021 Middle East Scholars Barometer found that 57 percent of scholars polled said that two states had become impossible, whereas another 40 percent said that solution was not probable in the next ten years. The two state solution may be dead, but its ghost remains—a floating illusion that distracts attention from the dynamics of the palpable fact that for more than a decade at least, a single state, Israel, dominates the life chances of all who live within the territory between the river and the sea. Contrary to the presumptions of the two state solution project, if change toward equality or higher levels of Israeli and Palestinian satisfaction can come to this reality, they will come not as the result of a negotiated delineation of the boundary between Israel and Palestine but as a result of social, economic, cultural, and political transformations inside the large but nondemocratic one state that now exists. Vested interests, cognitive biases, and emotional and psychological investments make it extraordinarily difficult for parties to the conflict and interested observers to accept or even see this new reality or think about its implications. Lustick concludes by urging a gestalt shift in how the political situation west of the Jordan River is imagined and illustrates its analytic and political payoffs.

In chapter 2, Gershon Shafir argues that, given the prevailing frame of the debate between two nation-states versus one, the civic state resolution to the Israeli-Palestinian conflict overlooks a third option. There is another one state genus: a single Jewish sovereign state from the sea to the river that not only privileges Jews but also imposes Judaic supremacy—a halakhically justified Jewish exceptionalism that rejects not just national but also political, social, and, in some cases, civic Palestinian rights. A Judaic supremacist regime inspired by the "pastoral power" of Religious Zionism is envisioned not only across the Green Line but also within Israel. Shafir charts the changes in uses of the historical halakhic legacy by Religious Zionist rabbinical authorities to address the modern dilemma of the status of "aliens" under Jewish sovereignty. The mostly accommodationist rabbis of the 1940s supported the recognition of Palestinian citizen rights. In contrast, the supremacist rabbis after the 1967 War, who rely on the same writings and even the same passages of the medieval sage Maimonides, deny the concession of any land to Palestinians and, subsequently, even their right to reside under Jewish sovereignty unless they accept Judaic supremacy. The pastoral power of the proponents of Judaic supremacy penetrates and shapes, though has not displaced, the Israeli state's "sovereign power" by creating a new universe of legitimate possibilities for rendering Palestinians invisible in a one state reality: a Jewish one.

In chapter 3, Yousef Munayyer argues that the settler-colonial framework, especially when compared to nationalism and occupation, provides considerable leverage regarding the formation of Israel/Palestine and the path forward. He traces settler-colonial processes, established more than a century ago in Ottoman Palestine by the Zionist movement, through various stages to illuminate a common trajectory over time built on principles of separate development that shaped and continues to shape various facets of the Israeli-Palestinian relationship. Munayyer concludes by arguing that the settler-colonial frame not only explains the history of political struggle in Israel/Palestine but also permits the vision of a path forward through decolonization and the principle of co-permanence.

The premise of part 2 is that we can best know what Israel/Palestine is not through any conceptualization but rather through its practices. Importantly, these practices did not begin with the one state reality but predated it and made it possible. This part does not attempt to provide a survey of all or even the most important factors that are responsible for producing the current reality. It avoids relitigating the history of who did what, when, and why; who is to blame for missing opportunities; whether actions were sincere or strategic at critical moments; and who is to blame for killing the Oslo Accords. Instead, its primary intention is to identify current forces of rule and the history of these practices; this is something of an archaeological endeavor, recovering the politics, economics, ideologies, and discourses that combined historically to produce the one state reality.

In chapter 4, Yael Berda begins with the observation that political membership—one's status as citizen, resident, subject, and foreigner—determines one's ability to move freely in the territory of the state. She argues that in many imperial, colonial, and modern state-building projects, mobility and status are intertwined, and in Israel/Palestine citizenship is organized not around rights but mobility. This mobility regime runs from before the origins of the state to the present one state reality. The British authorities used it in various colonies and in mandatory Palestine. In 1949, after independence and before enacting citizenship laws, Israel differentiated political status through a regime that restricted mobility. The bureaucratic structure that impeded Palestinian movement in the first two decades shaped the Palestinians' political membership in the independent state as a mobility regime, one that prevented their deportation and exile rather than granting rights. Parallel to the Oslo process, Israel extended its control over Palestinians throughout the territories through a permit system based on racial hierarchy and scales of suspicion, where separate rules and decrees are applied to different populations based on their identity and political belonging.

In chapter 5, Diana B. Greenwald explores the theme of "indirect rule," noting that it has been defined alternatively as a generic mode of decentralized state authority or as an explicitly violent form of despotism based on racialized hierarchies, most explicitly associated with European colonization projects. She situates the coercive institutions in the West Bank within existing theoretical frameworks of the origins, nature, and consequences of indirect rule. Central to all definitions of indirect rule is the idea of a principal-agent relationship: the stability of the incumbent, or occupying, regime relies on the comprehensive co-optation of indigenous agents. She argues that the latent stability of the Israeli regime in the West Bank has, like other settings of indirect rule, waxed and waned due to the varying threat of drift, or outright defection, from Palestinian agents. In particular, she explores the delegation of internal policing to the Palestinian Authority and the implications of these coercive arrangements for both regime stability and the existential security of the West Bank's population. Nonetheless, although indirect rule can be undermined by agent defection, she argues that certain features of indirect rule in the West Bank have contributed to regime stability by, for example, facilitating blame shifting and undermining collective action. The chapter concludes by asking, What are the possible trajectories for indirectly ruled populations and territories? Drawing on historical examples, she predicts that, rather than collapsing with the arrival of a sovereign Palestinian state, it is more likely that the institutions of indirect rule would be subsumed into future constellations of state authority in the West Bank and, as such, would persist as long-term targets of radical reform.

In chapter 6, Nathan J. Brown and Iman Elbanna explore how the one state reality has become insinuated into daily Palestinian life. Although many policymakers continue to cling in public to the idea of a two state solution for Israel and Palestine, observers increasingly speak of a "one state reality," with the land of mandatory Palestine and its inhabitants fully under the control of the Israeli state. Palestinians have long grappled with and adapted to this reality and now are gradually (and grudgingly) orienting themselves around the single state of Israel and away from the centrality of statehood to the Palestinian national movement. This chapter explores this aspect of the "one state reality" and the ways in which Palestinian collective structures inside the occupied territories, Israel, and across the diaspora have slowly shifted focus from the idea of statehood to dealing with Israel as their central reality, some much more reluctantly than others. This shift is accompanied by the decay of the authoritative national institutions that the Palestinians built (notably the Palestinian Liberation Organization and the Palestinian National Authority), the absence of strategies for pursuing Palestinian statehood, and the entrenchment of Israeli control—all of which have served to redirect the nationalist movement to grappling with the one state reality rather than forming an alternative to it.

Part 3's premise is that we can see the one state reality not from any declaration by governments, international organizations, or academics but rather by the effects it has on them. In other words, the members of the world polity may or may not agree that there is a one state reality, but they are often acting as if there is.

What will happen to the relations between Palestinians and other Arab and Muslim-majority countries, and how have Arabs and Muslims broadly conceived the Israel-Palestinian issue? Are we likely to see more Arab states recognize Israel's right to exist and establish relations? How are Europe and the United States responding to this new reality? What have been and may be the reactions and strategies of Jewish communities around the world, especially in the United States? Will international organizations, especially the United Nations, shift their positions in the face of the changing reality? What kinds of advocacy and activism are we likely to see? What forms of rule and resistance are likely to evolve? What kinds of coalitions are now possible or impossible?

This part begins with Mohanad Mustafa's and As'ad Ghanem's fascinating account of how Palestinians living in Israel are adjusting to and recalculating their politics and strategies in response to the one state reality. They argue that seven decades since the Nakba in 1948, Palestinians in Israel continue to suffer from the lack of a clear collective project. On the one hand, they were excluded from the Palestinian national movement, and on the other hand, the Palestinians in Israel, as a national indigenous minority, are separated from the rest of the Palestinian people and have failed to orchestrate a unique collective national project in Israel. Projects such as Equality in the Jewish State, the Citizenship Project, the efforts to collectively organize the community within Israel, and finally, the Joint List all collided at certain points with the ethnic structure of the state. In the shadow of the collapse of the two state option as a solution for the general Palestinian-Israeli conflict, the authors argue that it is time to formulate a new project that considers a wholesale restructuring of how the Palestinian people are politically organized, with the Palestinians in Israel as a constituent part of the same movement.

In chapter 8, Michael Barnett and Lara Friedman probe the past and contemporary moment to examine the conflict between Jewish Americans' attachment to Israel and their commitment to liberalism and democracy. It begins with a historical survey from pre-1948 through the early 2000s, highlighting how Jewish Americans attempted to square an identity that is liberal and democratic with a Zionist movement and a State of Israel confronting varying demographic pressures that potentially erode its liberal and democratic values. A central observation is that the current dilemmas are not new but rather bear a strong resemblance to those of the pre-statehood years, and many of the responses are likewise familiar. The chapter then offers four vignettes that illuminate ways that Jewish Americans and organizations have responded to what has become a one state reality: whether Jewish Americans are becoming more distant from Israel; how Prime Minister Benjamin Netanyahu's interventions in US politics transformed Israel from a bipartisan to a partisan issue and how the Netanyahu-Trump alliance caused Jewish Americans to question whether their values and interests continued to overlap with Israel's; how major defenders of Israel have made fighting the Boycott, Divestment, and Sanctions (BDS) movement a top priority and the parallel shift to defining criticism of Israel as antisemitism; and, lastly, how support for Israel potentially constrains and contorts how Jewish Americans position themselves vis-à-vis standard liberal positions, including civil rights and racial justice. They conclude by speculating about how the one state reality has reverberated in and across the different camps in American Jewry, forcing them to reconsider not only their relationship with Israel but also what it means to be Jewish in America.

In chapter 9, Nadav Shelef starts from the premise that, given the existence of competing nationalist aspirations by Jews and Palestinians, peaceful coexistence in a one state reality requires one or both nationalisms either to change these aspirations or redefine the political community in more inclusive terms. This chapter assesses the likelihood of such transformations and argues that the role of domestic politics in driving such changes means that those shifts, although possible, are also unlikely. It begins by outlining the ways in which nationalist ideologies evolve and describing the kinds of "denationalization" that would need to occur for there to be peaceful coexistence in a one state reality. The histories of Zionism and Palestinian nationalisms suggest that these kinds of denationalization are possible because some version of them has already occurred in the past, even on the question of how to define the nation's membership boundaries. The second part of the chapter briefly illustrates the balance of change and stability on this critical issue in both Zionism and Palestinian nationalisms. The process and limits of those transformations highlight the role of domestic politics and evolutionary processes in driving redefinitions of the nation. This, in turn, has two critical but conflicting implications for a one state reality. First, the kinds of fundamental transformations in the meaning of nationhood that are required for denationalization can occur even for Zionism and Palestinian nationalisms. Second, such transformations depend on the outcome of domestic political struggles that, at least at present, the denationalization projects among Israelis and Palestinians are poorly positioned to win. Denationalization, in other words, although possible, will not be the automatic consequence of a one state context.

In chapter 10, Shibley Telhami examines two central international arenas for Israel/Palestine: the Arab and American positions. The former has been central because the assumed international importance of the Palestinian issue has in part been predicated on it being important to the Arab world; US backing of Israel—which has shielded Israel from international consequences when it was seen to violate international law—has also been key. The international community broadly, including Arab states, has remained officially committed to a two state solution, but much has changed in recent years in both the Arab and American arenas. Several Arab states have made peace with Israel while ignoring the Palestinians, whereas the United States, during the Trump era, broke many of the norms and laws that had underpinned the international approach to Israel/Palestine. How will these shifts affect the status of Israel/Palestine? Based on a strategic and public opinion analysis, this chapter argues that these shifts further reduce the likelihood of a two state solution while strengthening the perception of the unacceptability of the status quo and the push for equality within a one state reality. There are signs of public opinion shifts that are more accepting of a one state outcome with full equality, but Arab and American ruling elites remain closely tied to the two state paradigm, with minimal indications of shift.

In chapter 11, Omar Rahman and Dahlia Scheindlin examine the historical trajectory of public opinion in support of the partition of Israel-Palestine into two states, commonly referred to as the "two state solution." The chapter identifies corresponding arcs in public attitudes from Israeli and Palestinian societies, which reached their respective peaks of support in the decade of the 2000s and have since been in gradual decline. Given the ebbing of support for two states, the authors identify the current period as one of "non-solutionism," in which no overarching political solution or constitutional arrangement enjoys majority support in either society, although for different reasons. Among Israelis, comfort with the status quo supplemented by unilateral Israeli action in the West Bank and Gaza Strip has largely replaced efforts to resolve the conflict with the Palestinians. For their part, Palestinians are increasingly concerned with internal dysfunction and the need to reframe the nature of their national struggle, with the focus on political solutions, as the two state outcome is increasingly viewed as an obstacle to or a distraction from the fulfilment of Palestinian rights. Finally, the chapter analyzes support for alternative constitutional arrangements for resolving the conflict, including equal and unequal single state solutions and confederation.

What is to be done? What can be done? Part 4 examines possible and plausible policy options given the current (one state or otherwise) reality. In chapter 12, Kevin Huggard and Tamara Cofman Wittes examine the future of US foreign policy toward the conflict. In recent years, the interests and capabilities undergirding American dominance of Israeli-Palestinian diplomacy have begun to change, and the dynamic between Israelis and Palestinians has likewise undermined prospects for negotiated resolution of their conflict. The renewed questioning about US policy has not, as yet, shaken the commitment of American policymakers and elected officials to the objective of a negotiated two state solution. This chapter reviews the history of American engagement with the concept of Palestinian statehood and with the Palestine Liberation Organization. The record reveals that US policymakers have always perceived Palestinian statehood as in tension with Israel's security, and thus their support for statehood was always and remains conditional. At the same time, US support for a two state outcome to the Israeli-Palestinian conflict coheres strongly with deep-seated American attitudes about national self-determination, identity conflicts, and democracy. Thus, even under present conditions, American policymakers continue to see the establishment of a Palestinian state alongside Israel as likely the only way to end the bloodshed of the conflict. Holding out the two state outcome as the objective of American policy—while allowing for flexibility in defining its parameters—remains attractive for US policymakers as a way to avoid conflict on both the domestic and the international fronts. Strong incentives push American policymakers to cling to the two state solution, but they will be increasingly challenged to do so. As the Israeli occupation of the West Bank enters its seventh decade, Israeli public opinion and policy preferences shift toward annexation, the US relationship with Israel becomes increasingly politicized both in Washington and Jerusalem, and America's wider interests in the Middle East recede, we are likely to see greater volatility in US policy toward the Israeli-Palestinian conflict. Domestic politics and political culture may play relatively greater roles in influencing US policy choices. The chapter concludes with some broad suggestions for how this altered environment might reshape US policy.

In chapter 13, Khaled Elgindy describes the demise of the Oslo process combined with the success of Israel's settlement enterprise and the collapsing political consensus around the goal of two states, as evidenced most clearly by the Trump administration; he argues that its demise requires us to rethink old assumptions and explore new possibilities beyond the classic two state model. Although a traditional two state solution remains theoretically achievable, it would require an entirely new approach to peacemaking by the United States and other international stakeholders based on upholding internationally accepted norms, altering realities on the ground, and promoting mutual accountability—all of which are likely to entail higher political costs than US decision makers are prepared to invest. Moreover, as the goals of territorial partition and demographic separation become increasingly unworkable, policymakers in the United States and abroad must begin exploring alternative paths by which to ensure self-determination for both Israeli Jews and Arab Palestinians, including the possibility of one binational state and hybrid models such as confederation. All three scenarios—binationalism, confederation, and the traditional two state model—would require a fundamental change to the power dynamics between Israelis and Palestinians. Indeed, any solution would require Israeli Jews, as the dominant group, to give up a measure of power and privilege, which represents the biggest single challenge to an equitable peace settlement. Only when Israeli leaders deem the costs of maintaining the status quo to outweigh the alternatives will a solution become possible.

In chapter 14, Muriel Asseburg observes that, even though dynamics in Israel/Palestine have rendered not only a two state settlement but also any agreed settlement of the conflict ever more difficult to achieve, Europeans continue to cling to the mantra of a negotiated two state solution, stressing that there is no alternative for resolving the Israeli-Palestinian conflict. As the 2007 intra-Palestinian split occurred, they added another mantra to their repertoire—the one on intra-Palestinian reconciliation—while erecting hurdles to achieving that goal. Consequently, the chasm between European rhetoric on conflict resolution and conflict realities on the ground has widened. This contribution analyzes European policy objectives and instruments concerning Israel/Palestine, explains why there is such a large gap between European rhetoric and actual policies, and discusses prospects for European policymaking on Israel/Palestine. It concludes that because Europeans are divided, on the defensive, torn between an allegiance to international law and a commitment to Israel as a safe haven for Jews, and thus resigned to a supportive rather than a formative role, it is unlikely that consensus will be achieved among the EU-27 on aligning their policies with their values and stated objectives. As a result, Europe is likely to remain wedded to the two state mantra without employing the means necessary to achieve progress. It will thus remain a payer that funds a game that cannot be reconciled with European values and interests.

In the conclusion, Marc Lynch reflects on three critical issues on which this volume seeks to move discussion forward. First, when we speak of a one state "reality," what is that reality that we insist be faced? Second, what is the effect of facing a reality that many have sought to avoid? Finally, what is likely or should be done in the policy arena, and what approaches might follow from acceptance of the reality that we claim should be acknowledged? He concludes with some observations on the relationship between normative and ethical concerns, on the one hand, and empirical concerns, on the other.

Part 1

CHARACTERIZING THE PALESTINIAN-ISRAEL REALITY

1

WHAT AND WHERE IS ISRAEL?

Time for a Gestalt Shift

Ian S. Lustick

Israel is one of the few states in the world that has never issued a postage stamp featuring a map of the country. Although most countries are proud of their shape and often use their map image on postage stamps and elsewhere as a unifying and iconic representation of national existence, that is not the case in Israel. The question of the country's exact territorial composition is, and always has been, too politically and ideologically fraught to enable its map image to be used in that way. But if the State of Israel dares not officially speak the name of its borders, that does not mean it does not have them. What it does mean, however, is that tracing where the borders of the state have been, and where they are now, requires an act of explicit and assertive analysis.

Because thinking productively about the future of a state means knowing what is inside it and what is outside it, we must ask what is it that lies between the Mediterranean Sea and the Jordan River. Is it a state named Israel, located in part of the area, with other parts of this territory existing outside it? Or does the State of Israel contain all the territories west of the Jordan River, even if those territories and the populations living in them are ruled differently? For a half-century the answer to that question in the minds of most (not all) of those living in this space, studying it, or seeking to change it was clear: the land west of the Jordan was defined as divided between Israel and not-Israel. For decades this was the solid ground of analysis and action: it contributed an unquestioned apprehension of reality to campaigns to bring about or prevent the establishment of a Palestinian state. The result was on-point journalism, energetic political mobilization, and much excellent scholarship.

But the world, including Israel, has changed in fundamental ways. Previously unquestioned assumptions now appear as highly problematic claims. Familiar categories fit uncomfortably with irresistible observations. Standard arguments seem hollow and lose their persuasive power. Intellectual and political moorings are loosened as unexamined premises and conventional beliefs no longer can enforce limits on discourse and discipline on the imagination. Those active in the communities of thought and effort based on destabilized first principles confront disorienting analytic, professional, and psychological challenges.

Struggles governed by differences in deep structures of thought are distinctive. They are, as Antonio Gramsci described them, "wars of position" involving fundamentally different ways of seeing the world expressed via questions posed, topics treated as trivial or crucial, and criteria for judging agendas for action and investigation as either necessary or irrelevant. Propositions made within one universe of discourse are difficult to challenge or even frame within another. This fundamental element of incommensurability springs from commitments that are not and, in the normal course of things, cannot be subjected to evidence-based criticism.

The purpose of this chapter is to highlight the stark discrepancy between perceiving West Bank and Gaza Arabs as if they are living outside the State of Israel and the actuality of their status as living within it. Thereby I hope to encourage a gestalt shift so that the area between the sea and the river can be seen for what it is, rather than how it must be imagined to justify continued work on behalf of a negotiated two state solution (TSS). For many this will pose an unsettling epistemological challenge. Is Israel a state that includes within itself all the territory and people west of the Jordan, or do those living "across the Green Line" (*ma'ever hakav hayarok*) live outside the State of Israel?

This is a question about the nature of political reality for Jews, Arabs, and others living between the river and the sea—a question that cannot arise within the discursive universe established and contained by the TSS. Accordingly, to engage with those whose assumptions forbid even posing the question, I need to establish a basis for thinking about how change occurs in beliefs that are so fundamental to systems of thought that they are not, and cannot normally be, exposed to criticism or demands for evidence. To do so I draw on the history of scientific beliefs as a model for understanding how dominant frames of reference can be replaced, even though the fundamental assumptions of their adherents forbid it.[1]

The problem is one of ontology. "Ontology" and "ontological" are big and somewhat mysterious words, but they have a very specific meaning. Ontology is the study of existence—of what constitutes reality. Ontological claims reflect judgments and apprehensions that precede theories, hypotheses, or even discrete perceptions. As unexamined and therefore unevaluatable assumptions, they establish what questions can be posed, what facts can be gathered to evaluate answers to those questions, and what kinds of change are and are not imaginable. In this sense they are preanalytic or "metaphysical." As key elements of a paradigm for thinking, they cannot be studied from within the paradigm but only from an external position animated by a framework of thought based on different ontological assumptions.

What does "ontological" mean in practical terms? Consider the case of fire. What is it? That is an ontological question. According to Aristotle fire is one of the four basic elements, along with earth, air, and water, that make up everything in the world with which we have direct contact. Burning was explained as the process by which fire, as an elemental substance, was released from things that contained it like wood. Renaissance revivals of Aristotelean ontology led to the theory of phlogiston as an invisible substance that yielded fire when things containing it were heated. Centuries of science and whole industries, such as metallurgy, were based on phlogiston. It took decades of dogged work by Lavoisier and others in the late eighteenth and early nineteenth centuries before a new paradigm for understanding chemistry arose that dispensed with phlogiston altogether. Instead, the whole idea of fire as a substance was replaced by metaphysics of an entirely different kind. Fire was not a thing itself, and neither was "air"—which was now understood as a mixture of "gases." Fire was but an effect of heated gases within fuel interacting with another gas, "oxygen." In the course of these interactions tiny things called "molecules" were broken and reformed, yielding another kind of highly energized "thing"—plasma—which is how we apprehend fire.

Just as the phlogiston paradigm for understanding burning and why some substances burned and others did not was based on a particular ontological view of the kind of thing that exists, so the two state solution paradigm is based on particular ontological presumptions, or "priors." Although many may be accustomed to thinking of the TSS as simply a scenario for achieving Israeli-Palestinian peace, it came to assume enormous importance both as a political *and* as a scholarly/social science project. Those who worked within it to either bring a TSS about, prevent that outcome, or simply understand it, adopted its ontological assumptions as their "priors." Chief among these was and continues to be that the land between the river and the sea comprises two fundamentally different kinds of spaces: territories and people within the State of Israel, and territories and people not within the State of Israel. Treating that principle as valid made perfect sense in the years and even decades following the 1967 War. But at least since the aftermath of the Second Intifada, palpable realities have made it impossible for scholars and political activists to treat the political separateness of the West Bank and Gaza Strip from Israel as an unquestioned fact, rather than as a claim that is at best problematic and at worst patently false.

Nevertheless, abandoning such a basic principle, even in the face of mounting evidence that contradicts it, is difficult. For many it entails the loss of hope for a long-cherished political utopia of two separate and independent national states. As is the case for anyone long committed to and heavily invested in an ambitious scientific or political project, this kind of change also threatens reputations, careers, and valued communities of mobilization and support. Faced with the terrible costs of paradigm exhaustion, adherents are caught in a painful predicament. Their analyses and policy recommendations can remain consistent with the old paradigm or they can grapple effectively with realities, but they cannot do both. To ignore the inadequacy of one's conceptual equipment means that work done will be repetitive, boring, and disconnected with ultimate political or intellectual purposes. Grappling with the invalidity of key assumptions means operating in unfamiliar territory and, perhaps, alongside former enemies rather than with familiar comrades and collaborators. At the same time, it can produce new insights and offer exciting prospects for scholarly and political progress.

We can learn about the challenges (and rewards) of abandoning an outworn paradigm and of adopting new ways of seeing and not-seeing the world by considering the history of science. At the core of that history are stories of how social, cultural, economic, political, or technological change and increasingly accurate observations regularly challenge prevailing paradigms. Upstart scholars, renegade scientists, and intellectuals with a greater taste for risk and less tolerance for analytic convention than most accelerate the decline and fall of established ways of thinking by identifying and questioning assumptions, destabilizing standardized ways of formulating questions and thinking of answers, and making it increasingly costly for defenders of the old paradigm to pretend to have faith in their doctrines.

Science and politics are conventionally characterized as dramatically different ways to approach the world. Accordingly, some may wonder how the history of science can be used to understand the changing character of a problem so intensely political as the Israeli-Palestinian conflict. Science, the systematic production and accumulation of knowledge, is normally figured as based on individually unselfish or disinterested curiosity sustained by a general commitment to the welfare of humankind or the planet. Scientific communities are thought of as sharing insights and data while arguing about which theories or models use fewer assumptions to explain more observations of interest than others. Good science, including good scholarship, is imagined as requiring a logical if not psychological separation between the values and preferences of its practitioners and the observations and analysis that are the primary focus of their work. The world of politics, in contrast, is generally seen as saturated with the pursuit of individual and group self-interest, however effectively it might be portrayed as serving the larger purposes of groups.

Politicians may compromise in their campaigns to achieve their goals and form partnerships and coalitions as key parts of those campaigns, but those alliances succeed not by satisfying curiosity but by winning power or implementing programs that serve their interests.

Science and politics do differ—in rhetoric, in expectations about how competition is to be regulated, in gatekeeping, recruitment, styles of communication, and so on. But there are fundamental similarities as well, arising from the identical predicament that both scientists and politicians confront. In their laboratories and libraries, scientists and scholars encounter the same overwhelming complexity and intractable uncertainty about how the world really works as do politicians in their legislatures, bureaucracies, smoke-filled rooms, and public arenas. Neither knows for sure what can happen and what cannot and, in the face of that uncertainty, what kinds of activity will prove either rewarding or not. To think and to act, both scientist/scholars and politicians/activists must treat the world as much simpler than it really is.

That simplicity is achieved by treating certain kinds of behaviors, data, observational opportunities, and questions as relevant and meaningful, relegating many alternatives to the category of meaningless or irrelevant. Without such limits on the imagination, no individual investigator could ever know where to begin a study or how to end one, and no community of scientists and scholars could ever form to discuss problems, findings, and new horizons for research. The same goes for politicians—who must effectively choose from a vast if not infinite number of logically possible appeals, postures, operational goals, and stratagems—if they are ever to be able to communicate effectively with masses or other ambitious elites about how to formulate, pursue, and achieve either individual or shared objectives.

Scientists and politicians solve the problem of simplifying the world enough to grapple usefully with it in the same way: by creating communities of belief and of fate whose members share fundamental presumptions about the world, how it works, and what is important within it. In this basic sense, successful scientific and political communities are both well-institutionalized "projects." Such projects impose on the intractable complexity of the world a stable array of rules for membership, large-scale challenges to be faced, and operational goals worth pursuing. To succeed as arenas for either science or politics, such projects must also offer a sustainable balance between opportunities for competition among individuals or teams of practitioners and boundaries or limits to acceptable behavior that protect the integrity of the community as a whole. In science and scholarship, the most successful projects are known as "paradigms." In politics, the most ambitious and successful of these projects are known as "states." In both realms successful projects take on a hegemonic aspect. In science, these are registered as metaphysical beliefs—unprovable or unproven claims, not open to testing. In politics, they are treated as self-evident truths, as in "We hold these truths to be self-evident . . .": they are beliefs requiring no justification and admitting no test as to their validity.

Of course, not all projects in science or in politics are successful. And no matter how much knowledge is produced or how much coordinated human activity is enabled, all eventually fail. Many promising projects, and almost all revolutionary groups, never enjoy the opportunity to fully test whether they hold capacities to explain or to govern that exceed those of reigning orthodoxies. Those projects that do succeed, however, that institutionalize themselves as robust scientific communities, academic disciplines, or regimes of political power, usually survive long after the questions and challenges they pose cease to be important and long after the answers and policies they enable cease to offer satisfaction or meaning.

Thomas Kuhn's seminal work, *The Structure of Scientific Revolutions*, popularized the concept of a paradigm as an all-encompassing framework of thought that isolates scientific discourses from one another by making claims based on one paradigm that are incommensurable with claims based on another. Progress in science, according to Kuhn, is thus marked by "revolution": disruptive breakthroughs involving the defeat or conversion of scientists from one way of looking at the world to another. Kuhn was explicitly dismissive of social science, even though he found himself unable to make his argument without drawing directly on both social psychology and political science theories of revolution. "At the heart" of his book, according to a recent study, is the "basic insight" that "scientific and political revolutions can be understood in important ways as the same thing."[2]

The saturation of science with politics and the importance of political maneuvering in the competition among scientific projects were key features of the thinking of another neopositivist philosopher and historian of science, Imre Lakatos. His theory of "research programs" built on Kuhn's provocative yet somewhat extreme and even confusing position. While using the terms "paradigm" and "research program" more or less interchangeably, I draw directly on Lakatos's dynamic account of how and why communities change in relation to the effectiveness of the work they can do within the paradigms that define them. His vocabulary offers an array of concepts particularly useful for understanding the trajectory of the TSS paradigm (or "research program") and the "morbid symptoms" that attend the increasing gap between reality and the way that reality must be depicted by those struggling to keep it alive.[3]

Lakatos asked what made scientific progress possible when the underlying assumptions guiding scientists can be exposed as fundamentally invalid. He was unsatisfied with Karl Popper's answers to this question and with the arbitrary and even nonrational image offered by Kuhn as to how one paradigm could be replaced by another. He strived for a theory to account for how new evidence could lead to the replacement of ineffective paradigms and, in a complex but somewhat orderly fashion, lead to more effective frameworks for pursuing knowledge.

Lakatos's theory emphasizes long-term processes of political and scientific competition among rival communities, each guided by its own productive or dysfunctional research program.[4] Although scientists working within separate paradigms cannot contradict or even learn directly from one another, science nonetheless progresses as communities working within these research programs either succeed or fail to attract sufficient resources, to pose problems that adherents feel compelled to address, and to generate answers consistent with basic assumptions. This competitive and evolutionary process is as much political as "scientific." As research programs and the communities that sustain them flourish, expand, stagnate, decay, disappear, or replace others, the process enables progress without guaranteeing it.

A key implication of this analysis is that the demise of once-flourishing paradigms is crucial for progress—whether in science or in politics. Adherents to a formerly dominant paradigm in either domain are required to abandon cherished beliefs and ask forbidden questions. The project's "negative heuristic," as Lakatos referred to the questions ruled out by ontological and other "metaphysical" assumptions, are, in effect, instructions to project adherents as to what *not* to think about or try to improve. The program's "positive heuristic," in contrast, are questions that communities are encouraged to find worthy of solving, goals they are urged to pursue, and methods they are authorized to use.[5] As long as the community's efforts, methods, and answers remain consistent with the assumptions that mark its discursive boundaries, conclusions and accomplishments can be celebrated by the project's community as valuable and as rendering the world more tractable to its purposes.

Maintaining the integrity of a research or political community requires the sense or at least the promise of progress. Occasional failures of analysis, persuasion, mobilization, or prediction can be rationalized as errors of measurement or technique, but sustained contradictions of expectations are serious threats. The key to project survival is to respond to such "anomalies" by ignoring them until their challenges can be explained or treated with authorized techniques and with basic assumptions still intact. Lakatos refers to the successful absorption of such anomalies as "progressive problem shifts," in which difficult-to-explain observations or events become exceptions that prove the rule, yielding new insights and provoking more interesting questions without contradicting core assumptions.[6]

But defense of a paradigm is often achieved in ways that are not progressive and indeed may undermine its vitality and competitive position. If experimental or predictive failures are repeatedly excused by specifying new assumptions, the paradigm quickly becomes more complex but less coherent and useful. As a "protective belt"[7] of conditions and assumptions expands to protect the "hard core" of the project's belief system, more and more work is required to make arguments that are less and less interesting or effective. A paradigm defended in this way narrows opportunities for success, discourages learning, and prevents discoveries. It also forces its adherents to rely less on evidence or on their ability to understand or explain events and data, and more on their faith in the truth of their theories and of the assumptions undergirding them. Less able to elicit excitement or satisfy curiosity, the project's theories become doctrines, orthodoxies that rely less on empirical results and more on political clout to fend off competition. In Lakatosian terms, the research program enters a "degenerative" phase, characterized by "sterile inconsistencies and ever more ad hoc hypotheses."[8]

The fact is that no successful system of belief, or paradigm, can have within it the means to quickly recognize when its time has passed or to establish procedures for discarding its assumptions when they become the obstacle, not the route, to progress. When contrary evidence becomes difficult to deny or ignore, both scientists and politicians have shown extraordinary ingenuity. They have offered brilliant strategies and arguments to extend the life of projects even in the face of seemingly stark evidence of error and failure. For example, phlogiston chemists long sought to ignore puzzling evidence that a burned substance weighed more, not less than it had prior to combustion, as if removing something made it heavier, not lighter. Eventually, when forced to acknowledge the accuracy of the measurements, some suggested that phlogiston had buoyancy—a kind of "negative weight"—that, when removed, increased the heft of the burned substance. Others hypothesized that disappearing phlogiston created air deposits that added more weight than was removed by its elimination. After decades of work, however, experimental chemists using radically new theories about individual gases produced a consensus that heat added mass from surrounding gases to combustible materials, rather than removing phlogiston from them. Only then did the ad hoc-ery and increasing complexity of phlogiston theory expose the degenerative character of that research program, leading to abandonment of beliefs that phlogiston even existed.[9]

Newtonian mechanics reigned supreme for two centuries on the basis of a robust positive heuristic that rewarded Newtonians with successful explanations of an amazingly wide variety of phenomena. This success protected scientists from having to ask how gravitational forces exerted themselves instantaneously over great distances, even as a hardcore assumption of the paradigm was the impossibility of "action at a distance." Their reputation also allowed Newtonians to avoid worrying over much about various anomalies—such as a glaring discrepancy between theoretical predictions and the observed orbit of the planet Mercury. Newtonian control of established institutions of science, and public belief in the deep connections between the truth of their theory and the truth of Christianity, bolstered their resistance to accumulating and powerful evidence in favor of Einstein's special and general theories of relativity. Eventually, however, advances in mathematics and scientific measurement enabled relativity to subsume and effectively replace the fundamental assumptions, if not most of the practical conclusions, of Newtonian mechanics.

The same pattern is observed outside the natural sciences. Core Marxian doctrine held that history was the unfolding of class struggle. This premise seemed fatally contradicted by the willingness of millions of workers to slaughter each other under national flags in World War I. In response Marxians quickly developed theories of nationalism as "false consciousness," thereby invoking psychology to protect their negative heuristic or hard-core assumptions, though at the cost of making fuzzy the orthodox commitments to materialism as the single basic driver of human history. Efforts to expand Marxism's "protective belt" also included Lenin's famous identification of imperialism as the final or "highest stage" of capitalist social organization, along with theories of the labor aristocracy and of the dynamics of "neocolonialism." These latter theories were developed to protect Marxian doctrine regarding the overexpansion and inevitable doom of capitalism via imperialism from being challenged by the success of European decolonization and the survival of capitalist powers.

In the middle decades of the twentieth century the "modernization paradigm" dominated social scientific approaches in sociology, economics, and political science to processes of change in Asia, Africa, and Latin America. The presumptive truths of this powerful research program and its associated political projects were that industrial technology would produce "modernity" in all "traditional" cultures and societies exposed to it. The irresistible and revolutionary changes that comprised this process of "modernization" would mold those societies and their political system, to conform to American and Western European models. Despite the obvious failure of their predictions, modernization theorists stuck by their assumption of a fundamental incompatibility between "traditional" and "modern" norms and organizing principles. For decades they offered elaborate, ad hoc subtheories and hypotheses to protect and save the paradigm. These included "breakdowns in modernization," "prismatism," "polynormativism," and "crises and sequences." Entire careers, projects, institutes, and subspecialties were built around these efforts to save modernization theory by protecting its hard core from the spreading failure of its key predictions. By the end of the twentieth century, however, little remained of the dichotomous ontology and technological determinism that lay at the heart of the modernization paradigm or of the expectation of convergence toward a single secular, rationalist, capitalist, and liberal democratic social order that it had encouraged. What began as a series of progressive problem shifts became, eventually, a flood of excuses, burdening remaining modernization theorists with the frustration, anomie, and sense of intellectual drift characteristic of a degenerative research program.

This pattern is as familiar in politics as it is in science. Projects move forward effectively toward analytic and political goals. The world changes or data available about the world improve, posing questions that cannot be answered or tasks that cannot accomplished within accepted and familiar categories. To protect cherished assumptions and agendas, adherents to the dominant political or research project avoid these questions. But if they cannot be dismissed as unimportant or turned into "confirming instances" with new theories that are yet consistent with the project's negative heuristic, the community faces a crisis. Loyalists who cling to the project risk frustration, boredom, cynicism, and departure from their ranks of the more ambitious and imaginative among them. In these ways we can see in the experience of the TSS paradigm what Lakatos and other historians of science have traced in the rise and fall of research programs in many different disciplines.

Although it later became a dominant paradigm, the TSS appeared, after June 1967, as a politically irrelevant fantasy, seen as impossible and beyond the moral pale of both Palestinian society and Israeli politics. By the 1990s, however, both elites and the informed public concerned with Israeli-Palestinian relations came to adopt the assumptions of its negative heuristic as boundaries on their thinking. They can be summarized as follows:

- The West Bank and Gaza Strip are temporarily occupied territories, held by the State of Israel but separate from it.
- Israel can withdraw from enough of the territory occupied in 1967 to make a negotiated "land for peace" deal possible.
- Two territorial states for two peoples in Palestine/the Land of Israel would be the basis for long-term acceptance by Palestinians and Israelis of a new and peaceful political status quo.
- The Arab and Muslim worlds and the wider international community would use this agreement as a legitimizing framework for the presence of a Jewish state in the Middle East.

Both analytically and politically, the TSS project scored tremendous successes in its rise to prominence and then dominance in the last decades of the twentieth century, marked by the enormous attention paid to its positive heuristic: its agenda for discussion, political calculation, and diplomatic action. Among other things, that agenda focused on the implications of settlements in the West Bank and Gaza and the meaning and presence or absence of a "point of no return"; the possibilities of dividing, defining, or sharing East Jerusalem; demographic trends and their political implications for Zionist values and Israeli interests; the likely importance of track-two versus formal diplomatic channels for facilitating negotiations; ways to finesse the refugee return question to suit political needs and public opinion on both sides; and strategies for bridging gaps between the "narratives" that Israeli Jews and Palestinian Arabs used to understand the tragedies and victories of their past relationship. The project's success resulted in vast numbers of news stories, research studies, conferences, political gambits, diplomatic initiatives, and fundraising activities, all linked to these and similar issues.

But in the twenty-first century the TSS project has analytically failed to account for or halt the passage of virtually every West Bank settlement milestone its advocates had historically established as capable of preventing the achievement of its central objective. In the early 1980s the number of 100,000 West Bank settlers was commonly used as a marker for a political reality that would render the two state solution an impossibility. There are now five times that number in the West Bank and seven times that number living across the Green Line—one out of every eleven Israeli Jews. This, however, is only one of the crucial anomalies the TSS project has been forced to (try) to ignore. Others include the rise on both sides and, in Israel, the ascendance of ultranationalist and fundamentalist views and programs; the vast and reliable support that Israeli Jews have given to governments wholly committed to de facto annexation; the miscarriage of dozens of international peace initiatives, including the Oslo process; the dominance among Israelis of beliefs in the absence of a Palestinian "partner for peace"; the failure of two generations of Israeli and Palestinian politicians who committed themselves to the banner of the two state solution; the near-evaporation of pressure on Israel from the Arab world and from Europe to agree to a Palestinian state; and the inability of even the most optimistic two state advocates to describe how coalitions capable of negotiating and implementing a TSS could come to power in Israel and within the Palestinian community.

One specific and important hypothesis underlying the TSS project has been that the United States would play a key role in pressuring Israel toward territorial compromise. Despite a record of active US diplomacy on the issue, however, the TSS paradigm has failed completely to explain why US administrations have not done so. Instead, they have moved from weak attempts to slow the West Bank settlement juggernaut (Obama 2009–2010), to phony or half-hearted efforts to achieve a TSS (Kerry 2013–2014), to a cynical and extravagant show of support for annexation and effective apartheid (Trump 2016–2020); and to lip service to a TSS goal unaccompanied by any hope or strategy for its achievement (Biden (2021–).

These are major anomalies for those expecting that the Israeli-Palestinian conflict can and will be resolved by negotiations leading to a viable Palestinian state in the West Bank and Gaza Strip. To save their paradigm, TSS adherents need to offer compelling explanations for these outcomes, and these accounts must inspire confidence and continued work toward the project's objectives. Instead, while the TSS's political leaders have either passed from the scene or abandoned the project—think of Yossi Sarid, Shulamit Aloni, Yossi Beilin, Amram Mitzna, Ran Cohen, Tzipi Livneh, Shlomo Ben-Ami, Amir Peretz, Haim Oron, Yuli Tamir, and Haim Ramon—its thought leaders have retreated to desperate defenses of their research program's negative heuristic. Instead of transforming these anomalies into "progressive problem shifts" (interesting agendas for research) or developing strategies for taking power, removing settlements, or starting negotiations, their attention is devoted to convincing themselves and followers that, in principle, it is not impossible (yet) for the dream of two states to be achieved, even if that might mean describing it differently, such as a confederation or as "parallel" states in the same territory.

Often these defenses of the paradigm's negative heuristic come down to an appeal to faith, hope, or to the logically problematic formula that because there is no (acceptable) alternative, the two state solution *must* still be available. Thus did a fundraising pamphlet issued by the Americans for Peace Now (APN) in September 2016 echo the haunting and fundamentally nonrational faith appeal of the *Ani Ma'amin* chant about the coming of the Messiah: "And even though he may tarry, with all that yet will I wait for him."[10] The APN request for donations concluded with this call by its vice chair Aviva Mayer: "You should believe in hope. I know that I do, even as I know that the peace process is currently non-existent. Should you wallow in despair? No, the time for peace will come . . . our time will come . . . My battered dream is better than no dream at all." The analytic version of this appeal to faith is well illustrated in a luxuriously produced 2017 plan for the two state solution, *2050 Strategic Plan: Between the Mediterranean Sea and the Jordan River.* Acknowledging that the region between the sea and the river "is too small to be strictly separated" and that "peace talks have stalled completely,"[11] the authors nonetheless offer detailed scenarios for development projects based on a declaration of faith made in the first sentence of the report: "We believe that by the year 2050 there will be **two sovereign states**, Israel and Palestine, living in peace with each other in the region that lies between the Mediterranean Sea and the Jordan River."[12] This "underlying premise" performs the same function of explaining how to achieve a two state solution as does the assumption used by the economist on the desert island who is asked how to open a can of food: "First, assume you have a can opener."[13]

When a paradigm is on the rocks, its adherents find it impossible to avoid engaging in forbidden behavior. For two staters, that means examining and trying to uphold the validity of assumptions that should be unquestioned starting points for discussion and work. Thus, for nearly a decade, the modal workshop, symposium, or panel discussion on or about the TSS has been framed as a question of whether it can ever be achieved or, in the metaphor of death that attends all these discussions, whether it should be considered comatose, on life support, "dying," "dead," or "dead but not buried."[14] It is also why, in April 2018, the Geneva Initiative (one of the TSS project's diehard organizations) launched its "Two-State Index," billed as "a monthly assessment of the road to the two-state solution." Until the announcement of its suspension in May 2021, the index offered graphical representations of monthly movement of a needle toward or away from prospects for success. No rules were offered to explain the relative importance of or relationships among different categories of developments deemed to be of importance ("Political and Public Arena," "Diplomatic and Legal Arena," "Reality on the Ground," and "Solvability of the Core Issues") or how events were coded under these headings as more or less positive or negative. In its report, in May 2021, the index stood at 5.68 (compared to 5.20 in April 2018); in other words, a little more than half-way between impossibility and accomplishment. But these numbers were much more instructive about the desperation of Geneva Initiative advocates than about the plausibility of progress toward a negotiated TSS. Note, for example, that the index was calibrated by treating the situation in 2018, when it was launched, as halfway to complete success instead of on the edge of complete failure.[15]

The function of a paradigm's negative heuristic, of its hard core of assumptions and truths, is to focus perceptions so that opportunities can be exploited while problems can be identified and solved. But for the last decade, at least, and probably since the second intifada, trying to see the Israeli-Palestinian conflict through the TSS lens has been like using a funhouse mirror to assess and navigate reality. So much effort has had to go into correcting the errors created by the lens that very little could be invested in advancing understanding or making progress toward desirable change. On the other hand, by adopting a new ontology, a new negative heuristic, and a new operating lens, questions of real importance, challenges of real significance, and opportunities of real promise come clearly into view. Those are the payoffs of flipping one's gestalt by seeing reality as one state ruling (if not governing) all those living between the river and the sea.

What happens when we start with the assumption that the State of Israel already rules the entire area between the river and the sea? First, it makes it easier to see just what being an inhabitant of the state means. Consider what political scientists mean by a "state." It is, fundamentally, an organization that enforces property rights. States appropriate property, but unless they appropriate all of it, they also enforce property claims of those ruled by it. If I can keep you off my property or even call property "mine" and have it mean something, that means there is an organization around that I think can enforce my claim to exclusive control of that property. If I do not believe that such claims can be enforced, then there is no state. If I and others are uncertain about the security of claims to property, then the state, such as it is, is weak.

Just as the property rights of Jews, wherever they live between the sea and the river, are a function of the power and policies of the State of Israel, so is that true of the property rights of Palestinians, such as they are, wherever they live west of the Jordan. No Palestinian property—no piece of land, no building, no home, no furnishings, no wealth of any kind—can be preserved in the face of an Israeli government seizure or demolition order. In that light, all Palestinians between the Jordan River and the Mediterranean Sea, whether denizens of Tulkarem, East Jerusalem, Gaza, or Jaffa, are living within the State of Israel. Saying that simplifies Israeli practices. Indeed, it is precisely what the Israeli Central Bureau of Statistics does when it classifies all Jews living between the river and the sea as living in the State of Israel. If all Jews living west of the Jordan River, including those in the West Bank, are counted within the total number of people living in the State of Israel, it seems natural to expect that all people living west of the Jordan would also be seen to live there.

For no matter where one lives in relation to the Green Line, the state that collects taxes, delivers mail, regulates trade, controls the airspace, and enables or prevents infrastructural development is Israel. This is not to say that Israel rules the fourteen million people living under its sway democratically or with the same laws and norms applied to all populations. It does not. A political caste system is in place. Ashkenazi citizen Jews occupy the highest rung; Gaza Palestinians are on the lowest. But regardless of how much political inequality exists within the state and how parochial is its application of the liberal and democratic principles it sometimes espouses, it is the State of Israel that is the apparatus of power and the arena of contestation determining who has what rights and who does not, who can travel and who cannot, whose lands can be possessed and used and whose are off-limits or confiscated, whose home can remain standing and whose can be demolished, who can be targeted for summary execution and who cannot. As measured by the State of Israel's impact on the intimate details of their lives and indeed on whether they live at all, Palestinians are as much its inhabitants as Black slaves were of the United States and as Africans in the Bantustans were of apartheid South Africa. The five-and-a-half-decade occupation of the West Bank and the fifteen-year blockade of Gaza, combined with the exposure to state violence that these populations regularly endure, do not mark their exclusion from the Israeli state: they are the crucial factors conditioning their incorporation within it.

If trying to see the situation in terms of the TSS paradigm produces anomalies, switching one's gestalt to a one state reality (OSR) paradigm eliminates them. From the OSR perspective it is not puzzling that no meaningful negotiations between Israel and the Palestinian Authority (PA), or brokered by the international community, took place over the last decade. If the PA, the West Bank, and Gaza Strip are within the State of Israel, why should one imagine otherwise? Similarly, that Israel arrests Palestinians in all areas of the West Bank virtually every night, or that it simply closes off whole sections of Ramallah or other West Bank cities at will, is not surprising. That is how Israel has long treated Arab, especially noncitizen Arab, inhabitants. That is to be expected given a OSR in which the dominant group in the state is threatened by a furious and subordinated population.

From an OSR point of view, Israelis living in the West Bank do not have to be treated "as if they are living in Israel": they are living in Israel. Within the context of the OSR, masses of East Jerusalem Arabs can improve their lot, and the city they share with hundreds of thousands of moderate Israeli Jews, by exercising their right to vote without fear of betraying their national cause. Liberal Jews can stop making a demographic argument that they know is racist but one that they used (in vain) to mobilize prejudice against and distaste for Arabs on behalf of territorial compromise. Given the impossibility of a land-for-peace deal, continued use of the argument only strengthens Jewish animus toward Arabs while blocking alliances with present and future Arab voters in a polity already inhabited by a majority of non-Jews (alliances whose political importance has become obvious in recent years).

Instead of desperately trying to see the Palestinian Authority as a potential negotiating partner or Palestinian state-on-the-way, it can be seen, much more accurately and fruitfully, as the functional equivalent of an Arab Department in Israel's "Ministry for Judea and Samaria"—a corrupt, alienated, and self-interested tool of discriminatory rule, used by Arabs to gain the (Israeli) permissions necessary to travel and by Israel to prevent popular resistance and lighten its administrative load. Increasingly, something of the same can be said about Hamas's position in the Gaza Strip. Chapter 4 by Yael Berda, which links the travel permit regime used to surveil and control West Bank and Gaza to its predecessor enforced by Israel via the military government that operated over Arab areas from 1948 to 1966, is an important contribution to understanding how the trajectory of Arab experience and struggle within the Green Line can illuminate the challenges and opportunities faced by those on the other side of it now and in the future.

Instead of chasing after a two state mirage or joining the ranks of the silent apartheidists who prefer pretending that the TSS might still be available to opening the door to struggles over Palestinian political rights, both Jewish and Arab progressives can work to end the occupation, not via withdrawal, but through full absorption of the territories and populations that Israel rules and the extension of equal citizenship to all. That is a real and, in the long run, attainable objective. In practical terms it means acting on the values that have led so many to support a TSS rather than acting to bring about the TSS itself. That means working in direct, meaningful, and satisfying ways to alleviate discrimination wherever it is found, increase political participation opportunities for everyone, and struggle against political disenfranchisement and economic inequality. In short, the OSR leads progressives toward democratizing Israel rather than wasting their time seeking to redesign its boundaries.

In chapter 7 Mohanad Mustafa and As'ad Ghanem discuss the "politics of hope" and document the shift among the "Arabs of '48" toward confidence in the mobilization of Palestinian political power within Israel and commitment to the democratization of the state. Although they are proud of the accomplishments of the Joint List, Mustafa and Ghanem make it clear that the new generation of Arab elites in Israel question the official line adhered to by their leader, Ayman Odeh, and look forward to a struggle not for a separate Palestinian state in the West Bank and Gaza but for a democratic state in the whole country.

Indeed, there are signs that increasing numbers of "liberal Zionists" and veteran two staters have shifted the focus of their hopes to the Joint List and, more recently, to Ra'am (the Islamist, Negev Bedouin party of Mahmoud Abbas) since the latter's split from the Joint List and its ascendance to power as a member of the Bennett-Lapid–led coalition government. It is impossible to say how many Jews in the large and mixed urban areas voted for the Joint List, but it is known that in the September 2019 election three predominantly Jewish areas contributed 10,000 votes to it. Five months later, in March 2020 that number doubled.[16] Meretz, meanwhile, which secured only four Knesset seats in the April 2019 elections, ran as a part of two different electoral unions in September 2019 and March 2020. In those elections Meretz representation fell to only three Members of Knesset. But in March 2021, embracing Arab voters more openly, it won six seats and entered the government. One of its three cabinet ministers was Issawi Frej, from the village of Kfar Qasim.

One grassroots organization, formed in 2015, whose composition, purpose, slogans, and tactics illustrate the OSR's implications for progressives in Israel, is "Standing Together." On its website, it states its core beliefs:

> We believe that every struggle that we face in Israeli society is connected—you cannot separate the struggle for peace, from the struggle for equality, from the struggle for social justice. If you are active in the fight for one of

> these rights in Israeli society, you are intrinsically connected to the fight for another one. Every person living in Israel, whether they be Arab or Jewish, male or female, living in the periphery or in a city center, is impacted by the government's refusal to afford us of these basic factors for happiness and security.
>
> The intersectionality of these struggles is undeniable—and when we fight for one, we fight for all. If we believe that we deserve to live in a society where peace exists, then we deserve a movement that presents a cohesive alternative to the right-wing in Israel which denies us this reality. That movement is us.[17]

Another specific example of this kind of struggle is the campaign against the 2017 "Law for the Regularization of Settlement in Judea and Samaria," aka the "Regularization Law." In 2017 President Reuven Rivlin sent shock waves through the country when he confronted a large meeting of settler activists with a speech framed in old-fashioned liberal Jabotinskian terms. Rivlin called for Israeli sovereignty to be fully implemented in the entire country, from the river to the sea, including the grant of equal citizenship to all its inhabitants. The occasion for the president's speech was promulgation of the "Regularization Law," which retroactively legalized the confiscation of Palestinian private property by Israelis in West Bank settlements. After passage of the law, more than a dozen Israeli organizations submitted petitions to the Supreme Court, sitting as the High Court of Justice, to overturn it. One of these organizations, Adalah: The Legal Center for Minority Rights, is staffed by Arab attorneys who are citizens of Israel. Adalah filed a petition on behalf of seventeen Palestinian village councils in the West Bank, and in 2020 the Supreme Court ruled in favor of the petitioners: it struck down the law as unacceptably discriminatory, mainly on the grounds of it contradicting not international law but rather Israeli constitutional principles of equality and human dignity.[18] Thus, as a result of a civil-society–based struggle launched by Arab activists, and supported by liberal Jews and by stalwart right-wing annexationists such as President Rivlin, not only was a measure of justice achieved but also a major precedent was set. All inhabitants of Israel, including noncitizen Arabs living in the West Bank, have rights under *Israeli* law enforceable in *Israeli* courts. The fight over this law foreshadows countless struggles that will ensue as the reality of apartheid in territories holding masses of noncitizens collides with global human rights norms and the legal and moral commitments of Israeli democracy, however limited that democracy may be.

The OSR is not a fully formed project or paradigm. The image of the future it implies is a contested future, not a settled outcome. Nor can one design a blueprint for the state that a majority of Jews and Arabs within it would endorse. But adopting the OSR as a fundamental understanding of what exists, and what does not, offers a secure place to stand and a much more productive and hope-enhancing framework of assumptions, categories, expectations, and questions than the TSS paradigm. And it can do real explanatory work. The puzzle I tried to solve in this chapter is why so many still imagine that the occupation of the West Bank and Gaza will end with Israel's withdrawal from those territories instead of ending, as the occupation of the Western and Central Galilee ended, by changing the terms of their absorption into Israel. By drawing on evidence for how and why deeply embedded scientific beliefs change slowly and jaggedly in response to contrary evidence, I explain why most of those devoted to the success of the TSS have been unable to respond in a timely way to realities that cannot be made to conform to their expectations and hopes. In doing so, my own hope is that disappointed two staters committed to democracy, equality, and mutual respect for nonexclusivist forms of national self-determination can be tempted to try to see the world differently, and thereby to stand as counterexamples to Max Planck's famous (paraphrased) dictum that "science advances, one funeral at a time."

2

FROM JEWISH PRIVILEGE TO JUDAIC SUPREMACY

The Religious Zionist One State Solution

Gershon Shafir

There is a call to abandon the two state paradigm as passé and view the de facto one state reality as the foundation for forward-looking research.[1] Ian Lustick leaves it up to the cunning of history to find the ways for expanding suffrage and citizenship in a single Jewish-Palestinian state.[2] Other advocates of the one state resolution to the Israeli-Palestinian conflict present two versions: the binational, in which each group enjoys cultural autonomy, and the one-person, one-vote model, which is commonly understood as a civic state of Jewish and Palestinian citizens who enjoy a full complement of equal rights and access to institutions. There has emerged, however, a third, diametrically opposed one state genus within the de facto one state reality: a single Jewish sovereign state from the sea to the river that not only privileges Jews but also imposes Judaic supremacy. This halakhically (the body of the written and oral compilation of Judaic law) justified Jewish exceptionalism rebuffs demands for and disregards not only national but also political, social and, in some cases, civic Palestinian rights. A Judaic supremacist regime is envisioned not only across the Green Line but within it as well. My aim in this chapter is to inform and warn of its growing sway, chart the trajectory of its emergence, and set out its main characteristics.

My thesis is that the halakhic one state model is best understood as an integral part and vital channel of the progression from laying claim to portions of Palestine by means of secular Jewish privilege to claiming all of Palestine as a matter of Judaic supremacy. Jewish immigrants constructed themselves, as the British had already defined them, as sovereignty-carrying settlers and *eo ipso* Palestinians as natives outside the moral universe of political rights. As the Yishuv grew and consolidated, so did its national consciousness, seeking to upgrade the British promise of the "national home" into a demand for independence and statehood, even if its expanse remained limited by demographic considerations. After the 1967 war, those impassioned by the prospect of normalizing further territorial expansion in disregard of Palestinian demography pitched a more sweeping religious justification. Although we may think of Zionism as nationalized Judaism, Religious Zionism—as part and parcel of the worldwide religious revival from the 1970s on—has diffused its halakhic doctrine by Judaizing that nationalism. Judaic supremacy renders Palestinian Arabs invisible or at least easy to ignore and has become the orthodoxy of Religious Zionists. In its most radical form, supremacy became the raison d'être of *hardalim*, a Religious Zionist group that is both more nationalist and Orthodox. Although Judaic supremacy has not yet captured the allegiance of Israel's large secular or traditional Jewish population, it has made significant inroads in the process of transforming Religious Zionism itself.

Part one of this chapter lays out my method of thinking about religious revival through the dual perspectives of Jewish exceptionalism and sovereignty. In part two I present its halakhic sources and examine the drastic transformation of the halakhic treatment of minorities by a sovereign Jewish state. In part three I examine the accommodationist halakhic interpretation, and in part four the radical turn.

Part One: Historical Legacy and Modern Dilemmas

How is the past made relevant to and formative for the living? Eric Hobsbawm and James Clifford offer two models of partaking in cultural traditions. Hobsbawm, the historian, views the selective invocation of time-honored cultural elements undertaken with the aim of advancing modern political agendas as an *invention of the tradition*. "'Traditions,'" he writes, "which appear or claim to be old are often quite recent in origin and sometimes invented."[3] Hobsbawm and his collaborators' cogent and insightful perspective on the uses and abuses of tradition, nevertheless, remains unduly narrow because of their focus on the rise of nineteenth-century nationalism. The anthropologist James Clifford also suggests the invocation of authenticity as a cultural ideal and directs our attention to *returns*: the rediscovery and reworking of a tradition. His subject matter—becoming indigenous in the twenty-first century by performing indigeneity—is, however, even narrower and more contemporary. In addition, although Clifford rejects Hobsbawm's narrowly political perspective, he avoids confronting the thorny intrusions of power into cultural matters.[4] For example, his presents-becoming-futures approach valorizes the invention of "post-vernacular languages" or the offering of "Exxon Mobil master artist classes" in the Alaska Native Heritage Center while ignoring, as he conceded, their destructive and homogenizing effects.[5]

Given the respective chronological limitations and one-sidedness of Hobsbawm's Marxist and Clifford's constructivist approaches, I prefer to follow in the footsteps of Tim McDaniel's Weberian analysis of the interactions of religion and politics. McDaniel queries the religious responses to the iconoclasm of modernity but within a *longue durée* time frame, all the while confronting head-on the push and pull of religion and politics.[6] My approach to the transformations of Judaism in its relationship with Zionist modernity is based on his work.

McDaniel supplants the broad concepts of religion and modernity with a pair of carefully crafted and focused analytic terms—the former with historical legacy, the latter with modern dilemmas—all the while concentrating on their interaction. He suggests that for any given aspect of culture to constitute a historical legacy, it must have significant historical roots and traction in the custody chain of tradition. To be transmitted to our period, such an aspect has to be accorded renewed significance because of its contemporary relevance or, in Max Weber's term, its "value relevance [*Wertbeziehung*]."[7] A historical legacy becomes relevant in our own time either as a "usable past" or an obstacle to a workable future. Either way, "historical legacies create modern dilemmas: either how to bring about change in accord with a past model or how to adapt or discard something from the tradition that no longer seems to make sense."[8] The modern use of an ancient cultural component in the context of a modern dilemma is likely to be messy and conflict ridden.

Historical legacies then are never simply invented or constitute a return, because they change in the process of being fitted for reuse while also changing the tradition into which they are fitted and its reusers who do the work of retrofitting. Comprehensive secular ideologies have fostered religious overtones without becoming religions, but as McDaniel observes, "It has been much less clearly perceived that religion can in turn develop many traits of ideology."[9]

The focus of McDaniel's study is the relationship between Islam and modernity, in particular the emergence of political Islam or Islamicism in the broader context of contemporary religious revivals. His central thesis is that within contemporary Islam there emerged, side by side with social fundamentalism, an ideological fundamentalism as an alternative to traditional, reformist, and modernist forms of Islam. The context for the ideologization within Islam has been its growing involvement in political and social struggles in search of a new social order in the present world; it consists of grafting novel elements to the Islamic religion "so that old concepts and patterns of action acquired new meaning."[10] Religious ideologization is a process that is politically engaged and inspired, and in many, though not all cases, religious revivals further nationalist projects even as they challenge their content. I suggest that the same development is observable within Judaism in Israel.

Part Two: The Historical Legacy of the Code of Maimonides

The sources of Judaic religious authority, what Foucault would call the disciplinary pastoral power of clerics over the laity, are diffuse and therefore pluralist.[11] Although Israel has a chief rabbinate, which is headed by a Sephardi Chief Rabbi whose office traces back to the Ottoman era and a Chief Ashkenazi Rabbi set up by the British Mandate, it is mostly an administrative rather than a pastoral body. The chief rabbinate supervises rabbinical courts, and its jurisdiction covers personal status issues, conversion, and services such as supervising kashrut and ritual baths. In the absence of religious centralization within Judaism, rabbis draw their traditional authority from a mixture of sources. First, graduation from a higher yeshiva affords a rabbinical certification. Second, prestige is bestowed by yeshiva affiliation; particularly prominent are those rabbis who establish their own yeshiva or are head of one. Third, some rabbis are viewed as possessing individual charisma or when they inherit their position, frequently within rabbinic dynasties, as having institutional charisma.

The final source of religious authority is the writing of halakhic works, from books through sermons to *responsa* addressed to followers outside the yeshiva. According to their literary output and quality, as well as their halakhic erudition, peers and lay audience rank their authors' reputations into a broad hierarchy very much like that of academic scholars in other fields.

This pluralistic halakhic legal framework was no match for the centralized legal system of a sovereign, nationalist, and democratic Jewish-majority state.[12] According to Alexander Kaye's pathbreaking study, Religious Zionist rabbis, who were well versed in Enlightenment norms, and in tandem with the other decolonizing states, offered their own version of legal centralism—the halakhic state—itself a modern creature conceived in the late 1940s. The main authority behind it was Rabbi Yitzchak Halevi Herzog, Israel's first Chief Ashkenazi Rabbi who constructed a halakhic constitution for Israel that, in his words, would have rendered Israel a "theocracy."[13] Despite the failure of Religious Zionists to transform Israel, "they never abandoned the principle that a legally centrist halakhic state was the ideal. The persistence of that idea continues to color Israeli political discourse."[14] Herzog's notion of the halakhic state reemerged two decades later on the back of another halakhic sea change: the religionization of Jewishness by placing at the center of the halakha the political aim of expanding the boundaries of the State of Israel by expanding Jewish sovereignty onto the historical Land of Israel, thereby challenging not only the rights but also the legitimate presence of Palestinians.

Though generations of Jews prayed for the rebirth of the State of Israel, for many religious Jews it has no religious significance because it is not a Judaic state but the "state of the Jews," whereas for many haredim it is an illegitimate attempt to usurp the messianic promise of divine restoration. At the end of the nineteenth century, Eastern European religious Jewry "lack[ed] the strength to respond to the iconoclastic challenges of the modern era" and the liberal, socialist, communist, and Zionist responses it generated. Those religious Jews who joined the Hovevei Zion and later the Zionist movement consequently remained its junior partners, nursing a deeply felt sense of inferiority that lasted until the second half of the twentieth century. For religious Jews, the State of Israel, as Israel's foremost sociologist of religious Jewry, Menachem Friedman explains, became a "theological dilemma," leaving them dependent on a social order that violated their beliefs.[15]

In contrast to the State of Israel, the Land of Israel under Jewish sovereignty following the 1967 war "is an original Jewish concept which has positive halakhic significance."[16] The modern dilemma of what should be done with the newly occupied territories offered a historic opportunity for Religious Zionists to overthrow their dependent status, and the commandment to inherit and settle Eretz Yisrael (Land of Israel) served as the historical legacy around which Religious Zionism underwent profound ideologization. Its rabbinical authorities politicized—in fact, nationalized—Judaism very much as secular Zionism had nationalized and politicized Judaism several generations earlier; they made the "Land of Israel" into the ideological battering ram of Religious Zionism's political struggle against Zionism's secular "State of Israel."

In the centuries from the end of the Judean Kingdom to the establishment of the modern State of Israel, rabbinic discourse about the place of minorities in a future Jewish state remained a barren field. After all, postbiblical halakha evolved in postexilic Judaism, and this topic was of no concrete or pressing concern in diasporic Jewish life. In addition, in the modern era the gap that opened up between halakhic study and the immense changes that had taken place in the structure and legitimacy of states "left a dearth of resources to study and elaborate on the halakha [concerning the running of a state]."[17]

When about 160,000 of the original 1.3 million Muslim and Christian Palestinian Arabs remained under the sovereignty of the new Jewish state at the conclusion of the 1948 war-generated Nakba, their presence and the protections and rights they should be entitled to posed a new theological dilemma for the rabbis of Religious Zionism. Against this background, the only available medieval treatment of *nokhrim* (aliens) under Jewish rule by the greatest medieval twelfth-century sage Maimonides (Rabbi Moshe ben Maimon; Rambam by his Hebrew acronym) has taken on exaggerated importance and remains the starting point of any halakhic analysis of the status of Israel's Arab minority. Its impact is enhanced by Maimonides's reputation as "the great eagle," a scholar revered as the most influential and prolific medieval Jewish halakhic author and codifier, and an outstanding philosopher conversant with the era's thriving Muslim scholarship and in dialogue with Greek philosophy. Adding further weight to Maimonides's rulings is that they are an integral part of his codification of the entirety of Jewish law in his fourteen-volume magnum opus, the *Mishne Torah*. Contemporary rabbinic authorities return to ground zero of the *Mishne Torah* as the focus of the halakhic endeavor that systematizes and rigidifies the historical legacy of Judaism on the status of nokhrim under Jewish rule in response to the modern dilemma posed by the conquests of the 1967 war.

My goal in this chapter is not to provide a textual exegesis of *Mishne Torah*. Nor am I concerned with the authenticity or even accuracy of halakhic analyses but only with their marked reinterpretation. The unit of my analysis, therefore, is not the idea or the text in which it is presented but a specific type of discourse: the rabbinic ruling (*psika*). Such rulings are viewed from within the tradition as theology, but because they are imparted to an audience, to students, to the faithful, and to fellow rabbis, they are best viewed from a sociological vantage point as teachings that carry influence. As such, their social transmission makes them potent by rendering ideas actionable. I aim to demonstrate how biblical and halakhic texts are reconfigured to replace claims of Jewish privilege with exclusive Judaic privilege over Eretz Yisrael and supremacy over both citizen and occupied Arabs. Reconfiguring a historical legacy as part and parcel of an ongoing political contestation of this-worldly concerns is the very process of dressing elements of a religious tradition in the armor of a political ideology.

Hebrew employs only the single designation "Jewish" (*yehudi*), whereas English and other European languages distinguish between two post-Enlightenment adjectives: the Jewish people and the Judaic religion, Judaism. I turn now to an analysis of two interpretive waves of Maimonides through the dual perspective of *Jewish sovereignty* and *Judaic exceptionalism*. Given that Jewish chosenness is to be preserved through Jewish rulers' careful management of foreign—that is, idolatrous—influences, these two halakhic motifs are joined in the treatment of nokhrim.

The subdivision and classification of nokhrim living under Jewish sovereignty by the halakha are every bit as detailed and complex as the immigration and naturalization laws of modern nation-states. Commandments concerning contacts and dealings with idolaters, according to *The Jewish Political Tradition* by Michael

Walzer and coauthors, are "anxious and wary, aimed at restrictions where that is possible, minimal accommodation where that is necessary."[18] Among the idolatrous nokhrim there is one subcategory—the seven original nations of Canaan—that are to be destroyed and not allowed to dwell (*lo techanem*) in Eretz Yisrael (Deuteronomy 7:2). The descendants of Noah's sons form another sweeping category. The halakha seeks to impose on them or claims credit for demanding that they adopt the seven Noahide commandments or duties: an exegetical invention of a code of law for humanity.[19] The most significant rubric for our analysis is the in-between category of the *ger toshav* (permanent resident; *gere toshav* pl.), who are allowed to reside alongside Jews in Eretz Yisrael but only under a set of detailed and harsh halakhic rules.

In their groundbreaking analysis of the concept of the "goy" from biblical through early rabbinical literature, Ophir and Rosen-Zvi emphasize the fluidity of the categories of the nokhrim who live around, in proximity to, and mixed in with Jews. The ger and citizen (*ezrach*) share certain aspects of social status (for example, in land inheritance) and holiness (e.g., in the performance of mitzvot): hence, they are not binary categories but gradations.[20] As a group Jews progressed from an endogamic kinship network, through communal life under Egyptian economic subjugation, to ethnic nationhood. It is not their separation from other nations per se but from those nation's gods, from idolatry, that is the key to Israel's exceptionalism.[21] Even then, the ger remains a dependent in the household of a Jewish patron and, as part of the community, does not become its Other, a stable pole of alterity.[22]

By the first and second centuries CE, however, the division between Jew and ger was not only sharpened but the ger was also understood only as a potential convert, leaving little or no room for the resident alien.[23] There is then, a flexible, nondualistic post-biblical tradition of the status of the ger, as well as an early rabbinic demarcation that places the ger toshav (unlike the ger tzedek, the convert) outside the bounds of the Jewish community.

Maimonides codified the list of halakhic rules to be followed by gere toshav as a precondition for residing under Jewish rule in two parts of *Mishne Torah*: as part of his treatment of idolaters (vol. 6: *Sefer Hamad'a, Avodat Kochavim* (Idolatry), chap. 10), thus labeling them as a potentially negative influence on Jewish chosenness; and under the category of kings and wars (vol. 14: *Sefer Hashoftim, Melachim Vemilchamot* (Kings and Wars), chap. 6), thereby identifying them as a prior and still potential enemy. As part of his interpretive framework, he emphasized those biblical commandments that are the closest to the binary rabbinic tradition. The gere toshav, Maimonides held, must accept both the payment of tribute and a "demeaning and humiliating (*sheyihyu nivzim veshfelim*)" subjugation. Neither were they to "lift their heads against Israel" nor "be appointed over a Jew in any matter whatsoever" (Kings and Wars 6:1). And yet, "for the sake of peace" (*mipney darkhei shalom*) or to prevent "hostility"—a common injunction to alleviate forbidding halakhic commandments toward aliens and thereby neutralize potential hostility—Jews are required to secure the well-being of the *gere toshav*; for example, by making available to them free health care, while poor idolaters should be provided for as poor Jews are (Idolatry, 10:2, 5).[24]

Maimonides's code, however, far from ending the discussion over the status of nokhrim, requires further clarification and leads to new questions. One of the oldest contentions is whether idolatrous nokhrim had to, as Maimonides required, accept the Code of Noah de jure, based on the conviction of Judaism's superiority (Kings and Wars 6:10) or, as Maimonides's greatest contemporary critic, Rabbi Avraham ben David (Ra'avad) argued, de facto, by behaving morally and recognizing god without reference to Judaism.[25] In addition to questioning how open to other religious belief systems Judaism should be, there is a tug of war between restrictive and expansive uses of the subcategories of nokhrim. Drawing transhistorical equivalence between modern and ancient identities and the redivision of the hierarchy of nokhrim and their attendant obligations is at the heart of the ideologization of Religious Zionism.

It cannot be emphasized enough that Maimonides's overall framework for allowing gere toshav to live in Eretz Yisrael is thoroughly political. The single axis around which the *Mishne Torah*'s stipulations revolve is whether Jews are sovereign rulers of the land. The restrictions imposed on idolaters listed earlier are in effect only when they rule over Jews, but "Israel has the upper hand, we are not allowed to let idolaters live among us even temporarily" (Idolatry 10:9). Jewish sovereignty is to be used to eliminate the risks of assimilation associated with living within a diverse population, and it overrides religious obligations, even overshadowing the "be kind to the stranger (ger) since you were a stranger in Egypt" admonition.

Not only were these injunctions political but ironically, Maimonides's presentation of the commandments concerning warfare against idolaters also possesses a striking jihadi quality. Whereas the Mishna and Talmud viewed Joshua's conquest of Canaan and battle against Amalek as "exceptional responses to divine command, Maimonides places them in continuity with the commanded wars of later kings."[26] His notion of religious war, adopted under the influence of Islamic scholarship—that is, war on behalf of religion and against hostile idolaters to bring them within the borders of a just polity—"remained idiosyncratic" among his contemporaries, only to become the standard and stand-alone interpretation in recent times.[27]

Part Three: The Modern Dilemma: Religious Accommodation

Religious Zionist aspirations for transforming the State of Israel into a halakhic state were achieved only in small but significant arenas. Israel is a halakhic state in terms of issues of personal status concerning marriage, divorce, and custody. The definition of Jewishness and, to a large extent, of national holidays, symbols, and the regulation of the public sphere are also determined halakhically. The extension of the halakha into other spheres of life and institutions received a major impetus after the 1967 war, when halakha itself was ideologized through its fixation on Judaic sovereignty over the Palestinian nokhrim under Israel jurisdiction.

The Yishuv and the State of Israel have twice reconfigured Maimonides's list of kingly, war, and idolatry commandments concerning Jewish exceptionalism and sovereignty, when two groups of Palestinians were placed under Jewish rule through the military conquests in 1948 and again in 1967. The first reinterpretation, stretching from the decade before establishment of the State of Israel to the 1967 war, supplemented the Maimonidean texts on the status of nokhrim under Jewish rule with meta-halakhic or nonhalakhic sources to bring them up to date with contemporary political theory, popular sovereignty, and human rights. Israel's first Ashkenazi and Sephardi Chief Rabbis were the most visible early articulators of this string of interpretation. They were intent on creating a modus vivendi between the newly formed state's legal framework and the halakha through proposed constitutional drafts.

Rabbi Herzog's assessment of the modern dilemma posed by Israel's attitude toward its minority population was pragmatic and motivated by a complex set of potentially contradictory considerations. Jews did not have "the upper hand" in the country, he argued, and mistreatment of Arabs might reflect poorly on diasporic Jewry. In addition, Israel's secular judicial system would not be based on the Maimonidean Code. Consequently, the State of Israel could not ignore the requirements of the post–World War II international legal order and enforce halakhic discriminations against *gere toshav*. This contextualization highlights the ad hoc character of his rulings, potentially limiting their historical scope. Rabbi Herzog presented his relevant rulings as a bridge between the halakha and democracy—as a Zionist halakha, so to speak. Consequently, he consented to equalizing Muslim and Christian Arab citizenship rights with their fellow Jewish citizens, including the rights to purchase land and serve in public office.[28]

Rabbi Ben-Zion Meir Hai Uziel, Israel's first Sephardic Chief Rabbi, also recognized the need to respect the legal obligations attendant on belonging to the UN. He reached very similar halakhic outcomes but from a very different starting point, under the influence of humanist and liberal values and cognizant of the constraints of international law. Uziel's proposed constitutional draft, in dialogue with the principles of liberal democracy, holds that all who live permanently in the country "are equal in rights and duties in all government ministries and courts, possess passive and active suffrage in municipal elections, and freedom of conscience and action according to the laws of their religion."[29] He also expressed opposition to declaring land whose Arab owners fled during the 1948 war as abandoned property as a step toward incorporating it into the new state's possession and, in essence, to the halakhic "right of conquest."[30] Uziel's approach was based on universal values; unlike Rabbi Herzog's formulation, it was not conditional until Jews gained the upper hand in Eretz Yisrael.[31]

Yet both Herzog and Uziel approached the status of Israel's Arab minority based on the broader belief that democracy could be reconciled with or even derived from halakhic principles. This starting point, though conditional for Herzog and partial for Uziel, led them to tone down Jewish exceptionalism as the guiding principle of the newly sovereign state. Israel's first request to be admitted to the UN was rejected, and it was accepted as a member state only in May 1949, after it promised to lift wartime restrictions on the liberty and property of its Arab minority.[32] Herzog and Uziel also felt compelled to accept these obligations. The Chief Rabbis' willingness to admit to the validity or at least the authority of human rights rendered overt and exclusive emphasis on Jewish exceptionalism suspect for the time being.

Between the 1940s and the 1970s, other Religious Zionist rabbis also propounded the accommodationist halakhic approach toward the Arab minority. For example, they made extensive use of the prudential injunction "for the sake of peace." Some went as far as viewing this as a foundational principle, rather than as a utilitarian device. Many also expressed concern that mistreating Israel's Arab minority could be used to justify discrimination against Jewish minorities around the world. Yet, the accommodationists and innovators were never a majority, and many Religious Zionist rabbinical authorities shared Herzog's view that accommodation was temporary until Israel had the upper hand over its Arab neighbors: it was appropriate for a weak Israeli state dependent on foreign succor and might change when Israel dominated over Arabs.[33]

Part Four: The Modern Dilemma: Radicalization and Ideology

A second interpretive wave of the Maimonidean Code reconfigured the halakhic position in a radically different fashion and provided a new answer to the dilemma of Jewish-Arab relations under Israeli rule. Taking its cue not from the

Universal Declaration of Human Rights but from military success, new halakhic interpretations gradually resurrected one section of Maimonides's code: his codification in chapter 6, "Kings and Wars," of the biblical commandments of conquests, in particular, "The Conquest of Canaan." The new approach, leaping over more than two millennia in the evolution of the laws of war and their most recent legislation in the Fourth Geneva Convention in 1949, is best described, as it views itself, as straightforward (*pshat*) or, as such approaches are commonly categorized in legal thinking, as "originalist."

We can best observe this metamorphosis by following the growing use of the *lo techanem* commandment and the changing meanings attributed to it. This commandment assumed new significance only after the 1967 war; although it was understood initially to refer to sovereignty over the Land of Israel, it was extended and refocused subsequently on its Palestinian Arab inhabitants. The institutional locus of reinterpreting the historical legacy of conquest was in the higher Merkaz Harav yeshiva. Its founder, Rabbi Avraham Itzhak Kook and his son Rabbi Zvi Yehuda Kook, were closer in spirit to the nationalist aims of Zionism than most of the Religious Zionist camp. Secular Zionists, in their view, were the unwitting tools of this messianic design, "whose beginnings were slow but [its] forward direction was certain."[34] It was Rabbi Kook *fils* who asserted in a thanksgiving celebration for victory in the 1967 war and the conquest of East Jerusalem that one was to brave martyrdom for the possession of all parts of Eretz Yisrael in disregard of the goyim. Such radicalization, however, was not limited to the Kookist teachings and rulings. Here we encounter the birth of a halakhic ideology, raising one religious commandment over all others in the service of an ultimate political end.

Specifically, Rabbi Zvi Yehuda Kook recalled the biblical proscription that regulated the permanent presence (*chanaya kvu'a*, referencing *lo techanem*) of non-Jews in Eretz Yisrael. He interpreted this prohibition as meaning that no sovereignty (*ribonut*) was to be granted to non-Jews, and should the Jewish leadership consent to such an outcome, it would be invalid.[35] His view was echoed in 1983 by his student and the editor of his works, Rabbi Shlomo Aviner, who bundled together the three ways Jews earn their exclusive privilege in Eretz Yisrael: as settlers, as the defenders of their national territory, and as members of the Judaic religion. A decade later, Rabbi Avraham Shapira, the successor of the Rabbis Kook at the head of Merkaz Harav and a Chief Rabbi, reiterated the halakhic rejection of the Oslo Accords because they were passed with the parliamentary support of Arab legislators and faithless Jewish MKs ignorant of the Torah and in disregard of the *lo techanem* commandment.[36]

This abrupt transformation is best observed in the radical reversal of the halakhic rulings of Rabbi Shlomo Goren, the Chief Rabbi of the Military Rabbinate and later Chief Ashkenazi Rabbi. In retrospect, he was a transitional figure, part of both the former and latter waves of Maimonidean interpreters. On the eve of Israeli independence, Goren's views resembled Rabbis Herzog and Uziel's inclusionary rulings. He rejected Maimonides's requirement that the Sons of Noah accept the seven universal commandments out of deference to Judaism in favor of those of the Ra'avad by arguing that Arabs enjoy civil rights even as he refused to view them as *gere toshav*.

After the 1967 war, Goren—even though he was not part of the Kooks's circle and differed from them in important respects—highlighted the commandment to settle Eretz Yisrael. Like Rabbi Kook, he based his ruling that "to turn over settlements land to Arabs is a double and quadruple offense" on the *lo techanem* prohibition.[37] Even though he was a former general in the IDF, he authorized soldiers to follow the halakhic ruling rather than the elected government and to disobey any order to cede Jewish land as part of a peace accord. By 1985, in a singular twist he not only demanded that the Muslims of Palestine accept Judaism as the authority for the seven Noahide commandments but that they also recognize Jewish entitlement to sovereignty in Eretz Yisrael and Israel as a Jewish state. The refusal to do so should deprive them both of the status of gere toshav and of the right to reside therein.[38] The drastic nature of this halakhic reversal cannot be overemphasized. *Lo techanem* came to exclude not only Arab sovereignty over land but also their very presence in Eretz Yisrael.[39] Although Religious Zionist halakhic authorities call on Nachmanides when asserting the commandment to settle the land (rather than on Maimonides, who did not list this requirement among his catalog of Judaism's 613 mitzvot), they turn to Maimonides to regulate the status of nokhrim under Jewish rule.

The "change in direction of halakhic rulings vis-à-vis aliens in the State of Israel," in Ophir and Rosen-Zvi's terminology, as Jews' Others, comes across most clearly in a 1987 publication by Rabbi Elisha Aviner, then a teacher in the Ma'aleh Adumin settlement's yeshiva and later its head; as a student, he had learned with his brother Schlomo in Rabbi Kook *fils*' Merkaz Harav Yeshiva. Aviner expresses the self-confidence typical of the post-1967 generation of rabbis. According to Ariel Picard, director of the Shalom Hartman Institute's Research Center for Contemporary Jewish Thought, Aviner's halakhic interpretations "express the political and ideological position of the majority of the Religious Zionist community's religious and civic leadership"; hence, they "did not generate objections."[40] It is the nationalist bent of Jewish exceptionalism that is given pride of place in his halakhic opinions. I focus my analysis of the halakhic turn on the status of Arabs under Israeli rule, as expressed by Rabbi Elisha Aviner and his contemporaries, because it is the mainstream view among Religious Zionists. This religious ideologization is spreading even further through its adoption as a central tenet by haredi Jews, as a result of the *hardalim*'s influence

Rabbi Elisha Aviner, like his brother, rejects the inclusionary approaches of the earlier generation of halakhic authorities because he views them as emergency measures whose validity has expired. Yet he goes even further, including, and sometimes singling out, Israel's Arab citizens in his scheme. Israeli Jews, he explains, are not commanded to provide social welfare to individual Arabs or to give them access to land. In his approach, Israel can also impose additional burdens and expectations on the cohesive Arab ethnic community that asserts its distinct nationality, according to Maimonides's *Mishne Torah*. "An alien national community that resides in our country," he expounds, "is not entitled to full civil rights." He demands that nearly the full list of Maimonides's restrictions on enemies defeated in war be implemented, requiring that Arabs under Jewish sovereignty "accept (*kabala*) of Israeli lordship, total surrender, namely reconciliation to Israeli sovereignty over all of the Land of Israel." Furthermore, Palestinians must relinquish expressions of their national identity and aspirations not only in their behavior but also in their consciousness.[41] They are to recognize Israel's god-given right to, well, Palestine. Consequently, their resistance to Israeli occupation and colonization becomes irrational and illegitimate.

Aviner goes further by holding that the *lo techanem* commandment is intended to forestall expanding the presence of aliens when Jews do not have enforcement powers, whereas another commandment—*lo yeshvu ba'aretz* (Exodus 23:33)—requires that their presence end when Jews rule the land. In short, he maintains that there is no place for Arabs in Eretz Yisrael.[42]

The exclusionary turn in halakhic reasoning vis-à-vis gere toshav and nokhrim relies on the Maimonidean approach to squeeze out other halakhic alternatives. Just as Rabbis Herzog and Uziel did in the 1940s and 1950s, Rabbi Raanan Mallek, coordinator of the Israeli Jewish Council for Interreligious Relations, suggests invoking Ra'avad's rival approach to liberalize present rulings, as would be the case under the pluralistic nature of halakhic interpretation.[43] But after the occupation of the West Bank and Jerusalem, the uses of the halakhic historical legacy to address the status of Palestinians living under Israeli sovereignty have gone in another direction. The predominant Religious Zionist and hardali approaches rigidify and ideologize the halakha as if Israel were already a halakhic state or en route to becoming one. Filtering the halakhic historical legacy through the political prism of Jewish sovereignty leads to rejecting not only halakhic pluralism but also the existence of alternative interpretive traditions regarding the Land of Israel and its Palestinian inhabitants.

Whereas Rabbi Elisha Aviner belongs to the Tzohar group of moderate Religious Zionist rabbis, the harshest and most detailed formulation for subjugating or forcibly removing Palestinians from Palestine was that of Rabbi Meir Kahane, leader of the vigilante Kach movement and one-term legislator in the Knesset.

Kahane's maximalist understanding of Jewish chosenness and resulting exceptionalism led him to minimize and sometimes collapse the distinctions between categories of non-Jews. In his approach, even the gere toshav remained a tolerated group to be segregated from Jews. Kahane placed Palestinians in the same halakhic status as the seven nations of Canaan.[44] The last article he wrote, just a few hours before his assassination, equated Palestinians and the seven nations of Canaan and concluded with this last sentence in bold print: "[The Canaanite status] is the clear halakhic status today of the Arabs, people who see the Jews as robbers and occupiers, who began wars with us and who thus are not to be trusted, and have lost the right to ever remain in the land."[45]

Adding a few incidental and short rabbinic pronouncements from the Jerusalem Talmud to Maimonides's *Mishne Torah* and other halakhic rulings, Kahane produced a tripartite division of "options" facing the indigenous inhabitants of Eretz Yisrael from the seven nations in Canaanite times to the Palestinian Arabs of today: leave the land, fight, or make peace. There is little need to explain what would happen to those who "choose" to leave, and Kahane devoted only three words to the response to those who fight back, which he equated with the biblical injunction "to be killed."[46] His focus was on the *gere toshav* on whom he placed the harshest restrictions, as enumerated by Maimonides. Their portion in life is "tribute and servitude," a proposal he shared with Rabbi Elisha Aviner, "and in their absence no members of the seven nations are to be left alive."[47] There is, then, a consensus within the broad swath of Religious Zionism that Jewish sovereignty over Eretz Yisrael is permanent, non-negotiable, and rooted in Judaic supremacy.

Kahane was an opponent of the Kooks, and his harsh approach has only gained influence decades after his death.[48] His perspective is reproduced in colorful language both by Bentzi Gopstein, his successor as the head of his vigilante organization now called Lehava, and by Baruch Marzel, a leader of the Kahanist Otzma Yehudit (Jewish Power) Party.[49] It is also, in laundered language, the core of the plan put forward by the hardali leader Betzalel Smotrich, a former transportation minister in Netanyahu's government and currently an MK of the Yamina Party.[50] Rendering Palestinians under Jewish sovereignty inconsequential is only a short distance from making them disappear. Though not part of the "mainstream" Kookist yeshiva, Goren, Kahane, and hardali religious and political authorities offered by and large concurring rulings.

The historical legacy of the second wave of Maimonidean interpretations differed radically from the first in addressing the modern dilemma of the Arabs' status under Jewish sovereignty. Elevating the military conquest of the West Bank into the rigid, ideological core of Religious Zionism justifies Jewish rule not just over a portion of Eretz Yisrael but also privileged and exclusive Jewish sovereignty over all of it. This second wave has taken another, even more hardline turn, rejecting on the basis of Jewish exceptionalism the very possibility of having Arabs, even as *gere toshav*, under Israeli Jewish control. The rabbinical authorities of the post-1967 years render equal access, treatment, protections, or rights under Jewish sovereignty no longer possible. Some explicitly reject Arab social citizenship rights to welfare, as well as political and national rights, but even to a national identity and ultimately their right to reside in their homeland, towns, and villages, now under Jewish sovereignty. All that is missing is chattel servitude, though Rabbi Aviner flags Nachmanides's even harsher interpretation: "enslavement is that every Jewish person can take one of them to become a hewer of wood and drawer of water and pay him proper wage."[51] In this interpretation, Israel is obliged to condemn Arabs under its rule to what Orlando Patterson termed "social death": the refusal to accept people as fully human by society.[52]

Final Reflections

Although the Netanyahu government's plan to annex parts of the West Bank under the aegis of the so-called Trump Peace Plan has been postponed and potentially abandoned, it is an appropriate context for assessing the significance and weight of the Religious Zionist and hardali interpretations of the Maimonidean code of the Land of Israel and the status of the Palestinians who live there. The Trump administration's strident support was viewed as an effective shield against the vocal opposition of most current and former leaders of the EU, the majority of Democratic members of Congress, Israel's neighbors, all other Arab countries, the organization of Islamic States and, of course, the Palestinian Authority and Hamas. What Netanyahu did not anticipate was the bitter antagonism from hundreds of rabbis, the Council of Yesha (Judea, Samaria, and Gaza), and hilltop youth and yeshiva students from both sides of the Green Line.[53] They objected to freezing settlement construction for four years, leaving a small number of isolated settlements outside the area over which Israel will impose its sovereignty and, above all, to the very idea that a Palestinian state would be established in the unannexed parts of the West Bank.

Blithely ignoring the vocal and determined Palestinian opposition to the one-sided plan, Religious Zionists were determined to reject even the slimmest chance of granting the Palestinian people any semblance of sovereignty and a political toehold. The intra-Israeli debate over the plan has taken place entirely within the right wing and religious camp. The Council of Yesha led by David Elhayani rejected any proposal that might not place the totality of Eretz Yisrael West Bank under Israeli sovereignty. Elhayani's opposition to annexation was not focused on the residents of Area C, nor was he concerned by the possibility of Palestinians receiving Israeli political rights. He said, "If the State of Israel has a problem with voting in Knesset elections, it will find a solution," citing options such as autonomy or residence rather than citizenship.[54] He correctly anticipated Prime Minister Netanyahu's position that declared that Palestinian locales, including the city of Jericho, in the Jordan Valley that Israel planned on annexing on July 1, 2020, would remain "Palestinian enclaves" and their residents would receive neither citizenship nor residence rights, but "will remain Palestinian subjects." In short, Israel retreated from the pattern of annexation in East Jerusalem and the Golan Heights where it afforded the residents residency rights.

The Religious Zionist and hardali parties and the settler movement do not set Israeli policy in the West Bank, but their halakhic solution to the modern dilemma of nokhrim under Israeli sovereignty has become one of its mainstays. Although international pressure and the half-hearted opposition of Benny Gantz have also played a role, Religious Zionism has proved itself capable of blocking the "fraudulent Trump Plan."

Ophir and Rosen-Zvi highlight and marvel at the "exceptional resilience" of the ancient figure of the goy, in this case as a ger who is treated as "our contemporary."[55] The goy, or nokhri, are not models that can be transported effortlessly across the ages. Indeed, in this chapter, I illuminate the interpretive work that was required to establish halakhic tools for addressing a modern dilemma. Forging a transhistorical history, the mainstream of Religious Zionism, including its hardali counterparts, squeezes flexibility and pluralism out of Judaism, turning it into an inflexible ideology, a political religion of nationalism. The clearest expression of this is the conflation of Rabbi Herzog's notion of a centralized halakhic state with the Kooks's ideologized Judaism in defining sovereignty and the status of the Palestinian nokhri in Judaic terms.

Transforming Jewish privilege into Judaic supremacy enables the imposition of tighter and harsher control mechanisms on Israel's Palestinian citizens and subjects. Since 1948, Israel has controlled its minorities by fragmenting them into subgroups—Muslims, Christians, and the Bedouin; after 1967, it extended this fracturing mechanism to the Occupied Palestinian Territories by affording different rights, protections, and types of punishment to the residents of East Jerusalem; Areas A, B, C, Hebron H1, and H2; and Gaza. Under the aegis of Judaic supremacy, the mechanism of fragmentation is being replaced with *lumping*, viewing all Palestinians as the same, with none entitled to citizen or national rights. Judaic supremacy offers a more extensive and exclusive form of Jewish privilege and sets up a less porous and more impenetrable barrier to Palestinians seeking their own rights.

Palestinians in the West Bank are, consequently, invisible to most Religious Zionists under the pastoral power of halakhic interpreters. The disciplinary influence of Judaic supremacy penetrates and shapes, although has not displaced, the

Israeli state sovereign power by creating a new universe of legitimate possibilities for rendering Palestinians invisible in a Jewish one state. Palestinian citizenship rights in Israel are equally threatened. From the perspective of the currently dominant halakhic historical legacy, Palestinians' very presence is illegal for prominent, central Religious Zionist rabbinical authorities.

The Religious Zionist halakhic one state also forestalls pathways to more equitable alternatives. The venue of denationalization on the road to a shared state, contemplated by Nadav Shelef in chapter 9, is even harder to envision when religion and nationalism not only intersect but religion and religious law also become a pathway to nationalism.[56] Israel's decolonization, the route offered by Yousef Munayyer (chapter 3) to a single state, would undoubtedly be a necessary step but runs up not only against the denial of colonization's illegality but also of the stripping of military conquest itself of any moral impropriety.[57] Linguistically, Hebrew does not dedicate separate words to conquest and occupation, using the word *kibush* for both. The halakha takes us even further by holding that conquest is legitimate, and consequently, occupation as such does not exist. Palestinian resistance renders them idolaters, and for some they are akin to the seven nations of Canaan. The prevalent reconfiguration of the Maimonidean historical legacy provides Religious Zionism with its own version of a "one state solution": a state based on Judaic supremacy and exclusive Jewish sovereignty.

3

ISRAEL/PALESTINE

Toward Decolonization

Yousef Munayyer

This chapter makes the argument for a specific analytical lens, settler colonialism, for understanding Israel/Palestine, how we arrived at the juncture we are at today, and how we can move forward to a more just and peaceful outcome. Understanding Israel/Palestine through a settler-colonial lens does not negate the value of an occupation framing or even a nationalist one; instead, it gives us a more encompassing vantage point through which we can holistically view the widest range of actors and stakeholders since the beginning of the confrontation between the Zionist movement and the indigenous population of Palestine. By gaining a sharper and more complete analysis of the problem, we are better positioned to think through solutions that right the most wrongs and protect the rights of all without negating the rights of any.

As a concept, settler colonialism is nearly absent in political science literature, although this is starting to change. Indeed, a search of five top journals in the discipline that have published thousands of peer-reviewed articles over the last several decades returned only eight hits for the term: all were published in the last decade and most in the last four years.

Surely, the dearth of focus on settler colonialism in western political science is in part a function of the reality that, as Jennifer Pitts writes "The key concepts and languages of European political thought—ideas of freedom and despotism, self-government, and the autonomous individual—were imagined and articulated in light of, in response to, and sometimes in justification of, imperial and commercial expansion beyond Europe."[1] Several studies have begun to chip away at this centuries-deep structure. Paul Keal's study looks at how the development of international law and political theory dispossessed indigenous people over time.[2] Aziz Rana's book examines how the very concept of freedom in the United States was tied to a settler colonialism that necessitated slavery and targeting of the native people.[3] In a study of comparative settler-colonial societies, Ivison and coauthors look at the role that political thought played in subjugating the indigenous communities.[4]

In addition to the deep contextual reasons for the lack of focus on settler colonialism in the literature, this concept falls in something of a gap between concentrations in the discipline. In international relations, for example, scholars are primarily concerned with the behavior of states and other global actors like international organizations and multinational corporations. Comparativists focus instead on dynamics within states. The politics around settler colonialism, however, is largely about the politics of or effecting the state*less*. As Hannah Arendt understood in her *Origins of Totalitarianism*, a work that appropriately has its place in the political science canon, citizenship and thus belonging to a politically sovereign state were what permitted "the right to have rights."[5] Similarly, settler colonialism and the politics of the stateless do not receive the focus they deserve in the literature precisely because they do not fit neatly into a discipline dominated by states. This chapter argues for an analytical lens that brings the stateless back in by going beyond a state-centric paradigm and, in doing so, provides a useful way to understand Israel/Palestine and imagine a path forward.

A Particular Colonialism

"We're not the British in India." Israel prime minister Benjamin Netanyahu said to a joint meeting of the US Congress in an address in 2011. He continued, "We're not the Belgians in the Congo. This is the land of our forefathers, the land of Israel, to which Abraham brought the idea of one god, where David set out to confront Goliath, and where Isaiah saw his vision of eternal peace."[6]

In something of a contrast, more than a century earlier, Theodor Herzl, the founder of modern Zionism, wrote to Cecil Rhodes, a contemporary who was the most well-known proponent of colonialism in the world, seeking his stamp of approval on the Zionist plan for Palestine. In his letter, which appears in his diary, Herzl wrote that the request might be unusual for Rhodes because it "doesn't involve Africa, but a piece of Asia minor, not Englishmen, but Jews." Yet he wanted Rhodes's support because "it was something colonial," and "it presupposes an understanding of a development which will take twenty or thirty years. . . . And what I want you to do is not to give me or lend me a few guineas, but to put the stamp of your authority on the Zionist plan. . . . What is the plan? To settle Palestine with the homecoming of the Jewish people."[7]

For Herzl, unlike for Netanyahu, there was no conflict between acknowledging the colonial process inherent in the Zionist plan to turn Palestine into a Jewish state and the idea that the land was a historic homeland for Jewish people. Indeed, at the early stages of the Zionist project in Palestine, the language of colonization was not taboo at all. Some Zionist organizations, like the Jewish Colonization Association, which was later reorganized into the Palestine Jewish Colonization Association, included the word in their names. Coverage of Zionist plans for Palestine in newspapers like the *New York Times* routinely described it as colonization.

Colonization is a process that produces structures. At some point between Herzl and Netanyahu, colonization became taboo, but the processes that were set in place by Zionism and the structures that they created continue to this day. This chapter focuses on several of those processes, the structures they created, the impact they had on Palestinians and how dismantling them can lead to a just and equitable outcome for Israelis and Palestinians alike.

Settler Colonialism as Process

Colonialism, writes Lorenzo Veracini, "is defined by exogenous domination."[8] But *settler* colonialism, the framework most appropriate for understanding Israel/Palestine, is something distinct. In this sense, Netanyahu is correct to say that the Zionists and later the Israelis were neither the British in India nor the Belgians in the Congo. The British and the Belgians came to economically exploit the indigenous populations and their land: the Zionists came to replace the indigenous population on theirs. Patrick Wolfe puts it succinctly, "Settler colonizers come to stay: invasion is a structure not an event."[9]

This structure is built by several processes of taking by the stronger group of land, rights, access, and identity from the weaker indigenous population over time. Because settler colonialism is an overall process of replacement within a physical space, perhaps the most important process is that of land taking. Other processes stem from or are related to this overarching process of wresting control of the land from one group and concentrating it in the hands of the other.

In Israel/Palestine, the settler-colonial process of land taking has been ongoing for more than a century and has taken various forms over time; yet all forms have contributed to the overall goal of putting increasing amounts of land under the control of the Zionist movement and later the State of Israel. Facilitating this process required political conditions that would ensure it could proceed largely unchallenged. These conditions, which limited the indigenous population's control over the actions of the state, first took shape under the British Mandate and then later under the State of Israel. Processes around rights, access, and identity supported the land-taking effort.

Pre-State: A Foundation of Replacement

The first Zionist settlements in Palestine preceded what became known as mainstream Zionism after the First Zionist Conference in Basel in 1897. But it was the organized political movement of Zionism post-Basel, defined by the Basel Program, that would shape the vast majority of Zionist settler colonialism in Palestine in the pre-state era.[10]

Three key developments were taking place during this time. The first was the culmination of the Zionist search for an imperial sponsor, settling on the British after failed overtures to both the Ottoman sultan and the German kaiser. The second was the socioeconomic direction of Jewish settlement during the second wave of Jewish immigration to Palestine from 1904–1914, which Gershon Shafir describes as a "separatist method of pure settlement."[11] Third was the official establishment of the Jewish National Fund at the Fifth Zionist Congress in 1901 as a corporation charged with procuring land in Palestine for the purpose of benefiting Jewish settlers. Herzl's vision was one of slow but steady and incremental growth "to create a germ cell out of which a state could grow organically," as he told a companion traveling with him to Palestine in 1898, who would later be a founding member of the Jewish National Fund. A land company "similar to that of Rhodesia" would be instrumental in the process.[12]

Shortly thereafter in the spring of 1899, Herzl wrote to Youssef Diya al-Khalidi, an Ottoman official and mayor of Jerusalem, about the good-natured intentions of Zionist land acquisition and how it could only benefit the native Arab population:

> It is their well-being, their individual wealth which we will increase by bringing in our own. Do you think that an Arab who owns land or a house in Palestine worth three or four thousand francs will be very angry to see the price of his land rise in a short time, to see it rise five and ten times in value perhaps in a few months? Moreover, that will necessarily happen with the arrival of the Jews. That is what the indigenous population must realize, that they will gain excellent brothers as the Sultan will gain faithful and good subjects who will make this province flourish.[13]

Zionist land acquisition, however, would have a very different impact on the indigenous population.

The Balfour Declaration, issued in 1917, made clear British intentions for Palestine; when the British became the Mandatory power that assumed control over the land after the dissolution of the Ottoman Empire following World War I, the political conditions were in place for accelerated Jewish immigration and colonization. In 1922, when the British Mandate officially began, the first census of Palestine recorded a Jewish population of about 84,000, which more than doubled to 174,000 by the next census in 1931. In the decade before World War II some 40,000 Jews immigrated to Palestine in the second wave of Zionist immigration. The third wave saw a similar number come in just a four-year span from 1919–1923 after the fall of the Ottomans. The fourth wave saw double this number, just over 80,000, arrive in the span of five years from 1924–1929.

Creating a "Jewish national home" as Balfour put it and establishing a Jewish state in Palestine as Herzl envisioned required a Jewish population. Economically sustaining a continued influx of Jewish settlers required jobs for them. Although the first wave of Jewish immigration during the Ottoman period used Arab labor, the second wave did not and sought instead to only use a Jewish workforce. In creating a firewall between the economies of the communities, the Jewish settlers were able to prevent competition between native and immigrant labor, despite the fact that the former were willing to work for much less. "It was this pure, or homogeneous, type of colonization" of the second wave "that won out," noted Shafir.[14]

Land acquisition in the 1920s by the various Zionist companies, including the Jewish National Fund (JNF) and the Palestine Jewish Colonization Association, continued to move forward premised on this separatist model. Thus, once land was bought for the purpose of Jewish colonization it was off-limits to the native Arab population, even as tenant farmers. This represented a change from earlier practice in which ownership of agricultural land did not necessarily mean that tenant farmers were prevented from working it. Poor economic conditions afflicting the agricultural sector in Palestine, combined with the finite arable land and the financial means available to the Zionist companies, led to them acquiring as much land as their budgets could finance.[15] A growing number of Arab farmers became landless, an issue that would continue to sow discontent among the Arab population toward the Zionist project as long as it proceeded. The decade culminated with the uprising of 1929, in which there were widespread Arab attacks on Jewish settlers and settlements followed by deadly British repression. Various British inquiries into the causes of the events pointed to the challenge that Jewish colonization and its exclusivist model were presenting to native life.[16] Charles Anderson notes that, by 1931, "no less than two-fifths of the agricultural population, and perhaps as much as half or more, were dispossessed."[17]

What is most consequential about this period is not merely the Jewish immigration or land-acquisition trends but the way in which they took place; that is, with an aim not of integrating into the local society but rather of replacing it. This process of replacement, most acutely through land acquisition and later conquest, continued to characterize each phase of Zionist settler colonialism in Palestine.

The most significant leap forward for the Zionist settler-colonial endeavor came with the establishment of the Israeli state and the depopulation of Palestine of the majority of its native inhabitants from 1947–1949. Processes that started before the state was formed were accelerated significantly in the early years after state formation. This period was instrumental in shaping the next seven decades of relations between the settler-colonial state and the indigenous population.

The Settler State: Colonizing Space

Of the 1.7 million Jewish-owned dunams by the late 1940s, some 500,000 were bought in the 1920s alone, before the 1929 violence. The British began to rethink land-acquisition policy in the uprising's aftermath and considered limiting Jewish immigrants, as well as their ability to purchase land. New ordinances were imposed in the 1940s that zoned territory to prevent the transfer of titles from Arabs to Jews in certain areas. By this point, however, the Zionist foothold in Palestine was already established, and the British Mandate was drawing to a close. After a half-century of land acquisition and on the eve of the war that would result in the mass depopulation of Palestine's native Arab inhabitants and the creation of the State of Israel, only about 7 percent of the land area of Palestine was owned by Jewish settlers or companies purchasing on behalf of the Zionist project.[18] The newly established State of Israel would act to accelerate significantly the taking of land.

During the Mandate period, the Palestinian Arab population doubled in size, while the Jewish population increased sixfold. Yet Palestinian Arabs still outnumbered the Jewish population nearly 2 to 1. This would change dramatically in a short period of time as the Israeli state was declared in mid-May 1948. By that point, some 400,000 Palestinian Arabs and 200 towns and villages had already been depopulated. By the time the war ended in 1949, nearly 800,000 Palestinian Arabs had fled or been forced to leave, and more than 500 villages had been emptied. By the end of 1949 Jews outnumbered the remaining Palestinian Arabs in the new State of Israel by nearly 5 to 1. Seemingly overnight, the population of the country was transformed, and swift changes in land acquisition would follow.

Starting in 1948 "the Israeli state used law, along with other means, to impose and legitimize Jewish political and territorial domination within its sovereign space."[19] By 1960, after a series of regulations and laws concerning land custody, the Israeli state came to "own" 93 percent of the territory, without there being transfers of title, despite only 7 percent of the land being owned by Jewish settlers or companies before the foundation of the state.

According to the Israeli Central Bureau of Statistics, the Jewish population of the state in the summer of 1948 was 716,000; by the end of 1951 it had doubled to 1.4 million. During the war, the new state used military ordinances based on colonial British Emergency Regulations to house many new immigrants in the properties of Palestinian Arabs who had become refugees. The suddenly available mass tracts of land, vacated by a nearly identical number of Palestinian Arabs forced into flight by the war and the attacks of the Israeli military, were crucial in situating the mass influx of immigrants. Soon after the war, the state began a process of legal land laundering through the passage of several laws. Military ordinances allowed them to seize and allocate "fallow lands" or "abandoned property," even though it was the military that had depopulated the lands of their residents and farmers and prevented their return. Laws passed in 1950, such as the Absentee Property Law, defined Palestinian Arab refugees as absentees and created a "custodian" to oversee their property in their "absence." The Development Authority Law of 1950 allowed those custodians of Absentee Property to "sell" the land only to the Development Authority. A 1951 state land law forbade the transfer of state-acquired land to anyone but the Development Authority or the JNF. A 1953 land acquisition law empowered the state to formally acquire land it had seized by military force if it claimed it was for development, settlement, or security purposes. In 1960, the Israel Lands Law was passed, formalizing all the previous changes in the newly created Israel Lands Authority, which controlled 93 percent of the land. In just over ten years, these various legislative mechanisms allowed the state to create a "closed reservoir" of land so it could "use appropriated Arab land to further Jewish interests in the country."[20]

The Settler State: Colonizing Belonging

The early years of the state were instrumental in demarcating not only who the land belonged to but also who the state belonged to. For the Zionist movement and its newly established State of Israel, the demographic upheaval brought about by the war and depopulation of Palestinian Arab towns and villages afforded them an unprecedented opportunity to further extend control over the territory. Advancing the settler-colonial project, however, required maintaining the new demographic balance and, if possible, increasing the Israeli population. A large number of Jewish immigrants entered the newly created state from 1949–1951, but this created a dilemma: How could the new state facilitate and welcome the arrival of Jewish immigrants, granting them citizenship, while denying repatriation to Palestinian Arab citizens who sought refuge during the war?

Answering this question required implementing what Shira Robinson characterizes as citizenship as a "category of exclusion."[21] Through another series of legislative moves, the state created a tiered system of belonging that effectively divorced nationality from citizenship, privileging the former over the latter. The Law of Return, passed in mid-1950, gave Jews from around the world the right to immigrate to Israel and become citizens. Once this legalized pathway to citizenship for Jews was established, the state turned to the broader question of citizenship, which was addressed in the 1952 citizenship law. This law repealed the 1925 Mandate-era British law on citizenship, effectively stripping citizenship from hundreds of thousands of Palestinians in exile; it also redefined citizenship to specifically exclude them. In doing so, the state afforded citizenship to the small number of Palestinian Arabs who stayed inside the borders of the new state during the depopulation. With the passage of these laws, someone could become Israeli citizen from anywhere in the world so long as he or she were Jewish, but to become a citizen as a Palestinian Arab, one had to have had Mandate citizenship, been registered as a resident in 1949 and when this law was passed in 1952, and had never left the country during this time. Israeli citizenship was crafted as a tool to exclude, rather than include, and was a function of a broader settler-colonial project of replacement.[22]

The Settler State: Colonizing the Discourse

From Australia and New Zealand to the United States, Canada, Zimbabwe, and beyond, settler- colonial projects have relied on and advanced some form of the *terra nullis* myth: the claim that the land they sought to colonize was empty, barren, underdeveloped, uncivilized, unused, and thus there for the taking. In almost all cases, the indigenous population, when not ignored completely, was presented as nomadic, uncivilized, and backward. In the Israeli context this mythology served an important purpose for the settler-colonial project: not only did it seek to provide a justification for a project that was destroying an existing society but it also gave the Israelis a framework within which to forge a national identity out of masses of immigrants coming from different national contexts. By rewriting physical space and consequently the historical narrative, reinforcing these changes through the education system, and shaping the media environment to fit the new narrative, all discussed later, the Israeli state also colonized the discursive space in the country.

Geography

After the establishment of the Israeli state in 1948 and the mass depopulation of the majority of the indigenous population, Israel proceeded with what amounted to a cartographic overhaul. Just as the landscape would have to change in the process of implementing the settler-colonial project, so too would the reference points for it across the map. Towns and villages that existed were physically erased, while scores of others that did not exist were being built. Places that continued to exist had their names changed. This cartographic rewriting served not only to facilitate the state-building project but also to perpetuate the founding myth of an unbroken link between the modern-day Zionist movement and biblical times. The physical evidence of an intermittent history in the two millennia between was systemically erased from the map. Hebrew names would replace Arabic names, as Nur Masalha notes,

> The Jewish settlement that replaced the large and wealthy village of Bayt Dajan (the Philistine "House of Dagon") (with 5,000 inhabitants in 1948) was named "Beit Dagon," founded in 1948; Kibbutz Sa'sa' was built on Sa'sa' village; the cooperative moshav of 'Amka on the land of 'Amqa village (Boqa'i 2005: 73; Wakim 2001, 2001a). Al-Kabri in the Galilee was renamed "Kabri"; al-Bassa village renamed "Batzat"; al-Mujaydil village (near Nazareth) renamed "Migdal Haemek" (Tower of the Valley). In the region of Tiberias alone there were 27 Arab villages in the pre-1948 period; 25 of them—including Dalhamiya, Abu Shusha, Hittin, Kafr Sabt, Lubya, al-Shajara, al-Majdal and Hittin—were destroyed by Israel. The name "Hittin"—where Saladin (in Arabic: Salah al-Din) famously defeated the Latin Crusaders in the Battle of Hattin in 1187, leading to the siege and defeat of the Crusaders who controlled Jerusalem—was renamed the Hebrew-sounding "Kfar Hittim" (Village of Wheat).[23]

Renaming the physical space helped the Israeli state develop social hegemony that simultaneously supported the settler-colonial narrative and unified its adherents while marginalizing and erasing the indigenous population. That hegemony would be continually reinforced by an education system that furthered the settler-colonial project.

Education

The national education system in Israel has, from the foundation of the state, been divided into two divisions: one for Hebrew education and one for Arabic education. Although the existence of a minority education system might seem like a pathway toward inclusivity and empowerment for that minority, its design and implementation in Israel resulted in anything but that. On the contrary, this majority-controlled education system has played a key role in the subjugation of the Palestinian Arab minority in Israel by systemically repressing "their collective culture, history and identity,"[24]

Although national Jewish narratives, including the settler-colonial mythology that underpinned the establishment of the state, is taught in both the Hebrew and Arabic systems, Palestinian Arab national identity is not cultivated in either system. The State Education Law of 1953[25] declared that the objective of the state education system was to inculcate "values of Jewish culture," "love of the homeland and loyalty to the State and the Jewish people," and even "pioneer training."[26]

The Arab school system does have its own curriculum, but it is supervised by the Ministry of Education in which "virtually no Arab educators or administrators have decision-making powers."[27] Universities within the Green Line are located exclusively in Jewish cities, and instruction is in Hebrew. Palestinians make up only 1 percent of faculty positions, despite being nearly one-fifth of the population. Unlike their Jewish counterparts, Palestinian Arab curricula and degree programs must be approved by the General Security Services before they can be employed. Thus, Abu-Saad concludes, "The separate school system, together with other mechanisms of control and discrimination, has succeeded in keeping the vast majority of Palestinian Arabs in subordinate, marginal positions in Jewish Israeli society."

Media

Israeli state media policy has also historically played an important role in shaping the discursive space in support of the settler-colonial project. Reinstatement of the 1876 constitution by the Ottoman sultan after the Young Turk revolution in 1908 created the conditions for a boom in journalistic activity in Palestine just as the confrontation with Zionism was in its early stages. Many newspapers popped up and were produced from Palestine's cultural centers in this period and throughout the Mandate.[28] Just as swiftly, however, the British repression of the 1936–1939 uprising and most significantly the war of 1948 decimated Palestinian cultural production and sent most of its cultural elites into exile. In the media space, just as with cartography, the Israeli state began to significantly reshape the Arabic media landscape. Only one Arabic-language newspaper, which was produced by the Communist Party, survived the Nakba.

In his work on the Arab public sphere in Israel, Amal Jamal writes, "The state of Israel transformed the media into one of its principal socializing mechanisms, second only to the education system, seeking to manufacture consent among the

Israeli public."[29] No Palestinian Arab nationalist papers were permitted in the years after the establishment of the state. The Arabic-language newspapers that did exist had to be approved by the state and were run primarily by Jewish immigrants from Arabic-speaking countries; the papers' editorial stances followed the state's line. When independent nationalist papers developed that sought to challenge the state-backed hegemony—for example, *al-Ard*—they were shut down and outlawed. Although the media space later opened up as technological developments outpaced the state's ability to control it and satellite television and the internet created new opportunities, the foundational decades of the state featured largely unchallenged state hegemony in the Arabic media spaces that did exist.

Martial Law

Martial law served as the foundation of nearly every step by the state to expand the settler-colonial project in the years after the establishment of the State of Israel. When the state was declared in May 1948, it announced it would carry over all Mandate-era laws except restrictions on Jewish immigration and land acquisition. This meant that the British Emergency Regulations, which amounted to martial law and enabled tremendous rights abuses and repression,[30] would become Israeli law as well.[31] Military rule over the Palestinian Arab population and the land that remained in their possession lasted until 1966. It was seen as "the best mechanism at the state's disposal block the return of Palestinian refugees to their lands; depopulate other Arab villages whose lands the sought to expropriate immediately; and to bring in Jewish immigrants to replace the original residents."[32]In addition, the geographic reality created by the movement restrictions of martial law shaped the separate school systems for Arabs and Jews and likewise empowered the state to shut down counter-hegemonic press when it emerged.

By the time the martial law regime ended in Israel in 1966, the state had effectively colonized the vast majority of the territory, controlling the land through a process of land laundering, denying repatriation to the vast majority of the native inhabitants, and debilitating those who had remained through restrictive policies affecting their education, media environment, and political mobilization. By 1967, a new frontier was opened when Israel occupied the Sinai, the Golan Heights, the West Bank, and the Gaza Strip; the latter three remain under Israeli control today. The British Emergency Regulations, extended from the Mandate period into post-Nakba Israel toward its Palestinian Arab citizens, would be extended again, this time into newly occupied territory—thereby setting the stage for the further expansion of the process of settler-colonial replacement.

The extension of martial law into this newly occupied territory opened a new chapter of settler colonization. Israeli settlements first began to be developed in occupied territory as military bases and then became civilian outposts.[33] After a seminal court ruling in 1979, by which time many settlements had already been established, the state was able to lay claim to territory in the West Bank on land considered "state land" by exploiting an 1850s Ottoman land law; this law enabled land to be absorbed by the custodian for absentee property and repurposed by other state agencies for exclusively Jewish development purposes, just as the state had done inside Israel from 1948–1967.[34]

The Result: One Settler-Colonial State

Between the Jordan River and the Mediterranean Sea, today there exists one state: the State of Israel. For the millions of souls who call the territory it controls home, their existence is shaped by structured inequality. These structures were created by processes that sought to facilitate the settler-colonial project of replacement by converting the territory from being under the control of the majority indigenous population at the start of the last century to the control of the Jewish population, nearly all of whom arrived in the course of that process. The rights, power, and access of Palestinians, across different political spaces, continue to be limited by these legal, political, and economic structures. From Palestinian citizens of Israel whose very citizenship was created as a category of exclusion, to Palestinian refugees who were denied repatriation so that the state could lay claim to and further colonize the land they inhabited, to Palestinians living under military occupation today where settlement expansion continues, mimicking the post-1948 processes, the legacy of settler colonialism shapes every dimension of their present lives.

The settler-colonial framework is an analytical and interpretive one that is most useful for understanding holistically the genesis of the current reality. Decolonization leaves room for national identity while also understanding that the specific historic process of national identity creation came at a cost that produced the structured inequality of today. In doing so, it keeps Israelis and all Palestinians in the frame. Unlike partition, which divides Palestinian stakeholders into various groups without collectively and comprehensively addressing their claims, decolonization offers an opportunity to right past wrongs.

Thus, decolonization could be a path forward that puts all inhabitants on the path toward an equitable and, therefore, more stable and peaceful coexistence in the state. It would require a dismantling of the structures that have been erected by settler-colonial processes over the past century. In the rest of the chapter. I discuss what decolonization could look like, with a focus on the features already mentioned, and how it could work.

Decolonizing Israel/Palestine

Although colonization, whether premised on exploitation or replacement, always has a devastating impact on the indigenous population, it takes different forms in different contexts. Likewise, decolonization as a process in Israel/Palestine would be unique to its context and thus may not follow the path other decolonization processes have taken elsewhere.

Decolonization in Algeria, for example, was the product of an insurrection that ultimately led to independence and the departure of the vast majority of French settler colonialists and their descendants who had come to Algeria during France's 130-year rule of the country. In South Africa, decolonization—known in that context as transformation—was the product of a lengthy internal and international struggle against Apartheid and did not bring about massive demographic shifts between the indigenous population and the settlers. In other settler colonies, such as United States, Canada, Australia, and New Zealand, the relationship between the indigenous communities and the settler communities varied, and each has decolonized to varying degrees—with much still left to be done.

Is decolonization in Israel/Palestine plausible or even possible? Before decolonization can begin, settler-colonial processes that continue to be in place must first cease, because decolonization by definition would require the reversal of several of these processes. The power dynamics are such now that this does not seem likely in the immediate future. Nonetheless, the trajectory that Israeli policy has set the state on has put it into a collision course with prevailing global values around democracy and human rights. Accelerating this confrontation is the growing global consciousness around the demise or unworkability of the two state solution. The question of when structural inequality between the river and the sea will be confronted is increasingly seeming like a question of when, not if.

When that confrontation does occur, what will decolonization mean for Israelis and Palestinians? There are no ideal models to look at for comparison. Unlike the French in Algeria, Israelis do not have a metropole to return to, and even though the State of Israel has only been around for half as long as the French presence in Algeria, Israelis have developed a distinct national identity, whereas in Algeria the *pied-noir* continued to be French. Further, in contrast to the United States, Canada, or Australia where centuries of settler-colonial policies have reduced the indigenous population to less than 5 percent of the total population, Palestinians today make up approximately half the population inside the country and significantly more when Palestinian refugees are counted. Decolonization in Israel/Palestine would take place in a context of near demographic parity, which makes it unique.

Replacing Replacement with Co-Permanence

For decolonization to be able to begin and for it to lead to an approximation of justice and not retribution, special emphasis should be given to creating guiding principles for the process that take into account Israel/Palestine's unique history and current reality. As the founders of Zionism understood, theirs was a colonial movement, even if Judaism was inextricably linked to the land. Decolonizing Israel/Palestine in a way that leads to justice should also recognize both these truths. Thus, decolonization cannot be a process of re-replacement. In contrast to settler colonialism that sought to erase the presence of the indigenous population to support its own claims to the land, the decolonization of Israel/Palestine should be based on the principle of *co-permanence*: the idea that the land is, and will always be, home to both peoples together and not for one at the expense of the other. This principle is a necessary antidote to the ideology of settler colonialism that establishes the permanence of one group through the erasure of the other. It should be at the foundation of the decolonization of various areas, including the law, land, and language.

Decolonizing the Law

As noted earlier, legislation was passed by the Israeli state to facilitate the settler-colonial project, and law from the pre-state era to the post-1967 era has been instrumentalized for this purpose. The Israeli declaration of independence called for a constitution, but lawmaking was instead done in an ad hoc fashion through basic laws to empower the state, enabling it to sidestep dilemmas that were inconvenient for the project. Decolonizing the law would require an end to this process and the rewriting of the law in a way that is based on the co-permanence of both peoples and for the purpose of facilitating decolonization. The constitution of the republic of South Africa could offer lessons here for how this can be done, as can the experiences of other multinational states, such as Belgium or Northern Ireland. In short, a new should uphold individual rights regardless of race or creed, while also creating space for collective rights for Palestinians and Israelis insofar as they do not trample on the individual rights of any person. This would mean making the law an instrument for upholding equality, instead of privileging one group over the other.

Take, for example, the issue of citizenship. In a new, decolonized constitution, citizenship could be defined as the preeminent category of inclusion, which is no longer secondary to the national category, and pathways to citizenship should be equally open to both peoples. Simultaneously, a policy similar to the Israeli law of return, affording an opportunity for safe haven for persecuted Jews or Palestinians through citizenship, can be implemented.

Communal self-determination can be legally safeguarded as well within a framework of universal suffrage. Constitutional provisions, which cannot be overturned without an overwhelming majority of votes that would require majority consent from both communities, can enshrine certain collective rights for both nations.

These changes can be implemented in various ways. South Africa's constitution, for example, establishes a parliamentary republic while granting provinces their own governments that have a voice at the national level through representation in the bicameral legislature. Similarly, the Swiss Federal system, which officially recognizes four language groups, has both direct representation and a high degree of autonomy for its twenty-six states.

Whatever form a constitution for Israel/Palestine would take, decolonizing the law would require fundamentally changing it from its present use as a tool of furthering replacement and ensuring it becomes instead the foundation of a system that actively seeks co-permanence. It is also the first and most important step in the decolonization processes from which other processes would follow.

Decolonizing the Land

Settler colonialism is rooted in the taking of land and resources away from the indigenous population, and it has had a deep impact in Palestine. A decolonization process rooted in co-permanence requires an end to and reversal of the process of land taking.

Land rights/use, repatriation, and reparation are key elements of these changes. First, the decolonization process must dissolve the current system of land custodianship that is premised on privileging Jewish nationals. A new land regulatory agency can be developed that is rooted in the legal foundations of the decolonized law: equality and co-permanence. Yet, before that is created, the settler-colonial process's disastrous impact on the relationship between the indigenous population and the land requires that there be a process of repatriation and reparations.

Repatriation in the case of Palestine is not a small-scale process precisely because the depopulation of Palestine was not a small-scale process. However, it does not need to embody the abruptness and chaos of the depopulation process. Instead, repatriation must be a careful, planned, and paced process, aimed at accommodating all who wish to return in a fashion that permits safe and sustainable living. The Badil resource center has done important work on learning the lessons of property restitution and repatriation processes in cases like South Africa and the former Yugoslavia and how they can be applied in the case of Palestine.[35] One key lesson is to ensure that repatriation is coupled with a process to support socioeconomic justice.

Studies estimate that the value of Palestinian land lost in 1948 was anywhere between $824 million and $2.1 billion in 1948 US dollars.[36] In 2020 dollars, this ranges from $8.7 billion to $22.6 billion. For perspective, the entire Palestinian GDP today is $14.5 billion.[37] The value of the land itself also does not account for any value produced from the use of that land over the time its Palestinian owners and occupants were denied access to it. The economic situation of Palestinians vis-a-vis Israelis today is a direct product of the denial of access to valuable and value-producing assets for decades and the redirecting of those assets, through settler-colonial policies, to the settler community. Repairing that disparity, through a process of reparations, will be a necessary component of decolonization that will help create a society with greater economic parity.

Decolonizing Language and Discourse

The settler-colonial process and the structures of inequality it created both enabled and necessitated a concurrent colonization of discourse.

Language, education, and media in the post-state era were all shaped for the purpose of advancing the project. Decolonizing language and discourse, rooted in co-permanence, would not be about removing the settler language but rather creating the space to permit indigenous language, education, and media to exist and thrive on equal footings.

Decolonizing the education system would require reforming the current system from one intended to support the Jewish state's hegemony into one that supports a binational citizenry. It could education curricula focused on cross-educating communities in the national narratives and history of the other, as well as enabling an honest telling of the history of the land without gaps. It would also likely require curricula on the human rights abuses committed during the previous regime. South Africa can offer some positive lessons here, and many other states can offer some negative examples. In short, a decolonized education system would be one whose aim shifts shifts from shaping loyalty to a Jewish state to shaping a cohesive citizenry loyal to perpetually overcoming colonization and its lasting impact on the present.

Decolonizing the discourse must go beyond reforming the education system and must also extend to language and media. The languages of Arabic and Hebrew, which are the two most widely spoken, would be official languages, and state agencies would facilitate the development of media outlets for both communities.

Truth and Reconciliation

A commission focused on truth and reconciliation could support the decolonization process by establishing an open, honest, and shared history of events and their impact on the human rights of victims in Israel/Palestine. Such commissions have played pivotal roles in the aftermath of oppressive episodes of mass human rights violations across the globe. Their goal is not merely to advance justice but also to address the legacy of injustice long ignored in a society, facilitating the healing of wounds and strengthening social cohesion. South Africa's Truth and Reconciliation Commission is well known, and others have been created in settler-colonial contexts; for example, the commission around the rights of indigenous children in Canadian schools. Although such processes are not without potential failings and are vulnerable to exploitation or criticism,[38] it would play a crucial role in moving Israel/Palestine forward through decolonization given the way in which rewriting the historical narrative undergirded the settler-colonial process.

Palestinian Views

Palestinians are increasingly coming to understand their current situation through the lens of settler colonialism, although aspects of this vantage point were evident earlier, although perhaps obscured by a discourse around statehood over the last three decades. Throughout the Oslo period—one that roughly began around the Madrid Conference in 1991 and ended after the Annapolis conference in 2007—slim majorities of Palestinian public opinion preferred a two state outcome, but importantly these respondents also regularly said a right of return for refugees was a top national priority and often opposed recognition of Israel "as a Jewish state." That the respondents—Palestinians from the West Bank, Gaza, and occupied Jerusalem—would prioritize the refugee return issue and oppose recognizing Israel as a Jewish state, even though they would be part of a Palestinian state in the two state scenario, suggests that they themselves understood their connection to Palestinians living in Israel and in the diaspora and that all were affected by a common force. Statehood, public opinion poll show, was always seen by the Palestinian public as a means toward the end of reclaiming their rights and not an end to itself. Thus, statehood proposals that specified an outcome that only benefited Palestinians in the West Bank and Gaza and neglected Palestinian citizens of Israel, Jerusalemites, and the diaspora, always polled more poorly.

In addition to the views expressed in public opinion polls, we have also seen Palestinian civil society creation of the Boycott, Divestment, and Sanctions movement in 2005. The call for international solidarity, which was put forward by a wide range of Palestinian civil society groups, urged that Israel be held to account until it met three basic demands: (1) an end to the military occupation of 1967, (2) a just solution to the refugee issue in accordance with international law, and (3) equality for Palestinian citizens of Israel. In doing so, the movement took a rights-based approach but also recognized that the confrontation between Zionism and Palestinians was not limited to, and could not be resolved simply in, 22 percent of the territory. The movement thus transcends Palestinian political divisions and instead focuses on the common threat facing all Palestinians; it is by far the most popular strategic platform among Palestinians.[39] Although the statehood project, now all but defunct, may have distracted Palestinian focus during the Oslo period, Palestinians are gravitating to a clearer analysis that includes all segments of the community—on both sides of the Green Line and both inside and outside Palestine.

Final Thoughts

A settler-colonial framework does not help us understand every dimension of Israel/Palestine, but it certainly helps us understand more than any other single framework precisely because it keeps most Israelis and Palestinians and most of the territory within the frame. The occupation lens falls short territorially, because it focuses on the 22 percent of Palestine occupied after 1967. Nor does this frame allow us to understand the connection between the happenings on both sides of the Green Line and how Israel's actions in the West Bank are connected to its actions elsewhere in the present and historically. Nationalism too falls short in descriptive leverage; even though it is more ambiguous on the territorial question, it fails to properly describe the problem facing Palestinians, both on the ground and as they see it: Palestinians are neither in search of an identity, nor is their conflict with Zionism rooted in their national identity. Rather the conflict is rooted in Zionism's insistence on dominating the territory in a specific way, which would persist regardless of how Palestinians identify nationally or whether they identified nationally at all. At its essence, the conflict with Zionism is about the denial of the rights of people who happen to be Palestinians because they are not part of the group that Zionism privileges.

Settler colonialism is the best descriptor of the interaction between Zionism and the indigenous population in Palestine and allows us to both best understand the scope, history, and scale of the problem and thus propose a path forward rooted in this understanding of the problem as it actually exists.

Yet, Israel stands today apart from some other settler-colonial states like the United States, Canada, and Australia because at this stage it has failed to accomplish what those states have done to the indigenous population: erase them until they exist at most as a marginal presence in the polity. It is this reality that prompted Israeli history Benny Morris, most well known for revealing the Israeli military's role in the "birth of the Palestinian refugee problem," to say that the mistake Israel made in 1948 was to not "complete the job" and cleanse "the whole country—the whole Land of Israel, as far as the Jordan River." Doing so, he said, "would have stabilized the State of Israel for generations."[40] Similarly, among his last recorded words, PLO Chairman Yasir Arafat said in 2004 that "90 years after the Sykes-Picot Agreement, Israel has failed to wipe us out. We are here, in Palestine, facing them. We are not red Indians."

This reality of a settler-colonial process that has failed to do away with the indigenous population—thus far—is in part a product of when the process is happening. Countries like the United States, Canada and Australia all had reduced their indigenous populations to below 3 perent by the time the Israeli state was established in 1948. The erasure of these populations took place in the preceding centuries, before such actions became crimes against humanity and taboo in the international order of the postwar era. In his 2003 article supporting a binational Israeli-Palestinian state, historian Tony Judt described Israel as "an anachronism." Although Judt was referring to Zionism as a ethnonational project "in a world that has moved on," the settler-colonial nature of Zionism is just as outdated.[41]

Today, half the population between the river and the sea is not represented by the Jewish state that rules them. Efforts at partition in recent decades have been primarily aimed at managing the situation and not resolving it. Even in the best-case scenario, a Palestinian state envisioned in partition plans would remain subsovereign in any real sense. Over the long term, the demographic blending would only increase, making the logic of a shared land practical even if such stop-gap agreements were achieved.

The settler-colonial processes of Zionism over the past century have structured the unequal and unjust present that Israelis and Palestinians live in today. Unlike today's Israeli leaders, early Zionists had no problem recognizing theirs was a settler-colonial project even as it was considered a "homecoming." A decolonization process, based on the principle of co-permanence, can help unravel the former while still acknowledging the latter, affording both peoples an opportunity to live freely and equitably in a shared homeland.

Part 2

WHAT HAS CHANGED AND WHAT HAS NOT

Key Drivers

4

CITIZENSHIP AS A MOBILITY REGIME

Yael Berda

Political membership—one's status as citizen, resident, subject, foreigner, or enemy—determines one's ability to move freely in the territory of the state. Freedom of movement is considered the primary right in liberal modern states, linking political concepts of freedom, security, and violence, as well as facilitating the exercise of all other rights.[1] Colonial and imperial histories of state-making underscore the role of mobility in the determination of boundaries and political memberships as part of the making of modern states and their efforts to consolidate identity through official documents, registration, and surveillance.[2] In Israel/Palestine, the ordering of movement has been central to the differentiation and segregation of populations, becoming an exemplary case for growing scholarly attention to racialized regimes of mobility in the making of the modern state, particularly how the state monopoly on the legitimate means of movement shapes citizenship.[3]

Mobility—and the prevention of it through the application of emergency laws—was a central feature of British imperial rule, used to facilitate economic extraction and to crush uprisings and intercommunal conflict. Since the British Mandate and to this day, mobility restrictions have been used consistently to control and govern Palestinians. In the last two decades, Israel has developed the most sophisticated permit regime in the world to control and monitor the movement of more than five million Palestinian subjects who do not have political membership in the state.[4] Yet the contemporary permit regime, well known for its checkpoints and separation wall, was not the first time Israel used a system of permits to control movement and define political status and political participation through impediments on movement. In 1949, after independence and before enacting citizenship laws, Israeli differentiated political status through a military government whose fulcrum of power was a regime that restricted mobility and prevented the return of Palestinian refugees. The permit regime from 1949–1966 was based on a repertoire of legal and administrative methods to monitor and restrict population movement developed in the British colonies during the interwar period. The trajectory of political membership of the Palestinians living within the borders of 1948 and considered citizens of Israel is key to understanding Israel's regime of political membership and population management, which is predicated on degrees of mobility rather than rights. The Palestinians of 1948 are the remainder of the Arab population of Palestine that was not exiled during the War of Independence/Nakba.[5] Those Palestinians who managed to remain in Israel were turned overnight from imperial subjects into a "dangerous population" under Israel's military rule and later into suspect citizens.[6]

The history of mobility restrictions, from British Mandate Palestine to the military government established in 1949 to the current permit regime, is central to understanding the current one state reality in which the Israeli government rules the undetermined political borders of Israel and the Occupied Palestinian Territories in the West Bank and Gaza. The Israeli government controls the population in this area through a sophisticated, graded, and racialized matrix of political membership in which one's political status, identity, and territorial location determine their political rights, which laws will apply to them, and their possibilities for mobility.

The racialized regime of mobility, a central feature of the one state reality, is the outcome or culmination—and not the repudiation—of the long process of partition from the proposed British colonial partition plan for Palestine to the failed Oslo process that was purported to be a pathway to a two state solution.[7] A comparative historical examination of bureaucratic practices of population management and the construction of permit regimes from British colonial rule to the present enables us to view political status in the entire territory of Israel/Palestine as it is lived and experienced on the ground, in a state that does not have formal borders defined by law but instead borders created by bureaucratic practices and technologies of rule.

This chapter investigates the legacy of British colonial emergency laws through the bureaucratic toolkits of the Israeli permit regime in the everyday bureaucratic practices of the state in its early years. The first part focuses on the origins of the mobility regime, a bureaucratic toolkit developed during British colonial rule in the interwar period in Palestine and India, and the way that the mobility regime—based on emergency powers and classification of subjects according to degrees of suspicion—created an organizational template that has structured the differentiated political status across Israel/Palestine. The chapter builds on scholarship on colonial legacies of surveillance and population control, the legal and administrative infrastructure of the military government, and recent studies on the settler-colonial citizenship of the Palestinians in Israel.[8]

Initially justified as security measures, permit regimes created the conditions in which official documents that enabled mobility became the necessary means for survival. This was not only the case in Israel/Palestine, which is the focus of this chapter, but also on the border of India and Pakistan, which I briefly reference throughout the chapter. Mobility regimes across the partition lines became the organizational building blocks of national belonging and citizenship. During the early years of the states, the absence of formal citizenship and nationality laws made it possible for bureaucrats to determine political membership in Israel and India through designations of mobility and suspicion. Implementation of the bureaucratic toolkit relied on the continuity of colonial emergency laws that the independent states chose to incorporate into the new regime. Situating the colonial military government over the Palestinians in a post-imperial context underscores the way in which bureaucratic practices and routines of spatial-legal surveillance were formative of citizenship as a regime of mobility, and not as citizenship might be conceived, namely as one of rights and political membership.

There is little doubt that the racialized hierarchy of citizenship and residency in Israel/Palestine led to differentiation in rights and opportunities, in which political status itself became a method of dispossession, a process Tatour aptly terms as "citizenship as domination."[9] However, if one views the entire territory through the institutional logic of the Israeli state, it becomes clear that the prevention, restriction, and monitoring of mobility are key to the differentiation between populations: differentiation between Jews and Palestinians living within the borders of 1948; between Palestinian residents of East Jerusalem and Palestinian subjects in the occupied West Bank and the besieged Gaza Strip; and between Palestinian refugees.

The chapter is structured as follows. After a brief genealogy of the development of the bureaucratic toolkit of emergency during colonial rule, it focuses on the military government's use of the inherited toolkit to control the movement of Palestinians and prevent the return of refugees from the aftermath of the War of Independence/Nakba until 1966. The final section addresses restrictions of mobility in the territories occupied in 1967 that differentiate among different Palestinian populations, linking political status to the limitations and prevention of mobility in the West Bank, East Jerusalem, and Gaza Strip. The chapter concludes with the theoretical implications of viewing citizenship as a mobility regime, rather than as a differentiation of rights.

The Origins of the Permit Regime: British Colonial Legacies

Post-independence Israel was deeply affected by the legacies of the broader British imperial context. The British imperial toolkit of emergency more broadly shaped imperial formations in Israel/Palestine by creating a sophisticated system that linked identity to mobility and exclusion from political rights.[10] Population management practices and colonial emergency laws developed in the horizontal circuits of the British Empire as the central method of rule, with its fulcrum located in Mandatory Palestine; there, inventories of knowledge and legal weaponry that harbored shifting imaginaries of racial ordering and schemas of "suspicious" populations were imported from India and Ireland directly or via correspondence with the Colonial Office adapted and innovated upon through the appointment and training of administrators, interrogators, and police officers.[11]

Fueled by the belief that any form of political activism toward liberation from British colonial rule was a threat to "peace and good government,"[12] British colonial governments developed a set of legal-spatial measures—bureaucratic practices of population control and surveillance—enacted through emergency laws. These developed into a repertoire of administrative tools to prevent and control mobility. Sociologists use the term "toolkit" to describe how people draw on elements from their culture to inform and justify their behavior, decision making, and strategies of action.[13] The bureaucratic toolkit of emergency not only defined what colonial administrators could do but also formed a set of scripts, templates, and classification to manage the population in times of crisis, using varying degrees of mobility restrictions as the fundamental element of control. These tools ranged from the confinement of bodies through preventive and administrative detention without trial to the confinement to a specific territory through curfews and closures. They included the monitoring of movement through blacklists, the declaration of whole towns and territories as "disturbed areas" and danger zones, public safety acts that could be accessed only with a specific individual permit from a district commissioner, and denials of the "natives of the colony" the right to enter or exit. Instead of the classical separation between the legal histories of criminal law, martial law, and the administration of the everyday state, an organizational vantage point on emergency laws reveals how the British bureaucratic toolkit of emergency that was formed during the British Mandate became the scaffolding of the state apparatus to govern Palestinians in Israel.

How did this process take place? During the Arab revolt in Mandatory Palestine in 1936–1939, the classification of political activists and militants, coupled with various counterinsurgency activities, augmented the enforcement of emergency laws. These bureaucratic practices transformed the binary opposition between "friend" and "foe" into an ever-expanding index of suspicion that conflated a security threat with a political threat.[14] This fluidity—the crux of British colonial bureaucracy—was achieved using demographic categories that effectively manipulated "intractably divisive primordial loyalties" for the surveillance and monitoring of colonized populations.[15]

Following Israel's independence and the Nakba ("the Catastrophe"), these practices became what I call an administrative toolkit of suspicion for the military government's relations with the Palestinians who remained. In India, a similar toolkit shaped the intimate relationship among citizenship, political opposition, and political violence by establishing a distinction between the sovereign people as a political community endowed with rights and those engaged in political violence—with the latter being governed by emergency laws that were sanctioned by the constitution and being excluded from the political community.[16] Even those who held formal citizenship became a class whose rights were at the discretion of bureaucratic officials.

The nascent Israeli state drew on certain practices of emergency and the repertoire of British colonial spatial-legal practices to govern civilian populations that had been developed and deployed throughout the British Empire.[17] The Israeli regime of emergency laws and military decrees established after the 1948 war used these emergency practices as a permit regime to compromise the claims on citizenship of the Palestinian population remaining in the borders of the new state. The bureaucratic structure developed in those first two decades impeded Palestinian political membership in the independent state through this regime that controlled their movement rather than granting rights. The permit regime evolved as a system of documentation and surveillance technologies that enabled the military government to exercise a high level of monitoring and control of the Palestinian population.

Partition, Prevention of Return, and the Legacies of Mobility Restrictions

The long shadow of the partition that never happened but enabled both the promissory note of an independent Palestinian state and the contemporary indeterminate occupation was fundamental to shaping the permit system and citizenship as a differentiated grid for mobility. The colonial practices that categorized populations as suspect and then created or adapted technologies to control movement formed an administrative repertoire of emergency. These sets of practices, the cultural-administrative scripts of the state, affected the structure of the permit regimes. Those regimes were formed through the practices copied and pasted from the procedures for monitoring foreigners, for managing a suspect list, and for confining or preventing people from entering their own districts.

Partition was devised as a solution to anticolonial and intercommunal conflict, along with the harsh measures of mobility restrictions and population control to quash insurgency. The desirability of partition had been first assumed by the 1937 Peel Commission.[18] The plan was written by a group of British colonial officers, and it was specifically couched in a security rationale. The basic question it was designed to answer was how to pacify "the Arab revolt" (1936–1939) and obtain regional stability. Its answer was to separate demographically, as much as possible, the Jews of Palestine from its Muslim and Christian inhabitants.

The political support for partition among Mandate authorities was thus a response to conflict, especially during the Arab revolt. Partition was perceived as a means of achieving national self-determination for communities, as empires were hammered into new nation-states. This solution necessitated carving up territory and inevitably transferring populations, along perceived religious or ethnonational divides.

In the aftermath of British colonial rule, partition plans played a crucial role in shifting the goals of the permit regimes away from what had been the focus of the colonial practices: security, surveillance, and gathering intelligence for the purpose of monitoring and controlling the population and preventing opposition to the regime. It did so by creating the demographic logic of "otherness" and an overarching, existential goal of achieving or maintaining a majority against a rival community. Partition, during this era, translated the principle of self-determination in international law into a project of massive population transfer and exclusion from citizenship that was perceived as legitimate to achieve homogeneous "national" majorities.[19] These principles had been incorporated into the political discourse of the Yishuv since the Peel Commission introduced the partition plan in 1937.[20]

After World War II, this plan was adopted by the UN General Assembly in Resolution 181, "the partition plan."[21] The resolution envisaged and indeed aimed to ensure freedom of movement and economic integration between the Jewish and Arab states. The way the separationist model played out on the ground, alas, defeated these objectives.

The partition that did not happen in Israel and the partition of India positioned the newly created minorities as problems that could not be addressed directly through formal law because both states after independence struggled to gain international and domestic legitimacy as democratic regimes governed by the rule of law. To get around the legalities of formal democracy, minorities were managed through administrative regulations, routines, and evidentiary demands. Partition plans legitimized the bureaucratic practice of exclusion intended to prevent people from demanding their rights. The transfer of Palestinians, the prevention of their return, and subsequently the denial of their citizenship were carried out by administrative means in the aftermath of mass violence.

British colonial rule governed subject populations defined by racial and ethnic hierarchies through a growing repertoire of emergency laws designed to control uprisings in response to the denial of equal citizenship. If race was the relational marker that made the colonies "safe" from the "dangers of universalism" by enabling the differentiation between citizens and subjects, as Laurent Dubois writes, then emergency was the method of maintaining that differentiation through the decoupling of an aspirational legal liberal discourse from everyday bureaucracy that operated to manage populations and repress struggles for equality.[22] Technologies of classification and surveillance, developed in the colonial state to monitor subject populations based on degrees of suspicion, were used by the newly independent states to exclude minorities from political membership by administrative means. Israel's permit regime, a main method of military rule over the Palestinians within the country's broader post-imperial context, follows the logic used to implement similar bureaucratic measures in the early days of independent India after partition on the frontier with Pakistan.

During the dramatic wars of independence and partition following British decolonization, massive numbers of people fled the territories that subsequently became Israel, India, and Pakistan. When they attempted to go back to their homes, permit regimes were enacted to block their return: a permit system on India's western frontier with Pakistan and one in the "security zones" of the military government that Israel established to control the remaining Palestinian population.[23] Having been transformed overnight from colonial subjects to refugees, these people were then classified by the new states as intruders, infiltrators, undesirables, and security threats. The story of the bureaucratic practices that turned refugees into intruders[24] and how this prevented people from claiming citizenship in the homes they had left weeks or months before underscores the intimate relationship between race, citizenship, and mobility.

Although there are multiple dimensions to these practices, I focus on the regime geared to restrict and prevent movement. Even though the prevention of movement enabled both military and civilian control over and appropriation of Palestinian territory, I argue that the institutional logic and organization of such prevention of movement are distinct from practices of the settlement and dispossession of land. The restriction of mobility for the dispossession of land entails the prevention of one's access to lands and land rights, but the restriction of mobility for the sake of surveillance and control constructed an administrative paper trail that subsequently determined one's possibility to claim political membership in the state. These practices of classification, registration, and monitoring of movement based on emergency laws had developed in the interwar period as colonial governments crushed anticolonial uprisings throughout the British Empire.

Development of the Bureaucratic Toolkit of Emergency

Governing through emergency laws was a central feature of British colonial rule. Beginning in the mid-nineteenth century, states of emergency were used in British colonies as an elastic repertoire of rule aimed mainly to ensure the preservation of colonial power, aiming at the crushing of strikes, riots, and insurgencies. Eventually emergency was used in "situations of danger that can never be exhaustively anticipated or codified in advance."[25]

During the nineteenth century, as security became an organizing principle of the colonial state, emergency laws allowed colonial bureaucrats, police officers, and military commanders to suspend rights, promulgate decrees, restrict movement in closed military zones, and grant impunity to military personnel operating within the civil population in "dangerous" and "disturbed" areas. The justification for using emergency powers drew on the rule of colonial difference: drastic measures were necessary "where a handful of white people need to maintain themselves against lawless, sometimes violent people"; that is, when confronting subject populations perceived as hostile.[26] Technologies of surveillance were created during these perceived "states of emergency" in the colonies, such as wars, uprising, and economic crises.[27] At first, temporary restrictions on movement were enacted through ad hoc practices and emergency decrees. Those restrictions gradually solidified into an apparatus to control movement across frontiers and within restricted areas.[28]

Emergency laws rarely specified the identity of the people for which they were intended; instead, they were worded to endow government officials with universal authority. In effect, emergency legal tools were mostly used to control minorities, and because the laws neither specified the conditions of their use nor their target populations, administrative classification of target populations was imperative for implementation. This necessity for regulation granted bureaucrats full discretion in defining dangerous and risky individuals or entire populations.

"Dangerous Populations" and the Axis of Suspicion

British colonial rule classified populations according to what I call an "axis of suspicion" determined by the level of their loyalty and potential security threat to the state; these categories were constituted by administrative and internal regulations, departmental directives, official recommendation forms, home department circulars, and intelligence reports.[29] Persons or communities were defined by their degree of loyalty on a continuum that included loyal subjects, subjects of doubtful loyalty, suspicious subjects, minor security threats, threats to the state, and enemy agents. These classifications were made by state officials, and they were fluid and changeable. Categories of suspicion upended colonial classification according to demographic characteristics, race, religion, region, or caste, which led to the application of differential administrative practices to individuals and communities that, in turn, led to disparities in access to rights guaranteed by the state.[30]

The organizational vantage point that traces the institutional logic of emergency laws and administrative practices provides a distinctively different account of the ways in which the "managed mobilities" of colonial rule are deeply intertwined with postcolonial citizenship.[31] In such a regime, bureaucratic routines structure political policies, rather than just reflecting and achieving them. Security emergency laws structure citizenship, rather than simply being tools for the suppression for the rights of citizens.

The axis of suspicion—the process of defining and classifying people based on the degree of their loyalty—was a prominent feature of British colonial bureaucracy that would later delineate the boundaries of citizenship in the new states.

The Military Government and the Administrative Prevention of Return

In the dramatic violence of partition, war, and the Nakba of 1947 and 1948, people fled India, Pakistan, and Palestine/Israel. That flight and forced exile would become defining events for the designation of the political status of those who fled or were exiled.[32]

But it was not the violence and exile themselves that created the long-term impact on political status and the making of citizenship.[33] Rather, it was the bureaucratic response to the violence and the subsequent exile and population transfer: the institutional routines in their aftermath created differentiated regime of citizenship for those who were designated as belonging to the "other side" of partition, whether in another state or one that was not yet created.

The military government was formative to Israeli state-making, setting clear boundaries of belonging based on race and constituting what Shira Robinson aptly describes as a "settler colonial liberal state."[34] The agglomeration of methods of colonial control, surveillance, monitoring, and coercion for collaboration, as well as the criminalization of political participation, formed a hierarchy of political status.[35] Palestinian citizenship has since been described as nominal, formal in an ethnocratic regime, second-class, conditional, or settler-colonial citizenship, assuming a categorical effect on all Palestinian citizens of Israel.[36]

The military government's permit regime aimed to achieve surveillance over population movement and to prevent changes in residency from one area into another. Another objective was to maintain the exclusion of Arabs from their lands; for instance, preventing internal refugees from returning to abandoned villages or preventing the return of land that had been declared "absentee land" and seized by the state. Some of these practices also aimed to control the flooding of the employment market in Jewish areas or to prevent Arabs from working in areas declared as security zones.[37] This last objective, which combined economic considerations with practices of segregation and the maintenance of suspicion, required procedures to prevent those named by the colonial government as involved in incitement or rebellious activities from moving outside their place of residency.

The Ministries of Interior, Minorities, and Immigration were all involved in the effort to impede mobility of returning refugees who had left the country and were now classified as infiltrators and intruders. In practice, soldiers and border police prevented people from returning, expelled many internally displaced persons, monitored the movement of the population, and prepared the conditions for excluding people from future citizenship laws by bureaucratic means.[38]

Recent innovative work on the military government has focused on its importance for the conquest and dispossession of territory and the promotion of settlement. Yet its formative role in population management and the making of political membership has been under-researched.[39] The military government and its permit system that monitored and controlled the movement of Palestinians defined the necessary documents for claiming citizenship. As Ballas shows, military courts that ruled by emergency laws established differentiated boundaries of citizenship.[40] This colonial military bureaucracy transformed political membership in the new Israeli state into a system in which a person's classification, according to degrees of loyalty and suspicion, would later determine their range of mobility. For Jews, citizenship entailed access to rights, affected and scaled by ethnic classifications. For Palestinians, citizenship was a mobility regime that granted nondeportability and protection from exile, though not from displacement. Nor did it offer political membership in a community that granted a "right to have rights," as Hannah Arendt famously articulated.[41] The promise of nondeportability was a way to rope in Palestinians as legal subjects of Israeli law and for government organizations to define their relationship to the state on a scale of suspicion.

As did India in the first years after the violence of independence, the Israeli state adapted the British colonial toolkit of emergency, which had been developed to govern the subject population, but this time the colonial toolkit was to enable the majority to rule over the minority population that remained within the boundaries of the independent state after the Nakba. With the institutionalization of control of suspicious and dangerous populations, temporary classifications and practices created during the emergency were transformed into permanent practices of the Ministries of the Interior and of Home Affairs.

The Israeli permit regime enacted in 1949 transformed colonial practices of population management that originated in the emergency laws forged between the two world wars into a method of administrative exclusion, thereby reducing the number of Palestinians entitled to claim citizenship once statutory citizenship laws were enacted from 1950 to 1952. The similarity between the Israeli case and the permit system in India underscores how ad hoc measures first justified by security reasons and an emergency situation following an influx of refugees were institutionalized into administrative routines. The organizational vantage point into the bureaucratic routines illuminates the practical experience of dispossessed remainder populations that became a minority after partition, in which security laws and perceptions of suspicion and threat carved out one's ability to move within the state and prevented deportation from it. The disparity between the institutional logics of the security forces that prevented people from returning to their land and homes, and the practices aiming at political exclusion through control of movement, suggests a flexible scale of control through political status defined by loyalty and suspicion. This flexible scale of control constructed citizenship as a complex set of rights defined by one's possibility for mobility.

The Bureaucratic Grid of Mobility under Occupation: The Permit Regime in the West Bank

From a legal perspective, and in contrast to the permit system of the military government that was based on the Emergency Defence Regulations of 1945, the permit regime in the West Bank is not a statutory regime based on formal rules. Yet it is not a lawless system, nor does it remain outside the Israeli legal system. The permit regime that governs the lives of millions of Palestinians in the West Bank deploys a patchwork of administrative decrees, internal regulations, and ad hoc decisions that have developed into an effective regime for the purposes of creating economic dependency and large-scale surveillance and segregation by administrative means. Space, race, and documents form the trinity of organizing principles of the permit regime. The first is spatial closure—the legal-spatial control and containment of the population within the territory; the second is the racialized exclusion from full citizenship; and the third consists of administrative practices that establish racial hierarchy through separate legal orders for different populations in the same territory. This trinity relies on two preconditions: "contained violence," physical violence through military force or the threat of such violence, which means the Israeli army and its Border Police can use lethal force against anyone attempting to move across the territory without a permit; and the enforcement of spatial closure, which was the driving force for change and development in the rules of the occupation of the territories conquered in 1967.[42] Although Israel ceded responsibility for administration of civilian affairs to the Palestinian Authority when closure was enforced, it increased and intensified its control over the daily lives of the Palestinians in the West Bank by slowing their movement and monitoring it through required documents.[43]

Even though the language of the Oslo Accords aimed to stimulate a free flow of workers and goods from the territories into Israel, the Oslo process introduced closure as the fundamental feature of Israeli governance, a process that renewed the gradual use of the bureaucratic toolkit of emergency. For example, in 1995 the number of Palestinian workers in Israel dropped by more than 50 percent due to closures. The disparity between the political discourse on free movement and free markets and the harsh realities of immobility, atomization, and poverty created fear and doubt about the accords among the Palestinians of the West Bank. In 1994 and 1995, suicide bombings in Israeli cities fueled the justification and enforcement of the closure policy that limited movement through an array of technologies of emergency, including manned checkpoints, earth mounds, Border Police and military patrols, and the expanding demand for documents. The Israeli army divided the West Bank into "territorial cells," which enabled it to impose more flexible and local limitations, such as "encirclement" (a blockade over a city) or "separation," the prohibition of movement between two or more areas. Thus, an entire system of special permits proliferated: permits for crossing a blockade, thirteen kinds of permits for the seam zone, permits despite a security ban, and so on. These technologies increased pressure on Palestinians to collaborate with the secret service in exchange for securing permits necessary for conducting daily life.[44] Despite these restrictions, the closure never brought about a complete halt to the movement of Palestinians, who found their own ways of entering Israel, establishing informal border economies.[45] The completion of the separation barrier in 2006 turned closure into a highly effective means of blocking movement, and the entry permit, combined with the Population Registry, became a vital document for sustaining even minimal living conditions.

In a way, the implosion of the Oslo Accords in the Second Intifada created a relationship between the Israeli state and Palestinians that resembled the situation of the Palestinians in 1948 after the Nakba and the failed partition. When the double-headed bureaucracy imploded during the Second Intifada, so did the administration of the Palestinians as a collective through organizations or the Palestinian Authority. The relationships that governed mobility were directly between Palestinian individuals and the Israeli state, which manipulated that power through the massive recruitment of informants who exchanged low-grade information for the ability to move. One might think of closure as applying to the territory, but it was, in fact, closure on a population, similar to the military government in 1949 that had jurisdiction over the Palestinian population and not over a bounded territory. In practice, closure meant that the movement of every Palestinian—whether seeking to enter Israel, moving within the occupied West Bank, or traveling between the West Bank and Gaza Strip—was constrained based on his or her identity. In contrast, the movement of Jewish settlers across the territories in the same closed military zones was permitted, so over time an entire system of administrative enforcement based on race was developed through documents, technologies, and infrastructures of segregation. Most of the military decrees limiting movement in the territories concluded in a clause stating they did not apply to Israelis. The category "Israeli" included Palestinian Israelis, but because those enforcing closure often found it impossible to apply the distinction between Israeli Palestinians, Palestinians of the West Bank, and Palestinian residents of East Jerusalem, Palestinian Israelis were often targets of monitoring and inspection as well. Therefore, the exemption of limitations on freedom of movement applied only to Israeli Jews, particularly Israeli Jewish settlers.[46]

The permit regime governing Palestinian mobility in the West Bank has fueled legal changes in the content of the rights of Palestinians of 1948, through amendments aimed at preventing marriages between Palestinians from the West Bank and the diaspora and through restrictions on mobility.[47] Like the separation wall, restrictions of mobility did not separate Jews from Palestinians, but Palestinians of different political status from each other.[48]

Palestinian residents of East Jerusalem are the exemplary population that experience the one state reality because of the annexation of Occupied East Jerusalem. Palestinian Jerusalemites are caught between exclusionary nationalism and bureaucratic inclusion in an urban citizenship that both denies political rights in Israel or self-determination in Palestine and yet provides a high range of mobility both in Israel and the West Bank.[49]

Citizenship as Mobility in the One State Reality"

Although citizenship as a mobility regime has been a continuous state project since its inception, it is by no means a stable regime from a legal and administrative perspective. Under constant construction and development, the permit system under the military government from 1949 to 1966 and the bureaucracy of the occupation of the West Bank and the blockade on Gaza are not results of policy design and constitutional infrastructure, as some scholars argue, but are forms of population management by administrative means.[50] They are enabled by the disparity between the formal liberal rule of law, the semblance of citizenship as equal status, and practices on the ground that delineate citizenship through security laws and matrix of graduated mobility. Citizenship as mobility was obscured by the effects of the partition plan and, later, the Oslo Accords that excluded Palestinian citizens of Israel and is therefore more visible in the contemporary one state reality.[51]

The one state reality is the result of an indeterminate occupation for more than a half-century, the expansion and normalization of settlements, and the permit regime in the West Bank and East Jerusalem that have developed the inherited British colonial toolkit of emergency into the most sophisticated surveillance and population management system in the world.[52] The failures of the Oslo process and the territorial, economic, and legal expansion of Israel's control over every aspect of Palestinian life have not only left a vacuum of rights but have also generated an excess of control, mostly through restrictions on movement: Palestinians are actively governed by the Israeli state apparatuses and markets yet are denied political participation in decision making. The recent threats of annexation de jure of the West Bank highlights Israeli citizenship as a mobility regime: Israeli citizenship provides freedom of movement, juxtaposed with the severe mobility restrictions that permeate every aspect of civilian life of those who are both stateless and have no political membership, Palestinians in the West Bank; these restrictions are in the form of total siege and blockade in Gaza. Israel's complete control over mobility in and out of the Gaza Strip is a critical component of the mobility regime, one that successfully segregates and separates Palestinian populations by graded access or denial of mobility.

The organizational vantage point presented in this chapter focuses on the role of bureaucratic and administrative practice legacies in the making of political membership in Israel/Palestine through the control of mobility and does not assume that political status grants rights. The focus on mobility as the key for understanding the patchwork of political status in the one state reality in Israel/Palestine incorporates the lived experience of the population into the categories of political membership we think by, while situating the contemporary moment within the colonial and imperial administrative infrastructures that have contributed to its making.

5

DELEGATING DOMINATION

Indirect Rule in the West Bank

Diana B. Greenwald

The state, or what James Scott calls that "vexed institution that is the ground of both our freedoms and our unfreedoms," is not only the primary unit of analysis in the study of international relations, but it also circumscribes political life for humans nearly everywhere that they live.[1] Israel, within its 1949 armistice lines, and the Occupied Palestinian Territories of the West Bank, East Jerusalem, and the Gaza Strip—are no exception. Although Palestinian governing authorities exist in parts of the West Bank and in Gaza, a single political organization—the State of Israel—retains a disproportionate capacity for wielding violence across the entirety of the land. For the more than fourteen million people who inhabit this land—whether they know it as historic Palestine, the Land of Israel, or something in between—it is the relatively coherent and unitary State of Israel that plays the greatest role in defining both their freedoms and their unfreedoms. Hence, the "one state reality" between the Jordan River and the Mediterranean Sea describes an empirical condition that motivates the analysis within this volume.

However, within the territory that is controlled or occupied by the State of Israel, Palestinians, who comprise nearly 50 percent of the population, face differentiated institutions of order, governance, and control.[2] The analysis in this chapter focuses on a geographically delimited unit—the contemporary West Bank, exclusive of East Jerusalem—and is mostly confined to the historical period from 1994 to the present, following the creation of the Palestinian Authority (PA) as a result of the Oslo Accords.[3] So defined, this territory is home to more than 2.8 million Palestinians and over 440,000 Israeli settlers at the time of writing.[4]

The political institutions that exist alongside Israeli military rule in the West Bank have often appeared to defy comparison to other cases, perhaps because of their geographic and legal complexity or the unique history that underlies them. One purpose of this chapter is to invite the contemporary West Bank into the comparative institutional literature on the state and modes of governance, rule, and domination.

As I elaborate later, existing analysis, often drawing on the perspectives of Palestinian residents of the occupied territories, has either implicitly or explicitly conceptualized the West Bank as a case of indirect rule. According to this understanding, the PA functions, at least in part, as an agent of or subcontractor to its foreign donors, Israel, or some combination of both.[5] In this chapter, I probe this analogy to assess the ways in which the PA conforms to or differs from existing conceptualizations of indirect rule. Although the delegation of authority is central to all definitions of indirect rule, scholars disagree on the importance of ideology and intent, elements that, I argue, are particularly consequential for thinking about the future of Israeli and Palestinian institutions in the West Bank. Further, I find that indirect rule within the West Bank exhibits several distinctive features, including the delegation of authority to former rebels; a relative emphasis on the delegation of political repression rather than resource extraction; and highly localized, urban–rural dynamics that contrast in some ways with traditional, colonial indirect rule. Considering these features, the chapter concludes by exploring what follows indirect rule and how it may shape future political and economic development. Rather than dissolving with the arrival of a sovereign Palestinian state, I suggest it is more likely that the institutions of indirect rule will be subsumed into future constellations of state authority in the West Bank and, as such, will persist as long-term targets of radical reform.

Background

The West Bank has been militarily occupied by Israel since 1967, when, in a matter of days, the Israeli military defeated Jordanian forces and seized control of the territory west of the Jordan River, displacing hundreds of thousands of Palestinians. For the first twenty-seven years of the occupation, Israeli troops directly policed and ruled the territory and its Palestinian residents, who numbered roughly 600,000 when the occupation began.[6] Although Israel relied, with spotty success, on local Palestinian authorities to ensure the provision of basic services to Palestinian towns and cities, Israel's military occupation took the form of a direct or relatively unmediated form of rule. State-backed settlement of the territory began almost immediately after the 1967 War and accelerated after the 1977 formation of a right-wing Israeli government under the leadership of the Likud Party. By late 1991, as the First Intifada waned and Israeli and Palestinian teams began negotiations at the Madrid conference, the population of Jewish Israeli settlers in the West Bank, excluding Jerusalem, had reached almost 90,000.[7]

The Declaration of Principles (Oslo I), signed by Israel and the Palestinian Liberation Organization (PLO), established the intent of the PA as an interim, self-governing body featuring a freely elected leadership. The PA was to govern Palestinians in the Gaza Strip and isolated population centers in the West Bank until future negotiations between Israel and the PLO resolved "permanent status" issues, such as borders, the status of Jerusalem, and the fate of Palestinian refugees. However, over time, it became clear that the PA, while engaging in certain forms of taxation, service provision, and regulation of the Palestinian economy, was not a vehicle for Palestinian political self-determination. Recruitment for the new Palestinian police forces was highly politicized, with selection heavily favoring loyalists to PLO leader and PA president Yasser Arafat's party, Fatah (H. arakat al-Tah. rir al-Watani al-Filast.ini, or the Palestinian National Liberation Movement), and elite positions were reserved for returnees from the exiled militant leadership.[8] By the late 1990s, it became clear that the sprawling PA police, security, and intelligence apparatus would be severed from democratic forms of accountability, ultimately taking orders from the PA's autocratic leadership and hamstrung by the need to coordinate its movements throughout much of the West Bank with Israel.

The Oslo regime broke down with the Second Intifada, as Palestinian insurgent attacks against Israeli targets mounted, and Israel responded by reoccupying major Palestinian cities, enacting strict curfews, and bombarding PA infrastructure. As for the Gaza Strip, its political trajectory diverged from that of the West Bank between 2005 and 2007, following Israel's withdrawal of its settlements, the 2006 victory of Hamas (H. arakat al-Muqāwama al-Islamiyya, or the Islamic Resistance Movement) in Palestinian legislative elections, and, ultimately, Hamas's seizure of power in Gaza. With Egypt's assistance, Israel has since imposed a blockade on Gaza, severely restricting the entry and exit of both people and basic goods; intermittent, devastating wars have erupted between Israel and Hamas since, most notably in 2006, 2008, 2012, 2014, and 2021. In the West Bank, Palestinians continue to live under the combined rule of the Israeli military and autocratic PA institutions. The latter were thoroughly overhauled beginning in 2007, with the support of the United States, to align Israeli and PA efforts to repress their shared opponents: Hamas, Palestinian Islamic Jihad, and other groups that rejected Oslo institutions as a betrayal of the national cause.[9]

What Is Indirect Rule?

Indirect rule is an elastic concept. It has been defined, alternatively, as a generic mode of decentralized state authority or as a violent form of despotism based on racial hierarchies, most explicitly associated with European colonization projects.[10] Importantly, every definition features a basic context in which a central state authority does not want to, or can only at great cost, produce some functions of governance over some subset of the population in the territory it controls. As described by Naseemullah and Staniland, citing Weber, "Direct rule represents the opposite condition, in which the state maintains and administers a monopoly of law, policy, and administration to the population without intermediaries, through bureaucrats without independent means of coercion."[11]

Thus, indirect rule captures a set of arrangements in which state decision makers selectively extend state institutions to—or withhold state institutions from—the population within the state's territory. Although proponents of indirect rule usually emphasize its connection to principles of local autonomy and empowerment, in practice indirect rule also evokes rules of exception, exclusion, discrimination, or neglect. This chapter's analysis is not concerned with whether indirect rule is normatively better or worse than direct rule, its conceptual counterpart; rather it seeks to understand the implications of indirect rule for populations, like Palestinians in the West Bank, who are subject to this configuration of state domination.

In one of the most frequently cited works on the topic, Mamdani describes indirect rule as a complex form of "decentralized despotism" that was initially deployed by Great Britain in India and, subsequently, in its colonies in sub-Saharan Africa.[12] It was soon emulated by other colonial powers such as France, Belgium, and Portugal and then refracted back to Britain's colonies in South Africa, where, Mamdani argues, it was later refined in the form of apartheid. Indirect rule entailed the application of so-called customary law in predominantly rural areas through the cultivation and sometimes creation of tribal chiefs, paired with civil law and methods of direct rule in the cities and areas of European settlement. In reading Mamdani, indirect rule emerges as an adaptive, yet intentional and strategic, framework for domination and extraction. The treatment of land, labor, and revenue depended on the most pressing needs of the colonial state and, where relevant, of the settlers. In all cases, indirect rule as practiced in the colonies in South Asia and sub-Saharan Africa was a form of despotism. It was highly racialized—even if it hid behind tribal, rather than racial, identity as the basis for administration and representation—and it was both implicitly and explicitly violent.

Mamdani's work contrasts with later, more strictly institutional definitions of indirect rule, such as that of Hechter, for whom indirect rule captures a variety of arrangements, including federalism, that make "the nation congruent with its governance unit," or of Gerring, Ziblatt, Gorp, and Arevalo who define it, simply, as decentralized rule, a concept that they argue can be applied to feudal, imperial, or contemporary states.[13] They note that "the principle of direct/indirect rule has rarely been applied in such a broad fashion" but argue "that there are sufficient commonalities across this heterogeneous set of governance relationships to justify their inclusion under a common theoretical rubric."[14] Thus, their framework applies to both imperial, nonconsensual forms of control and "constitutionalized (that is, formal, juridical, and largely consensual) arrangements" such as federalism. It is agnostic about the overarching objectives of the state and its leaders or is flexible enough to incorporate varied objectives (i.e., mere political survival, an agenda of racial supremacy, maximization of revenue, or something else). Finally, Naseemullah and Staniland use both formal legal arrangements and their implementation in practice to disaggregate indirect rule into three distinct types, each exhibiting different cost-benefit trade-offs for state leaders.[15]

The varied definitions presented here raise the question of whether ideological intent—particularly the emphasis on hierarchies of rights depending on ethnic, racial, or other identity-based traits—is an essential component of indirect rule. In fact, the answer depends on how one plans to use the concept. On its own, the institutional shell of indirect rule as, simply, a delegated or decentralized form of governance might not have sufficient predictive value. If indirect rule merely constitutes one administrative approach among many others, the ideological content of the regime—including those based in ethnic chauvinism, racial supremacy, or both—may condition the nature of resistance faced by the regime, its methods of responding to such resistance, and, ultimately, perhaps, the regime's survival or collapse.[16]

Principals and Agents in the West Bank

What all definitions of indirect rule have in common is an understanding of a fairly unified and dominant state—the principal, whether it is a colonial power, foreign occupier, or domestic state-builder—that employs indigenous agents to achieve its objectives. However, Mamdani cautions that a constitutive aspect of the regime was that these agents—chiefs employed by the colonial "Native Authority"—maintained some autonomy:

> To say that chiefs were autonomous is not to say that they were independent. It is not to claim that they did not act as intermediaries in implementing directives from the center, nor that they were not supervised by

> the organs of the central state, even closely. Their claim to independence was embedded in the demand that they be recognized as traditional and therefore hereditary authorities. . . . Once appointed, the personnel of the Native Authority were left to their own devices, unless they failed to keep order, to carry out orders (which included the demand for public labor and compulsory crops), or to balance their books. The autonomy and power of the Native Authority came to be crystallized in a decentralized despotism.[17]

Indeed, indirect rule operates in its smoothest and perhaps most brutal form when principal and agent interests are aligned in the maintenance of the regime. When indigenous intermediaries face divergent interests, including pressure from their own constituencies, "it will be extremely costly for the principal to apply sufficient rewards and punishments to make the agent comply."[18]

If indigenous intermediaries were often autocratic under the umbrella of British colonial rule, the autocratic nature of the PA, first under Yasser Arafat and, since 2005, under his successor, President Mahmoud Abbas, is no exception to this pattern. Central government institutions of the PA in the West Bank have been captured by the ruling party Fatah and the president's circle of loyalists. Yet the ideological intent underlying Israeli control of the West Bank, combined with the internationalization of authoritarian projects in the Middle East, introduces notable quirks to the form of indirect rule present in the West Bank since 1994.[19]

First, the conventional framing would suggest the PA is acting as an agent of Israel, the principal, in repressing opponents to Fatah, including those affiliated with Hamas, Palestinian Islamic Jihad, the Popular Front for the Liberation of Palestine (PFLP), and others who challenge Israel's occupation and Fatah's one-party rule. Indeed, informal discourse on the Palestinian case often seems to assume that the entire PA—from the president down to rank-and-file traffic cops—are agents of Israel. Although the PA's high degree of executive centralization might discourage defections, this is a probabilistic, not deterministic, outcome. In other words, even if they are exceedingly rare, defections may occur in the future and may take a variety of forms, from resignations to actively confronting PA forces. Abrahams, for example, finds that interest alignment between Israel and the PA in the late 1990s and again from 2007 to 2013 led to fairly robust cooperation in minimizing Palestinian violence against Israelis.[20] However, if Israel continues to deny Palestinian sovereignty, Abrahams predicts that it "is guaranteed to erode either the PA's security relationship with Israel or the PA's legitimacy among its own constituents, in the near future."[21] Indeed, we might not always predict that Israel and its PA agents will act in lockstep. Although the PA has threatened numerous times to suspend security coordination with Israel, the most notable period of agent defection in the Palestinian context was when Palestinian security forces participated in direct confrontations with the Israeli military and Fatah-affiliated militant groups staged violent attacks during the Second Intifada. The PA security services were thoroughly overhauled in the wake of the uprising and Yasser Arafat's death; as Abrahams describes, Israel reoccupied major Palestinian cities during Operation Defensive Shield and even directly attacked PA infrastructure.[22] Still, none of this guarantees that such defections will not occur in the future.

Further, even if we can assume that the PA is a fairly cohesive and unitary agent, it likely has multiple principals. The argument could be made that the PA is more an instrument of its largest donors, namely the European Union and the United States, than Israel. El Kurd, for example, argues that intervention by international patrons such as the United States in PA institutions "has the effect of making elite and public preferences diverge, thus separating political elites and the leadership further from the Palestinian public."[23] In this way, democratic forms of accountability between the PA regime elites and the Palestinian public are weakened. In El Kurd's analysis, the PA's largest international donors are where one should look for principal-agent dynamics of control to play out in Palestinian politics.

Finally, despite what El Kurd describes as the effective polarization and demobilization of Palestinian society under the Oslo regime, there may be domestic constituencies within the Palestinian population who might claw back some control over PA agents.[24] Until now, the most important coalition of Palestinians supporting the Oslo framework has been business elites who have been sustained through "crony capitalist" deals with Fatah's political elite.[25] While businessmen profiting from the indirect rule regime have no immediate reason to challenge it, the majority of Palestinians are cognizant of the elite pacts that facilitate the continuation of nondemocratic governance. In four recent surveys from the Palestinian Center for Policy and Survey Research in 2021, more than 80 percent of West Bank and Gaza respondents described PA institutions as corrupt.[26] Indeed, Nizar Banat, a frequent and vocal critic of the PA, was seized in the middle of the night from his home near Hebron and beaten to death by a squad of PA security agents in June 2021. Banat, a rising political figure, had often railed against PA corruption and coordination with Israel in his popular social media posts.

At the time of writing, Palestinians as old as thirty-three have never had the opportunity to vote in a national election, because none have been held since January 2006. Palestinians gathered for large-scale protests as news broke of

Banat's murder. Echoing a familiar rallying cry from the 2011 Arab uprisings, demonstrators chanted "the people want the fall of the regime."[27] After weeks of protests across the West Bank, during which numerous protesters were assaulted by plainclothes security forces, the PA announced it would charge fourteen of its own security officers with Banat's death, although, notably, they did not include the Hebron district head of the notorious Preventive Security apparatus or any of his superiors. It remains unclear whether Palestinian protests were sufficient to bring about the indictments or pressure from one of the PA's largest donors, the EU, was the pivotal factor.[28] Nonetheless, at the time of writing, accountability for Banat's surviving family members still seems only a distant possibility.[29] Yet, events elsewhere in the West Bank in mid-2022 demonstrated that past and present PA security officers are not a monolith. When a young Palestinian man from Jenin refugee camp opened fire on Israeli civilians in Tel Aviv, killing two, he was located and killed hours later by Israeli forces. Attention soon turned to his father, Fathi Hazem, a former officer in the PA security apparatus. Fathi spoke defiantly from his porch in the Jenin refugee camp in support of his son and continued militant resistance to the occupation. Still in hiding from Israeli forces seeking to arrest him at the time of writing, Hazem demonstrates that past employment within the PA security apparatus does not guarantee perpetual loyalty to the indirect rule regime.

In sum, our understanding of how much autonomy the Palestinian Authority's coercive agents possess must be grounded in a better empirical understanding of the principals—and possibly constituents—to whom they are responding. As Clarno writes in 2017, "Security coordination in the West Bank is one of the most sophisticated—and some would say successful—efforts to manage an unruly population. But tensions and contradictions undermine the illusion of stability."[30] In my own interviews with municipal-level politicians in the West Bank, I found that relationships between opposition leaders—those representing Hamas, PFLP, or smaller parties and independent lists—and PA rank-and-file police officers, whose political affiliations almost certainly lie with Fatah, are not universally uncooperative. Officers have collaborated with non-Fatah politicians at the local level in some settings; in others, the relationship has been more antagonistic. Further, the incentives of civil police officers versus PA agents within the Preventive Security or intelligence apparatus, for example, might be quite different. The indirect rule regime that protects Israel's military-backed settlement of the territory will rely on the continued cohesion of the entire Palestinian security sector, something that, as Abrahams observed, could become harder to maintain over time.[31]

Other Quirks of Indirect Rule in the West Bank

In addition to the complex questions around agency within the PA, a few other features of indirect rule in the West Bank distinguish it from more traditional understandings of the concept. First, it is notable that, in the Palestinian case, authority was delegated to former rebels who were militarily resisting the rule of the dominant state—Israel, in this case. Lia provides an illuminating overview of where the demilitarization of Fatah and its various militias succeeded and where it failed in the initial construction of PA coercive institutions.[32] Collaboration between Israel and the PA in the West Bank, particularly since 2007, has been heavily focused on demilitarizing armed factions affiliated with Hamas, Palestinian Islamic Jihad, and other militias that might challenge the regime. The assumption underlying this strategy has been that the PA would be able to prevent defections from within its own ranks. However, as described by Clarno, "The contradictory position of the PA troops who are drawn from the social milieus that they are expected to target" results in an inherently tenuous arrangement.[33] Should widespread violence erupt once again in the West Bank, there is no guarantee that the PA rank and file will continue to side with the regime at all costs.

Second, the functional modes of authority that the PA has assumed, in practice, do not include high degrees of economic extraction, whether in the form of revenue or labor, but instead emphasize political repression. Although monopolistic rent seeking is certainly a problem in key sectors of the occupied economy, less than one-third of the PA's revenue comes from taxation of Palestinians that it collects itself.[34] Regarding labor, unemployment rates are staggeringly high in the occupied territories, but they are largely attributable to Israeli-imposed restrictions on trade and development and the inhospitable environment for job creation amidst military occupation. The extent to which the Israeli–PA regime relies on the extraction of surplus value from Palestinian labor is a matter of scholarly discussion.[35] Finally, it is the Israeli state itself, not the PA, that is most involved in land expropriation. In summary, in terms of the despotic authorities delegated to the PA, the exclusion and repression of political opposition play much more central roles than taxation or labor extraction.

Of course, this delegation of coercive policing to the PA occurs within the context of Israel's disproportionately strong coercive capacity. Indirect rule, in the Palestinian case, did not represent a way to lighten the footprint of the coercive arm of the state: instead, it entailed a proliferation of coercive agents and opportunities for repression. In a moving reflection drawing on his own, multiple experiences with detention and arrest, Quran calls this the "Russian-Doll carceral state."[36] In this way, indirect rule over Palestinians adheres much more closely to its earlier colonial counterparts—those based on racialized domination—than the ideologically agnostic models put forward by later scholars. On the enforcement of customary law in British colonies, for example, Mamdani states it was done "with a whip, by a constellation of customary authorities—and, if necessary, with the barrel of a gun, by the forces of the central state."[37] This asymmetry in coercive capacity is also observed when one compares the Israeli military arsenal to the PA police force. The Interim Agreement (Oslo II) spelled out exactly how many rifles, machine guns, pistols, riot vehicles, and armored vehicles the PA was permitted to have, with the requirement that any updates to those allotments had to be agreed on by both Israel and the Palestinians. After Hamas's takeover of Gaza in 2007, US and European funding flowed into the PA security sector as part of the set of reforms advanced under PA prime minister Salam Fayyad. Although this influx of funds undoubtedly boosted the resources at the disposal of the PA police, security, and intelligence apparatus, their capacity remains dwarfed by that of the Israeli military. It is estimated that the PA security forces in the West Bank number more than 30,000. In contrast, Israel's armed forces contain more than 170,000 active officers, hundreds of thousands more in reserve, and in 2020, it dedicated an estimated 2,507 USD per capita to military expenditures, the highest of any country in the world.[38] The precise share of military spending that goes into West Bank operations is unknown, but their ground forces are equipped with advanced assault weaponry, artillery, armored vehicles, tanks, rockets, and more.

However, the Israel–PA relationship differs from traditional examples of indirect rule in where repression is deployed and by whom. This variation concerns the differentiation of urban and rural populations—the third way in which the case of the West Bank deviates from earlier colonial examples. Indirect rule regimes in a number of colonial examples feature more centralized and bureaucratic forms of rule in capital cities and more indirect, mediated forms of rule in the countryside. Since the signing of the Oslo Accords in the West Bank, the variation in authority across Palestinian populated areas has been the opposite: in the most densely populated centers of major Palestinian towns and cities such as Jenin, Nablus, Ramallah, Bethlehem, and (parts of) Hebron, the PA possesses the greatest authority. Much of this territory is designated as "Area A" under Oslo II, meaning the PA is the primary authority responsible for both civil and security matters. In the smaller towns and outlying villages, many of which are located in "Area B" and some of which cross into "Area C," the PA's policing capacity is explicitly constrained; Israeli-administered checkpoints dot major roads connecting Palestinian communities and Israeli military or border police actions occur much more frequently. For historical context, this Oslo-era arrangement follows an earlier, failed experiment by Israel in the late

1970s and early 1980s, when it established Palestinian intermediaries to assist in ruling the rural areas known as the "Village Leagues." Since Oslo, the Palestinian intermediary—in the form of the PA—has had disproportionate presence in urban areas. Direct rule in rural areas is primarily intended to protect Israeli settler communities and their access to resources. This strategy has meant that Israel relies on the PA to defuse urban mobilization, whereas Israel's own coercive apparatus—the military and border police, for example—most frequently responds to incidents occurring near the settlements.

The urban–rural segmentation of Palestinians in the West Bank under indirect rule is a specific form of the use of geography to, as Mamdani describes, "divide," "closet," or "containerize" the population.[39] Under British colonial rule in Africa, this tended to be done along ethnic or tribal lines, rather than territorial ones. Thus, the Palestinian population has been geographically "containerized" by Israel's occupation in unique ways. Even before the Oslo Accords, former prime minister Menachem Begin's formula that sought to promote "individual" autonomy for Palestinians emerged because there was no alternative method to efficiently divide and rule Palestinians. After Oslo, Israel has instead used region and geography to achieve a similar fragmenting effect—instituting the aforementioned division of Areas A, B, and C within the West Bank and maintaining and enforcing the separation of Gaza from the West Bank, the rest of the West Bank from East Jerusalem, residents of the occupied territories from Palestinian citizens of Israel, and Palestinians in the diaspora from historic Palestine. Because Israel has never successfully divided Palestinians by "tribe"—real or invented—instead they have often used geography.[40]

Looking Ahead

Mamdani asserts, "Every movement against decentralized despotism bore the institutional imprint of that mode of rule. Every movement of resistance was shaped by the very structure of power against which it rebelled."[41] The idiosyncratic nature of indirect rule in the West Bank has important implications for thinking about its long-term legacies. Indirect rule over Palestinians has meant an excess, not a dearth, of institutions. Further, despite the regime's persistent commitment to hyperlocal geographic fragmentation, it has done nothing to dampen nationalist identity and liberatory impulses among Palestinians. These features suggest that the struggle ahead will be a long one.

In considering the possible trajectories for indirectly ruled populations and territories, it is easier to observe the failure of indirect rule—most apparent in the collapse of colonial state-building projects that ultimately resulted in the independence of former colonies—than it is to conceptualize its success. From the perspective of the incumbent regime, success may be measured, at a minimum, as holding the sovereign state together. Few would argue that Israel's project of indirect rule in Palestinian communities of the West Bank (and arguably in Gaza) has been an unqualified success. The absorption of territories into European states or the gradual formation of the United Kingdom might meet some such standard. However, the longer Israel maintains its highly complex, modernized regime of ethnic separation and delegated coercion in the West Bank, the less relevance these historical examples may hold for sketching out the political future of the region.

For example, some research identifies indirect rule with weaker developmental outcomes than in regions that were directly ruled. Work on British indirect rule in India has linked the outsourcing of authority to weaker economic growth and even to a greater risk of insurgency.[42] In addition, Lange holds that British colonies governed under direct rule were more likely to experience postcolonial development, whereas those ruled indirectly were more prone to despotism after independence.[43] His argument rests on the directly ruled states' superior "legal-administrative" capacity, infrastructural power, and social inclusiveness that promoted developmentalism. However, in each of the first two areas wherein indirectly ruled regions are expected to have less state presence, the West Bank does not seem to fit the mold. PA courts are being increasingly usurped by executive authority, while Israel's parallel military court apparatus ensnares thousands of Palestinians each year. As described by the Israeli human rights organization B'Tselem,

> To all intents and purposes, the Israeli military court appears to be a court like any other. There are prosecutors and defense attorneys. There are rules of procedure, laws and regulations. There are judges who hand down rulings and verdicts couched in reasoned legal language. Nonetheless, this façade of propriety masks one of the most injurious apparatuses of the occupation. The military orders are all written by Israeli soldiers and reflect what they consider to be harmful to Israeli interests. Palestinians have no way of influencing the content of the military orders that rule their lives. The military judges and prosecutors are always Israeli soldiers in uniform. The Palestinians are always viewed as either suspects or defendants, and are almost always convicted.[44]

In this sense, the legal capacity of the West Bank is high: the outputs of the legal system are closely aligned with the ideological intent of the regime. Infrastructural power is similarly high in the West Bank, with an emphasis on structures that achieve extremely localized segregation in access to land, resources, and urban centers. On social inclusiveness—or "the inclusion of societal actors in policy-making and policy implementation"—this is obviously low in political institutions of the West Bank, where accountability to the Palestinian population is largely nonexistent.[45] Thus, the prospects for development "after" indirect rule in the West Bank force us to reckon with a familiar dilemma: Is it the institutional capacity of the existing state that is most critical for predicting later development, or is it the fundamental content and nature of the regime, such as its ideological intent and its degree of inclusion or exclusion of various segments of society? As an interesting counterpoint, using a geographic regression discontinuity design within Cameroon, Letsa and Wilfahrt find that indirect rule improved local development when compared to direct rule by, they argue, facilitating localized political action.[46] These questions about the predictors of long-run development after colonialism or indirect rule go beyond contemporary Palestine. However, the previously described quirks of the Palestinian case—the delegation of authority to former rebels, the disproportionate weight attached to coercion and internal policing, and the particular geographies of division and urban–rural dynamics—mean that generalizations from prior historical cases should be pursued with caution.

When considering the legacies of indirect rule for the state itself, rather than for economic development, broadly speaking, the Palestinian experience might provide more grounds for optimism. For example, in their analysis of the case of Sierra Leone, Daron Acemoglu and coauthors theorize that indirect rule contributed to state weakness after independence. However, one of the pathways by which this occurred is that indirect rule "mitigated against the construction of a national identity so that politics stayed local and parochial" because of the tribe-centered modality of indirect rule.[47] Elsewhere, Hechter has provocatively claimed that the decentralization of power that comes with indirect rule can ultimately reduce demands for national sovereignty from ethnic groups within the state.[48] However, in the Palestinian case, indirect rule, in the form enshrined in the Oslo Accords, came well after Palestinian national identity had been constructed and advanced. Indirect rule under the Oslo formula has neither reduced demands for Palestinian sovereignty nor the salience of national identity for Palestinians. Thus, decades of bifurcated authority in the West Bank might have different, and perhaps less severe, implications for Palestinian institution building in the future.

The Palestinian case forces us to consider what institutions might look like if the "one state reality" persists and is formalized in the future. Indirect rule in the West Bank has entailed a multiplicity of principals, uncertainty about the coherence of the PA as a unitary agent, and a highly modern infrastructure of geographic segregation and discrimination. Nonetheless, throughout the post-Oslo period, Palestinian national identity has not diminished, and although there are a diversity of views on the one state versus two state future, the overarching political demand of the Palestinian national movement—the right, quite simply, to stay and to belong, as Erakat has eloquently argued—has not changed.[49] If the one state reality becomes formally institutionalized, the vestiges of indirect rule will most likely remain as instruments of state domination and discrimination. Thus, it would be no surprise if they were to face continued campaigns for their dismantling.

6

THE THOROUGH INSINUATION OF THE ONE STATE REALITY INTO PALESTINIAN POLITICAL LIFE

Nathan J. Brown and Iman Elbanna

On May 19, 2020, Mahmoud Abbas, president of the State of Palestine and of the Palestinian National Authority, chair of the Palestinian Liberation Organization, and head of Fatah (Movement of Palestinian Liberation), affirmed the goal of seeking a state in the West Bank and Gaza—but also announced that the road to that end ran through an insistent acknowledgment of the Israeli occupation. He also seemed to disavow any responsibilities that flowed from the multiple authorities he had, instead proclaiming that "the Israeli occupation authority, as of today, has to shoulder all responsibilities and obligations in front of the international community as an occupying power over the territory of the occupied state of Palestine."[1] Even though he seemed to be handing responsibility for Palestinians over to Israel, he was not denounced by critics as abandoning national goals but instead was lauded. Palestinians and others peppered him with questions about whether he really would follow through on dismantling the security, economic, and political arrangements that had sustained Palestinian leadership structures, in their constrained form, for a quarter-century. His recognition of the one state reality came reluctantly and very late—so that he seemed less to be leading Palestinians as much as following them. And indeed within less than six months, he quietly bowed to reality as he seems to have perceived it, resuming the suspended cooperation with Israel. A year after the Palestinian president appeared briefly to bow to the one state reality, Palestinians in the West Bank, Gaza, and Jerusalem launched a series of demonstrations and strikes that their leaders struggled (often unsuccessfully) to get in front of—almost as if the harshly enforced fences, walls, and zones could be surmounted by loosely coordinated action.

Grappling with Reality

When observers speak of a "one state reality" they generally are speaking from some combination of diplomatic, geographic, and demographic vantage points. Diplomatically, there is no viable process that would lead to a two state solution; geographically, there is a single sovereign state that controls the entirety of Mandatory Palestine; and demographically, the Israeli presence across the 1967 borders seems unlikely to be reversed.

In this chapter, we explore a different aspect of this one state reality—one that flows in part from the others but may also be more profound in its implications: the way in which Palestinian collective structures have sometimes imperceptibly but still very deeply oriented themselves around the single state of Israel.

Of course, Palestinians have always been aware of Israel's existence, whatever they felt about it. But Palestinian nationalism was not merely about Israel; it was about realizing a Palestinian nationalist vision in the form of a state. In recent years, Israel has loomed steadily larger, and Palestinian statehood has receded in Palestinian national identity and political horizons. In Palestinian political discussions, there has long been growing talk of both a "one state solution" and a "one state reality." Less noticed has also been a slow reorientation of the nationalist movement away from the centrality of any kind of statehood, as themes like "rights" or "the end of occupation" have edged out concerns about sovereignty and borders in internal debates. The center of gravity of the national movement—embodied in some authoritative and even governmental structures (the PLO, the PNA), political factions (Fatah, Hamas, and smaller groups), formal organizations (student associations), and informal or loosely organized tendencies (the BDS movement)—seems to be shifting away from the overriding goal of Palestinian statehood. For some Palestinians, this is a deliberate calculation or strategy, but even for those who do not make such a conscious choice, the idea of statehood seems to be receding in salience: in people's discussions, in their imaginations, in the symbols that resonate, and in voicing aspirations.

In its place, something new has arisen, though many would be loath to admit it: the State of Israel is now the central reality toward which most collective Palestinian organizations are oriented. This is even true—actually, it is especially true—for those organizations that are self-consciously national in nature and were designed originally to pursue Palestinian statehood, the independence of Palestinian decision making, national unity, or various conceptions of national identity.

This development has been gradual, and it involves as much coping with the one state reality as embracing it. Although there is increasing talk among Palestinians about a "one state option," it is not at the core of what we are examining in this chapter. Instead, the deep entrenchment of Israeli control, the decay of cohesive national institutions, and the absence of strategies for realizing Palestinian statehood in any form have combined to force Palestinian political actors to recalibrate their short-term horizons—and move toward far greater agnosticism about the ultimate form that Palestinian nationhood should (or will) take.

It should therefore be no surprise that this orientation toward the one state reality is rarely discussed or proclaimed. Indeed, the phenomenon is clearest most of all when viewed in a long-term historical perspective: Palestinian organizations soldier on, but almost all have come to accept—at least for tactical reasons and sometimes with considerable bitterness—that Israel lies at the center of their political lives.

National Institutions

Over the past century, Palestinians have built a variety of national institutions designed to speak for them as a national entity. The purpose of most of these has been to prepare for some form of statehood, to form the kernel of a governing state, or even to proclaim "Palestine" as a state. Most retain that nominal goal to this day but effectively show no credibility to deliver it; they sometimes seem to operate only to manage the occupation while denouncing it, and their ability to present themselves as steps to statehood has withered. The atrophy has been slow, but in historical terms it is dramatic.

The international context for Palestinian national efforts to build proto-state institutions over the decades has varied; sometimes these efforts were praised and even supported regionally (in the Arab world) but not globally; sometimes they were viewed with more suspicion regionally; and some clawed their way to achieving some form of global status. Yet historically, most were oriented around the idea of establishing, asserting, gaining recognition, or taking the necessary practical steps for attaining sovereignty and statehood for the Palestinian nation.

The Arab High Committee pushed for the end of the Mandate so a state of Palestine could emerge (with a significant Arab majority); the All-Palestine Government of 1948 claimed to replace the Mandate with an assertion of sovereignty over all of Palestine. The Palestinian Liberation Organization (PLO) sought recognition as "the sole legitimate representative of the Palestinian people," with its leaders and constituent groups arguing about the form of statehood but none departing from the position that a Palestinian state of some sort was the national goal. When the PLO and the assembly that presented itself as representing the Palestinian nation—the Palestinian National Council—declared independence in Algiers in 1988, they did so in a manner that reluctantly allowed for partition of the territory of Palestine precisely to purse the goal of Palestinian statehood. In signing the

Oslo Accords in the mid-1990s, the PLO leadership secured some administrative authority in parts of the West Bank and Gaza but portrayed the accords only as an interim measure on the road to statehood. They made clear at the time that the goal was not to run municipal services but to achieve a measure of self-rule over portions of the area that the PLO saw as the territory for its partitioned state. The administration immediately began referring to itself as the Palestinian *National* Authority (PNA) and pushed the idea of Palestinian statehood anywhere it could, either in matters permitted by the Oslo Accords (postage stamps) or by seizing on their silences (by establishing "State Security Courts," for instance). PNA leaders, mostly drawn from the PLO, made clear that the PNA's purpose was to move from *al-thawra ila al-dawla*, from the stage of revolutionary movement to that of state-building. Any symbol of statehood was sharply resisted by both the United States and Israel through the 1990s, whose leaders treated the idea of a Palestinian state as literally unspeakable until the early 2000s, but Palestinian leaders ignored these protestations wherever they could.

Most of these national institutions soldier on today. The All-Palestine Government is forgotten except by historians, but the PLO and PNA remain very much in existence. Indeed, these two bodies have worked to build an entity designed eventually to succeed and absorb them, the "State of Palestine," and references to the PNA by its own leaders are increasingly replaced by references to the State of Palestine.

The oft-proclaimed State of Palestine exists primarily in institutional forms that are indistinguishable from the PNA and PLO in practical terms in all but stationery, but it is the title under which Palestinian efforts to attain international recognition for statehood are now made. Yet Palestinians find their PLO, PNA and State of Palestine, in their various forms of existence, increasingly weak and progressively decaying. And their failings and state of disrepair—acknowledged even by those working to support them—may actually be less significant over the long term than a subtle but fundamental change in their focus, which has increasingly moved to coping with Israel rather than building an alternative to it.

This is most obviously the case with the PNA. When the PNA was launched, it immediately took on oversight of administrative, social-service, and adjudicative bodies serving Palestinians in the West Bank and Gaza. It added to these security bodies an elected assembly, which assumed legislative and oversight functions, and a set of ministries. Most of these bodies were granted generous international financial and diplomatic support so long as they operated within the limits circumscribed by the "peace process"—a set of diplomatic initiatives that initially studiously avoided any reference to Palestinian statehood but then, working to avoid collapse in the early 2000s, embraced a hitherto unmentionable "two state solution."

For Palestinians who were governed by these structures and for those designated to lead them, it seemed in the 1990s that a Palestinian state might be coming into being. That effort was shaken by the decay of the peace process and the Second Intifada but emerged from these crises with a renewed commitment by the leadership to building "reformed" institutions—which initially meant less corrupt, more efficient, and more democratic ones. When Hamas won parliamentary elections in 2006, the leadership's commitment to democratic procedure was quickly buried (again, with significant international support for placing democracy into hibernation), but a more technocratic effort to make institutions function more effectively survived for some years. This approach of constructing a Palestinian state on the back of a technocratic leadership led to an atrophy of politics and accountability and ultimately ran out of steam—although it did keep PA institutions alive and allowed for continued donor support and even a deepening of an international rhetorical commitment to Palestinian statehood.

The failure of the effort to convert the PNA into the basis of a state had a slow and generally unnoticed effect: it led to a divorce between the PNA and the quest for statehood, thus fostering a gradual reorientation of the increasingly non-authoritative Palestinian Authority (and all its constituent parts) toward simply managing degrees of autonomy under Israeli control. Of course, critics had always charged that the Oslo process had entailed merely "subcontracting the occupation," in a frequently used phrase. But PNA leaders and those they administered slowly began to drop any pretense that the PNA was anything else. For a time, some senior leaders had a strong interest in developing some of the institutional bases and practices of a state that international assistance supported so heavily. But although they did not abandon the search for statehood, by the mid-2010s, they no longer behaved as if building strong PNA institutions was a critical part of that effort. The PNA was no longer the kernel of a state but instead became an orphaned interim structure that was increasingly disrespected for its unplanned non-obsolescence.

For Palestinians, the problem was deeper than just the policy inclinations of their leaders; it involved the nature of the formal leadership of the national movement that, over the past two decades, has decayed and lost much of its ability to shape Palestinian political horizons and strategic thinking. Palestinian leaders and institutions do little policymaking, pursue no coherent ideology, express no compelling moral vision, are subject to no oversight, and inspire no collective enthusiasm.

So, what purpose does the PNA serve currently? It continues to manage security coordination with Israel and does so very clearly as a way to protect whatever pockets of Palestinian autonomy remain. That autonomy, the social services it enables, and the employment it generates are all dependent on a continued relationship with Israel and with "movement and access"—as the phrase that is used internationally puts it—not only between Palestine and the world but also among Palestinian enclaves. That movement and access are largely determined unilaterally by Israel. But what of other Palestinian national structures? What has happened to the PNA has dragged down the PLO and other Palestinian bodies along with it.

The PLO itself had been brought back to Palestine (where it was founded in 1965) when most of its leadership moved to Ramallah to establish the PNA in the mid-1990s. Its leadership and that of the PNA were often difficult to distinguish because the same figures often had leading positions in both, with Yasser Arafat and Mahmoud Abbas heading both bodies. Small parts of the PLO did remain in the diaspora, but those largely withered.

Under the Oslo Accords, the PNA was not permitted to carry out foreign affairs (except to receive international assistance, which is why its de facto foreign ministry was long termed the "Ministry of Planning and International Cooperation"). The body representing Palestinians internationally was still to be the PLO; over time, the PLO became the international face of the same leadership, and indeed, the PNA de facto foreign ministry became to call itself one formally in 2003. The effect was to give Palestinians a set of voices, sometimes competing and sometimes overlapping, when acting internationally. As recognition of the "State of Palestine" made some limited progress, PLO/PNA leaders and diplomats learned to style their business cards and stationery according to the legal status of Palestinian representation in the international body or diplomatic mission they were leading. But in all cases, the leadership could be traced back to the same set of offices in Ramallah, sometimes reporting to the PNA, sometimes the PLO, and sometimes the State of Palestine.

And the task of the international representatives increasingly became persuading international actors to pressure Israel, the central focus of the Palestinian leadership's attention. In the mid-2010s, an effort to secure international recognition for the "State of Palestine" occurred to be sure, but its victories seemed to be symbolic ones that did not so much promise the independence of Palestinian decision making but seemed to be devices to annoy the Israeli leadership and communicate to it that other options might be available. Meanwhile, other Palestinian bodies—labor unions, writers' association, and student unions, among others—built since the 1950s either withered or became so thoroughly intertwined with the PLO that they limped on as appendages to that national body that was itself an appendage to a PNA.

The inability of the Palestinian senior leadership to deliver statehood is thus now taken for granted in most Palestinian political debates. Some institutions retain some administrative ability but not of a kind that is evolving toward a state—or even one that can lead Palestinians to any kind of outcome. The inability of the national movement to articulate a clear strategic goal is now deeply embedded in Palestinian political expectations. Whatever initiatives and ideas arise come from other parts of Palestinian society and the national movement. In the remainder of this chapter, we look beyond the would-be state to see how Palestinian political movements and Palestinians outside the West Bank and Gaza have been reacting to the decay of the central leadership. Some remain active in various ways, but all increasingly seem more oriented toward the existing one state reality than in forming an alternative to it.

Political Movements

In the 1960s and 1970s, Palestinians of various ideological stripes built a series of movements—often collectively referred to as "the factions"—that sought to organize and mobilize Palestinians for various forms of "resistance" in support of the nationalist cause. Those movements quickly moved to the center of both action in support of statehood and debates about the form it should take (and strategies for getting there). None seems to have any clear vision now—and again, although this failure is taken for granted in Palestinian discussions, it happened so gradually that it often escapes notice. If the factions show any vitality at all, it is in how to manage relations with Israel, determining what blend of coordination, modus vivendi, and resistance strategies will work under whatever constraints and opportunities exist at any particular moment.

Initially, the factions were generally anchored primarily (even exclusively) in the diaspora. Some smaller ones took on a pan-Arab orientation, but those tended to fade over time. The exceptions were small leftist movements, such as the Popular Front for the Liberation of Palestine, which sought to align itself with revolutionary forces in the Arab world. With the defeat of Palestinian factions in Jordan in 1970 and their marginalization in Lebanon over the subsequent decade and a half, those groups survived only as Palestinian factions, rather than as parts of broader Arab movements.

The most successful faction by far was Fatah, a movement that resonated among Palestinians precisely because it prioritized Palestine as a cause: it anchored itself in an Arab nationalism that largely (though not always) sought to work with existing regimes that its more radical Palestinian competitors sought to undermine. Able to strike deep roots in selected locations—Jordan until 1970, Lebanon until 1983, and Kuwait until 1990—and successfully parachuting into PLO leadership in 1969, Fatah was able to present itself as the centerpiece of the Palestinian national movement that could participate in both "armed struggle" while also organizing Palestinians wherever they could and staffing PLO bodies that aimed to build the embryo of a state.

Although anchored in the diaspora, these movements reached out to the West Bank and Gaza and then stepped up their activity in Palestine in the 1980s; the motivation was partly competition with each other but also the fear of a separate and autonomous leadership arising in territories occupied by Israel that might incline toward a separate peace that stopped short of Palestinian national goals (and cut the diaspora out as a part of the Palestinian nation). These factional efforts were supported in part by assistance from Arab states for Palestinian institutions in the West Bank and Gaza after Egypt signed a separate agreement with Israel. Because that aid came from existing Arab regimes and was funneled through a channel overseen by Jordan and the PLO, it had the effect of cementing the factions' reorientation away from challenging the Arab order and toward building a Palestinian political order.

In the 1980s, the older factions were joined by a new one, which was built on Islamic social service organizations, religious networks, and remnants of the Muslim Brotherhood scattered in the West Bank, Gaza, and a few Arab states. The new faction, Hamas, began with a far stronger anchor in Palestine than in the diaspora; although it sometimes aligned itself in regional terms with other Islamist movements (and for a while dabbled with a "resistance axis" that included Hizbullah and Iran), it has generally insisted that its horizons were centered on Palestine.

Thus, by the beginning of the First Intifada—and continuing throughout its duration and then through the era dominated by the Oslo process—the factions competed (and occasionally coordinated) within a Palestinian political arena. They drew on external support to be sure, but those outside geographic Palestine moved most of their operations there, each pursuing its own vision of national liberation. For Fatah, that vision shifted to negotiation and state-building, although parts of the organization felt a need to keep a "resistance" option alive. For Hamas, the emphasis was reversed: it focused on "resistance" but considered the idea of joining the emerging Palestinian political entity (and finally plunged fully into local elections in 2004–2005 and parliamentary elections in 2006). The smaller factions often criticized the Oslo process but offered no viable alternative. In the 1990s they were pulled in the direction of the state-building process.

In 2000, with the eruption of the Second Intifada, all factions, large and small, joined in resistance, once again seeing it as a means of national liberation. The strategy of the various factions was a bit unclear and indeed was the subject of disagreement even within them—was it to drive out Israel, provoke international intervention, or strengthen the Palestinian negotiating position—but securing some kind of Palestinian political entity was something that they shared.

But as the Second Intifada ebbed in the mid-2000s, national liberation began to recede with it. The Second Intifada itself had focused far more on tactics, and with its end—and the failure of resistance, diplomacy, or any combination to bring a Palestine into political reality—no strategic vision emerged to respond to or counter the deeply entrenched reality of Israeli control. The split between Gaza and the West Bank has meant that any unifying national strategy is beyond reach, but both leading factions, Fatah and Hamas, have individually and gradually but unmistakably shifted their energies to coping with and resisting the occupation, rather than finding any path toward ending it.

No longer does any viable strategy for statehood motivate or guide any factional efforts, with the result that they are left to focus far more on Israel than on a prospective Palestinian state. To be sure, there is some discussion of ends (the "one state" alternative) but most action and energy are devoted to managing and mitigating the effects of occupation. Fatah, whose top leadership is melded with the PNA, can focus only on keeping its grassroots alive while trying to secure more favorable policies from Israel. When its leadership and focus shifted, its diaspora presence atrophied. The movement thus is sustained largely by its claim to PNA and PLO leadership, combined with its presence in the West Bank that occupies social and political space. But it remains without a clear strategy, ideology, or reason for existence. Fatah has never been a coherent organization, having always been divided among local leaders, large egos, and internal fiefdoms. But its formal procedures live on, with periodic party congresses and local meetings that provide an opportunity for activists again to discuss the meaning of resistance, elect leaders, and argue over governance structures. But there is no disguising the fact that the movement cannot marry its strong claims to leadership with any clear strategy or even set of tactics for securing nationalist goals.

But if Fatah's gravitation from national liberation to fending off some effects of the occupation is unsurprising, the shift in Hamas has been more dramatic. Like Fatah, it has not repudiated any past positions: its ideological program makes hints in various directions but commits the movement to no fundamental change in strategic goals. But its administration of Gaza has led the movement to a very different daily, even monthly, or yearly focus. Especially after the fall of the Muslim Brotherhood in Egypt and several rounds of brutal fighting with Israel, Hamas's energies seem devoted to managing the affairs of the Gaza Strip and on negotiating with Israel (sometimes through Egypt and sometimes negotiating with Egypt as well) in support of that task. Israel–Hamas negotiations are not about a diplomatic resolution of the conflict between the two but about managing what goes in and out of Gaza and what the terms of an indefinite ceasefire should be. These are not dramatic Camp David-style negotiations about an end to the conflict, national reconciliation, or peace; they are about managing the one state reality in a manner that allows Hamas to administer Gaza without challenging overall Israeli control.

Smaller factions—the Popular Front and Democratic Front, among others—carry on primarily to serve collectively as some form of national conscience; because they retain seats in PLO structures, they are possible minor allies in the Fatah–Hamas rivalry. What they share with those larger movements is the reality that Palestinian political movements have not merely reversed the Oslo PNA slogan of "from *al-thawra* to *al-dawla*" by abandoning any real state-building efforts but also focus now not on liberating or building Palestine but on administering and managing pieces of it under ongoing occupation. They do not do so publicly or even seem to acknowledge this shift to themselves. But having presented itself for years as the authoritative face of Palestine internally and externally, Fatah finds itself now only operating effectively in the West Bank and then within limits set by Israel. Hamas, which presented itself as the un-Fatah that is unwilling to negotiate with Israel, now negotiates regularly with Israel (if generally indirectly) over borders and security issues. For neither movement is this situation perceived as acceptable. But accept it they do, making Israel the center of their efforts.

Palestinians inside Israel

Palestinian citizens of Israel have long had to grapple with the State of Israel as a central reality, but their relationship with the Israeli state has changed over the years with varying degrees of political participation and engagement. Today, that engagement reflects two general trends that seem contradictory but are not: an increasing insistence both on Palestinian nationality and on participation in Israeli political life.

The relationship between Palestinian citizens and the Israeli state has been defined by the pursuit of rights for Palestinians as a minority, who make up around 20 percent of the population. For Israel, Palestinians are effectively an ethnic minority but not a national group with the right to self-determination, which is reserved for Jewish citizens of Israel, as made official under the Basic Nation-State Law passed in 2018. Indeed, Palestinian citizens are not always treated even as an ethnic group but instead as separate non-Jewish communities—Muslim, Christian, and Druze—and even informally as "bedouin" and non-bedouin. Despite (or actually because of) this political fragmentation and marginalization, Palestinians have become increasingly engaged civically and politically inside Israel.

Over the years, Palestinians have oscillated between political participation and electoral boycotts at different junctures of Israeli history. Many have taken part in national elections since 1949, but a large number also abstained from a lack of interest or resisted participation for ideological reasons to avoid granting legitimacy to the State of Israel. Despite some ideological boycotts, significant numbers of Palestinians continued to participate in Israeli elections at the national and local level. But they have been met with structural discrimination, voter intimidation, and legal challenges by the Israeli government to limit their inclusion—challenges that continue today. Despite this history of exclusion, Palestinians in Israel have gradually inched into the Israeli political system and are now far more active in their political participation and engagement.

After the creation of Israel in 1948, Palestinian citizens had little to no political presence at the national level, with the population under martial law from 1948 to 1966. Yet, voting participation records during that time show unusually high turnout in response to pressure by the military government to vote for Zionist parties. Authorities exercised tight control over national and local elections and Palestinians' broader political activity. The relaxation of martial law in the 1960s spurred Palestinians to begin developing their own parties, although the Israeli political system remained largely exclusive. The first formal Palestinian party that ran in national elections, Al-Ard in 1965, was later banned by the Israeli Central Elections Committee, which prompted electoral boycotts in response. Many Palestinians remained hesitant to participate in Israeli politics given such experiences.

But as time went on, new parties and local institutions began to develop that took more active positions or placed the interests of Palestinian citizens on the local or even national agenda. The National Committee of the Heads of Arab Localities (NCALC) was created in 1974 as part of a drive by Palestinians to establish institutions and organize Palestinian society inside Israel. These networks were initially stronger at the local level but eventually led to the establishment of the High Follow-Up Committee for Arab Citizens of Israel in 1982, a broader umbrella organization that was created to organize these new institutions and represent Palestinians at the national level. Israel refused to recognize the legitimacy of the extraparliamentary committee because it was seen as an attempt by Palestinians to establish autonomy.

Independent Palestinian parties continued developing along various ideological and religious lines, expanding significantly in the 1980s and 1990s after the First Intifada and Oslo Accords. The Oslo negotiations and peace process evoked notable engagement and influence from Palestinians inside Israel on critical national questions. For the first time in Israel's history, Palestinian parties recommended a candidate for Israel's prime minister, Yitzhak Rabin, in 1992, following his pledge to pursue peace. These parties later helped the Oslo Accords secure passage in the Knesset. During this time, Palestinian participation in national elections crept upward from 70 percent in 1992 to 77 percent in 1996 and 75 percent in 1999. However, voter participation plummeted to just 18 percent in 2001 following a widespread boycott of the elections in response to the Second Intifada and Israeli forces' crackdown against protests and strikes organized by Palestinian citizens inside Israel (most notably in October 2000 when police killed thirteen Palestinians).[2]

Although the wider Palestinian cause influenced the political participation of Palestinians inside Israel during the 1990s, the parties began to focus more narrowly on calling for the full equality of the Palestinian population inside Israel in the 2000s. Politicians continue to advocate for an end to Israel's occupation of the Palestinian territories, but political matters inside Israel have edged out concerns related to the wider Palestinian cause in recent years. In the process, Palestinians have challenged their marginalization in Israeli political life—so much so that their growing activism has been used by right-leaning Israeli groups to mobilize their own supporters. By closing ranks and encouraging participation, Palestinian parties have become a national political factor even as other parties have managed to keep them away from a seat at the table.

Palestinian parties make up a key part of the opposition inside the Israeli Knesset and have seen recent electoral success following the creation of the Joint List. This alliance of four small, predominantly Palestinian parties with distinct ideologies—Hadash, Balad, the United Arab List-Ra'am, and Ta'al, led by Ayman Odeh of Hadash—formed in 2015 in response to a change in Israeli law that raised the electoral threshold for entering the Knesset from 2 percent to 3.25 percent. The measure was seen as an attempt to prevent smaller Palestinian and other opposition parties from entering the Knesset. The move toward unity was thus sparked by tactical concerns and indeed seemed fragile—but it produced results. Voter turnout among Palestinians increased from 56 percent in 2013 to 63.5 percent in 2015 in response to the formation of the Joint List, which emerged as Israel's third largest political party. Political infighting, however, led to a split in the alliance ahead of the April 2019 elections, leading voter turnout to decline to just 49 percent before recovering and increasing after reunification of the Joint List during the September 2019 and March 2020 elections.[3] After the September 2019 elections, the Joint List seemed poised to play an active role in Israeli coalition building and moved to recommend Benny Gantz as the next Israeli prime minister—the second time in Israel's history that Palestinian parties made such a recommendation. Even though this move angered some of the Joint List's members and supporters, its recommendation and campaign tactics showed Palestinian parties' willingness to become more deeply involved in the Israeli political system.

This fragile (and sometimes fractious) unified leadership has worked to cross the national divide by expanding outreach to left-wing Jewish voters, who have turned to the Joint List amid a shift amid the rightward shift of the Zionist parties. The Joint List has also expanded outreach to other marginalized Israelis, such as the ultra-Orthodox Ethiopian and Russian communities, campaigning on shared issues like opposition to compulsory military service, police brutality, and broader discrimination. The result has been a more inclusive message to other Israelis to challenge structural discrimination of the country's minorities.

Although its focus is on domestic concerns inside Israel, the Joint List maintains ties to the Palestinian political leadership and includes in its political platform support for a "two state solution" and an end to the Israeli occupation of Palestinian territories. PA president Abbas has repeatedly expressed support for the Joint List and encouraged Palestinians in Israel to take part in national elections, and Joint List leaders like Odeh and Ahmad Tibi engage in regular contact with PNA and PLO officials.[4] Tibi himself previously served as a special adviser to Yasser Arafat in the 1990s before running for the Knesset. Continued political ties with Palestinian officials inside the West Bank have provided additional fodder for the Israeli Right's criticism of the Joint List, but its leaders stress that their overwhelming focus is on internal matters and the Palestinian population inside Israel as they try to expand their influence domestically.

The willingness to engage national political issues has attracted attention and voters but has not led to any significant degree of national political power. Structural obstacles to political inclusion remain a challenge at the national level where, despite recent political successes, Palestinian politicians remain largely excluded from the cabinet or any governing coalition. Zionist Jewish parties have even less of an appetite to form an alliance with Palestinian parties due to the rightward shift of Israeli politics. During recent elections, then Prime Minister Benjamin Netanyahu and his right-wing Likud party made a point of accusing the Blue and White Alliance (Kahol Lavan) of cooperating with "Arab parties" to strengthen support for their right-wing base. Despite these obstacles, Palestinians continue to adapt inside the Israeli political system and push for a seat at the table.

By the time of the March 2021 election, Israel's fourth in just two years, Netanyahu and some right-wing Israeli politicians changed their tune and indicated a willingness to work with Palestinian parties, specifically Mansour Abbas's conservative Islamist party, Ra'am, after it controversially split from the Joint List. Abbas engaged directly with Netanyahu in the lead-up to the vote, stating his party was willing to work with anyone who could help address the Palestinian community's needs. The strategy was successful enough to win the party four seats in the Knesset, but at the cost of weakening the Joint List and branding Abbas as a "traitor" by some Palestinians.

After another inconclusive election result, Abbas emerged as a possible kingmaker between the pro-Netanyahu and anti-Netanyahu blocs. Days after the vote, Abbas delivered a speech in Hebrew in which he emphasized that he is "a proud Arab and Muslim," while stating that "what unites us is stronger than what divides us" and indicating his willingness to participate in a right-wing government.[5] After all, Abbas's party aligns with socially conservative right-wing Jewish parties on several issues, including opposition to gay rights.

Ultimately, Ra'am became the first Palestinian party to join a governing coalition in more than forty years and the first to play such a critical role in the coalition's formation, which was confirmed by lawmakers on June 13, 2021. Abbas joined forces with the anti-Netanyahu bloc that consisted of eight parties from across the political spectrum, led by Prime Minister Naftali Bennett's ultranationalist Yamina Party and Yair Lapid's centrist Yesh Atid.

Ra'am's successful entrance into the coalition overshadowed the fact that the 2021 election saw a steep decline in voter turnout among Palestinian citizens of Israel, which dropped by 20 percent.[6] As Israeli and Western media lauded Ra'am's success as an example of coexistence in Israeli society, many Palestinians rejected Abbas's cooperation with right-wing Zionist parties that support discriminatory policies toward Palestinians in Israel and settlement expansion, occupation, and even annexation of the West Bank. Abbas's and Ra'am's political platform was viewed as abandoning the Palestinian cause and avoiding the structural issues that perpetuate Palestinian exclusion and discrimination, such as the 2018 Basic Nation-State Law, which Ra'am no longer demanded to revoke. So, although Ra'am went as far as joining a governing coalition, the 2021 election proved there are still limits to meaningful Palestinian participation and inclusion at the national level. Given that the rest of the Joint List rejected and criticized Abbas and many Palestinian voters avoided the polls, the election also proved there are still limits to how far most Palestinians are willing to get involved in day-to-day Israeli politics.

At the local level, Palestinians are far more politically engaged, often more than Jewish voters, with high levels of voter turnout for local elections inside Palestinian and mixed municipalities in Israel. Here, Palestinian politicians and voters have found greater political space to address their concerns, as well as those of the Bedouin community. Local-level politics demonstrates how Palestinian citizens of Israel have found ways to integrate into the Israeli political system while still maintaining some degree of autonomy and influence over their communities.

Inside Israel, Palestinians primarily live in mostly Palestinian cities and towns in the Galilee in northern Israel, the "Triangle Area" in central Israel, and the Negev in the south. The rest live in mixed cities like Haifa, Tel Aviv-Jaffa, Acre, Ramla, and Lod. In mixed cities, there has been greater cooperation between

Palestinian and Jewish politicians to push for equal rights, although tensions over national identity and national-level politics remain an issue. Inside Palestinian cities and towns, politicians and local councils have worked to address issues of poverty, underdevelopment, crime, and socioeconomic marginalization for the Palestinian population and other minorities. Appeals for greater funding and resources from the Israeli government have been included in their efforts, with varying degrees of success.

Local and national leaders have also sought to organize themselves through institutions like the NCALC and the High Follow-Up Committee that represent Palestinian politicians at the local and national levels. Membership is drawn from the heads of Palestinian political parties, local leaders, civil society organizations, and other groups that act as representative bodies for Palestinian citizens. These coordinating bodies have strengthened attempts to coordinate the Palestinian political landscape and respond to the needs of Palestinians, including most recently, through efforts to respond to the COVID-19 virus.

As Palestinians integrate further into Israeli politics and society, local cultural institutions have expanded their efforts to promote Palestinian identity through the preservation of Palestinian history and culture. More overt campaigns reinforcing a distinct Palestinian identity have led to friction with the Israeli government at times, while also deepening a shared national identity with Palestinians outside Israel, despite limited political ties. These institutions are crucial in ensuring Palestinian cultural representation inside Israel, despite government restrictions and broader discrimination against the population. The use of the term "Palestinian" itself or Palestinian-Israeli has gained currency as a conscious decision by Palestinians to reinforce their identity, culture, and heritage, thereby challenging non-Palestinian use of the term "Arab."

These grassroots campaigns set the stage for one of the strongest showings of Palestinian identity in years with the broad-based, youth-led mobilization of Palestinians in solidarity with Jerusalem in May 2021. Palestinians united across historical Palestine and in the diaspora to protest Israel's planned expulsion of Palestinian families in the East Jerusalem neighborhood of Sheikh Jarrah, as well as violent crackdowns by Israeli forces against worshipers at Al-Aqsa Mosque. Protesters raised the Palestinian flag across cities such as Lod (Lydd), Haifa, Akka, Ramla, Jaffa (Yafa), Nazareth, and the Negev (Naqab) in an assertion of Palestinian identity and opposition to Israel's discriminatory policies. These demonstrations built on previous protest movements in Umm al-Fahm against police violence and violent crime and in Yafa against evictions targeting Palestinian residents, viewed as a form of "ethnic cleansing," which drew parallels to Sheikh Jarrah. Violent Israeli crackdowns and hundreds of arrests fueled greater participation, with young activists using social media to coordinate demonstrations and call for action, including a general strike across all of historic Palestine on May 18. Palestinians also organized a "National Economy Week" in June to encourage people to buy from Palestinian-owned businesses and boycott Israeli products in both Israel and the Palestinian territories.[7] The campaign was followed by a "Unified Palestinian Culture Week" in July in which various cultural institutions, associations, universities, and museums hosted events promoting Palestinian identity and rejecting Israeli policies.[8]

But even as their Palestinian identity strengthens, Palestinian citizens are starting to feel a greater sense of belonging within Israel as Israeli citizens, as they demand greater inclusion. A survey from the Israel Democracy Institute's Guttman Center for Public Opinion and Policy Research conducted in April 2020 showed that 77 percent of "Arab Israelis" feel that they are part of Israel and share in its problems: this is the highest level among Palestinians in the past decade.[9] The prevailing attitude—which might be termed "highly critical engagement"—amounts to a willingness to protest exclusion and insist on a greater role in Israeli politics and society while still asserting a Palestinian identity and pushing to open the political space.

Jerusalem

That Palestinians in Jerusalem constitute a separate category at all is testimony to the centrality of Israel.

When the PLO signed the Oslo Accords with Israel, it took great pains to preserve the linkages between Palestinian Jerusalemites and those in the West Bank and Gaza. Of course, Israel defined the contours of that category: Palestinian Jerusalemites were those within the municipal borders unilaterally imposed by Israel and accorded Jerusalem identity cards by Israeli authorities. But the Oslo Accords permitted Jerusalemites to vote in PNA elections (though at post offices rather than other polling centers), and an initially secret side letter allowed Palestinian institutions to continue operating in Jerusalem. Elections are now a distant memory, however, and those institutions have been closed. In addition, as West Bankers lost access to Jerusalem, social and especially cultural ties between Palestinian Jerusalemites and the West Bank have withered. And although few Palestinians in Jerusalem have accepted Israeli nationality, they cling to the Israeli privileges they do have: access to the Israeli health insurance system, ability to travel through Israeli airports, and license plates that greatly ease internal mobility.

But if they partake of Israeli society when they are ill, fly, or drive, they have not entered Israeli politics in the way that Palestinian Israelis have done. Jerusalem is a notable exception to trends of political engagement in the Israeli system at the local level: there, most Palestinians have boycotted municipal elections since Israel's occupation and annexation of East Jerusalem in 1967. (A small number of Palestinians held Israeli citizenship by virtue of residence in the western part of the city before 1967, but the vast majority reside in East Jerusalem and surrounding areas that were annexed in 1967 to the Jerusalem municipality). When the Israeli government integrated large swaths of territory into the jurisdiction of its Jerusalem municipality, it gave Palestinians "permanent resident" status that allows them to vote and run in municipal elections even if they are not Israeli citizens. However, for similar reasons as the Palestinians who boycotted elections inside Israel after the state's establishment, Palestinians inside East Jerusalem have historically refused to participate in Jerusalem's municipal elections to avoid granting legitimacy to Israel's claim of sovereignty over the city and the occupation. Palestinian politicians both inside and outside the city support and encourage the boycott, including Joint List member and Jerusalem resident Ahmed Tibi (born in al-Tayyiba, a town in northern Israel and thus an Israeli citizen), who rejected a call to run for mayor of the city in 2018, stating that doing so would "grant legitimacy to a city under occupation."[10]

But even in East Jerusalem, some Palestinians are inching toward participation in municipal elections in the hopes of addressing discriminatory policies and decades of neglect that have left much of the Palestinian population impoverished and without access to basic services. In the 2018 municipal elections, civil engineer Ramadan Dabash became the first Palestinian candidate to run for Jerusalem's city council since 1967 on a platform focused on improving the living conditions of Palestinians in the city.[11] His campaign faced fierce opposition from both Israeli authorities and Palestinian politicians, and he ultimately did not garner sufficient votes. Still, Dabash's decision to participate highlights the precarious position of Palestinian Jerusalemites who oppose Israel's occupation and annexation but continue to experience deteriorating living conditions as a result, leading some to grapple with engaging in Israel's political system.

At the grassroots level, East Jerusalem emerged as a center of Palestinian resistance and mobilization against Israel's discriminatory policies with the uprising in May 2021—a sudden wave of protest that erupted from a months-long campaign against the expulsion of Palestinian families in East Jerusalem, not only in Sheikh Jarrah but also in other neighborhoods such as Silwan. Young Palestinian Jerusalemites, such as the al-Kurd twins, broadcast crackdowns by Israeli forces, attacks by settlers, and other daily challenges from their social media accounts—strategically in both Arabic and English—to millions of followers around the world. They shared images from court hearings and explained the intricacies of the Israeli legal case to expel them from their homes. What was new was the publicity, not the resort to the courts: Palestinians in Jerusalem have long participated in the Israeli legal system to oppose their expulsion, knowing that prospects for any success are precluded, as Palestinian researcher Dr. Yara Hawari described.[12]

This sort of participation is thus opportunistic; it is not built on any sort of acceptance or recognition of the Israeli system or pursued to the exclusion of other paths but has by now evolved into a tactic to delay or prevent the expulsion of Palestinians while mobilizing local and international support. In short, engagement with Israeli structures is not an alternative to but a part of a diverse set of tools whose use is shaped tactically.

The Decay of Expatriate Institutions and the Birth of a New Generation of Activism

It is striking—though rarely remarked—that when a Palestinian voice is heard in discussions outside Palestine, it is generally an intellectual or an activist rather than a diplomat of the State of Palestine or an official of the PLO who speaks. This was not always the case. But it is a sign that the shift in orientation from the idea of statehood has been particularly pronounced within the Palestinian diaspora.

The PLO, although founded in Jerusalem, anchored itself for almost all its first three decades in the diaspora, where it worked to present itself as a placeholder for Palestinian statehood—and where it proclaimed a state (in Algiers in 1988). It established itself symbolically as the "sole, legitimate representative of the Palestinian people." On an institutional level, it gathered many Palestinian institutions and structures under its umbrella. But its influence outside Palestine substantially weakened since the signing of the Oslo Accords in the 1990s, leaving the diaspora today largely unorganized and less engaged with a unified Palestinian national project. In its place, grassroots movements centered primarily in the West have expanded, focusing on campaigns to pressure the Israeli government using a rights-based discourse.

In short, when Palestinians and their supporters are active internationally, the thrust of their efforts have shifted: they no longer serve as supporters (or even initiators) of the effort to achieve a state of Palestine. Instead, official diaspora efforts have atrophied to the point that they are an appendage of the PNA, which itself is effectively oriented toward managing the terms of the occupation. Newer efforts—such as the BDS campaign—aim less at establishing a political entity of Palestine and more at insisting on some alternative to Israeli occupation. Indeed, Palestine's supporters are likely to speak more among themselves—and to find their calls resonate outside their own ranks—to the extent that they emphasize combating occupation or apartheid than realizing Palestinian statehood.

Matters were different a generation and two generations ago. The Palestinian diaspora previously served as the center of Palestinian political activity through the PLO and other institutions emerging from the diaspora and based outside Palestine for years. After their expulsion from Israel in 1948, Palestinians in the diaspora began building networks and institutions to support the population and the nationalist struggle. Activity was largely unorganized early on and took a back seat to Arab countries' fight against Israel and lead in seeking a resolution to the Palestinian plight. Their failed efforts and infighting spurred Palestinians to take matters into their own hands, leading to the rise of a Palestinian national movement anchored in the diaspora. More radical factions leading the resistance movement garnered support, but eventually, Palestinians began to refocus the national movement on the idea of statehood.

The emergence of the PLO in 1964 (and the degree of freedom it secured from Arab states in the aftermath of the 1967 War) helped organize the diaspora through an emphasis on institution-building to govern Palestinian political, economic, cultural, educational, and military activities. From the Palestine Red Crescent (PRCS) to the General Union of Palestinian Workers (GUPW), the PLO oversaw the creation of a variety of institutions, including political councils and committees, various unions and professional organizations, medical and health care providers, and cultural institutions. The reach of these organizing structures spanned the diaspora, primarily in other Arab countries, and served to deepen a shared sense of national identity and kickstart state-building efforts.

The Palestine Martyrs Works Society (SAMED), for example, provided vocational training, workshops, and job opportunities to Palestinians, particularly in Lebanon in the 1970s. SAMED also served an important cultural function through the creation of a cinema production sector that expanded in the 1980s, in cooperation with the Palestinian Cinema Institution. Unions were organized under the Department of Mass Organizations and included branches wherever Palestinians were located. By the 1980s, the GUPW had branches in thirteen Arab countries, as well as in Germany, Sweden, Denmark, Australia, and Belgium.[13] The General Union of Palestinian Students (GUPS) previously served as a center for youth engagement with the PLO and national movement. Unions in general had significant representation within the PLO and therefore helped maintain political influence and engagement across the diaspora with the broader Palestinian national movement.

Leading up to and following the Oslo Accords, however, the focus of political energy and initiative shifted to Palestinians in the West Bank and Gaza with the return of the PLO and its state-building efforts. The PLO still maintained ties to the diaspora, but its influence outside the Palestinian territories gradually declined throughout the 1990s and 2000s, especially given the weakening of

Palestinian national institutions inside the Palestinian territories over the years. As a result, most of the PLO's institutions abroad have become largely defunct or otherwise limited in their activity and influence. GUPS, for instance, which served as an incubator for many Palestinian leaders, has decayed, with only a few chapters still functioning.

There have been efforts to reactivate the Palestine National Council (PNC), which is made up of a significant number of Palestinians in the diaspora, along with those inside the Palestinian territories. But its position as representing Palestinians everywhere and its role as the constituting body of the PLO make it too central a body for the existing leadership to allow it any freedom.

The PLO and the PNC are thus indispensable—but for those who cling to its leadership, their indispensability makes them too important to allow these institutions to become independent of their control. Agreements to bring in new groups or to hold elections are periodically proclaimed but never executed. A full quorum of the PNC convened in Ramallah in 2018 for the first time since 1996.[14] But this meeting was largely seen as an effort to consolidate Mahmoud Abbas's power, and Hamas and several other factions boycotted the meeting. Additionally, both the PLO and Hamas have floated inclusion of the Palestinian diaspora in general elections at times, but no serious attempt has been made to do so, just as attempts to organize general elections within the Palestinian territories have failed in recent years.

Yet the decline and decay of Palestinian institutions in the diaspora have not led to total passivity. Indeed, the most notable signs of life for the Palestinian national movement comes outside its traditional channels—a feature that often escapes attention.

In the wake of the decay of institutions born to pursue some form of Palestinian statehood, more diffuse grassroots campaigns to support Palestinians have emerged, ones that are inherently oriented to the State of Israel. These campaigns are primarily centered in the West but maintain ties to Palestinian civil society both inside Israel and the Palestinian territories, as well as across the diaspora. There is a strong irony here: Palestinian nationalism in the West is less expressed in clearly national institutions like GUPS but is more powerfully supported by broader coalitions. And they are more distant from the PLO umbrella and often disdainful of the traditional (now quite senior) national leadership. They aim at mobilizing against Israeli policy more than they seek to build Palestinian national institutions in preparation for statehood.

The most influential of these campaigns has been the Boycott, Divestment and Sanctions (BDS) movement, which emerged in 2005 from the call of some leading Palestinian civil society groups to target Israel, invoking similar boycott movements against apartheid South Africa. The failure of the diplomatic process and the ebbing of the Second Intifada led some Palestinians to search not only for new strategies but also for new tactics. Diplomacy and armed struggle were the property of the old movements and leaders, but younger ones arose with new avenues in mind. BDS grew slowly, but it has emerged as a leading face of the struggle for Palestinian rights in the diaspora. The movement is focused on Israel and demands that the Israeli government end its occupation of the Palestinian territories, grant full rights and equality to Palestinian citizens of Israel, and respect the rights of Palestinian refugees to return.[15] The movement has garnered support from dozens of Palestinian unions, professional associations, refugee networks and other civil society groups.

And it has crossed the divide between Palestine and the diaspora. Although born in Palestine, it first grew rapidly outside its borders. Over the years, the BDS movement has expanded inside the United States and Europe through the support of the broader International Solidarity Movement, as well as student groups like Students for Justice in Palestine, which is active in college campuses across the United States and several other countries. These groups, made up of both Palestinian and non-Palestinian members, have worked to promote BDS by pushing universities, other institutions, and consumers to boycott and divest from entities tied to the State of Israel or companies seen as complicit in the occupation of Palestinian territories, such as those that operate inside Jewish settlements. The BDS movement also organizes cultural and academic boycotts, including high-profile campaigns to prevent musical artists from performing inside Israel. Notably, American Jewish groups opposed to the Israeli occupation and treatment of Palestinians like Jewish Voices for Peace (JVP) have been instrumental in supporting BDS and the work of pro-Palestinian groups.

In addition to BDS, broader Palestinian solidarity networks around the world are engaged in political and cultural educational campaigns and workshops that adopt a rights-based discourse to raise awareness of the Palestinian plight. Although these networks work to preserve and promote a Palestinian national identity at times, ideas of sovereignty and statehood are no longer central themes. The focus is instead on Palestinian rights and ending Israel's occupation of Palestinian territories. In fact, many of these networks have more openly oriented themselves toward the one state reality and have led calls for equal rights for all Palestinians under Israeli control and occupation.

Living with Reality but not Liking It

As talk of a "one state reality" grows, Palestinians are already adapting to a new reality, even though it is not one of their own creation. Shifts in political activity, the decline of the national movement, and the decay of institutions previously centered around the idea of statehood have given way to a new focus on a single State of Israel, whether deliberately or out of resignation to circumstances on the ground. The trajectory of Palestinian political activity inside the Palestinian territories, Israel, and within the diaspora over time demonstrates a gradual shift and understanding of Israel's central role in which even the recent uprising in May 2021 was driven not by any sort of national political project but rather in response to shared struggles against discriminatory Israeli policies and violence.

In the Palestinian territories, prospects for sovereignty and statehood have never been dimmer, though Palestinian officials are only now starting to publicly acknowledge this reality; this is despite the fact that Palestinian institutions and factions have long been focused in practice on managing the occupation and Israel, rather than pursuing any viable strategy for achieving statehood. Politically, civil society groups and Palestinian youth are adopting a similar rhetoric as external groups centered around individual rights and securing civil liberties, with a focus on Israel as the leading violator of these rights.

Inside Israel, Palestinian citizens' decades-long fight for inclusion in the Israeli political system and society demonstrates a story of growing integration in the face of discrimination and exclusion that could provide insight into future struggles for Palestinians living under occupation as Israel moves to annex new territories. Issues of identity remain a challenge, but Palestinians are increasingly finding ways to assert their identity as both Palestinians and citizens of Israel as they move toward greater political participation and demand inclusion.

Caught in the middle is East Jerusalem, where Palestinians mostly continue to boycott municipal elections following Israel's annexation in 1967. Yet, a decline in living conditions, expanding Israeli encroachment, and a weakening of the PA's influence are leading some to reconsider their refusal to participate in the Israeli political system much in the same way that many Palestinians inside Israel previously did.

Palestinians in the diaspora have been more deliberate in their recognition of the one state reality and shift in orientation toward Israel, evidenced by the collapse of networks and institutions to support statehood and the rise of a rights-based discourse to address Israeli occupation and discriminatory practices. The diaspora's role is no longer that of an anchor to the national movement but has instead broken into various networks working to help Palestinians adapt to their new reality.

What may be happening at the current moment is that leaders—and international diplomats—are gradually catching up with their followers (or the subjects of their diplomacy). The change is imperceptible in public: most Western diplomats cling to the two state solution as a way of avoiding grappling with the existing one state reality. The senior leadership seems to pursue that solution not out of conviction but out of a lack of alternatives. But private conversations are more realistic. And at all levels below their senior leadership, Palestinians have been learning to cope with a single state for decades.

"One state" is thus not so much a political program for settling a conflict; the oft-stated claim by proponents of the Oslo process that "one state" is not a practical solution misses that point. Of course, it is not a solution to all Palestinian national aspirations. But it is a lived reality for Palestinians, one that has become so entrenched that the various strands of the national movement have wound themselves around it despite themselves. Achieving national goals and a just order runs through, rather than around, that fact.

Part 3
CHANGING ATTITUDES
Drivers and Limits

7

PALESTINIANS IN ISRAEL AND THE ONE STATE REALITY

Mohanad Mustafa and As'ad Ghanem

This chapter aims to clarify how the Palestinian citizens of Israel contribute to the shaping of an "one state reality" (OSR) as part of the general framework of the Palestinian-Israel conflict since it began and particularly in the post–Oslo Accords era.[1] We demonstrate a number of key claims that confirm the role of Palestinian citizens of Israel in shaping the post-Oslo reality in "Historical Palestine." In the first part we describe the demographic and geographic distribution of Palestinian citizens of Israel, as part of the Palestinian people's dispersal—in contrast to the Jewish Israeli demographic and geographic reality—as material evidence for a mixed Palestinian and Israeli OSR, both geographic and territorial-geographic throughout the territory, from the Mediterranean Sea to the Jordan River.

In the second part of the chapter, we present our main argument that political developments concerning Palestinian citizens of Israel since 1948, including state policies toward them, have evolved from recent historical developments, the general development of the intractable Palestinian-Israel conflict, and the failure to achieve a just and reasonable solution to that conflict. In parallel to the failure to take practical steps, advance the two state project, and establish a Palestinian state in the West Bank and Gaza, there is another "failure." Because they are citizens of Israel, the goals of the Palestinians as a national minority in the State of Israel and living in a collective reality differ from those of the other dispersed Palestinians; they aim to attain equal individual and group rights, including autonomous cultural and educational control, and this goal too has not been realized. The population of Palestinians in Israel has been distanced from the rest of the Palestinian people as part of a broad process of localization of the Palestinian identity and its disintegration. In addition to the Israeli state and political system intensifying the exclusion of Palestinians in Israel, thereby pushing them to the margins, a Judaization process has been developed at various levels and in different areas, to which the Palestinian leadership in Israel has failed to design a serious response.

In the third part, we address recent developments that contribute to the integration of the Palestinians in Israel into the complex Palestinian-Israeli OSR between the Mediterranean Sea and the Jordan River. Although this process is slow and marginal relative to other processes and developments described in other chapters in this volume, its direction is quite clear. First, we examine a very recent development in Israeli politics: the integration of a Palestinian party, the United Arab List (UAL), into the current post-Netanyahu coalition government as a reflection of the general Palestinian political situation. We then argue that the political separation of Palestinians Israeli citizens from Palestinians in the West Bank, Gaza, and Jerusalem presents a serious challenge for all Palestinians. We point to the events of May 2021 as evidence of the beginning of a process of change that connects the situation of the Palestinians in the Occupied Territories with that of the Palestinian citizens of Israel. In fact, these events clarify that the rift in historical Palestine is not between Israeli citizens and the stateless Palestinians in the West Bank, Jerusalem, and Gaza but between two ethnonational groups: one that enjoys ethnic supremacy and control and makes daily efforts at all levels to establish control and superiority, thereby consciously creating an apartheid regime, and the other that remains in a position of inferiority and constantly struggles to achieve genuine change toward a state of democracy and balance between the two peoples.

Demography and Geography of the Palestinians in Israel and the OSR

The material foundations for the development of the OSR are rooted in a demographic and geographic reality shaped over more than a hundred years of struggle between Palestinians and Jews in the area of what was known as the Holy Land—the former Palestine Mandate territories. During the last century, Jews and the Zionist movement encouraged and in various ways facilitated several waves of Jewish immigration from all over the world to Palestine\Israel. The first wave was from Europe and then from North and South America and Asia. After the establishment of the State of Israel a huge wave of *Mizrahi* Jews immigrants arrived from Arab countries. From the 1970s "Russian" Jews or their close relatives from Eastern Europe emigrated, especially after the break-up of the Soviet Union. The

Jews lived in different parts of the country, with most choosing to live in settlements built specifically for their absorption and that still today are considered "Jewish" settlements and some living in mixed localities historically dominated by the indigenous people, the Palestinians.

In the war of 1948, most of the Palestinian Arab majority population either fled in fear or was expelled, leaving behind an Arab minority in the newly created Jewish state, a process described as ethnic cleansing and remembered by the Palestinian Arabs as the *Nakba* (catastrophe). This was a key event in the deployment of the Jews in the country and in the creation of the OSR as we see it today, including in localities that until the Nakba were considered purely Palestinian. The Judaization process was accelerated after the deportation or flight of most Palestinians, as the state worked hard to change the demographic and geographic reality. This process was accelerated by the 1967 Six Days' War when Israel occupied the West Bank, East Jerusalem, and Gaza. In these areas, too, the state worked hard to encourage Jewish settlement and takeover of territory, in practice applying a Jewish-Palestinian reality to these areas that since have become part of the OSR.

The geographic and demographic distribution of Israeli Palestinian citizens is fundamental to the shaping of the OSR. The Palestinians in Israel are part of the Palestinian people, although in comparison to those in Gaza, Jerusalem, and the West Bank, they are more a part of the "Jewish" reality within the Green Line, the 1949 armistice line defining Israel's eastern border after the war of 1948. As noted, following the Nakba and the expulsion of the majority of Palestinians from their homeland, a small and powerless minority of 150,000 Palestinians remained and became Israeli citizens after establishment of the State of Israel. On December 31, 2020, the number of Palestinians in Israel was around 1,956,000, constituting 21 percent of the total Israeli population.[2]

Although the birth rate among Palestinians in 2005 had declined to 4.3 babies per woman compared to an average of 9.0 children in the 1960s and 5.0 children in the early 1980s, it still was much higher than the average birth rate among Jews of 2.6.[3] In 2018, the average fertility rate decreased even more: among Christians it was 2.06 children per woman, compared to 3.2 for Muslim women, 3.17 for Jewish women, and 2.16 for Druze women; thus the gap between the Jewish and Muslim fertility rates has narrowed greatly.[4] This is mainly due to two developments. First, the changes in the status of Muslim women towards modernization and integration in work outside their homes, and second, the increased birth rate among Haredi Jews.

The gap in the birth rates, especially up until the 1990's, and as a result of its higher birth rate, the Palestinian population in Israel is younger than the Jewish population. In 2016, 43 percent of Arabs in Israel were age eighteen or younger, compared with only 32 percent of Jewish Israelis.[5] In addition, 3.2 percent of Palestinians in Israel are sixty-five years or older versus 11.8 percent of Jewish Israelis.[6]

In addition, the Israeli official inclusion of almost 300,000 Palestinians living in Jerusalem to this demography contributes significantly to the growth of the Palestinian population. Population growth led to the expansion of Palestinian towns and their transformation into cities. In comparison to 112 Israeli towns with populations of 5,000 or more, there are currently 41 Arab towns, of which 15 have more than 10,000 residents. In some places, a geographic contiguity exists between Arab towns. In Nazareth, Sakhneen, the Wadi Aara area, Majd Al-Kurom, and Tamra-Shfa'amr, the Palestinians make up the overwhelming majority. In addition, some Palestinians reside in coastal cities together with Jews. Approximately 87 percent of Palestinians live in 107 Arab localities, 8 percent live in mixed areas, and the rest, almost 5 percent, live in villages that have yet to be recognized by the state.[7]

The Palestinians in Israel live mainly in three geographic areas. A majority (56.6%) live in the Galilee. This region spans from Haifa in the west and Beit She'an in the east and to the Lebanese border in the north. Some 23 percent live in the Triangle, a region close to the West Bank border that runs parallel to the coastline. It extends from southeast Haifa to east Tel Aviv. Another 12 percent of Palestinians live in the Negev/*Naqqab*, specifically, in the Be'er Sheva area. The rest (about 8.5%) live in the mixed coastal cities, such as Akka (Acre), Haifa, Lydda, Ramla, and Jaffa.[8]Palestinians in Israel belong to one of three religions. Nearly 85 percent are Muslim; they live mostly in Arab villages and cities located throughout all the areas of the state. The Druze are the second-largest group, constituting 7.8 percent of the Palestinian population and residing almost entirely in the Galilee and the Carmel. Christians comprise 7.4 percent of the Palestinians in Israel,[9] and the vast majority live in the Galilee. The Christians are divided into several sects, including Catholic, Orthodox, Maronite, Armenian, and Protestant.

The Political Dimension

As noted earlier, after the Palestinian Nakba of 1948, around 150,000 Palestinian Arabs remained in their homeland within the borders of what became the State of Israel and became Israeli citizens. Those who remained in Israel lost their political and cultural elite, as well as their middle class. Theirs was a society in ruins, with few financial or cultural resources at their disposal.[10] Within a year of the state's creation and lasting until 1966, the military government imposed strict controls and restrictions on their movement and activities, which had a severe impact on socioeconomic development and greatly impeded political activity and organization.[11] The military administration sought to incentivize Palestinian cooperation by using a system of "favors" that were distributed via traditional *Hamula* (extended clan) leaders; these favors mainly related to education, employment, and the issuing of travel permits subject to Israeli "security considerations."

During the years that it was under military governance, the Palestinian community in Israel was transformed from a rural agrarian society into a proletarian society. Zureik described this process as one of "deserting agriculture."[12] In the absence of an Arab national economy and an Arab bourgeoisie, laborers moved from working the land in their villages to working in the manual labor market in Jewish cities. Their isolation from the outside world, in particular from the rest of the Palestinians and the Arab world, meant that they endured a twofold marginalization: as a marginal population within the Israeli state, they were also marginal participants in the wider Palestinian national movement.[13] This remains true to this day.[14]

The unique situation of the Palestinians in Israel after the Nakba and the establishment of Israel is an integral part of the overall "Palestinian Question." Relations between Palestinians in Israel and the rest of the Palestinian people and their representative organizations have always been problematic, exacerbated by the hostility of the Zionist movement toward the Palestinian national movement. Before the 1993 Oslo Accords, Israel considered the PLO to be a terrorist organization, and thus any contact between the PLO and Palestinians living in Israel was considered a violation of the law, tantamount to treason. Although some did establish contact with the PLO before the signing of the Oslo Accords, the subsequent peace process facilitated the establishment of closer relations with the Palestinians of the West Bank and Gaza Strip and with the PLO and the Palestinian National Authority (PNA).

Even though mainstream Israeli Jewish opinion continued to characterize Palestinians in Israel as posing a potential threat to the Israeli authorities and wider public,[15] the signing of the Oslo Accords in September 1993 between the PLO and Israel and the mutual recognition that followed constituted a significant event for Palestinian citizens of Israel. It greatly affected state–community relations, as well as Palestinian political activity and discourse in Israel. It coincided with other international political and economic trends that also affected Palestinians in Israel, such as the rapid acceleration of globalization in the 1990s. These changes have had a significant impact on the political development of the Palestinians in Israel over the last two decades, culminating in the growth and consolidation of Palestinian human capital and in the deployment of this human capital as the basis for a new "politics of hope."[16]

The first decade after the Oslo Accords saw an unprecedented growth in the level of political organization of the Palestinians in Israel. It resulted in the rise of a distinct Palestinian civil society in Israel, alongside the emergence of a pluralistic Palestinian political culture based on three principal ideologies: nationalism, communism, and Islam.[17] Palestinian voting patterns in Knesset elections changed, with a higher voter turnout for Arab parties and a sharp decrease in support for Zionist and Jewish parties.[18] There was also widespread involvement in protests that reached their peak during the Second Intifada (uprising) in October 2000. This event and the "marches of return" to displaced villages that preceded it are seen as turning points in the history of the Palestinians in Israel.

In our recent book charting the rise of the "politics of hope" among Palestinians in Israel, we highlighted six factors that significantly influenced developments in the political life of this community: the emergence of a new discourse of defiance against Jewish hegemony, the emergence of a new leadership, the organization of civil society, an energized political Islam, the publication of articles and manifestos laying out visions for the future (hereafter, "Future Vision documents"), and finally the formation of the Joint List.[19] The Palestinian community in Israel, supported by demographic, cultural, and political shifts, thus experienced a surge in confidence in its own strength and ability to actively pursue its aims.

A contrasting viewpoint sees the Palestinian national movement as characterized by dissolution and failure, in which the general Palestinian "reality" is marked by a loss of hope and trust and a decline in the collective action of Palestinians in Israel, both internally in the community and at a general level across Israel and Palestine.[20] In the next section we discuss the failure of Palestinians in Israel in the political domain as reflected in the political conduct of the Arab Joint List.

The Performance of the Joint List and Its Foundations

After more than seven decades as a Palestinian Israeli minority group, the economic development, achievements, and lifestyles of Palestinians in Israel seem to be advancing rapidly, but as a collective, they are regressing. This regression is the result of failures to attain collective achievements in three arenas. First, they failed to attain a just and civil equality and to introduce substantive changes needed to transform Israel into a democratic state. Second, they failed to reunite with the Palestinian people and its national movement, insisting on seeing themselves as a unique Palestinian group living in Israel and separate from the rest of the Palestinian people. Third, they failed to establish a separate national minority group that could confidently seek to achieve its collective demands and to construct the essential institutions of a national community; at most they built weak collective institutions that have not evolved since their establishment but instead have retreated and weakened as the years progressed. These failures are clearly manifested in the recent scourge of violence within Palestinian communities and the lack of self-efficacy of this society to combat this violence, which weakens it from the inside. They are also reflected in the establishment of the Joint List that, despite its electoral achievements, reflects subordination to the Jewish and Zionist center and a return to the discourse of "marginal belonging to the Jewish state" after it was rejected by broad Palestinian consensus in the publication of "Future Visions."[21]

The formation of the Joint Arab List in 2015 is considered an important political moment in the history of Palestinians in Israel. After a decades-long political and public debate over the collaboration of Arab parties in the Knesset, the Joint List was a political experiment that expressed hope in the midst of division and fragmentation in the general Arab and Palestinian arena; it included the active parliamentary political movements in Arab society—the communists, nationalists and Islamists. It was aimed to represent the collective civil and national demands of Palestinians in Israel.

The formation of the Joint List imposed a greater internal challenge to the Arab public, particularly in relation to the internal challenge of organizing Palestinian Arab society in Israel, building its national institutions, and leading mass action and popular struggle; its role was not to be limited to traditional parliamentary work. However, the Joint List was a positive model of unity for Palestinians in the West Bank and the diaspora, to be emulated and so end the division in the Palestinian political arena between Hamas and Fatah. The Joint List represented hope not only to Palestinians in Israel but also to Palestinians in general.

Yet, after its formation, the political domain of Palestinians in Israel has been greatly affected by the emergence of new economic, social, and political power relationships with the Israeli political system in a neoliberal context. In its electoral campaign, the Joint List focused on civil issues, emphasizing the importance of Arab representation in weakening the Israeli Right and countering racist laws. However, there was less discourse on Palestinian national identity and collective rights. The Joint List has so far—seven years since its formation—failed to bring about any tangible changes, neither in weakening the Right or in preventing racial laws. In this context the Joint List has also attached itself to the Israeli Left as if it were an Israeli party competing with the rest for power in Israel. The List also jeopardized and undermined its power when it insisted on endorsing Benny Gantz (of the Blue and White Zionist party) to head the government, after Gantz had rejected this support, fearing that association with an Arab party would deter his voters.[22]

In addition to some of the political decisions made by the Joint List, the following factors have led Palestinians in Israel to lose hope, a process that may also have engendered an increase in Palestinian citizens' "de-politization" and "Israelization" and a sharp decline in Palestinian collective political action in Israel:

- The rise of the Israeli Right, which increasingly applies policies that deny the basic needs of Palestinians everywhere, including those who are citizens of Israel. This legislation and policies make official the marginalization of Palestinian citizens while elevating the status of Jews, in a state that since 2018 defines itself as the state of the "Jewish People" with the passage of the-Nation State Law.[23]
- The general decline of the Palestinian national movement, augmented by aggressive corruption and division in the Palestine National Authority. From the time of the First Intifada (1987–1992), the Palestinian national movement was a source of inspiration for Palestinians in Israel; it helped strengthen their sense of their Palestinian identity and contributed indirectly to the efforts of those trying to establish and consolidate important collective institutions, such as the Committee of Heads of Local Authorities, the High Follow-Up Committee for Arab Affairs in Israel, and others. However, the failure of the Palestinian national movement to make major gains and the steady decline in its performance led to it ultimately fading as a source of inspiration. This also accelerated the process of Israelization, a process that can also be discerned in some of the policies and positions of the Joint List, as we explain later.
- The failure of the Arab revolutions (Arab Spring), and the loss of hope for change and self-confidence that they had initially inspired. Palestinians in Israel were deeply interested in the Arab revolutions, considering them as significant historical events not only in the region but also as a source of inspiration for change in the Palestinian cause in Israel and in the territories occupied in 1967. The faltering of the revolutions and in some cases their disastrous results contributed both to political frustration and to internal political polarization within the Palestinian community in Israel, particularly over the issue of the Syrian uprising and civil war.[24]
- Neoliberal economic orientations within the Palestinian community, supported by successive Israeli governments, that aimed to integrate Palestinians into the liberal capitalist market as individuals, thus magnifying perceptions of personal achievement and excellence. This phenomenon runs alongside the continued strengthening of the Jewish community's ethnoreligious character, for example, through the Nation-State Law.
- The failure to develop a collective political project, or more precisely, the absence of a unified Palestinian national movement inside Israel that

sees itself as part of the Palestinian national project, while also championing the collective political interests of its constituents in the Israeli political sphere.[25]

- The decline in faith in the ability of collective action to effect change, observable in the decline in numbers of those involved in protest movements and the lack of affirmative action. It can also be discerned in the lack of trust that political leaders and organizations will maximize and contribute to collective political action.[26]
- Increased distrust and fear in the social domain, exacerbated by the notable increase in intercommunal violence and crime in Palestinian communities in Israel. There is a sense of helplessness when it comes to trying to address this issue.[27]
- A notable deterioration of trust in the Palestinian political leadership and political organizations, due to the public's impression that they are not working seriously toward solving their electorate's problems and that they have limited their tactics to merely denouncing and condemning Israeli policies and actions rather than taking action.[28]

Epilogue

In 2021, Palestinian society in Israel witnessed two important events: the United Arab List (UAL) headed by Mansour Abbas, separated from the Arab Joint list and created a new list that run separately in the Knesset elections and entered the government coalition headed by Naftali Bennett, the head of an extreme right-wing party, and there was increased "unification" with Palestinian people throughout the region and their struggle for the right to self-determination. That "unification" was expressed by the participation of Palestinians in Israel in the popular uprising in May 2021 in the wake of Israeli actions taken to dispossess Palestinian residents of their East Jerusalem homes, police actions on the Al-Aqsa site, and the war on Gaza.

The participation of the UAL in the current Israeli government coalition is a historic development in Palestinian political action in Israel. It is the first time that an Arab party in the Knesset has entered the government coalition made up of centrist and right-wing Israeli parties that reject the right of self-determination for the Palestinian people and the establishment of a Palestinian state and call for the annexation of Area C of the West Bank. This coalition was established despite the ideological disparities between the position of the UAL and its sponsors, the Southern Islamic Movement, and the orientations of the future prime minister Naftali Bennett and other coalition members. We argue that the decision to enter the government reflects a high level of frustration regarding the few political choices that were and still are available and realistic in the Palestinian political scene in general, and among Palestinians in Israel in particular.

Support for the UAL reflects a loss of trust in the political ability of the Palestinians to change the status quo, whether by altering the Jewish character of the state, challenging the identity of the "Jewish state" and its politics, or reaching a reasonable settlement of the Palestinian-Israeli conflict. The Palestinian political programs and orientations that exist among the Palestinians in Israel, such as the decolonizing Israel, achieving a "state for all its citizens," empowering the Arab community's collective action apart from the state, or solving the Palestinian question within the framework of the two state solution are no longer feasible in the current OSR; it no longer makes sense to wait for the realization of these aims before integrating into the Israeli political system. From the UAL's viewpoint, the remaining options are full integration in the political system through participation in the government coalition and attempting to influence its decisions from within.

The UAL's new political approach is based on the assumption that a two state solution is no longer feasible. It therefore chooses to engage in a government that does not consider the issue of a peace process with the Palestinians among its political priorities, but rather maintains the status quo and supports settlement in Area C. In other words, this step represents "stabilization" and a deepening of the OSR.

In contrast, the popular uprising in May 2021 by Palestinians in Israel reflects the conviction among the Palestinians in Israel, especially the younger generation, that there is a close connection between what is happening in the areas of the West Bank, East Jerusalem, and Gaza beyond the Green Line and what is happening inside the Green Line. The popular outburst protested Israel's processes of colonization, Judaization, and settlement in Jerusalem, especially moves to dispossess Palestinian residents in the Sheikh Jarrah neighborhood. It also reflected Palestinians; realization that Israeli Judaization policies and practices are commonly applied not only in the state's actions in the West Bank and East Jerusalem but also in the Palestinian areas of Israel, especially in the mixed cities and the Negev. The same processes of colonization, Judaization, the systematic support of settlers, locating yeshivot (rabbinical seminaries) in Palestinian neighborhoods in mixed cities, attempting to control and seize Arab lands in the Negev, and narrowing the public space for Palestinians in all areas are taking place within the Green Line. In practicing these policies, Israel does not differentiate between Palestinians in the West Bank and East Jerusalem and areas and places of residence of the Palestinians within Israel.

Palestinians in Israel protested, demonstrated, and confronted Israeli security forces in solidarity with the Palestinians in the West Bank, who were demonstrating on their side of the Green Line; this represented a new trend of "unification" of the different parts of the Palestinian people. In a poll conducted by Mada al-Carmel Center in Haifa on the key cause of the popular uprising, 62 percent of the Palestinians in Israel indicated that the events in Jerusalem, including the storming of Al-Aqsa Mosque during Ramadan, and the case of Sheikh Jarrah, were the main reasons for the outbreak of the Palestinian popular uprising inside Israel.[29] The Israeli government and the security services tried to suppress the popular uprising of the Palestinians in Israel with almost the same tools that they use to suppress the Palestinian protest in the West Bank—closing Arab towns, arresting hundreds of young people, making administrative arrests of some young citizens of Israel—without making any effort to deal with civil protest through "civil means."

In essence, the popular protest among the Palestinians in Israel represents frustration with the inability of political agendas in the Palestinian scene to change the status quo and the conviction that Israel itself has deleted the Green Line and considers it nonexistent in its dealings with all Palestinians, thus contributing to the consolidation and deepening of the OSR. The UAL participation in the governmental coalition and the popular uprising in May 2021 reflect two contradictory facets of the same Palestinian reality in Israel that enhance the OSR in Palestine\Israel.

Final Thoughts

Seven decades after the Nakba in 1948, Palestinians in Israel, as a national indigenous minority separated from the rest of the Palestinian people, have failed to create a collective national political agenda in Israel. This does not mean that there have not been political achievements on the ground, or that awareness about the situation of Palestinians in Israel has dissipated. On the contrary, several collective agendas have played a major role in the development of the community's political awareness and have helped the struggle for national and civil rights in the face of the rigid ethnic structure of the state. Agendas such as Equality in the Jewish State, enhancing civic status, the efforts to organize as a collective community within Israel, and finally the Joint List have all at certain points confronted the ethnic structure of the state. These experiences may facilitate creating a new agenda that considers a wholesale restructuring of Palestinian political organization, with the Palestinians in Israel playing a key role in a shared political situation.

In this context, we can understand the rapid changes in public opinion of the Palestinians in Israel regarding a possible solution to the Israel-Palestinian conflict. The two state solution is still the most popular solution among the Palestinians in Israel, as consistent with their integrative orientation. Yet, the percentage of those that support this solution is only 50 percent which indicates a significant decline over the last thirty years, and there has been an increase in the percentage of supporters of the one state solution. For example, during the past three years, the percentage of supporters of the one state solution rose from 19 percent to more than 25 percent.[30]

In this context, the similarity between the Palestinian situation in general and that of the Palestinians in Israel is extremely pertinent. Three issues now challenge the Palestinian national movement: the political split between the West Bank and Gaza, reinforced by geography more than by ideology; the absence of a common national program, a joint strategy, and more, importantly, an inclusive national vision; and weak leadership, as reflected in the ongoing decrepitude of the Palestine Liberation Organization, which has been superseded by the Palestinian Authority. For Palestinians within Israel, division and disagreement over the course of collective action has reached its peak in recent years and will very likely worsen in the coming years. This similarity between the Palestinian reality within and beyond the Green Line only reinforces support of the OSR.

8

AMERICAN JEWRY AND THE ONE STATE REALITY

Michael Barnett and Lara Friedman

From the earliest years of Zionism, most Jewish American supporters of Israel held the nearly sacrosanct aspiration that Israel would be Jewish, democratic, and liberal, reflecting both their ideals and will on them as Jews and as Americans. Standing between aspiration and reality has been a very real problem: depending on the historical period, anywhere from a significant minority to a near-majority of the people living under Israeli control have been non-Jewish; that is, Palestinians (Israeli citizens and noncitizens). As long as non-Jews were a relatively small minority (and were citizens), Jewish Americans could comfortably regard Israel simultaneously as a Jewish state and a state with a democratic and liberal character.

The 1967 war and Israel's occupation of territories that were home to a sizable (and growing) Palestinian population, however, increased tension between Israel's insistence on its Jewish identity and its claim to being a state defined by liberal and democratic values. Full enfranchisement of Palestinians would mean an end to Israel's identity as a Jewish state; permanent disenfranchisement of a large population of non-Jews living under Israeli control would challenge Israel's claim to being a democracy. In the context of a peace process launched in 1993, and after long rejecting the idea of a Palestinian state, Jewish Americans' increasing appreciation of this tension led to the widespread acceptance that a two state solution—a Jewish democratic State of Israel existing alongside a sovereign state of Palestine—was desirable and indispensable to maintaining Israel's Jewish, democratic, and liberal identity.

More than twenty-five years after the start of that peace process, and nearly twenty years after President George W. Bush embraced the two state solution as the official goal of US policy, the one state reality has arrived. Israel has, de facto and increasingly de jure, decided to retain its Jewish character at the expense of liberal democracy. Now, Jewish Americans must decide how to respond to Israel's choice and what it means for their relations with Israel and their own identity. There is much unknown about how this will play out, but three things are certain. There will not be one American Jewish position; there will be many. The arguments around those positions will be exceedingly emotional because: many Jewish Americans have a deep attachment to Israel and view liberalism, pluralism, and democracy as quintessential Jewish values.[1] And the debate will be fierce and long-lasting—opening, exposing, and inflaming deep rifts; dividing families and communities; and complicating relations between Jewish Americans and their non-Jewish compatriots.

This chapter uses the recent past and the contemporary moment to examine the conflict between Jewish Americans' attachment to Israel and their commitment to liberalism and democracy. The first section surveys how, from pre-1948 through the early 2000s, Jewish Americans attempted to square an identity that is liberal and democratic with a Zionist movement and a State of Israel that confronts varying demographic pressures that potentially erode its liberal and democratic values. The current dilemmas bear a strong resemblance to those of the pre-statehood years, as do many of the responses.

The second section offers four vignettes that illuminate ways that Jewish Americans and organizations have responded to the emerging and existing one state reality: (1) whether Jewish Americans are becoming more distant from Israel; (2) how former Prime Minister Benjamin Netanyahu's interventions in American politics have transformed Israel from a bipartisan to a partisan issue and how the Netanyahu–Trump alliance caused Jewish Americans to question whether their values and interests continue to overlap with Israel's; (3) how major defenders of Israel have made fighting the Boycott, Divestment, and Sanctions (BDS) movement a top priority and the parallel shift to defining criticism of Israel as antisemitism; and (4) how support for Israel potentially constrains and contorts how Jewish Americans position themselves vis-à-vis standard liberal positions, including civil rights and racial justice.[2] We conclude by speculating about how the one state reality has reverberated across the different camps in American Jewry, forcing them to reconsider their relationship with Israel and what it means to be Jewish in America.

American Jewry and the Idealized Jewish State

Historically speaking, the views of Israel held by Jewish Americans have been refracted by their own ideals, identity, and ideas about what it means to find security through acceptance in their "golden land" of America.[3] From the start, Jewish Americans saw American values of liberalism, pluralism, and democracy as central to their American identity, consistent with their identity as Jews, and key to their strategy of security through acceptance. Encountering Jewish nationalism, they wanted a Zionism—and an Israel—that shared these values. There were moments when some segments of American Jewry worried that Zionism and the establishment of a Jewish state—with the political and moral perils that would accompany what might resemble a colonial project—were at odds with their values and might disrupt or threaten their own integration into American society. There were other periods when they saw Israel and the United States sharing fundamental values and interests, which made them feel good, proud, and secure.

1880s–1948: From Wariness to Fondness

Acceptance and security were the primary challenges facing Jews in the United States from the start of large-scale Jewish immigration through the era of the establishment of the modern State of Israel. As a minority that had experienced persecution in Europe and Russia, Jews came to the United States in search of safety, religious freedom, and economic opportunity. Knowing the deep-seated suspicions and prejudice that followed them wherever they went, the growing number of Jewish Americans sought to inoculate themselves against antisemitism by demonstrating that they were proud, patriotic Americans. They rejected particularism in favor of universalism. They denied they were "chosen." They repudiated insinuations that they had dual loyalties and pledged allegiance to the United States as their "golden land."[4] Nonetheless, there was a clear uptick in antisemitism in the United States beginning in the late nineteenth century, as a wave of Jewish immigration from eastern Europe and Russia upset a Christian America that accused Jews of bringing backward traditions, disease, criminality, and dangerous political views such as anarchism and socialism.[5]

The desire to integrate and find security through acceptance explains the initially cool response of Jewish American religious and lay elites to Zionism; they saw the explicit claim of Zionism—that Jews were a separate nation needing a state of their own—as directly undermining their campaign for acceptance in the United States.[6] A major gathering of Reform Jewish leaders in Pittsburgh in 1885 issued a statement denouncing Zionism. Of the two hundred attendees at the first Zionist Conference in 1897 in Basel, Switzerland, there was only one Jewish American, and at the time many Jewish American thought and religious leaders condemned the conference and Zionism.[7] They wrote and spoke of Zionism as if it were nearly as great a threat to their safety and existence as antisemitism—which, in their view, it was, because it reinforced many classic antisemitic tropes.

Beginning in World War I, Jewish Americans began to support an Americanized Zionism that included the belief that Palestine was a homeland for the Jews that would support equal rights for all its inhabitants.[8] This Americanized Zionism, however, soon crashed into the reality of the Nazi era. As circumstances grew more dire for European Jews, and as the United States and other countries refused to open their doors to Jewish refugees, Jewish Americans accepted the idea of a separate Jewish state in Palestine. In 1947, Britain announced its imminent departure from Palestine, and the United Nations voted to carve Palestine into three parts: a Jewish state with a slight Jewish majority, a Palestinian state with a large Arab majority, and an internationalized Jerusalem. The 1948 war buried those plans: the war ended with Israel controlling more territory than originally assigned to it; hundreds of thousands of Palestinians fled or were forcibly displaced; and Jordan extended its sovereignty over Jerusalem's Old City and the remainder of what was to have been the Palestinian state, now known as the West Bank.

1948–1967: From Fondness to Infatuation

Between 1948 and 1967 Jewish Americans viewed Israel like a distant relative. Few emigrated from the United States to make their homes in the new Jewish state, and surprisingly few even visited. They did, however, provide considerable financial and political support, lobbying Washington to extend economic, political, and military assistance. In making their case, Jewish Americans proudly celebrated Israel as the miracle of the salvation and rebirth of the Jewish people after the horror of the Holocaust, as the only liberal and democratic state in the Middle East, and as a country that shared American values, struggling for its survival against radicalizing and increasingly pro-Soviet Arab states. The US government listened sympathetically but saw greater benefit keeping Israel at arm's length as it cultivated closer ties with the geopolitically more important and oil-rich Arab world.

From the start, Israel's democratic character had its challenges, but Jewish Americans barely noticed them, which was understandable given that Israel was established in the trauma of war and the Holocaust, faced impossibly rapid population growth as Jews poured in from European and Arab countries, and was surrounded by enemies that still openly sought its destruction. Israel proclaimed itself a liberal democracy and granted citizenship to the Arabs who constituted 18 percent of its population. But equality had its limits, and Israel's Arab citizens confronted myriad legal and extralegal restrictions, usually justified on the grounds of national security. From 1950 to 1966, Israel maintained Emergency Laws that profoundly curtailed the rights and freedom of movement of its Arab citizens. Additionally, Israel enacted laws that stripped Arab citizens of their property and carried out a national mapping project that literally erased Palestinian villages from the map. But from the perspective of Jewish Americans, Israel's democratic status was unimpeachable.

1967–1990: From Infatuation to Idolatry

The 1967 and 1973 wars sparked Jewish Americans' love affair with Israel. In spring 1967, skirmishes between Syria and Israel escalated into a broader confrontation between Israel and surrounding Arab states. With Arab states mobilizing for war and announcing that Israel's destruction was at hand, Israel turned to the United States and the United Nations for support, but neither was prepared to pressure the Arab states to shift course or to offer Israel military support. Jewish Americans watched the events unfold, seeing a replay of every nightmare of Jewish isolation, victimization, and vulnerability. For Israel and Jews around the world, Holocaust analogies were immediate: the world was abandoning Israel at the very moment that Arab states were vowing to throw the Jews into the sea. But Israel flipped the script, transforming a possible nightmare into a Quentin Tarantino-esque Jewish fantasy of strength and victory. Launching a preemptive attack on June 5, in six days Israel destroyed three Arab armies and captured the Sinai Peninsula and Gaza Strip from Egypt, the Golan Heights from Syria, and East Jerusalem and the West Bank from Jordan.

This stunning victory made a deep impression on Jewish Americans. Whereas once Jewish Americans sought security through assimilation, now they shared Israelis' sense of security grounded in the military prowess of a Jewish army. Whereas once Jewish Americans invented comic book characters to imagine themselves as superheroes, they now had Israeli soldiers achieving heroic feats in real life. In addition to making Jews proud, Israel also became central to their identity, and it became nearly impossible to be considered by the Jewish American community as a good Jew without also pledging nearly unconditional support for Israel. Conversely, dissent became tantamount to treason and risked ostracism from the Jewish community. Coinciding with a time when Washington was discovering Israel's strategic value as a pillar in its containment policy, Jewish Americans formed a formidable and sophisticated lobby, led by the increasingly prominent AIPAC (American Israel Public Affairs Committee).[9]

After the 1967 war, any thoughts that Israel and the Arab states might exchange land for peace were quickly dashed by both sides, reopening a question that had lain quietly for almost two decades: What are Israel's borders? In the absence of any peace process that might immediately return the territories, Israel began establishing control over them. The Israeli government annexed East Jerusalem and its environs. Almost as soon as the dust settled from the war, some Israelis began lobbying to establish settlements in the West Bank; in September 1967 construction began on a new settlement in the southern West Bank. Although some Israelis warned that occupation would poison Israel, a growing constituency of Israelis marveled at the opportunity. For some religious Jews, the heartland of the West Bank had far more religious and historical resonance than Tel Aviv, and its return to Jewish hands was seen as reflecting God's will for Jews to control all the biblical land of Israel, Eretz Yisrael. Others saw Israel's conquest of the West Bank and Gaza as the natural continuation of the "Yishuv," Zionism's original state-building project. Many military and security officials viewed the newly captured territory as providing vital strategic depth for Israel, envisioning civilian settlements on hilltops as a means of policing Arab villages and refugee camps and defending Israel's frontiers. Regardless of the varying rationales for keeping and settling the land, the occupation began the process whereby Israel would govern a large, mostly disenfranchised Palestinian population and encounter a demographic dilemma. Beginning in 1967, Israel governed Palestinians in the West Bank and Gaza through an ad hoc combination of British Mandate-era Emergency Regulations, Jordanian law, and Ottoman law—variously selected and applied to suit Israel's objectives. These were complemented by an ever-expanding body of regulations issued by the Israeli military in its role as the occupying authority.

Perhaps the original moment of the postwar demographic dilemma was Israel's annexation of East Jerusalem, defined by Israel to include the Old City, its adjacent Palestinian neighborhoods, and close to thirty square miles of the West Bank.[10] Whereas Arabs who remained within Israel's borders in 1948 had to become citizens, in 1967 Israel conferred the status of legal "residents" on those Palestinians who now found themselves living in what Israel considered its sovereign territory. Like any other legal "residents" of Israel, Palestinian residents of Jerusalem have the right to apply for Israeli citizenship, but few have done so because it would be a tantamount surrender of their rights as Palestinians and would further normalize Israeli control over East Jerusalem; in any event, most who have sought citizenship have been denied.[11] This anomalous situation remains, with hundreds of thousands of Palestinians of East Jerusalem residing in the city without rights as Israeli citizens or comparable legal protections. Palestinian residents do not have the right to vote in national elections and know that their residency can be revoked at Israel's discretion for numerous reasons, including security, being out of the country for too long, or accepting citizenship in any other country. By choosing to deal with East Jerusalem this way—annexing the land but not the people—Israel sought to prevent the erosion of its Jewish demographic majority but created a new problem: how to be simultaneously democratic and rule over a large disenfranchised minority.

Israel's early actions in the occupied territories triggered little opposition from Jewish Americans. One reason is that the Labor government did not publicly endorse the idea of a "Greater Israel," even as it laid the conditions for achieving this objective. Some Israelis and Jewish Americans warned that settlements were violations of international law, could create friction for Israel in the international community, and could become an obstacle to peace. But these concerns were largely overridden or ignored. Settlements continued to expand under the next government, led by Menachem Begin, who lauded a Greater Israel. This development led more Jewish Americans to voice their opposition to settlement expansion on many of the same grounds—and adding the worry that demographic trends would erode Israeli democracy. Yet, once again, their voices were marginalized or silenced by a more dominant Jewish American constituency that presumed that almost anything Israel did was ipso facto necessary for its security. In general, major American Jewish organizations, through their financial and diplomatic support and policing of dissent, preserved the status quo.

A key factor in American Jewish organizations' uncritical support for Israel in this era was the reframing of the Holocaust in the American Jewish psyche that occurred in the wake of the 1967 and 1973 wars. Jewish Americans recognized the enormity of the Holocaust before 1967, but after that war and even more so after 1973, it became absorbed into their identity, almost to the point where the Holocaust ("they tried to exterminate us"), twinned with the existence of Israel ("but we survived and thrived"), defined American Jewish identity to the exclusion of Judaism itself. The extreme illustration of this coupling was the idea that Arabs and Palestinians are latter-day Nazis. This equation had existed before 1967 but became a pronounced pattern afterward. The 1967 war was replete with Holocaust references by Israeli leaders, and the 1973 war, with the surprise attack that threatened Israel's survival, fused images of Israel's vulnerability with the Holocaust for Jewish Americans. In this view, the PLO and Arab states came to be seen as attempting to finish what Nazi Germany started. Accordingly, any sort of compromise by Israel was seen as tantamount to assisted suicide; anyone in the United States and Israel who criticized Israel or entertained the idea of a land-for-peace solution risked being accused of being a modern-day British prime minister Neville Chamberlain seeking to secure "peace in our time" by appeasing an Arab Hitler.

The first cracks in the wall of Jewish American support for Israel occurred because of Israel's invasion of Lebanon in 1982. Major American Jewish organizations continued to defend Israel "right or wrong," but images coming from Beirut were hard to dismiss. Israel's "war of choice" and then its bombardment of Beirut were difficult to justify as self-defense and undermined the Israeli army's image "as the most humane in the world" among Jewish Americans. Israel's complicity in the massacre of Palestinians in the refugee camps of Sabra and Shatila further sullied its image. A few years later, the outbreak of the First Intifada in 1987 had a shattering effect on many Jewish Americans. Israel and Jewish Americans had touted Israel's occupation as benign. If so, how to explain the mass unarmed protests that included women and youth? Or the photos of Israeli soldiers breaking the bones of Palestinian protesters, apparently ordered to do so by Defense Minister Yitzhak Rabin?[12] A growing Israeli peace movement began to offer direct evidence that countered Israel's insistence that it ran a humane occupation, used force only when absolutely necessary, and would do whatever it could for peace.

1990–2000: From Blind Adoration to Mature Love

The end of the Cold War and Saddam Hussein's invasion of Kuwait unleashed new momentum to solve the Israeli-Arab conflict. American president George H. W. Bush attempted to leverage his military victory over Iraq to restart negotiations between Israel and its neighbors. Neither PLO chairman Yasir Arafat nor Israeli prime minister Yitzhak Shamir were thrilled, but they had little choice but to accept the American invitation. In 1992, Israel elected Yitzhak Rabin, who ran on a platform in support of negotiations. Shortly thereafter, Israel and the PLO, aided by the Norwegian government, established secret backchannel talks that led to mutual recognition and adoption of a statement of principles for further negotiations. With the formal signing on the White House lawn on September 13, 1993, the parties pledged to finalize a negotiated peace agreement within five years.

The Jewish American community responded to this sea change in Israeli-Palestinian relations with mixed emotions. Polls showed that most Jewish Americans supported negotiated agreements between Israel and its neighbors, but major Jewish organizations, including AIPAC, maintained the views they had formed during the Likud years, including the position that the PLO is a terrorist organization driven to destroy Israel. These differences of opinion between Jewish American groups and Rabin led to considerable strain, with Rabin often making known his irritation with these Likud-friendly opinions. Importantly, Rabin's desire to find a resolution to the conflict was driven not only by Israeli security concerns but also by preserving Israel's Jewish, liberal, and democratic identity; he believed that only a peace agreement would allow Israel to escape the demographic timebomb that was ticking ever louder.[13] Rabin's assassination in 1995 by a right-wing Israeli extremist did not formally end the peace process, but subsequent negotiations under three Israeli prime ministers—Benjamin Netanyahu, Ehud Barak, and Ehud Olmert—failed to achieve any real progress. Seven years after the signing of the Israel-PLO agreement, the parties were arguably farther away from a deal than when the process started.

2000–the Present: It's Complicated

The Oslo Accords were already on life support when the Second Intifada broke out in September 2000, shifting the ground from a status quo of stalled negotiations, intermittent violence, and constant settlement expansion to open conflict. In 2002, President George W. Bush raised expectations for serious US engagement with the peace process when he laid out a vision for peace that included a two state solution—the first time the United States had supported a Palestinian state as a matter of US policy—and the demand that Israel freeze settlements.[14] His efforts failed, settlements continued to expand, and the occupation deepened. In 2009, President Barack Obama made achieving Israel-Palestine peace a top priority from the moment he took office, but the same failure, further settlement expansion, and a more entrenched occupation. Picking up the baton in 2017, President Donald Trump trumpeted his intention to make the "deal of the century" and then abandoned the very principles on which the peace process was based and aligned US policy with the aspirations of American and Israeli Greater Israel ideologues.

This period—marked by the receding viability and credibility of the peace process, a rightward shift in Israeli policies and politics, and an increasingly partisan feel about Israel in the US political debate—has produced a level of political and intellectual ferment in American Jewish politics unseen since the early pre-1948 debates about Zionism. In this context, four important constituencies have coalesced regarding the once and future Israel, which we present in order of those that most favor to those that most oppose the existing status quo. The first is a relatively small but growing number of Jewish Americans, most of whom are Orthodox, that champion a Greater Israel. This constituency enjoys outsized prominence and influence on US policy because it shares ideological and political affinities with Christian evangelical Zionists.

A second constituency, and the dominant camp in Jewish American politics, includes AIPAC and other major Jewish organizations who mirror the Israeli government's "hasbara" script of defending and supporting whatever Israel does. In addition to giving Israel a nearly free hand to de facto pursue a pro-Greater

Israel agenda, this camp mobilizes to deflect criticism with an arsenal of talking points that blame the Palestinians for all failures of peace efforts. Whereas once AIPAC and other like-minded Jewish organizations could legitimately be called nonpartisan, both in their base of support and policies, since the start of the peace process and particularly with the election of Barack Obama as president, they lean Republican.

A third constituency, which has risen in political power and prominence over the last decade, consists of Liberal Zionists for whom support for a two state solution is central to their view that Israel can and must be both Jewish and democratic. Important American Jewish voices and organizations (like Americans for Peace Now) have long supported this outcome, but this constituency took on greater political relevance with the creation of J Street in 2007. Capitalizing on Jewish American support for Obama, growing unease with Israeli pro-settlement policies and creeping annexation, and fears that the demographic dilemma was increasingly eroding Israel's liberal and democratic character, J Street has become a gathering place for mainstream progressive Jews who continue to support the peace process and are uncomfortable with AIPAC's conservativism. Voices in this constituency have increasingly become mainstreamed within Jewish communities around the United States. Wielding the language of shared values and shared interests, they urge constructive US leadership and engagement toward a two state solution and beseech Jewish Americans not to give up on hope for peace. Although they are critical of Israeli policies, they emphasize their support for Zionism and love of Israel and try to balance criticism of Israel with criticism of the Palestinians. This camp generally shies away from supporting coercive pressure on Israel, including the use of economic tools, but increasingly considers whether and how to use aid to Israel to halt Israeli policies that are anathema to two states.

The fourth constituency is the newest one and consists of more progressive Jewish organizations—like Jewish Voices for Peace, which has existed as a grassroots movement for decades, and If Not Now, which emerged out of J Street's youth activists.[15] These organizations, whose leaders and supporters tend to be younger, include Liberal Zionists, post-Zionists, non-Zionists, and anti-Zionists, and generally frame their views on Israel-Palestine not in terms of love of Israel but in terms of defense of universal values, whether as Americans, Jews, or both. As such, they function less as a part of the Jewish communal world and more as part of a broad ecosystem of mutually supportive social justice movements in the United States. They challenge what they view as the hypocrisy of self-identified progressives in the Jewish American community whose values extend to every issue but Israel/Palestine. They do not necessarily reject a two state solution but are open to various binational options. And their view is that if it takes extraordinary pressure on Israel to bring about change, including conditions on or cuts to aid, sanctions, and boycotts, so be it. Although this camp is often dismissed or derided by members of the other camps, its appeal to fundamental values of right and wrong and to building "intersectional" ties with progressive movements across the political landscape makes it arguably the one best positioned to deal coherently with the one state reality in which all these different camps find themselves today.

The One State Reality

Regardless of whether Jewish Americans call the current Israel-Palestine status quo a one state reality—and many do not—it is this reality that is shaping today's debate and exposing deep fault lines within among Jewish Americans, as they are forced to contend with an Israel in which "liberal" and "democratic" are sacrificed in favor of "Jewish" and "Greater Israel." In this section we explore how Jewish Americans have responded to the demographic dilemma and one state reality by surveying four issues and their corresponding effects: Jewish Americans' attachment to Israel, the Trump-Netanyahu alliance and the increasingly partisan divide over Israel, BDS and the weaponization of antisemitism, and the movement for social justice and Black Lives Matter.

Social Distancing

Since the 1990s, a frequently made observation by Jewish Americans and Israelis across the political spectrum is that Jewish Americans are losing their love for Israel. There is considerable debate about this trend and how to capture feelings of attachment.[16] Whose attachments count? Does it depend on self-identification or belonging to a synagogue?[17] Or is it about whether Jewish Americans support this or that Israeli policy or attend pro-Israel rallies and festivals?

Jewish Americans have identified more or less with this observation at different times but are arguably more ambivalent about Israel today than at any time since 1948. Why this is the case is also a matter of considerable debate. Ardent defenders of Israel are apt to argue that this ambivalence has little or nothing to do with Israel's policies or actions and everything to do with what they see as negative changes in the identity of Jewish Americans, including the rise in assimilation and intermarriage, the increase in the number of nontraditional families, and declines in membership in synagogues and enrollment in Jewish day schools. Their conclusion is that there is a direct cause–effect relationship between the declining role of traditional Judaism and Jewish institutions in the lives of Jewish Americans and the declining centrality of Israel in Jewish Americans' identity.[18] As further evidence, they point to the countertrend in Orthodox Jewry, where more traditional Judaism, anchored in resolutely conservative social, cultural, and political worldviews, is accompanied by ever-stronger and more unwavering attachment to Israel.

Although some of these internal developments might indeed contribute to a decline in attachment and an increase in ambivalence, the overarching factor affecting Jewish Americans' views about Israel relates to values. As discussed earlier, Jewish Americans have agonized over Israeli policies and positions that, in turn, have raised questions about whether Israel's values coincide with their own. These values tend to be measured against three features of state–society relations. The first is the Israeli state's relationship to religion. Whereas religious authority plays an important role in Israel, Jewish Americans understand and emphatically defend the importance of separation between religion and the state. This is not just a principled debate, grounded in concern for Israel's treatment of non-Jews, but also a personal one. Israel's religious authority is in the hands of the Orthodox, who tend to treat the Judaism of Jewish Americans as second-rate. The demographic dilemma fuels the other two features. As a Jewish state, Israeli grants Jews privileges and rights not accorded to non-Jews, which contradicts Jewish Americans' sacrosanct belief in equal rights. And the growth of the Palestinian population means that a (near) majority of the population living under Israeli control lacks the right to vote, a reality that cannot be reconciled to Jewish Americans' commitment to democracy. Jewish Americans have noticed this value divide. In one survey of Jewish residents of nations around the globe, the most frequently cited reason for their alienation from Israel was "the political aspect of the State of Israel," the runner up was "religious coercion," and garnering honorable mention was the feeling of Jewish peoplehood that "opposed the global/modern spirit."[19]

Whatever one sees as the reasons, dissensus is growing among Jewish Americans with respect to Israel. There appear to be three schools of thought on what can be done about it, which align, not coincidentally, with views on Israel. One school believes little can be done because the split is no longer personality or policy driven but rather identity driven.[20] According to this view, Jewish Americans and Jewish Israelis are just different, and their differences have become more pronounced over the years.[21] Another school suggests that the solution is for Jewish Americans to save Israeli Jews from themselves. Adherents to this view, including many in the center left, want to salvage Israel's liberal and democratic character at all costs—perhaps even at the expense of Israel's Jewish identity.[22] The third school exhorts Jewish Americans to accept their differences with Israeli Jews, set aside their value-based concerns and judgments, and support Israel: this demand is often framed in terms suggesting that Jewish Americans are overly judgmental of

Israel or are ignorant about the realities that Israel faces, or that living in the United States where they do not face the same reality as Israeli Jews, they should not be criticizing Israel at all.[23]

The growing unease among many Jewish Americans regarding Israel's values and discriminatory rule over non-Jews, including even among staunch loyalists such as AIPAC, was on display in May 2021 when Israeli authorities attempted to evict Palestinians from their homes in East Jerusalem. Defenders of Israel insisted that the issue was a mere real estate dispute and that the proposed eviction was "legal," whereas Palestinians and Palestinian rights activists countered that Israeli law structurally disadvantages Palestinians, violating their property rights and their basic human rights. On the ground, the dispute sparked a new Gaza War, widespread Palestinian protests—including rioting and violence—on both side of the Green Line, and in some Israeli "mixed cities," Jewish Israeli rioting and anti-Arab vandalism and violence. Many Jewish American supporters of Israel began using the language of apartheid to describe Israel's rule over the Palestinians. With prospects for the two state solution long gone, others began insisting that Israel must respect the human rights of Palestinians. President Biden, a strong supporter of Israel, refused to criticize Israel in public, which earned him criticism from some fellow Democrats.

Trump–Netanyahu Alliance and Partisan Politics

Most Jewish Americans are registered Democrats who describe themselves as liberal. In 2008 and 2012 they voted in large numbers for President Obama. In contrast, Prime Minister Netanyahu all but endorsed Obama's Republican opponents in 2008 and 2012, and during Obama's eight years in office, Netanyahu and the Israeli public displayed unreserved suspicion, hostility, and contempt toward him. In the 2016 presidential election, Jewish Americans voted in large numbers for Hillary Clinton. They strongly opposed President Trump for his policies, his values, and his willingness to be an accessory to the surge of antisemitism during his term. In contrast, beginning with the 2016 election campaign and running throughout his term, Netanyahu and the Israel public warmly embraced Trump—not just as a true friend of Israel but also as "the best friend Israel has ever had in the White House."[24] During the 2020 election a majority of Israelis strongly supported President Trump over Joe Biden, and when Trump lost, some right-wing Israelis publicly took up the narrative that the election had been stolen from him.

With respect to views on Obama and Trump, differences of opinion are not solely or even mainly rooted in a disagreement over Israel-related policies. Many Jewish Americans who loved Obama had reservations about his Israel-Palestine policies, and many Jewish Americans who loathed Trump were sympathetic to some of his shifts in Israel-Palestine policy. Rather, at its core this disagreement discloses a profound and growing dissonance between Jewish Americans and Jewish Israelis regarding the values and interests that define their identities. Regardless of their views of his policies on Israel, most Jewish Americans viewed Trump as a threat to their values and held his presidency responsible for stoking or inflaming antisemitism. In contrast, Netanyahu and most of the Israeli public viewed Trump's beyond-their-wildest-dreams support for Israel as something to celebrate; his illiberalism failed to alarm them because it aligned with domestic political trends.

This dissonance was already reflected in Netanyahu's treatment of Jewish Americans during his 2009–2021 tenure as prime minister and has arguably contributed to Jewish Americans' growing ambivalence toward Israel. Most obviously, Netanyahu's open hostility toward Obama, which included siding with Republicans in Congress against Obama on Iran, coupled with his warm embrace of Trump, aggravated what was already a strained bipartisan consensus around Israel. Netanyahu's venture into an increasingly polarized American political scene was not an accident but rather a political calculation, reflecting his own preference for dealing with illiberals and evangelicals who do not bother him with concerns about human rights, international law, or the imperative to make peace. In short, Netanyahu appeared to have decided that if Jewish Americans would not offer unquestioning, unconditional support for Israel, he could find other Americans who would.[25]

One of the great feats of Jewish Americans after 1967 was the establishment of a "special relationship" between the United States and Israel that enjoyed strong bipartisan support. Netanyahu's interventions in American politics undermined that relationship, with the prime minister of Israel over the course of more than a decade publicly treating the Republican Party as Israel's true ally and courting its conservative evangelical elements. Old Guard Democrats mainly responded defensively by insisting that Democrats are just as pro-Israel as Republicans—and by trying to score pro-Israel points, for example, by supporting ever larger aid to Israel or taking ever stronger stances against BDS. Over time, this approach became more difficult as Israel, with Republican support, moved to jettison even the pretense of supporting the policy framework that still enjoys wide Democratic support; that is, the two state solution. Even after Netanyahu's loss of the premiership in 2021, this approach is close to becoming untenable, with the rise of a new generation of progressive Democrats aligned with a progressive, social justice-oriented grassroots. These progressives, who represent a small but growing cohort in Congress, reject an Israel exception to the ideal of free speech and openly challenge their party's unconditional support for an illiberal Israel.

Netanyahu's nearly unconditional support for Trump was especially disturbing to progressive Jewish Americans, given the surging antisemitism that his presidency unleashed and fueled. Not only did Trump trample the values that they hold dear and consider central to their own security, but he also did so while trafficking in antisemitism and dog-whistling to white nationalism and right-wing movements that are a direct threat to Jewish Americans. Trump failed to immediately and categorically condemn the antisemitic demonstration at Charlottesville, Virginia, in August 2017. American Jews were unnerved by the silence of the White House and Netanyahu.[26] In response to the October 27, 2018 massacre at the Tree of Life synagogue in Pittsburgh, Israeli officials gave the impression that they were more worried about the possible harm done to Trump than the assault on American Jews: "Israel defends Trump amid synagogue shooting criticism."[27] These were among the many moments during the Trump presidency when Israel appeared to be indifferent to the safety and security of Jewish Americans, and even an accessory to their insecurity, shattering the long-standing understanding that Israel would never engage in behavior that would put their safety at risk.

Even as Trump contributed to the normalization of and attacks against Jewish Americans, he sought to use his support for Israel—and Netanyahu's support for him—to inoculate himself against charges of antisemitism. At a Sheldon Adelson-backed summit, Trump accused some Jews of not loving Israel enough, characterizing them as the ones who did not support settlements or him.[28] And if uncritical support of Israel equates to "not antisemitic," it is only natural to equate criticism of Israel with antisemitism. Trump did just that, weaponizing the rhetoric of opposing antisemitism to attack Democrats who questioned Israel's policies or called for consequences, slandering progressive activists who were criticizing Israel, and pandering to those who wanted to quash criticism of Israel on college campuses and beyond.

For many Americans Jews, Netanyahu's embrace, support, and legitimation of Trump—with apparent indifference to what Trump's presidency meant for Jewish Americans—were disconcerting and amplified the dilemmas they face regarding their relations with Israel.[29] The election of President Biden did not automatically reset the relationship: profound and lasting damage has been done. After four years of the Trump–Netanyahu bromance, most Jewish American see Israel differently and are more attentive to the gulf between their and Israel's values. Politically, Israel has for now been cemented as a partisan issue, and even though both Biden and Vice President Harris are vocal supporters of Israel, some progressive members of Congress, working with an energized progressive grassroots that includes Jewish voices, are pushing for US policies toward Israel that align with progressive values, including support for Palestinians' civil and human rights, and that more strongly challenge continued occupation and settlements.

BDS and the Definition of Antisemitism

Since the start of the peace process, neither the process, nor the United States, nor any other international actors ever managed to curb Israeli policies that violated Palestinian rights or that, by changing facts on the ground, undermined the achievement of a negotiated agreement. This failure over time led advocates of Palestinian rights and some supporters of the two state solution to search for new tactics to pressure Israel to change its behavior. The most significant of these efforts is the Boycott, Divestment, and Sanctions (BDS) movement. Launched in 2005 by Palestinian activists and modeled on South Africa's anti-apartheid campaign, over the past fifteen years BDS has grown into a worldwide network of organizations and supporters, aiming to use popular boycotts, divestment, and sanctions to promote Palestinian rights on both sides of the Green Line, including a full Palestinian right of return. The latter demand has been seized on by many supporters of Israel to argue that the movement's real goal is to attack Israel's very existence.

Almost from the start, major American Jewish organizations and the Israeli government labeled BDS an "existential threat" and successfully exploited the "existential threat" argument to both try and use BDS to exonerate Israeli policies and to attack critics of Israel, regardless of whether they support BDS.[30] Based on this reasoning, President Obama enacted two federal laws that, in effect, make it US policy to oppose boycotts of both Israel and settlements; as of this writing, more than thirty states have adopted laws penalizing those who boycott Israel or settlements by denying them the ability to conduct business with the state.[31] All these laws were lobbied for and applauded by many Jewish American organizations. Furthermore, this weaponization of BDS has escalated over time from attacking the motives behind BDS to alleging connections between BDS and terrorism.[32] In parallel, accusations of support for BDS have become a powerful tool of partisan warfare, used against candidates in the 2018 and 2020 elections and against sitting members of Congress.[33]

The categorical rejection of BDS—both the movement and its tactics—by mainstream Jewish American groups and the Israeli government has put many Jewish Americans in a bind. On the one hand, they view boycotts as political free speech protected by the Constitution and see divestment and sanctions as legitimate protest tactics. On the other hand, they recognize that, in the context of protest against Israel, embracing or even defending these tactics risks censure and attack.[34] There is some evidence that the strong-arm tactics used by mainstream Jewish American groups and the Israeli government are alienating some Jewish Americans,[35] who reject giving up core democratic values of free speech and the right to protest in order to insulate Israel from pressure. To avoid the appearance of proposing the sacrifice of free speech rights for Israel, many American Jewish groups have reframed the battle against BDS as being not about defending Israel but about fighting antisemitism.[36] For many Jewish Americans this is not a huge leap; attacking critics of Israel or advocates of Palestinian rights as antisemitic (or, if they were Jewish, as self-hating Jews) is commonplace. The difference in recent years is the emergence of an international movement—of scholars, activists, public intellectuals, Jewish and evangelical Christian defense groups, Israeli-government supported organizations, and governments—promoting the idea of a "new antisemitism" that is first and foremost about criticism of Israel and anti-Zionism.[37] This approach is increasingly used to delegitimize and stifle criticism and popular activism targeting Israel under the guise of fighting antisemitism.[38]

The International Holocaust Remembrance Alliance (IHRA) is arguably the most powerful expression of this development.[39] Established in 1998, it unites government representatives and Holocaust scholars from thirty-three countries "to spread and institutionalize teaching and research on the Holocaust, commemorate the Holocaust, and struggle against antisemitism."[40] In 2016 it adopted a "working definition" of antisemitism.[41] That definition does not explicitly mention Israel, but its explanatory language—widely treated as integral to the definition—includes both a statement that not all criticism of Israel is antisemitic and examples of when criticism of Israel is antisemitic that are so broad that they have been used by defenders of Israel to argue that virtually any criticism and activism challenging Israel or its policies, or even any expression of a Palestinian narrative of history is antisemitism. This definition gained the weight of US law in December 2019, when President Trump issued his Executive Order on Combating Anti-Semitism to widespread praise from Jewish American groups and leaders.[42] That order made the IHRA definition, including its Israel-related examples, part of Title VI of the Civil Rights Act of 1964. Since then, bills have been introduced in various state legislatures seeking to codify the IHRA definition and its Israel-related examples into hate crimes and civil rights laws.[43]

With the IHRA definition as the touchstone, in May 2020, an organization called "stopantisemitism.org" named the US representative of the Israeli human rights group B'tselem its "Anti-semite of the Week" for having defended the legitimacy of boycotts (even though she opposed the BDS movement).[44] In July 2020, a report by the Amcha Initiative reported a surge in antisemitism on campuses—largely glossing over its own findings of a drop in "classic" antisemitism on campuses to highlight Israel-related antisemitism, as defined by the IHRA.[45] Even challenging the definition is problematic. In August 2019, Daniel Blattman, a Holocaust historian at the Hebrew University of Jerusalem and chief historian of the Warsaw Ghetto Museum, suggested that Israel has exploited the IHRA definition for political purposes; in response, another prominent Holocaust scholar, Yehuda Bauer, accused Blattman of antisemitism.[46]

The battle between Jewish American organizations and BDS has been especially fierce on college campuses. President Trump's executive order on antisemitism, in practice, has been used mainly if not exclusively to target activists and professors who criticize Israel and support BDS, following in the tradition of attacks against them for years.[47] In May 2020, George Washington University came under attack for appointing as interim dean of the Elliott School of International Affairs a highly respected (Jewish) professor who supports BDS.[48] That same month, a American lawyer who specializes in cases targeting critics of Israel, working with an Israeli group tied to the Israeli government, petitioned the IRS to revoke the nonprofit status of a US foundation over its support for Students for Justice in Palestine (SJP), alleging SJP's support for BDS qualified under law as antisemitic discrimination.[49] And then there is Canary Mission.[50] Funded by conservative Jewish donors and organizations, Canary Mission monitors college professors, administrators, or students for criticism of Israel and support for BDS or Palestinian rights; it then posts profiles online attacking offenders, including with accusations of antisemitism. Canary Mission seeks not only to "name and shame" but also to scare individuals into silence. A student who ends up on its watchlist, for instance, might have greater difficulty getting a government job or a security clearance or being allowed to enter Israel or the West Bank.[51]

The battle over defining "antisemitism" continued and intensified after Trump left office, most notably with the publication of two definitions—produced by two separate groups of prominent experts and scholars of antisemitism, Jewish history, and the Holocaust. The Jerusalem Declaration on Antisemitism and the Nexus Document, each, in their own ways, were explicitly crafted to either replace or complement the IHRA definition, by challenging the IHRA definition's conflation of antisemitism with criticism of Israel or rejection of Zionism.[52] In an exchange that exemplified the gulf between progressive Democrats and the Democratic Old Guard, in May 2021, a group of progressive members of Congress wrote to the US secretary of state urging that, as the Biden administration carries out the task of fighting antisemitism, it considers these two definitions alongside the IHRA definition.[53] In response, the State Department sent back a letter reiterating—and doubling down on—the Biden administration's embrace of the IHRA definition.[54]

American Jewish progressives have historically been fierce defenders of free speech. Yet, the desire to insulate Israel from criticism or to remain inside the tent of mainstream Jewish American organizations has led many to accept a redefinition of antisemitism or a narrower definition of the First Amendment to create a free speech exception for Israel. In doing so, on this issue, the mainstream American Jewish community has stood against traditional allies such as the American Civil Liberties Union and aligned instead with right-wing Israeli political forces and their US supporters.[55]

Social Justice and Black Lives Matter

Most Jewish Americans see themselves and their community as fighting for the rights of all minorities and vulnerable populations, pointing with pride to the role of Jewish Americans in the US civil rights movement. In reality, that role was more complicated than many Jews today understand, with Jewish Americans standing on both sides of the color line.[56] Still, Jewish Americans participated in the civil rights movement in numbers that exceeded their percentage of the population; two Jewish civil rights workers were murdered during the 1964 Freedom Summer; Martin Luther King was often in the company of rabbis and leaders from the Jewish community; and the legendary Rabbi Abraham Joshua Heschel was a highly visible participant in the civil rights movement. Jewish Americans' support for Blacks, "a group stigmatized and despised by the American mainstream," derived from their own sense of self and aspiration for an America to be their one and true home.[57] Many Jewish Americans saw the cause of civil rights and racial justice as rooted in their belief that they had special obligations to others fighting for freedom and equality. The American Jewish Committee, for instance, became a leading Jewish organization in the struggle for civil rights largely out of the belief that minority survival should be a concern of all minorities.[58] Some Jews felt a further connection to the civil rights struggle because the African American community looked to Jewish history for inspiration.[59]

The failure of Black Americans to support Israel during the 1967 war and its aftermath left many Jewish Americans feeling betrayed, contributing to the fraying of their alliance with the civil rights movement. Martin Luther King's shift from focusing on civil and political rights to economic rights, and the movement's gradual identification of economic issues—including small business ownership, property rights, and access to loans—as targets of protest moved to more controversial ground for Jews, as they saw themselves and their property threatened. Notwithstanding their shared identification with the Democratic Party, over time many Jewish Americans became concerned about a perceived African American strain of antisemitism through which growing tensions became increasingly refracted; this was often related to views on Israel held by African American leaders like Malcolm X, Stokely Carmichael, Louis Farrakhan, and the Reverend Jesse Jackson.[60]

Today, most Jewish Americans still view themselves as committed to racial and social justice, but for many, uneasiness about perceived antisemitic tendencies among African American activists has deepened, largely linked to racial justice leaders' and movements' criticism of Israel and identification with the Palestinians. That tension—between principle and politics—is embodied most clearly in hostility from some Jewish Americans toward the Black Lives Matter (BLM) movement. BLM was born in 2013 in response to the acquittal of George Zimmerman in the 2012 shooting death of the African American teen Trayvon Martin. A year later, it rose to national prominence as it rallied the grassroots in response to the deaths of two African Americans in Ferguson, Missouri. It soon developed dozens of chapters across the United States and became involved in the 2016 elections.

From its inception, BLM welcomed supporters of Palestinian rights, with both groups viewing this alliance as a natural reflection of a common struggle for rights, equality, and justice. Images of IDF troops acting against Palestinians in the West Bank, or cases of the IDF killing Palestinians who posed no apparent threat, resonate powerfully with the experience of many Black Americans at the hands of law enforcement. The occupation's systematic granting of power and privilege to Jewish settlers in the West Bank, at the expense of the rights and dignity of the indigenous Palestinian population, carries powerful echoes of slavery, Jim Crow, and apartheid. BLM's first platform, published in 2016, reflected this sense of common cause, with language supporting BDS and accusing Israel of perpetrating genocide against the Palestinians.[61] In response, many leading Jewish American organizations attacked BLM as antisemitic.[62]

As long as BLM remained just one of many players in the US movement for racial and social justice, American Jewish organizations could still support racial justice without having to identify with it. However, the outbreak of mass racial and social justice protests, led by BLM in the wake of the George Floyd's murder on May 25, 2020, made that no longer possible. Most major Jewish organizations, and especially those that have come to define fighting BDS as central to their mission—including the Anti-Defamation League—confronted a dilemma: how to support racial justice when the movement that is leading the fight, BLM, insists on seeing Palestinians too as victims of racial injustices that, like those facing Black Americans, must be overturned.

For some, the answer has been, in effect, to support BLM "with conditions."[63] Others, especially those aligned with the cause of Greater Israel, have doubled down on attacking BLM. For example, in July 2020, a US legal group that focuses on fighting BDS asked the Department of Justice to investigate BLM, alleging that, through its link to BDS, it is tied to terror.[64] Others, including some voices from Israel that appear to be actively trying to aggravate relations between Jewish Americans and BLM, have sought to use progressives' support for BLM to score political points. For example, in July 2020, a former member of the Israeli Knesset published an article in a New York Jewish outlet arguing that BLM is "structurally anti-Semitic" and suggesting that Jews who work with BLM are "part of the problem." That same month, the Jerusalem Center for Public Affairs, run by former Israeli ambassador to the United States, Dore Gold, warned that the alliance between BDS and BLM (and Antifa) "demands that Jewish Americans sacrifice their liberal and progressive worldviews."[65]

Since Biden took office on January 20, 2021, the issue of Black support for Palestinian rights has gained even greater political salience, and the trend that began under Trump, wherein defenders of Israel joined with Republicans to denounce virtually any criticism of Israel by members of Congress of color as ipso facto antisemitism, has only intensified. For example, even though major Israeli human rights organizations now describe Israel's rule over non-Jews as apartheid, when congressional members of color used the same term some fellow Democrats denounced their statements as "antisemitic at their core" and said they "contribute to a climate that is hostile to many Jews."[66] Similarly, following the May 2021 war in Gaza, a relatively large number of congressional Democrats, including Rep. Yarmuth, a Jewish Democrat from Kentucky, criticized Israel's actions; yet, the Republicans and mainstream Jewish American organizations singled out Representatives Alexandria Ocasio-Cortez (D-New York), Rashida Tlaib (D-Michigan), Ayana Pressley (D-Massachusetts), and Ilhan Omar (D-Minnesota).[67] Asked why these members were censured for criticizing Israel when other Democrats who voiced similar criticisms were not, Yarmuth replied, "Well, I'm neither Black, nor female, nor a Muslim."[68]

The Challenge of Divergence

The one state reality poses a profound challenge to Jewish Americans' relationship to Israel and their self-identity. At the foundation of their embrace of Israel was the belief that Israel shared their liberal, democratic values. That foundation is collapsing under the weight of Israel's increasingly open embrace of illiberalism, particularly with respect to its treatment of Palestinians. It is no longer easy for Jewish Americans to rationalize Israeli policies on the grounds that the occupation was benign or temporary, or that a separate Palestinian state is in the offing. Israel's de facto and increasingly de jure control over the territories has created something that undeniably resembles an apartheid state.

Jewish Americans have cherished liberalism and democracy for both principled and political reasons that are connected to their values, security, and survival. As a religious minority, they have viewed liberalism and democracy as essential to their strategy of security through acceptance. An Israel that allies with illiberal and openly antisemitic leaders, including those who traffic in white supremacy and Holocaust denial, reveals a gulf between the values and interests of Jewish Americans and those of Israelis that is so large as to be, for many, unbridgeable. Although there is nothing new in right-leaning American Jewish groups and leaders welcoming these strange bedfellows, in the Trump era the cognitive dissonance reached new heights as some defended the likes of Steve Bannon and Sebastian Gorka on the grounds that support for Israel is the same as support for Jews or were silent as Trump cultivated antisemitism and as white nationalists like Richard Spencer used Israel and illiberal policies such as Israel's Nation-State Law as a model for the kind of ethnonationalism he imagined for the United States.[69]

This clash of values and interests is playing out in several significant ways, including the changing nature of Jewish Americans' views of their relationship with Israel.[70] Jewish Americans are not just increasingly distant but are also increasingly divided over the relationship with Israel, both in partisan terms and within the ranks of Jewish Democrats. Many Jewish progressives are increasingly frustrated by the failure of their party to adopt policies on Israel consistent with their values, including with respect to social justice and human rights. In this view, it is Israel's Jewish American defenders, not its critics, who are guilty of using a double standard. A consequence is that as a group, the progressive credentials of Jewish Americans are increasingly challenged, as is their place alongside, and the authenticity of their solidarity with, other minority groups with which they traditionally shared many of the same concerns. This development is not the result of antisemitism, as the term has been traditionally understood, but reflects the fact that, based on the values they hold dear, social justice groups are often sympathetic to the Palestinians and hostile to those who defend Israeli (or, for that matter, American) policies that deprive Palestinians of rights and dignity, regardless of those defenders' faith or ethnicity. Some Jewish Americans and Jewish organizations have responded to this challenge by compromising their values, doubling down on support for Israel "right or wrong," and increasingly accusing critics of Israel of antisemitism.[71]

One final consequence of the strain between Jewish Americans and Israel is that it has encouraged many Jewish Americans to reexamine the relationship between their identity as Jews and their views about Israel.[72] For some, harsher criticism of Israel, support for concrete consequences for illiberal Israeli policies, and even anti-Zionism do not necessarily require turning their back on Judaism but rather require them to reimagine their Jewishness in a way that prioritizes their values over the very specific form of Jewish nationalism that animates Israel and its supporters today.[73] This, in effect, represents a return to the intellectual and moral place where Jewish Americans stood on the eve of Israel's birth, when many were reluctant to embrace Zionism and Israel until they were certain that doing so reflected their liberal, democratic values—and therefore would reflect well on them and their interests as Jewish Americans. Jewish Americans overlooked the possible fault lines in Israel's liberal democracy because of the memory of the Holocaust and Israel's just wars for survival. Today, in contrast, with Israel embracing illiberalism at home and abroad, the clash of values and divergence of interests will not be so easily papered over.

9

LESSONS FROM HOW NATIONALISMS EVOLVE FOR A ONE STATE REALITY

Nadav G. Shelef

Given the existence of competing nationalist aspirations by Jews and Palestinians, peaceful coexistence in a one state reality requires that one or both of these nationalisms either change these aspirations or redefine the political community in more inclusive terms. This chapter assesses the likelihood of such transformations and argues that the role of domestic politics in driving such changes means that, although possible, they are unlikely. It begins by outlining how nationalist ideologies evolve and describing the kinds of "denationalization" that would need to occur for peaceful coexistence in a one state reality. The brief discussion of the contestation over how to define the nation's membership boundaries in Zionism and Palestinian nationalism in the second part of the chapter highlights the role of domestic politics and evolutionary processes in driving redefinitions of the nation. This, in turn, has two conflicting implications for a one state reality. First, the kinds of fundamental transformations in the meaning of nationhood that are required for denationalization *can* occur even for Zionism and Palestinian nationalism. Second, such transformations depend on the outcome of future domestic political struggles—struggles that, at least at present, the denationalization projects among Israelis and Palestinians are poorly positioned to win. Denationalization, in other words, although possible, will not be the automatic consequence of a one state context.

For all the ups and downs of the last 150 years, the fundamental problem facing Jews and Palestinians in the area of Mandatory Palestine remains rooted in the conflicting aspirations of Zionism and Palestinian nationalism. Like all nationalisms, both make the same basic claim: "We are a distinct people and, as such, we deserve control over our political destiny." The conflict arises because the definitions of national membership and desired forms of control are (or at least have largely been) exclusive, yet both nationalisms want to establish this control in the same geographic space.

Given this diagnosis, the idea that creating two states could provide a path to peaceful coexistence was built on the assumption that dividing geographic space is easier than relinquishing national aspirations. As the Peel Commission argued almost a century ago, because the "National Home cannot be half-national" and the "national aspirations [of Jews and Arabs in Palestine] are incompatible . . . the only hope of a cure lies in a surgical operation."[1]

As the contributions to this volume note, however, Israelis and Palestinians increasingly find themselves living in a reality that makes this particular treatment harder to implement. The underlying diagnosis, however, has not changed. Can this circle be squared? Can the nationalist ideologies that constitute the basic reason for conflict change in such a way that enables the emergence of a peaceful society in which neither group subjugates the other? If so, how do such changes come about? And how likely are they in this context?

This chapter answers these questions in three steps. First, it abstracts away from this case and argues that nationalisms can change even their most fundamental aspects. Such changes, however, are not automatic reactions to experienced reality but are more properly understood as the product of unguided, "evolutionary" mechanisms. The second part of the chapter returns to the history of Israeli and Palestinian nationalisms to demonstrate that changes in the membership boundaries articulated by these nationalisms can occur and that unguided domestic political dynamics, rather than new realities per se, drove these prior transformations. Building on these lessons, the third part of the chapter argues that although changes of the kind that would be necessary for peaceful coexistence in the context of a one state solution *can* occur, they are unlikely to be the automatic consequence of the reality in which Israelis and Palestinians live. A one state reality, in other words, will not necessarily produce the denationalization required for peaceful coexistence.

How Nationalism Evolves

At its core, nationalism is a political project that seeks to endow a group (the nation) with control over its political destiny. As part of this project, all nationalisms must answer at least three basic questions: Who is included in the nation? Where should the nation assert control over its political destiny (i.e., where are the borders of its homeland)? And how should this control be exercised (in an independent state, autonomous province, etc.)?

The political projects providing answers to these questions actively work to naturalize themselves, to turn their socially and politically constructed answers into self-evident truths.[2] These efforts notwithstanding, nationalism is not, in fact, immutable. The possibility of change is afforded not just by virtue of nationalism being a social construct but also because, quite often, various political movements offer different answers to these cardinal questions.[3] When such variation is paired with political competition those bundles of answers that are relatively more successful politically tend to displace less successful bundles over time. In short, given variation, competition, and time, nationalism evolves.[4]

Importantly, this conception of change in nationalist ideology is situated at the movement and elite levels. These elites are the people who direct the movements that create, take over, and legitimate states. They write the history textbooks, plays, poetry, novels, and propaganda that provide the building blocks with which everyone else imagines the nation. Although individuals may select from among the definitions available to them and sometimes even recombine them in novel ways,[5] elites play a much stronger role in defining the available meanings of nationalism and in managing the coordination around particular definitions of the nationalist project.

The evolution of nationalism applies to each of the three cardinal questions that nationalist projects need to answer—including how to define the national "we." Variation on the question of who should be counted as part of the nation exists because drawing the line between insiders and outsiders is not always obvious. Sometimes this is the case because individuals are potentially members of more than one nation. In such contexts, nationalist projects must convince individuals to see themselves as belonging to one nation rather than to the alternatives. For example, in Czechoslovakia in the early twentieth century, competing German, Czech, and Jewish nationalist movements openly lobbied to "persuade individuals of their so-called true nationality much as they would in an election campaign."[6] In the waning days of the Austro-Hungarian Empire there were so many disagreements about the national membership of individuals that the Imperial Court of Justice ruled that official determinations of nationality took precedence over individuals' self-declared nationality.[7] In other contexts, nationalist movements fought to categorize children as members of a particular nation, even against the parents' insistence that they belonged to another.[8]

Variation can also be driven by disagreements about the criteria that should be used to distinguish insiders from outsiders. In some contexts (such as those noted earlier), the debate was over which nominal identity category—often language or religion—ought to be the one that is activated.[9] In other contexts, the lines of debate are between those who argue for the use of a particular identity criterion—for example, race in the United States or religion in India—and those who promote a civic membership rule that includes everyone within a given territory.[10]

The existence of movements articulating different answers to the key nationalist questions allows for the occurrence of at least two kinds of evolutionary transformation. In the first kind, a nationalism is transformed when one nationalist movement wins the domestic battle for hegemony and is thus able to set the tone for the nation as a whole. Here, change is the product of a particular bundle of answers (aka a particular nationalist ideology) displacing others. When a movement with a particular nationalist ideology has control of a state, it can use the state apparatus—including the educational system, the military, domestic political economy, and the census, among other components—to "homogenize" the population by eliminating movements articulating alternative bundles of answers and by incentivizing individuals to switch their allegiance from one such movement to another.[11]

A second kind of transformation stems from the process of domestic political competition itself, rather than from its outcome. Domestic political competition can induce modulations to the answers that nationalist movements give to the three key nationalist questions when doing so is politically advantageous in the short term. For example, political movements may reframe the community's membership boundaries or modulate the presentation of their goals to appeal to a needed constituency or to enable cooperation with a rival with which they otherwise disagree. When politically successful, the political returns generated by such modulations increase the costs of abandoning them. This dynamic essentially traps these movements into promoting what was initially understood as a temporary, even insincere, modulation as the new ideological orthodoxy.[12]

The incentives that individuals have for identification with particular political projects shape both kinds of nationalist transformation. Individuals can shift their allegiance from one bundle of nationalist answers to another in response to the perceived costs and benefits—for example, in terms of economic opportunity or its limitation, increased or decreased status, or more or less security—of doing so.[13] When enough individuals shift their allegiance, the newly activated identity or goal can cascade to become the dominant one in their society.[14] Sometimes, these changes are assumed to take place over generations, if only because children born in new contexts may have a different repertoire of available identities than their parents.[15] However, such changes can also occur much more rapidly.[16]

The possibility of change in the meaning of nationalism illuminates the kinds of transformations that would be needed for a peaceful and equitable one state reality to emerge. In short, for this to happen, Palestinian, Israeli, or both nationalisms would have to change their conception of who is part of the political community or of what would count as fulfilling their national aspirations. Such changes would be so fundamental that is useful to think of them as forms of "denationalization."

Building on Benedict Anderson's canonical definition of nations as "imagined political communit[ies] . . . [that are] imagined as both inherently limited and sovereign,"[17] I suggested elsewhere that such denationalization can take three forms: (1) substitution of the current criteria used to determine national membership with the membership criteria of another new or previously existing nation; (2) replacement of a political community that is imagined as inherently limited with one that is either imagined as universal or concrete and limited; or (3) downshifting the collective aspiration from total control over a group's political destiny (sovereignty) to partial forms of such control.[18] For a one state reality to lead to peaceful coexistence, one or both of the nationalist projects involved would need to denationalize in at least one of these ways.

The first form of denationalization changes the criteria used to decide national membership by substituting a new criterion for the prior one. Denationalization by substitution is an integral component of both the assimilationist projects undertaken by nationalizing states and the separatist projects of secessionist movements.[19] The former projects seek to substitute the membership criteria of the assimilating nation for those of the assimilated; the latter seek to substitute the membership criterion of the nation seeking independence for that of the nation from which they seek to separate. One way in which a one state reality could conceivably produce peaceful coexistence is through the substitution of a single, common, national identity for the currently distinct Israeli and Palestinian identities.

Whereas denationalization by substitution focuses on activating other nominal national identities in an individual's repertoire of possible identities, the second form of denationalization—denationalization by replacement—focuses on making non-national identities the politically relevant ones. These non-national alternatives can include universal ones, based on, for example, religion or notions of a "global citizenship," or concrete identities such as one's locality.[20] Both Israeli and Palestinian societies contain political projects promoting denationalization by replacement. These projects often advocate replacing national identities with non-national religious ones. Radicals in both Israeli and Palestinian societies also often assume that the other group would denationalize by replacement in a one state reality that they would control. These predictions are embedded in the frequently made promises to "permit" Palestinians or Jews, depending on who is making the argument, to live in peace so long as they organize their identity along religious or local, rather than national, lines. Ironically, a similar assumption is made by those, usually on the other side of the political spectrum, who assume that the salience of national identification will decline, thereby solving the root cause of the conflict.

The third form of denationalization (by downshifting) involves changing how the aspiration to control the nation's political destiny is enacted. In an extreme form of denationalization by downshifting, a group stops mobilizing for any collective control of its political destiny, effectively transforming itself into a "mere" ethnic group.[21] In a more moderate (and likely) form, groups downshift their goal from independent sovereignty to autonomy within a state controlled by a different national group. This form of denationalization is considerably more relevant for nations that do not yet have sovereignty, although in principle it could also apply to sovereign nations. The successful emergence of a single state in the area of Mandatory Palestine based on some consociational power-sharing arrangement between Jews and Palestinians requires that at least one, if not both, of the nationalist movements in the Israeli–Palestinian space downshift their aspirations in this way.

Change and Stability in Definitions of National Membership

The histories of Zionism and Palestinian nationalism suggest that these kinds of denationalization are possible because some version of them has already occurred in the past, even on the question of how to define the nation's membership boundaries. This section briefly illustrates the balance of change and stability on this critical issue. Both Zionism and Palestinian nationalism have been characterized by strikingly parallel internal disagreements over whether to distinguish between co-ethnics in Mandatory Palestine and those outside it, and between advocates of ethnic (specifically, religious) or of civic membership criteria. In the Zionist context the first disagreement was over whether diaspora Jews were equally part of the nation, whereas Palestinian nationalism contended with the extent to which the Palestinian nation was distinct from the Arab one. On the second axis of disagreement, although relatively civic ways of conceptualizing national membership emerged in both Zionism and Palestinian nationalism, ethnic definitions of national membership continue to dominate.

The process and limits of those transformations highlight the role of intragroup politics and evolutionary processes in driving change, which, in turn, have two critical but conflicting implications for a one state reality. First, the kinds of fundamental transformations in the meaning of nationhood that are required for denationalization *can* occur even for Zionism and Palestinian nationalism. Second, such transformations depend on the outcome of future internal political struggles, which, at least at present, the denationalization projects among Israelis and Palestinians are poorly positioned to win. Denationalization, in other words, although possible, will not be the automatic consequence of a one state context.

Localizing the Nation in Zionism and Palestinian Nationalism

All Zionist movements initially conceived of the nation as including all Jews, regardless of where they lived. This principle was reflected in, among other things, the prominence given to "ingathering the exiles" as the paramount nationalist mission and the concomitant negation of diasporic existence. However, starting in the early 1940s, one Zionist political movement, the central stream of the Labor Zionist movement, began to see American Jews as "allies," "partners," or "friends," rather than as part of the "us" being formed by the Zionists in Palestine. By the 1960s, Jewish communities outside Israel were recategorized from existing in purgatory to being viable and legitimate entities. Jews in the dispersion (a phrase that increasingly replaced "exile") were still potential members of the political community, but they would not become actual members of the collective unless they made the individual decision to physically join the community in Israel.[22]

The relegation of diaspora Jews in the Labor Zionist movement's thinking was driven by their need to secure the support of American, including non-Zionist, Jews for the nationalist project. In the process of securing this support, Labor Zionist leaders modulated their definition of the boundaries of national membership to accommodate two demands made by organized American Jewry: (1) that their continued existence in the Diaspora be recognized as legitimate and (2) that they be excluded from the scope of automatic membership in the Jewish state so as to avoid accusations of dual loyalty. This modulation was reflected in the rhetorical distinction between "exile," which continued to refer to Jews in the Displaced Persons camps in Europe, behind the Iron Curtain, and in the Arab states, and "dispersion," which was applied to Western, especially American, Jews. Jews in "exile" were seen as automatically and appropriately part of the nation, whereas Jews in the "dispersion" could become part of the nation if they decided to do so as individuals.[23]

The mutually beneficial nature of this modulation fostered its institutionalization as the new ideological standard within the Labor Zionist movement. It enabled non-Zionist American Jews to fend off the threat Israel posed to their American identity, and the mainstream of the Labor Zionist movement to secure the material and political resources it needed to establish the state of Israel, entrench its defenses, and undertake the ingathering of the Jewish communities that were still considered to be in exile. These successes, in turn, enabled the Labor Zionist movement to dominate Israeli politics for almost thirty years after the establishment of the state. These positive returns also made abandoning the (new) way of delimiting the national boundaries costly, even long after the initial reason for the modulation was no longer relevant.[24] In fact, the heirs of the Labor Zionist movement continue to speak of the "dispersion" rather than exile today.[25]

Several factors suggest that this transformation occurred because of the evolutionary pressure exerted by domestic political success, rather than by other potential mechanisms, such as generational change or acceptance of a new reality. First, it was undertaken by the traditional leadership of the movement rather than by a new cohort. Second, it began before any of the significant changes to reality, such as the Holocaust or the establishment of the State of Israel, occurred, though these realities reinforced the change that was already underway. Finally, the Labor movement was the only main Zionist movement to change on this dimension. Despite experiencing the same reality, the right-wing Revisionist Zionist movement and the Religious Zionist movement, for example, persisted in articulating a vision of national membership that automatically included all Jews, regardless of where they lived. The absence of change in the ideology of these other movements reinforces the lesson that even if a new political context, like the creation of the State of Israel, might reinforce the prospects of a particular ideological modulation, its impact is not deterministic. This is why, still in the late 2010s, the wider impact of the change that took place within the Labor movement was mixed at best. One survey found that 74 percent of Israeli Jews agree that they share a common destiny with their American coreligionists, whereas another found that only half of Israeli Jews believe that the impact of Israeli decisions on diaspora Jews should be considered when formulating policy.[26]

Palestinian nationalism also contended with a debate about whether the nation's membership boundaries included all co-ethnics or only those in Palestine. This debate raged between movements that prioritized membership in the wider Arab nation and those that emphasized the narrower, specifically Palestinian one.[27] For the Arab nationalist movement in Palestine—including the Istiqlal party in the 1930s, the Arab National Movement (ANM) in the 1950s and 1960s, and the Popular Front for the Liberation of Palestine (PFLP) in the late 1960s—Arab unity was a prerequisite for the defense (and later, liberation) of Palestine, but Palestinians were not a distinct people separate from the Arab nation. Instead, all Arabs comprised a single nation, even if they were temporarily divided into separate states.[28] For Palestinian nationalists, in contrast, the unique Palestinian experience distinguished Palestinians from other Arabs. As a result, they saw the defense and liberation of Palestine as paramount, even if some hoped these would contribute to a wider Arab unification as well. Even though a Palestinian-centric nationalism predated it, Fatah has been the most successful movement articulating this view. Emerging in the late 1950s, Fatah was singularly focused on the activation of a specifically Palestinian national identity and the emphasis of Palestinian, rather than Arab, action to liberate Palestine.[29] In practical terms this meant both demonstrating that there was a distinct Palestinian nation whose desire for national self-determination needed to be acknowledged and constantly guarding against the subordination of Palestinian identity to an Arab one.

The political struggle between these ways of defining the nation's membership boundaries was critically shaped both by the way external events affected their respective political fortunes and by the need to secure popular support in Palestine itself. The separation between Syria and Palestine as a result of the Sykes-Picot Agreement, as well as the failure of Faisal's attempt to establish a state of "Greater Syria," reinforced a specifically Palestinian nationalism at the expanse of a pan-Syrian one in the 1920s because the latter became less plausible and was thus less able to garner support.[30] The pan-Arab definition of national membership, however, experienced a resurgence in the 1930s as the Palestinian-centric nationalist movement was severely weakened by the exile of much of its leadership in the aftermath of the 1936–1939 Revolt.[31] As a result, the Arab nationalist variant dominated organized Palestinian politics until the 1960s.[32] Subsequently, Arab nationalist movements were politically weakened by the collapse of the United Arab Republic in 1961 and the Arab defeat in 1967. These developments reinforced the appeal of the Palestine-centric approach promoted by Fatah, allowing it to rise to control the PLO in 1968 and to dominate Palestinian nationalism into the twenty-first century.[33]

The denationalization by substitution evident in the PFLP's emphasis of a specifically Palestinian identity in place of the wider Arab one illustrates the critical role both of political competition and of the unintended consequences of ideological modulations undertaken for short-term gain in shaping the balance between Palestinian and Arab nationalism. This change did not occur smoothly or in a linear reaction to the consequences of the 1967 war, as we might expect if external realities were deterministic. As Asʿad AbuKhalil noted (though in a different context), "their [Arab] nationalist convictions were too strong to be overcome by one . . . stroke."[34] In fact, the PFLP's leaders articulated both Palestinian and Arab nationalist sentiments well into the 1980s.[35]

Instead, the transformation began with the PFLP's 1969 adoption of a Marxist explanation for the failure of the Arab nationalist project.[36] According to this diagnosis, Arab unity was impossible until a successful class struggle first unseated the reactionary "Arab bourgeoisie" in every Arab state.[37] Even if the adoption of this perspective by some PFLP leaders was of questionable sincerity,[38] it nonetheless legitimated the deemphasis of the pan-Arab conception of national membership and the prioritization of a local, Palestine-centered one by localizing the class struggle within state boundaries. Over time, the need to compete with Fatah for the support of the Palestinian population itself reinforced the utility of constraining national membership to the Palestinian rather than Arab one.[39] Substituting a narrower definition of national membership for the wider one enabled the movement to better appeal to the Palestinians in Palestine (and especially in the West Bank and Gaza Strip): motivated by the desire to get out from under the occupation, this population was less receptive to subordinating the immediate Palestinian cause to long-term dreams of Arab unity.[40] In the course of this competition, the PFLP thus effectively came to define the boundaries of the nation according to "the narrow *qutri* (limited to one Arab country) borders that only the day before were considered 'the artificial creation of imperialism.'"[41]

The Persistence of Ethnic Definitions of National Membership

The narrowing of the membership criterion to "local" co-ethnics in Palestinian nationalism and, to a more varied extent, in Zionism might have fostered a concomitant shift to a civic definition of national membership based on the borders of the polity each sought. Yet, despite significant incentives to do so and the potential of some modulations to foster this change, ethnically exclusive notions of national membership continue to dominate. Even though ideological modulations that were consistent with a civic definition of membership emerged, they were never politically successful enough to become institutionalized as the new ideological status quo.

In Israel, the main Zionist movements all articulated an ethnic definition of the nation, one that prioritized Jews and excluded the local Arab population. This ethnic definition of membership persisted despite tremendous pressure by the international community, political incentives for inclusion, and the desire to reconcile the tension between this exclusion and the state's democratic self-image.[42]

These pressures, however, did lead to some modulations in the conceptualization of the nation that, had they generated meaningful domestic political returns, might have transformed an ethnic definition of national membership to a civic one. For example, starting in the 1920s, the Labor movement argued that the polity it sought would belong to "the Hebrew nation and . . . the Arabs who reside in it," implying the possibility of full and equal membership.[43] Likewise, the Zionist Left embodied in the Meretz Party and the heirs of the liberal tradition in the Likud, like Reuven Rivlin, Israel's former president and long-time Likud politician, have consistently argued for the civic equality of Jews and Arabs in Israel.[44]

These potential openings for a civic conceptualization of national membership never displaced ethnic ones, either within the movements in which they were articulated or in the body politic writ large, because they never produced significant positive domestic political returns. These modulations were never embedded in any institutions or alliances whose success could generate the returns that would have reinforced their appeal and incentivized actions consistent with them. In other words, there was little at stake in the domestic political game that could reinforce and promote the articulation of a civic notion of membership at the expense of an ethnic one. As a result, advocates of civic notions of membership consistently lost the political struggle, both in the competition between parties and in the internal debates within parties. In a sobering lesson for the future, the reality of the nationalist conflict played a key role in their weakness because it fostered the construction of intergroup relations in zero-sum terms and made it difficult for civic notions of membership to gain traction.

Moreover, in both the Zionist Left and the Zionist Right, the consistent losses in the intra-movement political battle led advocates of civic notions of national membership to cede the fight to advocates of ethnic notions of membership. On the Left, enticed by Israel's low electoral threshold, these advocates often formed their own splinter parties rather than fight within the main parties. These efforts, however, proved largely unsuccessful, because they were ultimately unable to gain either significant popular support or to build meaningful coalitions across ethnic lines.[45] On the Israeli Right, advocates of civic notions of membership were historically sidelined. This was recently evident, for example, when Benny Begin, the veteran Likud member and son of the party's founder, was forced out over his opposition to the 2018 Nation-State Law that institutionalized an ethnic notion of national membership in Israel.

Paradoxically, the terms with which Zionist advocates of the two state solution supported their arguments also reinforced the exclusion of Palestinians from the scope of the Israeli nation. These advocates, ranging from traditional Labor Zionists like Shimon Peres and Yitzhak Rabin to former right-wing Revisionist Zionists like Tzipi Livni and Ehud Olmert, justified their acceptance of partition in terms of maintaining the ethnic conception of national membership. A two state solution, they repeatedly argued, was necessary to maintain a demographic Jewish majority in Israel. The use of this rationale—that withdrawing from the territories was needed to preserve the fundamental Zionist goal of a Jewish majority—made it difficult to simultaneously integrate citizen Palestinians as appropriately part of the Israeli nation. This helps explain the apparent paradox that the increasing willingness to disengage from the territories and to countenance the emergence of a Palestinian state was not correlated with a concomitant acceptance of citizen Palestinians as appropriately part of the Israeli nation.

In Palestinian nationalism, the debate between civic and ethnic notions of national membership largely revolves about the extent to which Islam is a marker of national membership and therefore whether Christians and Jews can be fully Palestinian. As in the Zionist context, over time, ideological modulations potentially consistent with civic notions of membership emerged in the pattern of articulations of some of the main Palestinian nationalist movements. Yet, here too, these potentialities were not actualized because the advocates of these perspectives remained politically weak. This weakness was driven by the growing competition between secular forms of Palestinian nationalism and religious ones and by the framing of a two state solution as the alternative to a secular democratic state.

Perhaps the most important modulation in the discourse around national membership in the Palestinian arena has been the retreat from the explicit exclusion of Jews. Although some distinguished between Jews and Zionists, all the organized Palestinian groups, apart from the Communists, initially had, in Yezid Sayigh's words, "little room for the Jews" in their vision of the Palestine they sought to create.[46] Since their emergence, however, the main strains of Palestinian nationalism have modulated their rhetoric in ways that are more consistent with civic notions of membership, although at different times, to varying degrees, and with varying levels of institutionalization. This variation, importantly, also suggests that these changes were not the product of an automatic reaction to any new reality.

Among Palestinian religious nationalists, there have been at least two, limited, modulations on this score. First, like other Palestinian nationalists, Hamas has shifted, at least in some of its pronouncements, from framing the nationalist conflict as against Jews qua Jews to it being against Zionism.[47] In this vein, Hamas spokesmen now frequently appeal to the history of religious tolerance under the Ottoman Empire as evidence for the compatibility of their vision with coexistence.[48] These modulations notwithstanding, non-coreligionists still fit uneasily into their vision of the nation.[49] The religious sanctity they imbue in the land means that, even if non-Muslims may have a right to live there, they do not have the right to rule over Muslims and thus face intrinsic limits on the extent of their inclusion.[50] In fact, the appeal to the Ottoman experience to highlight their tolerance paradoxically reinforces the exclusion of Jews and Christians from national membership, given that the Ottoman system institutionalized the lower status of (monotheistic) religious minorities by requiring them to pay for internal religious autonomy with political quiescence and additional taxes.

Nonetheless, even this limited modulation was the result of Hamas's struggle for domestic and international legitimacy and for breaking out of the isolation imposed on it in the Gaza Strip, rather than an inevitable consequence of some objective reality.[51] Its ability to continue to spread within the movement depends, therefore, on Hamas's ability to secure the political returns that triggered the modulation. At least to date, their inability to do so has inhibited the spread of this view among religious Palestinian nationalists.

A second ideological modulation within Palestinian religious nationalism that might be more consistent with civic notions of national membership allows for a multisectarian order as a fundamental aspect of creation. Here, full equality is theoretically possible because religious diversity is itself seen as part of the natural order of the world. This strain, which emerged in response to the need to compete more effectively with the appeal of secular nationalism,[52] however, has yet to win the political battle within Palestinian religious nationalism or with its secular counterparts. To the extent that its advocates remain politically weak or disengaged, this ideological modulation is not likely to spread.

Secular Palestinian nationalism has also offered an ideological modulation, embodied in the notion of a "secular democratic state" that, were it to receive sufficient political returns, could theoretically enable a civic notion of Palestinian national membership to displace the dominant ethnic one. This view has, over time, become most strongly articulated by the heirs of the secular, formerly Arab-nationalist variants of Palestinian nationalism. Their secularity, as well as persisting class commitments, more easily accommodates the inclusion of individuals regardless of their private religious beliefs.[53] Although initially this openness was extended more easily to Christian Arabs than to Jews, today PFLP and Democratic Front for the Liberation of Palestine spokespersons routinely articulate visions of national membership that explicitly include Jews, Muslims, and Christians.[54] The wider impact of this shift, however, has been limited partly because its advocates also remain committed to other ideological stances, such as Marxism and, for the PFLP until relatively recently, opposition to the two state solution, that are relatively unpopular among Palestinians in Palestine. As a result, these parties, together with their potentially civic notions of national membership, remain marginal and ultimately unable to decisively shape the way in which national membership is conceptualized.[55]

Fatah too appeared to shift away from its initial exclusion of Jews and marginalization of Christians when it adopted the rhetoric of a "secular democratic state" in 1968. Even if this formulation of their goal was initially tactical, it nonetheless created the potential for a civic conception of national membership. This potential, however, was not actualized for many of the same reasons driving the political failure of civic notions of membership in the Israeli context. Despite their expectations that this framing would resonate with the international community, it was not until Fatah accepted partition in place of a single state that they received significant international recognition. Partly as a result, this modulation did not yield the political returns that might have led to its institutionalization as the ideological status quo.

Second, in this arena as well, the context of a nationalist conflict made it very difficult politically to simultaneously fight against the occupation and remain open to the full inclusion of the occupying Other. This is perhaps why all streams of Palestinian nationalism continued to condition the inclusion of even individual Jews on their rejection of Zionism.[56] The inclusion of this caveat may have been politically useful in the context of domestic Palestinian political contestation, but it made it quite difficult to build cross-national alliances that might have been able, if they had secured meaningful political returns, to foster the spread of the more inclusive notion of national membership.

The institutionalization of the potentially civic notion of national membership within Fatah was also undermined by its competition with a resurgent religious nationalism. As a result, Fatah deviated from its commitment to a nonsectarian nationalism and increasingly framed its appeal in religious, Muslim, terms.[57] Not only was this a persistent source of tension with Christian Palestinians but it also reinforced the utility of an ethnic (religious) notion of membership at the expense of a civic one.[58]

Finally, like in the Israeli case, Fatah's turn toward a two state solution also undermined the political standing of those arguing for a secular democratic state within the movement because the two were (and continue to be) presented as mutually exclusive alternatives.[59] A side effect of this framing was to make it difficult to envision the inclusion of Jews in the Palestinian state that would be the product of the two state solution. This was one reason why Fatah leaders consistently rejected proposals for a two state solution that would have kept Jewish settlers in the new Palestinian state.[60] Today, for most Fatah leaders, the ideal thus remains an ethnic Palestinian state, even if some are willing to consider a "single democratic state" if that project fails.[61]

Lessons for a One State Reality

This history, and the role of short-term political success in shaping the balance between stability and change in the conceptions of national membership, carries two, somewhat contradictory lessons for the prospects of the denationalization required for a one state reality to lead to peaceful coexistence: denationalization is possible, but it will not be automatic.

The historical experience of Zionism and Palestinian nationalism shows that the kinds of denationalization required for peaceful and equitable coexistence in a one state reality are possible because similar changes have previously occurred. If Palestinian nationalism could be substituted for Arab nationalism, and a localized (though still ethnic) definition of national membership could replace a wider one for Labor Zionists, a change to a notion of the membership boundaries of the political community that includes both Jews and Palestinians is also theoretically possible. As Ian Lustick has recently argued, a one state reality has the potential to change the character of the domestic political struggle in ways that could facilitate cross-national cooperation, reinforce positive-sum framings of group relations, and potentially create positive political returns to formulations of national membership in civic terms.[62]

However, this same history also calls for a sober assessment of the likelihood of these transformations. Just as the role of politics in driving the evolution of nationalism makes denationalization possible, it also reinforces just how difficult its actualization is likely to be. As shown earlier, although institutional and political contexts do shape the fortunes of political movements and ideological variants, their impact is not deterministic. Even if new alliances are made and ideological modulations consistent with peaceful coexistence emerge, such changes will not spread unless they are politically successful enough to generate substantial political returns or to win the domestic political fight.

If nothing else, future projects of denationalization will be starting from a position of significant political disadvantage. Fewer than 20 percent of Israeli Jews and fewer than one-third of Palestinians in the West Bank and Gaza Strip currently support one state solutions, solutions that by definition would require some form of denationalization.[63] Even this level of support may be overstated. A 2019 Palestinian Center for Policy and Survey Research (PSR) poll found, for example, that although 31 percent supported abandoning negotiations and demanding a one state solution, only 13 percent believed that a single state with equal rights for Palestinians and Jews was the best way to achieve peace (in contrast, 49% believed that a two state solution was the best way to do so).[64] Omar H. Rahman and Dahlia Scheindlin's review of public opinion on this question in chapter 12 in this volume comes to a similar conclusion. The reality that such solutions garner a relatively small following, even among the Palestinians who have comparatively more to gain from them and in a context when a two state solution is unlikely to emerge, suggests that denationalization projects have a steep hill to climb.

Although constituencies that support projects of denationalization may become large enough to reward political movements that cater to them, the contribution to this volume by Mohanad Mustafa and As'ad Ghanem (see chapter 7) highlights some of the difficulties involved in crafting a sustained coalition of these groups. In short, the deep religious, ethnic, class, and ideological divides that characterize potential supporters of denationalization projects make it less likely that proponents of denationalization will be able to appeal to all of them simultaneously. As a result, even if projects of denationalization have a constituency that is theoretically sympathetic, their political path to victory appears to be quite narrow.

A one state reality could theoretically shape this political calculus. Such a state could, for example, promote alternative visions of the nation and use the tools available to any state to, over time, denationalize the population by substituting a different nationalism for Zionism and Palestinian nationalism. Importantly, however, for all their power, states are not omnipotent in this regard. If they were, we would not have any secessionist movements. As illustrated earlier, even the Labor Zionist movement, despite its decades-long control of all state institutions including education, was unable to impose its relatively narrower vision of national membership boundaries on the Jewish Israeli population more broadly.

Moreover, to succeed, such an effort by the (one) state would need to overcome the inevitable attempts of currently mobilized nationalists to derail such a project and would require erasing the economic distinctions between Jews and Palestinians to drain (existing) nationalist mobilization of its appeal. Neither, in my view, is particularly likely.

Adherents of mobilized nationalist movements are likely to resist attempts to coerce or incentivize them into denationalization by either substitution or replacement. In part, this is the case because it would require abandoning the fundamental raison d'être of Zionism and the currently dominant Fatah-led version of Palestinian nationalism. Both are fundamentally based on the call to recognize that their people constitute a nation deserving of self-determination. The sacred value of this nationalist conception means that material incentives are unlikely to facilitate their transgression.[65] In other words, material cost-benefit calculations may be less relevant in inducing denationalization among those already committed to it than in incentivizing the uncommitted to opt for it in the first place. This could take place if, for example, advocates of denationalization are able to convince their audiences that giving up this sacred value enables the achievement of another sacred value, such as the unity of the land or democracy. To date, however, such attempts have not resonated broadly.

The persistent material inequality between Jews and Arabs in a one state reality is also likely to undermine the political plausibility of denationalization projects because it will foster the continued resonance of nationalist stories linking this inequality to national difference. Any project of denationalization by substitution or replacement would depend on the extent to which individuals are fully accepted in the new arrangement.[66] Continued blocked opportunities for mobility and the persistence of systematic economic differences between groups are likely to inhibit denationalization by making it easier for advocates of nationalist political projects to argue that continued injustice is linked to nationality and that, to improve their lives, the group requires gaining or maintaining control of its political destiny. In other words, for denationalization to succeed, it must limit the ability of the currently dominant nationalist projects to provide a reasonable and resonant explanation of lived reality. This is likely to be a significant challenge in any single state reality that aspires to overcome the conflict between Israelis and Palestinians.

Denationalization by replacement does not seem any more likely. Indeed, the failure of such projects to date underscores the power of the existing nationalist projects. Among Palestinians, the emergence of Hamas in the late 1980s reflected the subordination of a non-national religious identity to Palestinian nationalism, rather than the victory of a non-national identity. Non-nationalist Islamists do exist, but where they are politically quiescent, they are, by definition, less inclined to engage in the political struggle that would be needed for this perspective to spread at the expense of the nationalist alternatives. Those who are politically active, including in the projects promoted by al-Qaeda and the Islamic state, have garnered only negligible support among Palestinians. Among Jews, even the haredim, once fiercely antinationalist and insulated from mainstream Israeli society, are increasingly adopting a nationalist perspective. Indeed, about half of the Israeli Jews who self-identify as haredi also identify as Zionist.[67]

In this context, the inclusion of the United Arab List in the governing coalition formed after the 2021 elections is a potentially significant development. Although Arab political parties have been part of Israel's parliament since its establishment, this is the first time that one of these parties has been included in the government. To the extent that the inclusion of the United Arab List yields tangible political and material benefits both for its constituency and for the Jewish parties allied with it, such an alliance could foster the institutionalization of a civic identity in Israel. At the same time, it is not an accident that the first Arab political party formally included in an Israeli government is an Islamist rather than a nationalist one. Indeed, the leader of the United Arab List is quite comfortable with advocating a denationalization by replacement and envisioning a future where religious identity is more relevant than national identity.[68] As a result, the success of this alliance could also be consistent with a vision of a one state reality in which Jews dominate and Palestinians are included to the extent that they reorganize their identity along religious rather than primarily national lines. Time will tell.

Denationalization by downshifting seems somewhat more likely, though it too faces significant hurdles. There are important historical examples of nationalist movements that have experienced such downshifting, including the Quebecois in the 1980s, the Catalan national movement under Franco, and the Sikhs in India, to name a few.[69] Zionist history also contains a legacy of framing the operationalization of control over political destiny in terms other than full sovereignty.[70] In this volume in chapter 6, moreover, Nathan J. Brown and Iman

Elbanna suggest that such downshifting—a move toward claiming collective rights, rather than independence—may be occurring among the Palestinians.

Yet, comparative research suggests that denationalization by downshifting is not common. Only around 20 percent of movements for national self-determination that seek independence subsequently downshift to seek autonomy.[71] In a non-negligible proportion of these cases, moreover, such downshifting was only of limited duration (as in, for example, the Catalan experience). Importantly, although successful denationalization by downshifting may enable the peaceful cohabitation of nations in a single state, it simultaneously reduces the likelihood of denationalization by substitution. This is the case because power sharing itself reinforces the benefits of identifying as part of a group that shares power and therefore inhibits the elision of meaningful differences among the groups.[72] Moreover, to the extent that, for Israelis, denationalization by downshifting necessarily means the loss of some autonomy, we can expect the prospect of such a loss to lead to significant resistance.[73]

In sum, a one state reality may shift the political landscape in such a way that strengthens the political prospects of the denationalization projects required for the peaceful coexistence of Jews and Palestinians in a single state. However, the very character of the one state reality that is emerging contains elements that are likely to reinforce the purchase of existing nationalist projects (including political and economic inequality and entrenched benefits from the status quo). Given that the prospects of denationalization are linked to the outcome of the domestic political fight between nationalist and denationalization projects, and nationalist projects are starting from a clearly dominant political position, it is not at all clear that the painful conflict that will take place in a single state reality will yield a better outcome than territorial surgery. At the end of the day, both partition and continued conflict appear to be more likely alternatives than a peaceful and equitable one state reality.

10

ARAB AND AMERICAN DIMENSIONS OF THE ISRAEL/PALESTINE ISSUE

State Policies and Public Views on One State, Two States, and Beyond

Shibley Telhami

The international context of Israel/Palestine cannot be understood without two central elements: Arab and American attitudes. The first is central because, international law and norms aside, interest-based global policies have assumed that Palestine has been central to Arab publics, if not to their governments. This presumed importance inclines states with interest in the region to fear that certain thresholds cannot be crossed without jeopardizing their interests in the Arab world. The second, the American role, is central not only because United States has been the principal global power since the end of the Cold War but more so because it has also been Israel's principal enabler by providing Israel with a technological military edge over any combination of Arabs and by shielding Israel at the United Nations and other international organizations. But are these two central international elements shifting in their view of the current reality on Israel/Palestine, their advocacy of a two state solution to the conflict, and their openness to a one state outcome? How would a shift in their view of reality to that of a one state alter public and ruling elites' positions?

Analyses and public opinion polls indicate bigger shifts in American public opinion than in Arab public opinion on likely and preferred outcomes in Israel/Palestine, as well as smaller shifts in Arab and American ruling elites' positions, because any shift in policy from two state frameworks forces choices that most do not want to make.

The Arab Dimension

At Israel's inception, the conflict with the new state was an Arab-Israeli, more than a Palestinian-Israeli, conflict even as Palestinians paid the heaviest price. For decades after 1948, the liberation of Palestine was invoked as a central Arab cause, especially during the era when the Arab national movement was led by Egypt's Gamal Abdel Nasser. Certainly, the strategic importance of Palestine in the Arab world decreased with the decline of Arabism, the signing of the Egypt-Israel peace treaty in 1979, and the end of the Cold War between the United States and the Soviet Union. Yet, even after these transformative events, Palestine continued to be central in direct and indirect ways.

It was not that Palestine was ever genuinely the driving issue for Arab governments; rather, it was deemed central to Arab publics and even to Arab identities, and that encouraged Palestine to be invoked and used by rulers, often for competing ends. As I pointed out years ago, Arab rulers behaved *as though* Palestine was important to their publics, whatever their real priorities were. And despite much tumult in the region in the ensuing decades that was unrelated to Palestine—the Iran-Iraq War, the 1991 Gulf War, and the 2003 invasion of Iraq, for example—there was reason, bolstered by public opinion polls, to term the Palestinian issue as the "prism of pain" through which many Arabs saw the world.[1]

But much has happened since. The twin earthquakes of the 2003 Iraq War and the Arab uprisings that began in 2010 profoundly affected the calculus of Arab rulers and Arab publics in a manner that was bound to affect the salience of the Palestinian issue in regional politics.

The core impact of these events has been on the Arab regimes' sense of security and on how they see events beyond their borders affecting this security. Take, for example, Saudi Arabia, which, in addition to facing the impact of these weighty external events, awakened to the fact that its citizens had the lowest identification with the state of any in the Arab world, defining themselves instead mostly as Muslims or Arabs and thus being highly sensitive to Arab and Muslim events outside their own boundaries.[2] Much of the recent discourse has focused on the personality of Crown Prince Mohammed bin Salman to explain what seem to be extraordinary changes in Saudi foreign policy. But the connection between these changes, the Iraq War, and the Arab uprisings is often missed.

For decades, Saudi foreign policy had two central security features in the Gulf region and domestically: relying on the United States and maintaining a balance of power between Iraq and Iran to assure that neither could pose a threat to Saudi security and interests in the region. That environment allowed Saudi Arabia to avoid being directly dragged into conflict and to use its economic and political assets to influence events as needed. Before the Islamic revolution in Iran, Saudi Arabia had an amicable relationship with the Shah's Iran, because it balanced a radical Iraq. After the rise of Ayatollah Khomeini, Riyadh backed Saddam Hussein's war against Tehran, fearing the expanding influence of revolutionary Islamist Iran. When Iraq invaded Kuwait in 1990, the Saudis relied on the United States to reverse Iraq's invasion. But following that war, Saudi animosity toward Saddam Hussein did not reverse Riyadh's strong preference for maintaining Iraq as a balancer to Iran. And even though groups like al-Qaeda—which had some roots in Saudi Arabia—still posed threats, the broader regional environment assured that most of its bases were in Afghanistan, far away from the Saudi neighborhood.

The 2003 Iraq War had three predictable consequences. It created so much instability that al-Qaeda and later ISIS could thrive right next door, first in Iraq and later in Syria and Yemen, which posed greater threats to the Saudi homeland. Second, the war ended any prospect of Iraq serving as a balancer of Iran just as Iranian power was on the rise. Third, the extraordinary costs of the failed Iraq War, both in blood and treasure, led to an antiwar sentiment in the United States that undermined Saudi confidence in the US willingness and ability to intervene effectively if and when the Saudis felt it was needed. These events generated significant insecurity within and outside Saudi borders. The advent of the Arab uprisings that toppled seemingly entrenched rulers, including close Saudi allies, intensified Saudi insecurity at home and in the neighborhood, at a time when the anchors of Saudi security policy were significantly undermined by the war; this forced the Saudis into a higher degree of self-reliance than they were accustomed to or were good at.

Thus, Riyadh became far more interventionist in foreign policy, even before the rise of King Salman and his son, Crown Prince Mohammed bin Salman: engaging in attempts to influence politics in Iraq to limit the rising influence of Iran, heavily investing in Lebanon to counter Hizbullah's influence, working clandestinely and aggressively to organize and support opposition to the Bashar Assad regime in Syria—and certainly in leading a war coalition in Yemen. It was not that Saudi Arabia had failed for decades to use its economic and political influence to affect regional politics; it was that the degree to which it was doing so, including taking initiative and using enormous resources, reflected a sense of strategic urgency.

Although in different ways, one can also argue that similar, though not identical, strategic imperatives also affected oil-rich states like Qatar and the United Arab Emirates, leading them to adopt more aggressive regional policies in an attempt to control their political environments. Thus, both were actively involved in Syria, Libya, Yemen, and beyond. The net result was that these strategic imperatives in and of themselves reduced the centrality of the Israeli-Palestinian conflict to key Arab states.

The changed strategic calculus, especially among Gulf Arab states, inclined them to coordinate relations with Israel, regardless of the absence of any progress toward the two state solution that they have continued to advocate officially, and even as their constituents increasingly discounted its prospects. Although these governments' actions suggested resignation to the improbability of ending the Israeli occupation in the West Bank and Gaza in the foreseeable future, their official positions of advocating such an outcome were unlikely to change, given their inability to formulate a realist alternative. The question is whether their policies and efforts to influence Arab public opinion have worked.

Arab Public Opinion

Over years of public opinion polling, Arab attitudes toward the Arab-Israeli conflict have remained consistent, even after the Arab uprisings. Generally, a two-thirds majority of Arabs in the six countries polled—Egypt, Saudi Arabia, Jordan, Morocco, the United Arab Emirates, and Lebanon—supported the two state solution.[3] The problem is that most Arabs have come to believe that such an outcome will never happen.[4] What has kept the two state solution alive is that Arabs could not imagine a realistic alternative. When asked what the outcome for the Middle East would be if the prospects for a two state solution collapse, most predicted sustained conflict for years to come. Nor did the public in the Arab world see any serious prospects of a one state solution, in which Arabs and Jews would live as equals in the same territory.[5]

The question remains whether the actions of Arab states in the past few years—including the Abraham Accords between Israel and the UAE, Bahrain, Morocco, and Sudan—to lower the centrality of the Palestinian issue have affected public views, including receptivity to the existing reality, even if seen as that of one state with severe inequality. Analysis and public opinion polls in recent years suggest little change beyond the lowering of the Palestinian issue in Arab public priorities.

Even without any attempt by Arab regimes to affect Arab public opinion on Palestine, there were objective reasons to conclude that the issue had declined in Arab public priorities. The Iraq War and the Arab uprisings combined to create pressing priorities for most Arabs—many of whom had to be concerned about daily existence—regardless of their views on the Israeli-Palestinian conflict. And with the lack of active visible conflict—except for brief Gaza wars—the urgency to resolve the issue was not evident. The very existence of the Palestinian Authority (PA) after Oslo and the pretense of semi-statehood also undermined any message of urgency. The unpopularity of the PA and the deep division between Fatah and Hamas made it even harder for potential supporters of the Palestinian issue to determine what and whom exactly to support.

Except for this decline of Palestine in Arab public priorities, there is little evidence that principled Arab public support for the Palestinians in their conflict with Israel has lessened. Have active attempts by Arab regimes to affect public sentiment affected the direction of Arab public sentiments on Israel/Palestine, decreasing their support for Palestinians and increasing their openness to Israel?

Palestine and Arab Regimes' Reponses to the Arab Uprisings and the Abraham Accords

The information revolution—both satellite television and the internet—were key mobilization weapons used against Arab governments and took them by surprise, leading up to and during the Arab uprisings. Understanding this reality, some Arab rulers, especially those in Egypt, Saudi Arabia, and the UAE, coordinated efforts to counter the information revolution, using their resource advantages and the very same information tools to their benefit. Arab governments took steps to control the content of websites and social media.[6] They used Israeli technology to spy on their opponents, including hacking the phones of Al Jazeera journalists, and murdered Saudi journalist Jamal Khashoggi.[7] They assembled armies of trolls on social media to create a sense that their agenda was popular and to harass those with different views.[8] Rulers in Saudi Arabia, the UAE, and Egypt saw Al Jazeera television as the biggest threat to the picture they were trying to portray, and confronting it became one of the thirteen key demands they made of Qatar as they boycotted the emirate.[9]

The Palestinian issue was increasingly seen as an oppositional issue: it negatively affected their cooperative relationship with Israel, and it also played into the hands of the Islamist and Arab nationalist groups they sought to confront.[10] Although, in the past, Arab governments confronted opposition groups advocating for Palestine by portraying themselves as the true champions of the cause, this time around there were efforts to downplay the importance of Palestine or even to attack Palestinian leaders and others, and, in some cases, even the cause itself.[11] They broadcast television shows during Ramadan 2020 that were more sympathetic to Israel and less sympathetic to the Palestinians, as well as interviews, such as one with Prince Bandar of Saudi Arabia attacking Palestinian leaders and providing uncomplimentary historical narratives.[12]

The peace agreements between Israel and the UAE and Bahrain were unprecedented in the way in which they bypassed the Palestinians, breaking with the 2002 Arab Peace Initiative.[13] Egypt was the first Arab state to make peace with Israel, going against not only the Palestinians but also against the collective Arab position, yet it had compelling national interests to do so: regaining the Sinai peninsula that Israel had occupied since 1967 and ending the state of war that has been devastating the country, which had already fought four large-scale wars with Israel. The second Arab state to make peace with Israel, Jordan, did so with the approval of the Palestinians and only after the latter signed their own Oslo Accords with Israel; there was also a benefit to both the Palestinians and Jordan in that the deal weakened Israeli far-right advocates of the idea that "Jordan is Palestine." In the case of the UAE, there were no compelling bilateral benefits, especially because it had been openly coordinating and cooperating with Israel, including on Iran, even without a formal agreement: this is why it is reasonable to see its peace deal with Israel as a sign of the diminishing weight of the Palestinian cause in the calculus of Arab rulers.

Since the 2020 Abraham Accords, the war of narratives against the Palestinians has expanded, especially after Palestinian leaders harshly criticized these agreements. For example, the UAE cut back support for UNRWA, drastically decreasing its allocation from $51 million in 2019 to $1 million in 2020; criticized Palestinians directly by demanding apologies from Palestinian leaders for criticizing the normalization deal, developed trade relations with Israeli settlers in the West Bank through an import deal with Tura Winery in the Rehelim settlement, and hosted a delegation of Israeli settlers in November 2020.[14]

Given these developments, two questions arise. First, have the efforts of Arab rulers to write a new narrative on Israel/Palestine swayed Arab public opinion? Second, to what extent were Arab rulers' attitudes driven by the Trump administration, which made the pursuit of an agenda in harmony with the Israeli Right a surprising priority, on which it expended unprecedented resources and leverage, thereby making this agenda central in the bilateral relationships with key Arab states?

The verdict is still out on the effects of the Abraham Accords and efforts by key Arab states to affect Arab public opinion on the Israeli-Palestinian conflict. Polls conducted so far have not been conclusive. Surveys by the Doha-based Arab Center found little change in Arab public attitudes on the issue of Palestine and continued opposition to normalization with Israel until a final settlement between Israel and the Palestinians is reached.[15] A poll for the Arab American Institute conducted by Zogby Analytics showed increased Arab public openness to normalization with Israel, but concluded it is seen by the public as a possible means to advance the Palestinian cause, not hurt it.[16]

In the two states that signed peace treaties with Israel decades ago—Egypt and Jordan—there has been little evident shift in public attitudes toward Israel/Palestine, despite the interests of their governments in increasing normalization with Israel. Egyptians continue to display opposition to normalization with Israel, reflected in the public discourse and the positions of civil society organizations, as well as in the low number of public visits—which are sometimes accompanied by public shaming.[17] These public attitudes have withstood not only warm strategic and official cooperation between the Egyptian and Israeli governments but also attempts by the Egyptian government to directly affect the public and media discourse.[18]

The American Dimension

For years, American public opinion polls showed solid support for a two state outcome in Israel/Palestine, bolstered by bipartisan support by American political elites ever since President George W. Bush expressed his backing for it after the 9/11 attacks. But a shift started to take place during the Trump years: about as many Americans wanted US diplomacy to push for a one state outcome with equality as a two state outcome. Much of this change seemed to be linked to Trump's own position early during his administration in which he suggested exploring alternatives to two states. But the pushback against a one state solution was strong across the American political spectrum, even among Trump allies such as Senator Lindsey Graham. As a result, the Trump Middle East plan ultimately reverted to recommending a two state solution, although one in which the proposed Palestinian entity lacked any attributes of sovereignty.[19]

When Joe Biden began his presidency in January 2021, he returned the American position to strong advocacy for two sovereign states, bolstered by widespread support for this option among the Democratic political elites. But shifts among Democratic progressives, as well as reports by human rights organizations, especially Human Rights Watch, describing the current situation in Israel/Palestine as one that fit the legal definition of apartheid, began to raise some doubts among some mainstream Democrats.[20] In an October 2021 confirmation hearing for the proposed US ambassador to Israel, Thomas Nides, Democratic senator Tim Kaine of Virginia questioned the Biden administration's focus on two states, noting its diminishing prospects.[21] In general, however, Democratic political elites remain officially committed to two states for reasons that become clear by analyzing shifting American public attitudes in Israel/Palestine.

What Has Changed and What Has Not

In recent decades, Israel has played an important role in American politics, bordering on being a domestic issue, as noted by Obama's deputy national security adviser Ben Rhodes.[22] But rarely, at least since the end of the Soviet-American Cold War, was Israel as high a priority for the White House as it was in the Trump era. The Trump administration elevated Israel to unprecedented levels of importance in US foreign policy priorities, despite the absence of an immediate crisis or compelling strategic interest.

The American strategic focus on the Israeli-Arab conflict broadly began after the 1973 war and the subsequent Arab oil embargo during the Cold War. These events led the United States to conclude that the only way to reconcile American support for Israel with important strategic interests in the Arab world was to solve the Arab-Israeli conflict. Yet, the 1979 Egypt-Israel peace agreement, the end of the Cold War, and the declining importance of regional energy to the United States combined to substantially reduce the American strategic urge to act.

In fact, ever since the Clinton administration, which focused on domestic priorities after the end of the Cold War and the 1991 Gulf War, attention given to the Israeli-Palestinian issue has been primarily a function of the bilateral US-Israeli relationship, as sometimes heightened by external events like 9/11 and the 2003 Iraq War. As noted in *The Peace Puzzle*, Clinton focused on this issue largely in response to the urging of the Israeli government, which he saw as an extension of domestic American politics; in fact, domestic politics drove many of his critical decisions as he attempted to mediate between Israel and the Palestinians.[23] In the end, the fact that the Israeli-Palestinian issue was not a top strategic priority for his or any of the successive administrations before Trump was one reason for their failure to effectively mediate the conflict.[24] The elevation of the Israeli-Palestinian issue in the Trump administration's priorities was itself an aberration in American history, a historical accident driven by a president who delegated this issue to his Jewish son-in-law and top aide, Jared Kushner, who personally prioritized it and mobilized the president behind his efforts.[25]

The return to the usual US diplomacy on Israel/Palestine during the Biden administration was not unexpected, especially its advocacy of a two state solution, which had become the key talking point in the mainstream American discourse. But Biden's priorities and his posture of maintaining earlier policies have led to a severe asymmetry of power between Israel and the Palestinians: maintaining the Israeli regional military edge by providing Israel with top technology and shielding Israel at the United Nations and other international organizations from sanctions for possible violations of international law and UN resolutions make it impossible to see where the external leverage to achieve the two state outcome would come from.

Regardless of its prospects—as noted in the introduction to this volume, it is hard to see how repeating the same approach over and over will yield different results—the two state solution has served as a "psychological trick" that achieved two objectives for American elites. First, the idea that this outcome might be achieved enabled elites to pretend that the glaring inequalities of what now exists in Israel/Palestine is temporary, to be addressed later when a final settlement is reached. Second, the idea of two states helped resolve the conflict between the advocacy of democracy, on the one hand, and support for the Jewishness of Israel, on the other.[26] This comfort zone of the American political mainstream is unlikely to shift quickly unless there is a shift in American public attitudes. Analyses of polls in the past several years suggest some discernible changes in public opinion.

Polarization in American Attitudes

Over the past decade, there have been some important shifts in the American public's attitudes on Israel/Palestine that could influence government policymaking. In this section I address several issues that are relevant to the nature of any likely outcome—one state, two state, or the status quo—in light of developments since the Trump administration and the Abraham Accords. There are reasons to conclude that meaningful and potentially consequential shifts in American public opinion toward the Israeli-Palestinian conflict are unfolding.

The most important change over the past decade has been increased partisanship on an issue that had historically been bipartisan. In my thirty years of conducting public opinion polls on this issue, it has always been the case that a large majority of Americans, around two-thirds, did not want the United State to take either side of the Israeli-Palestinian conflict. That has not changed.[27]

What *has* changed over the past decade is that Republicans have expressed increased desire for the United States to take Israel's side instead of being neutral, with our recent polls showing a slight majority of Republicans choosing that option. In fact, in our June 2021 poll,[28] 51 percent of Republicans responded this way. In contrast, consistently, Democrats—73 percent in June 2021—supported neutrality, with those wanting the United States to take sides leaning more toward Palestinians (18%) than Israel (10%) in recent years (and among young Democrats aged 18 to 34, 35% wanted to lean toward the Palestinians compared to 9% toward Israel).

When I started observing these trends during the Obama administration, I also noted that the gap between elected Democrats and their constituents on this issue was increasing, with constituents growing more critical of Israel than politicians.[29] I address whether this gap has been sustained in the final section.

There are several issues on which polarization in American public opinion has been notable. One is support for the United States taking action against Israeli settlements in the West Bank. For the past several years, polls have consistently shown a majority of Democrats wanting to take action against Israeli settlements, including imposing sanctions, whereas Republicans and independents want to do nothing or to limit US opposition to words.[30] Another polarizing issue is the Boycott, Divestment, and Sanctions (BDS) movement aimed at Israel. Until the fall of 2019, the University of Maryland (UMD) Critical Issues Poll had not probed directly about the BDS movement, because it was not on the radar screen of most Americans. However, emerging debates in Congress and elsewhere raised the profile of the issue.

The October 2019 poll included questions probing the extent to which respondents had heard of the movement.[31] Nearly half of respondents said they have heard about BDS at least "a little." Among those respondents, almost half, including a large majority of Republicans (76%), said they opposed the movement. But the story was different among Democrats who said they had heard at least "a little" about the movement: about half said they supported the movement, whereas only 15 percent said they opposed it.[32]

Importantly, majorities of Democrats (80%), Republicans (62%), and independents (76%) indicated their opposition to laws penalizing people who boycott Israel, principally because these laws infringe the constitutional right to free speech and peaceful protest.[33] These attitudes are starkly at odds with the expressed sentiments among elected officials, including many Democrats.

One State, Two States: Israel's Democracy versus Its Jewishness

One of the notable trends, starting with the Obama administration and strengthening under Trump, has been the decrease in the number of Americans choosing a two state solution as a preferred aim of US diplomacy. In the October 2019 poll, we found that Americans are evenly divided between those who back a one state solution (33%) versus those who support a two state solution (36%) to the Israeli-Palestinian conflict.[34]

This is a significant increase in support of the one state solution, as compared with the UMD Critical Issues Poll of November 2017, which found that 41 percent of respondents supported a two state solution versus 29 percent in favor of a one state solution.[35] In the Trump administration, the two state solution came under assault from both the Left and the Right, for different reasons and to achieve different visions. It is noteworthy, however, that most of those who prefer a two state solution say that if two states were no longer possible, they would then support one state with equal citizenship.

A strong majority of Americans are more supportive of Israel's democratic aspects than its Jewishness. In March 2020, when asked whether they value preserving Israel's democracy more than its Jewishness in the event that a two state solution is not an option, 63 percent of all respondents say that they favor Israel's democracy more than its Jewishness, even if that means Israel would no longer be a politically Jewish state.[36] More than one-quarter (29%) would choose preserving the Jewishness of Israel, even if that means that Palestinians are not full citizens.

Finally, there has been a growing sense that the Israeli government has "too much influence" on US politics and policies, as my 2018 poll showed: 38 percent of all Americans (including 55% of Democrats and 44% of those under thirty-five years old) say the Israeli government has "too much influence" on the US government, compared with 9 percent who say it has "too little influence" and 48 percent who say it has "about the right level of influence."[37] When we asked this question in March 2020, we found yet another increase, to 42 percent, in the number of Americans who say that Israel has "too much influence."[38] This includes a majority of Democrats (63%), 42 percent of Independents, and 20 percent of Republicans.[39]

Do these Changes in Public Opinion Matter for US Politics and Policy?

As Jon Krosnick and I suggested in a 1995 article, the segments of the public that matter most for the electoral process and elections are those who rank the issue in question high in their priorities.[40] Over the years, I have thus probed how respondents prioritize the Arab-Israeli issue. Although a majority of Americans over the past quarter-century have favored US neutrality on this issue, those who ranked the issue among their top priorities tended to favor Israel more. Has this changed?

In a September 2019 poll, we found that, overall, 60 percent of respondents wanted the United States to take neither side in the conflict. Yet, 52 percent of those who ranked the issue among the top three issues in their priorities wanted to take Israel's side, compared to 35 percent of those who ranked the issue among the top five, and 23 percent among those who did not rank the issue among the top five.[41]

In March 2020, as criticism of Israeli policy became more pointed in the US House of Representatives after the 2018 midterm election, we added a question about respondents' views of this criticism.[42] We found that two-thirds of Americans, including 81 percent of Democrats, say that it is "acceptable" or even the "duty" of members of Congress to question the Israeli-American relationship.[43] Among those who ranked the Israeli-Palestinian issue among their top five priorities, only 64 percent said it was either "acceptable" or the "duty" of Congress to question this relationship.

In what may seem to be a counterintuitive result, among Democrats in September 2019 who ranked the Palestinian-Israeli issue as their first or among their top three priorities, a large majority (62%) still wanted the United States to be neutral in the conflict: this is lower than the 80 percent of *all* Democrats who want to take neither side. Those who ranked the Israeli Palestinian issue high on their priorities (and whose views are thus more relevant for the electoral process), were almost equally divided among those who want the US to lean toward the Palestinians and those wanting to lean toward Israel.

The bottom line is that Democrats want US evenhandedness on this issue, even among those who rank the issue high in their priorities. On specific policy issues, such as sanctions on settlements, BDS, and opposing laws prohibiting sanctions against Israel, they have strong views. Will these views matter at least in the Democratic primaries?

The Israeli-Palestinian conflict is hardly a central issue in American elections, and certainly it was not so in the 2020 presidential race, where the stakes were so high on core matters of the American political system and the future of the country. It is not likely that a significant number of people would base their votes (or financial contributions) principally on the candidate's position on this issue. But there are other ways in which public opinion on this issue matters for Democrats.

Candidates who reflect public opinion closely are more likely to energize their supporters; those who take a position that is substantially at odds with public opinion may lose credibility and appear less authentic. Among Democrats, positions on Israel-Palestine may have become part of a candidate's authenticity check, either discounting them in the public's mind or enhancing their stature. These positions likely are not based on stances toward BDS specifically but on broader issues like tying aid to Israel and its policies toward the Palestinians. Arguably, when Bernie Sanders spoke publicly in favor of Palestinian rights (as well as Israelis') during the 2016 campaign, it helped his credibility among supporters and energized his base. He followed a similar pattern during the 2020 presidential campaign, as did several other candidates.[44] As a candidate, Joe Biden chose a different path, criticizing Sanders on this issue by saying, "In terms of Bernie and others who talk about dealing with Zionism, I strongly support Israel as an independent Jewish state."[45] But even Biden, in the Democratic debate held after his criticism of Sanders, seemed to go out of his way to criticize Israeli prime minister Benjamin Netanyahu, saying, "Bibi Netanyahu and I know one another well. He knows that I think what he's doing is outrageous."[46] The outcome of the presidential primaries was hardly determined by the candidates' position on this issue, but those who embraced public sentiment stood to gain more, and those contradicting it risked having their authenticity questioned.[47]

Solidifying the mood critical of Israeli policy among Democrats was the perception of a strong alliance between the Israeli government and President Donald Trump. This was particularly visible in the Democrats' immediate critical reaction to Trump's Middle East plan.[48] As the Israeli government appeared poised to annex parts of the West Bank in harmony with Trump's plan but in clear violation of international law, pro-Israel Democrats opposed the move, and even AIPAC sent out a message that it would not lobby against those who expressed such criticism, perhaps as a preemptive move given that criticism became inevitable.[49]

Even though the outcome of the 2020 presidential election had little to do with the issue of Israel/Palestine, the nature of the conversation about Israel and US-Israeli relations has changed, most notably among Democrats, as reflected in an increasingly visible way in the 117th Congress.[50]

Key Takeaways

Shifts in Arab and American politics, including shifts in public opinion, have combined to weaken the forces pushing for a two state solution, even as that goal remained part of official policies. The Abraham Accords, which bypassed Palestinians altogether, played into the hands of the Israeli Right, which saw in them evidence that Israel can have normal relations with Arab states without withdrawing from Palestinian occupied territories. As achieving the outcome of two states became increasingly harder—given the increase in Israeli settlements in the West Bank, the asymmetry of power between Israel and the Palestinians, and diminishing Arab leverage on behalf of the Palestinians—US strategic incentives to muster the resources required to push in that direction also diminished. Despite the Biden administration's revival of the two state solution in Israel/Palestine, it was hard to see what would be the incentives to implement it. If one considers that the previous Democratic administration of Barack Obama—which came before the setbacks to the two state solutions of the Trump administration and which publicly placed more emphasis on Palestinian-Israeli peacemaking—still failed to make progress in that direction after eight years, it is very unlikely that Biden can succeed where Obama failed.

At the same time, there is growing recognition that what we are witnessing in Israel/Palestine is a one state reality with severe inequalities, if not apartheid. This may have led to the removal of the fig leaf that Israeli occupation and its glaring inequalities are temporary, thus increasing the focus on these inequities; as a result, the Israeli-Palestinian conflict was increasingly seen by Democrats (and even by young evangelicals) through the prism of social justice, highlighted by the prominence of the Black Lives Matter movement.[51] In the American arena, public passion is to be found especially among Democrats. Yet, because, in the absence of a two state solution, two-thirds of the American public, including most Republicans, prefer a democratic Israel with full equality to a Jewish state without equality of Jews and non-Jews, American political elites find it easier to stick with the framework of two states, regardless of its prospects: its abandonment would force uncomfortable political choices.

11

ISRAELI-PALESTINIAN CONFLICT RESOLUTION AND PUBLIC OPINION

Changing Realities, Shifting Perceptions

Omar H. Rahman and Dahlia Scheindlin

In the years following the Oslo process that began in 1993, the two state solution emerged as the primary approach for resolving the Israeli-Palestinian conflict. However, by 2021, the conflict appears to have reached a new level of intractability. The most recent negotiations with any realistic chance of yielding a two state agreement were held in 2008, more than a dozen years ago. There have been no formal bilateral negotiations at all since the collapse of the last US-led process in 2014.

During the intervening years, political and physical developments have effectively superseded the once paradigmatic two state solution: these dynamics may have become irreversible. As a result, the two state solution has been publicly and repeatedly eulogized by analysts, academics, and citizens alike.[1] The one state reality appears to be replacing the two state solution in practice, although public discourse is ambiguous about naming and acknowledging the changes.

What do the people of the region think? Public opinion is essential not only for assessing the range of movement for elite decision making but also matters as the voice of the people most directly affected by the outcome. As the two state solution became paradigmatic, its supporters often presumed, hoped, or worked to ensure that it had the stalwart support of the Israeli and Palestinian public. Over time, the public on both sides has shown dynamic changes with regard to the two state solution as a framework for resolution.

This chapter examines the course of Israeli and Palestinian public opinion toward the "two state solution" over time and the relevant political circumstances in the region affecting this approach. Through this examination, it seeks to assess the role of the public in supporting or undermining peace. The inquiry is predicated on the understanding that public opinion has some bearing on conflict resolution and can play a role in the success or failure of negotiations aimed at resolving conflict.[2] Public opinion is understood to have an impact on both domestic and foreign policy.[3] Some studies show that public opinion is often "ahead" of leadership: changing public attitudes therefore can precede, or perhaps lead to changed policies.[4]

Public opinion can evolve over time; on controversial or divisive policy issues such change can occur slowly or suddenly. For example, support for LGBT rights in the United States grew over the course of decades through sustained public activism and broader changing social norms.[5] This can be contrasted with Israeli attitudes toward withdrawing from the Sinai as stipulated under the peace agreement with Egypt in 1979; they changed rapidly as a direct result of a leader-driven breakthrough that yielded a dramatic peace accord.[6]

Similarly, public attitudes of Israelis and Palestinians toward the two state solution have taken the form of a dynamic arc, rather than the stable foundation of support that is often presumed retroactively. It is important to recall that the notion of a solution based on sovereign Palestinian statehood in the West Bank and Gaza Strip was only adopted by both sides at official levels during the 2000 Camp David negotiations; it was named as the vision for peace by UN Security Council in 2002, and President George W. Bush was the first American president to adopt the language for US policy, as stated in the 2003 Roadmap.[7] The PLO only formally adopted the concept of a Palestinian state limited to the 1967 occupied territories in 1988.[8]

For these reasons, we view the two state solution as a window as much as a paradigm. Many use the window metaphor to warn of its closure, often forgetting that the window only opened at a certain point in history: during the earliest years of the conflict, the two state solution—as it is understood today—did not exist. It opened decades later, but has been closing for some years, and the closure is now nearly complete. Whether the window may one day reopen in the public mind is unknown, and by that time, developments on the ground may have overtaken attitudes.

The assessment of public opinion among Israelis and Palestinians on modes of resolving the conflict therefore predates the two state solution and goes beyond its apparent expiration date. We necessarily provide analysis that goes beyond polling, because people had opinions well before systematic survey research was available on both sides. Meanwhile, alternate scenarios and possible paths forward are at a nascent stage, and polling has only partially kept up.

The limited scope of this chapter requires that we narrow the chronological focus to attitudes regarding the Israeli occupation, which began with the Six Day War in 1967. Although the conflict stretches back to the late nineteenth century, the 1967 war reshaped the political forces in Israel/Palestine and the Middle East at large: it changed international understandings and legal developments, prompted the international community to recognize Palestinians as the agents of their own destiny, and galvanized the Palestinian national movement. Therefore, the year 1967 is a logical, if limited, starting point.

The structure of this chapter is as follows. In the first section, we track documented public attitudes regarding the approach that would eventually come to be known as the two state solution, from its modern inception through to the present. To do this, we identify the various iterations of the two state concept, even in nascent forms, and seek relevant documentation of public attitudes where available. This section shows the emergence and legitimization of the idea among large sections of both publics, reaching majority support on both sides for a specific period.

In the second section, we explore current public opinion dynamics, analyzing the broad decline in support for the two state solution over the last decade, the roots and reasons for this decline, and what it means. We characterize the present as a time of "non-solutionism" and examine the factors contributing to this status among Israelis and Palestinians.

In the third and final section, we address public opinion on both sides toward alternative approaches for resolving the conflict. These range from one state to a confederation and reflect more or less democratic visions of various political camps. In the conclusion, we summarize the rise and fall of the two state solution in public opinion while observing that no clear alternative solution has yet taken its place and what the implications are for the future.

Historical Attitudes: The Arc of the Two State Solution

The availability of polling or its absence can tell a story about evolving understandings of the relationship between the Israeli and Palestinian communities. The questions asked or not asked, or other expressions of public discourse when polling was not available, showed two communities speaking two different languages at the political level. Over time, these languages began to converge around the idea of two separate states. Public opinion rose alongside the political discourse in support of such a solution, eventually reaching an auspicious phase of mutual support—and then began its decline. The most apt metaphor is that of an arc.

Palestinian public opinion surveys are not broadly available before the 1980s; among Israelis, public opinions surveys are available from the late 1940s, but the concept and language of a "two state solution" is nearly absent until decades after the 1967 war. Therefore, the data we present are not linear; rather, we draw on other contextual indicators, such as political developments and civil activity, as well as related public opinion surveys and election results, to create a composite picture of the two societies attitudes toward a political endgame.

During the first decade following the 1967 war, the evidence from each side shows significantly diverging political goals; the main common element appears to be mutual disregard for the political consciousness of the other side.

In Israel, surveys available at Data Israel from shortly after the war through the late 1970s tested numerous items related to the occupied territories but little by way of a direct comprehensive political agreement with Palestinians.[9] These questions focused largely on negotiation strategies and territorial concessions, including how much of each territory the public would be willing to concede ("some, part, all . . .") regarding each territory separately—the Gaza Strip, the West Bank, the Golan Heights, and Sinai—and whether Israel should declare a willingness to return territory as the basis for negotiations.[10] These were surveys of the Jewish public only, not inclusive of Israel's Arab citizens.

These questions indicate that Israeli discourse centered on the transactional land-for-peace concept implicit in UN Resolution 242, without considering the final political status in any areas of the West Bank or Gaza that would be "returned"; nor did the questions specify to whom the land would be returned. Indeed, Israeli Jews had barely internalized that Palestinians had a distinct national identity at all; when asked in 1969 whether the "Arabs in the territories" were a distinct people from Arabs of other Arab countries, 73 percent disagreed (Data Israel G0301).

Yet Palestinian national consciousness and political organizing were present at least as early as the start of the twentieth century and the end of World War I.[11] The Palestine Arab Congress was held seven times between 1919 and 1928, and in 1948 an All-Palestine Government and National Council were established. The Palestine Liberation Organization was formed in 1964, espousing the goal of establishing a single, democratic, and secular state in all of historic Palestine.[12] At the time of Israel's occupation of the West Bank and Gaza Strip in 1967, the Palestinian national consciousness was well developed—a discourse that either was lost on Israelis or one they actively rejected.

By the early 1980s, the Jaffee Center for Strategic Studies (now the Institute for National Security Studies; INSS), began asking Israeli Jews regularly whether they support or oppose a Palestinian state. The question did not provide information about negotiations or an agreement between Israel and Palestinians to reach this solution. Neither did it use the terminology of the "two state solution" nor give details about the terms and contours of a Palestinian state. Similarly, in 1985 Professor Sammy Smooha of the University of Haifa asked the Jewish public a

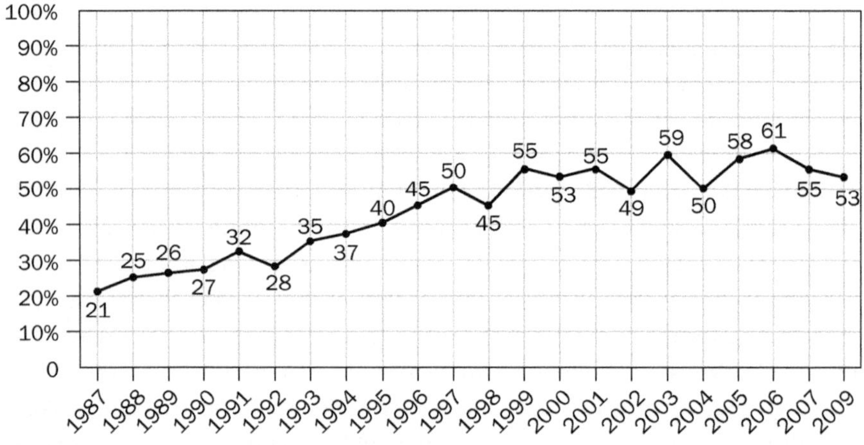

FIGURE 1. Support for the establishment of a Palestinian state, 1987–2009 (percent).

(Source: Ben Meir, Bagno-Moldavsky, 2010)

concept-only question with no detail: "Are you for or against the establishment of a Palestinian state in the West Bank and Gaza Strip alongside Israel?" (Data Israel J0009). Just 5 percent supported the idea unconditionally, and another 23 percent selected the response "under the right conditions."

The Jaffee Center/INSS surveys' tracking of a single question over time provides valuable and clear insight about the legitimization of the idea at different phases (see figure 1). The data show low support among Israeli Jews for a Palestinian state at the start of the research. The outbreak of the First Intifada in late 1987 and the PLO's declaration in 1988 of a Palestinian state in the West Bank and Gaza were likely catalysts for a modest but consistent rise in Israeli support for the two state framework. Theories about the growth in support range from the idea that Israelis gradually believed the conflict could not be controlled through military force, that the Intifada meant it was unlikely the status quo could continue, and that political solutions might be needed. Yet an overall assessment of public opinion found that attitudes did not broadly shift to a "dovish" direction; rather they became more polarized.[13]

By 1993, when the first Oslo Accord was signed, the portion of Israeli Jews who supported a Palestinian state stood at only 35 percent. Another survey from the Guttman Institute in 1992 shows support for a direct question about Palestinian statehood at just 19 percent (Data Israel G1045, series 264). It asked, "In the current situation, do you agree or oppose [sic] the establishment of a Palestinian state?" This question was very general, lacking even the geographic detail found in Smooha's 1985 survey.

The Oslo process demonstrates the power of leader-driven policy to change attitudes on both sides. From the early 1990s, Palestinian public opinion began to be measured far more regularly, and, although joint surveys had not yet begun to ask identical questions, the trends can be more easily compared. The Oslo process was the first direct, bilateral negotiations leading to an agreement between the two societies, and it was grounded in a broad vision of separation as the key to peace—at least from the Israeli perspective.[14] Attitudes toward the Oslo agreements and the negotiation process can be viewed as a proxy, even if imperfect, for public opinion regarding the general separation paradigm.

From 1993, Israeli Jewish support for a Palestinian state climbs steadily upward, despite major turmoil within Israeli society—from the first wave of suicide bombings by Hamas against Israeli civilians to the assassination of the prime minister in 1995. Palestinian attitudes also underwent a major shift.

An academic survey conducted in 1986, two years before the PLO declaration, showed that the large majority (78%) of Palestinians in the West Bank and Gaza saw a "democratic Palestinian state in all of Palestine" as their preferred solution; only 17 percent preferred a democratic state in the occupied territories, which the PLO would embrace just two years after the survey.[15] Thus, the policy reflected in the declaration itself drew significant internal opposition from Palestinian factions.

Yet polling from the Palestinian Center for Policy and Survey Research (PSR) on the eve of the 1993 accords showed that nearly two-thirds supported the agreement (referred to in the September 1993 survey as "Gaza and Jericho First," though the annex by this name would be signed only in May 1994), and a plurality of 45 percent believed that it would lead to a Palestinian state (34% said it would not, and 20% were not sure; PSR#1). Once again, this finding should not be seen as equivalent to an endorsement of the two state solution. But the Oslo Accords built on the 1988 declaration, which opened the way toward negotiations over separation or partition, along lines roughly defined by the 1949 ceasefire lines (the Green Line). Palestinians broadly interpreted this as the process that would lead to a Palestinian state.

Jerusalem Media and Communication Centre (JMCC) tracking polls show similarly high support at the start of the Oslo process: nearly 70% either "supported" or "strongly supported" it (see figure 2). An absolute majority, more than half of the respondents, continued to support the Oslo Accords throughout the 1990s (JMCC 2013).

During the Oslo years, the two communities experienced very different realities. Palestinians faced the segmentation of their territory, the increasing restrictiveness of the permit regime and movement constraints imposed by Israel's military government, deteriorating economic conditions, continued settlement expansion, and early-stage authoritarian tendencies of the newly

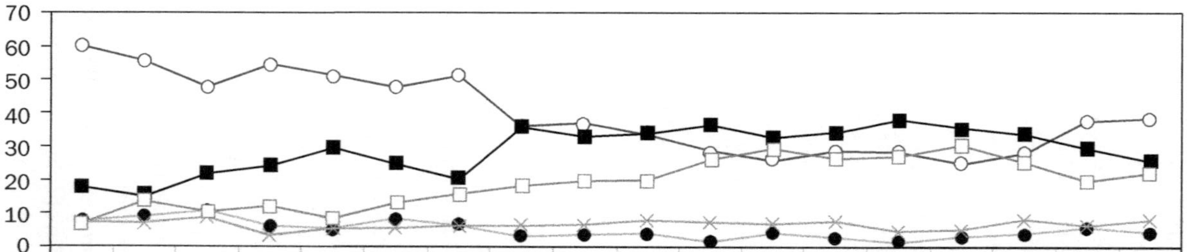

	Dec-97	May-98	Jul-98	Feb-99	Mar-99	Dec-99	Jun-00	Dec-00	Apr-01	Jun-01	Sep-01	Dec-01	Mar-02	May-02	Sep-02	Dec-02	Jun-06	Mar-13
Strongly support	7.8	8.9	11	5.9	5.2	8.3	6.6	3.2	3.8	4.2	1.6	4.4	2.9	1.7	3.4	4.2	6.3	4.6
Support	60.3	55.6	47.9	54.5	50.9	48	51.3	35.8	36.6	33.9	28.1	26.6	28.7	28.4	25.1	28.3	37.8	38.5
Strongly oppose	18	14.9	21.9	24	29.8	24.6	19.9	36	33	34	36.4	32.5	34	38.1	35.5	33.7	29.7	26
Oppose	6.7	13.6	10.2	12.3	8.3	13.4	15.9	18.5	19.9	19.9	26.5	29.6	26.5	27.2	30.8	25.4	19.6	22.3
No answer	7.2	7	9	3.3	5.8	5.7	6.3	6.5	6.7	8	7.4	6.9	7.9	4.6	5.2	8.4	6.6	8.3

FIGURE 2. What's your opinion of the Oslo agreement? Would you say that you strongly support, support, oppose, or strongly oppose it?

(JMCC Table, 2013)

formed Palestinian Authority.[16] Over the course of the 1990s, the JMCC data show a steady decline in Palestinian support, though a majority of Palestinians continued to support the peace process.

Israeli Jews, as noted, also experienced deep trauma and ruptures during the 1990s phase of the peace process. Yet both support for a Palestinian state and for the Oslo process increased: Israeli Jewish support rose, from roughly half in 1994 to a peak of 58 percent on the eve of the Camp David negotiations in 2000.[17]

The Palestinian Intifada that began in September 2000 was a watershed for both communities, and their favorable attitudes toward the negotiation framework dropped simultaneously. Among Palestinians, support for the process fell in 2000 and would never again reach a majority through 2013, according to JMCC's tracking data.[18] Israeli attitudes toward Oslo followed almost an identical pattern—falling sharply after the Intifada to well below half by July 2001 and failing to approach 50 percent for as long as Peace Index surveys continued to test that question, until July 2009.[19]

Despite falling support for the peace processes of the Oslo and then Camp David negotiating frameworks, the concept of a political solution based on two states continued to gain legitimacy. During the 2000s, the term "two state solution" began to be commonly used by both sides; this was also the decade when support from Israelis and Palestinians for two states would reach its peak (see figure 3). In 2001, the JMCC began tracking the question of two states, comparing it to a one state solution and other approaches throughout the decade. The findings show that this approach had become the clear favorite among Palestinians. In every survey, they preferred the two state solution by a wide margin over one equal democratic state and the less equal options proposed by some interviewees. Through most of the decade, support for two states regularly attained support from an absolute majority of more than 50 percent, with support in the low 40 percent range at the low points.

Among Israeli Jews, the INSS data show that, from 2001 onward, support for a Palestinian state generally reached a majority, falling below half just once—to 49 percent in 2002 when the number of suicide bombings in Israel peaked during the Second Intifada. The INSS tested the concept using the terminology of the "two state solution" for the first time in 2006 among Israeli Jews and found that fully 70 percent supported it. As with the earlier questions reviewed here, the new INSS question offered little explanation for two states, asking, "Do you support or oppose the solution of two states for two peoples?" They tested it again in 2007 and 2009, finding support from 63 percent and 64 percent of respondents, respectively.[20]

The Peace Index tested the most detailed version of the two state solution as a concept (as opposed to examining the details of an agreement): "Do you support

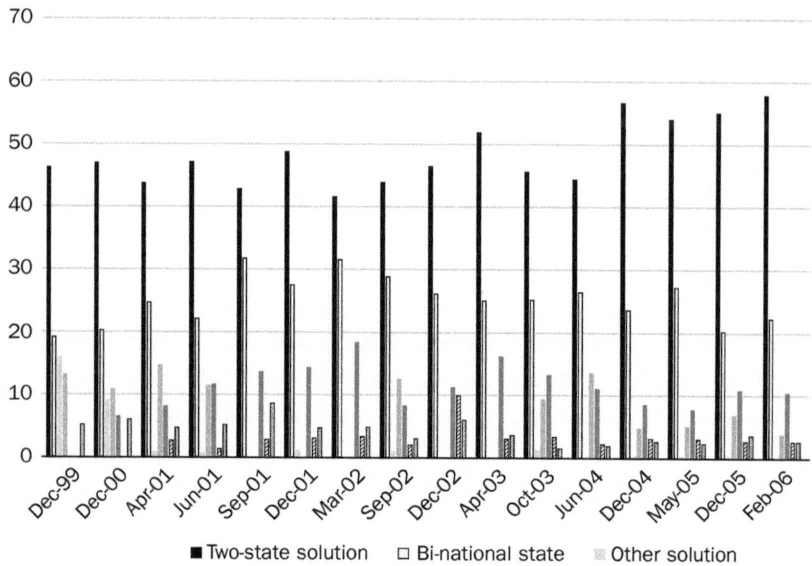

FIGURE 3. The most preferred solution for the Palestinian-Israeli conflict.

(JMCC, 2001–2010)

or oppose the solution to the Israeli Palestinian conflict according to the formula of 'two states for two people,' meaning an end to Israeli control over the territories and the establishment of a Palestinian state?" (Data Israel). A time-series comparison from 2002 shows that Jewish Israelis supported the broad concept at a high rate, ranging from 56 percent to nearly 70 percent through 2009 (falling to the low 40% range when the question stipulated compromises to be made to reach this outcome).[21]

The decade of the 2000s therefore represented the peak phase of support at the conceptual level for the two state solution. It was the decade during which this language became paradigmatic, when the most elaborate policy proposals for reaching two states were developed in and out of negotiations, and when negotiators came closest to agreement (2000 and 2008).

However, it is important to note that going back to the 1980s, when opinion for a Palestinian state was first tested in Israel, and continuing until the 2000s, public opinion research offered respondents little detail on what a Palestinian state meant in practice and tested the notion very broadly. Thus, responses would indicate that people supported or opposed the concept in principle, rather than reacting to specific policy details. Those details would be elaborated far more extensively in surveys following the negotiations in Camp David in 2000 and

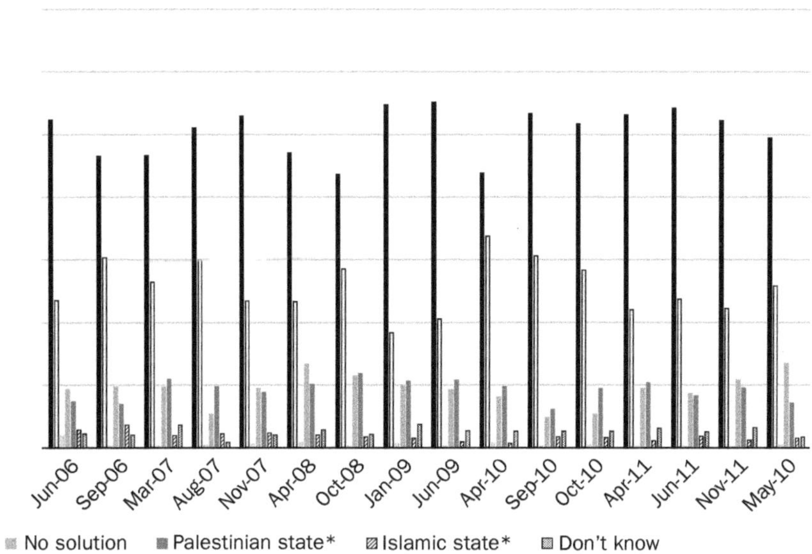

the subsequent Taba negotiations and Geneva initiative in 2003. Those phases of survey research provided detailed prospects for compromises and contours of a solution and eventually tested them in more elaborate ways as well.

The next decade, from roughly 2009–2019, saw the decline of all circumstances conducive to a two state solution, both on the ground and in the political landscape. Simultaneously—and perhaps rationally—both Israelis and Palestinians showed a slow, incremental, but consistent downward turn in support. On both sides, different polling projects tested the two state solution in varying ways, yielding somewhat different levels of overall support, but the downward trend over time was consistent.

JMCC, for example, continued to ask respondents to indicate their preference between two states or one state (see figure 4). Its surveys showed that the preference for two states was consistently higher than for one state; the peak of support—nearly 60 percent—was found in 2006. From 2009 and 2010, with slightly erratic changes, the choice of two states declined consistently; from 2013 onward, it remained below 50 percent (we discuss the trajectory of support for one state and the alternatives in the next section). In the INSS surveys of the Jewish Israeli public, responses to the simple question, "Do you support a two state solution?" showed a downward trend from the peak of support in 2006 (71%) to 58 percent in 2018.[22]

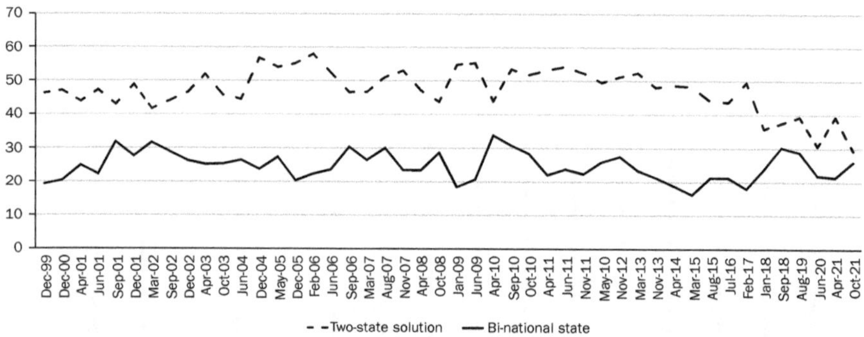

FIGURE 4. The most preferred solution for the Palestinian-Israeli conflict—two states versus one bi-national state.

(JMCC table, 2020)

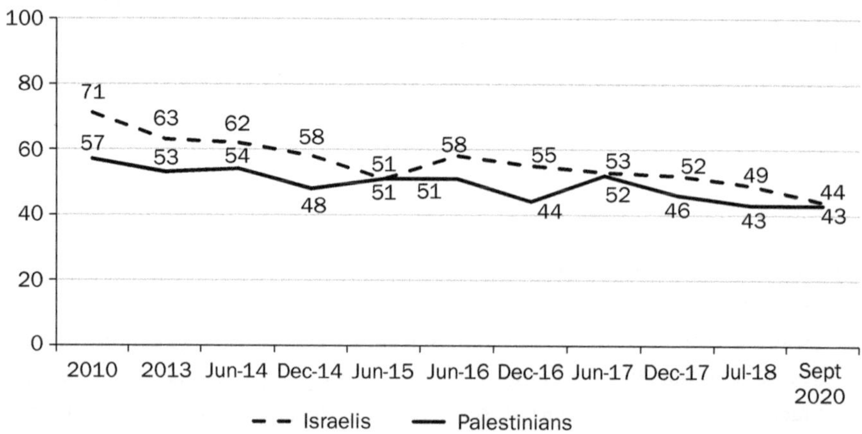

FIGURE 5. Changing support for two states: all Israelis and Palestinians. "Do you support or oppose a solution based on establishment of a Palestinian state, the two state solution?" (%, time series).

(PSR/TAU Palestine-Israel Pulse, 2016–2020)

Yet the clearest indication of the mutual and consistent decline spread over the second decade of the twenty-first century is the joint Israeli-Palestinian polling conducted by PSR and several Israeli institutions: the parallel question put to both sides, which included the entire Israeli population, rather than just a Jewish sample, was, "Do you support or oppose a solution based on the establishment of a Palestinian state next to Israel, known as the two state solution?" (see figure 5).

Since the question was asked with identical wording over the course of the decade (from 2010), the findings are therefore consistent across polls and populations. Further, in 2018 the Jewish Israeli population and the Palestinian population of the West Bank and Gaza show identical levels of support.[23] In Israel, the consistently high support of Arab Palestinian citizens in the joint survey—often more than 80 percent—increases the overall average.

The joint polling led by PSR devoted significant attention to questions that examine the details of a two state "package," testing the main items of an agreement as worked out in previous rounds of negotiations.[24] Generally, after respondents learn of the specific items and compromises, support for the overall package is lower than for the general question about the concept. The detailed "package" testing, item by item, is an important indicator because it ensures that all respondents are reacting to the same interpretation and description of what a two state solution would mean in practice. These studies can therefore offer a more precise picture of support for the policy needed to reach a two state solution, whereas the broad, generalized question helps define broad ideological camps.

Elaborate experiments testing additional incentives for a two state solution succeed in changing minds among some respondents and increasing support to a majority on both sides—but these are theoretical poll exercises that have not yet been tested by reality.[25]

Since 2018, separate polls on both sides show that support falls within the upper 30 percent to mid-40 percent range among Israelis and Palestinians alike. In October 2019, the Peace Index found that 44 percent of Israelis supported the establishment of a Palestinian state as the solution to the conflict; this support dropped to only 40 percent among the Jewish sample. In February and June 2020 PSR polls, 39 percent and 45 percent of Palestinians supported the two state solution, respectively. In the most recent joint survey by PSR together with the Evens program at Tel Aviv University, 42 percent and 43 percent of Israeli Jews and Palestinians, respectively, supported the general question about a two state solution. For the first time, support among Palestinian citizens of Israel declined precipitously, from 82 percent in 2018 to 59 percent in September 2020.[26]

Thus, the trajectory of public opinion regarding a two state solution can be understood as an arc—from the historic phases during which neither side supported two states nor thought of them as a solution, to the rising tide of support, leading to the current stage of decline. On the Israeli side, public opinion shows a clear upward trend of growing support for the establishment of a Palestinian state during the 1990s, whereas Palestinian indicators show a shift of national goals from a single state encompassing historic Palestine to a Palestinian state within the areas Israel occupied in 1967—although the available polling data are less linear. The first decade of the 2000s represents the normalization of the concept of a "two state solution" in which majorities on both sides regularly displayed conceptual support—representing both a peak and a plateau of support within each community. Yet, during this same decade, support for or belief in the efficacy of a negotiation process to reach such a solution declined rapidly. Circumstances clearly explain the decline—in fact, public opinion on both sides reflected an accurate reading of the political context and the inauspicious environment for successful negotiations.

At the same time, perhaps in hindsight, the concepts of "support" or "oppose" need to be understood critically. Given the significant erosion of support over the years, it is worth considering that support is not the same as enthusiasm, desire, or a willingness to take action on behalf of the policy. Perhaps such enthusiasm would be found among sharply defined ideological communities such as Palestinian citizens of Israel or the Jewish Left; yet it is likely that when support was at its highest—approaching 60 percent—a large portion more likely merely tolerated the idea when they selected the "support" option. For this reason, some peace- and conflict-oriented surveys test emotions toward a policy, on a scale such as "essential, desirable, acceptable if necessary, or unacceptable," but these are rarely implemented with consistent tracking potential.

Eventually, the increasingly remote chances of reaching a two state solution began to drive away earlier supporters in both populations. The trend was augmented by the growing political clout of those camps who were ideologically opposed to this outcome: religious and far-right forces in Israel, religious and Hamas supporters among Palestinians. The combination of the physical spread of settlements and permanent entrenchment of Israel's presence in the West Bank with the concerted separation policy between Gaza and the West Bank—overlaid with political paralysis between Hamas and Fatah—led many to drift away from even supporting the two state solution, losing faith in its feasibility. Surveys show that the loss of feasibility and the loss of support are closely linked.

It is also valuable to note how the surveys themselves—their availability and the questions they ask—can reflect aspects of the political reality at the time. Surveys conducted before the Oslo years reflect elements of the political reality they describe, regardless of the findings. There was a paucity of available data on Palestinians in the West Bank, Gaza, and Israel; the population of the West Bank and Gaza was perhaps not considered an independent group with agency by any of the researchers conducting polls during this time. Israeli survey research rarely examined Palestinian-Israeli attitudes systematically until the mid-1980s. In addition, the content of the questions—crude assessments of support for a Palestinian state or for negotiations—reflect very incipient notions of how to engage with the other side: the idea of two states living side by side through agreement, as a solution, had not yet emerged in public discourse.

Public Opinion in the Present: Non-Solutionism

If support for the two state solution has followed the trajectory of an arc, which is now in a historic decline, how are Israelis and Palestinians thinking about their present and future? In this section, we review trends characterizing the current moment.

At present, eroding support among both publics for the classic two state formula, matched by an inauspicious political environment at the elite level, has led not to the emergence of a new substitute framework for peace but rather to divergence between the two sides and fragmentation within each. We refer to this context—in which the two state solution no longer enjoys a majority on both sides but no other framework has garnered sufficient support in the public imagination to replace it—as "non-solutionism." It appears to be a product of the fragmentation of support for various outcomes among some groups and the belief of others that there is no permanent solution to the conflict that would be acceptable to both sides. Although the reasons for the emergence of non-solutionism and its manifestations differ for Israelis and Palestinians, there is evidence that it has taken hold among both sides.

Non-Solutionism in Israel: Support for Half-Measures and the Status Quo

As Israeli support for the two state solution has declined, the other alternatives regularly tested in public opinion research have won only small increases in support and in an inconsistent manner. No alternative—neither the frequently tested one equal state, one unequal state, or confederation—has superseded support for the two state solution, even though fewer than half of Israelis support the latter.

Notably, some survey questions have found, at times, explicit Israeli support for the status quo in which the conflict remains unresolved; however, the preference for nonresolution is most evident in Israeli voting behavior, in which voters have consistently elected parties and leaders who steadfastly reject seeking a peace agreement with Palestinians. Surveys also regularly show the general decline in the salience of peace in rankings of items on the Israeli national agenda.

In that regard, although Israelis still express higher support for two states in principle than for other solutions, these trends suggest a strong interest in maintaining current structures indefinitely. At best, various political figures in Israel have advocated interim steps that avoid resolution of "final status" issues, such as the question of borders, how to allot sovereignty over Jerusalem, or what is meant by an overall "end of conflict." The government that replaced Benjamin Netanyahu's long rule in June 2021 provided a clear example: early in his term, Prime Minister Naftali Bennett advocated "shrinking the conflict," widely understood as making incremental material improvements for Palestinians in the occupied territories, while explicitly opposing negotiations toward an agreed comprehensive political solution.[27] Perhaps more fundamental was the fact that the precarious coalition was only established on the implicit bargain that the United Arab List, the Islamist party representing Palestinian citizens, would refrain from demanding major changes regarding the conflict, in exchange for improvements in Palestinian life within Israel.

Within Israeli society, broad support for the status quo makes logical sense in a way that it does not for its Palestinian counterpart, owing to obvious differences in the quality of life for each society under present conditions. For Israelis, maintaining the status quo does not require difficult choices or concessions in the name of peace, defers risks, and preserves the benefits of exclusive sovereignty, making it attractive even as a plurality of Israelis espouse support for a two state outcome in polling.

The appeal for Israelis of maintaining the status quo also draws from widespread pessimism over past negotiating failures; the collapse of the peace process and the violence of the Second Intifada; the consequences of withdrawing settlements from Gaza from the Israeli perspective, including the Hamas takeover there; and a prevailing notion that a Palestinian state would inevitably be hostile or at least a bastion for hostile substate actors: Peace Index surveys throughout the decade have shown that only a minority of approximately one-quarter or slightly more expect negotiations to succeed (Peace Index surveys 2010–2021). Furthermore, among Israelis who support a maximalist vision of Greater Israel, the status quo provides the opportunity for continued acquisition of Palestinian land in the West Bank through the conduit of Israel's military occupation, which has successfully facilitated the land appropriation enterprise for more than a half-century.

As such, the status quo is itself a misnomer and one that masks processes that are constantly reshaping the present. Within an emerging context of non-solutionism in the aftermath of the Second Intifada, Israeli leaders enjoyed broad support for taking major unilateral action, declared or de facto. During that time, there has been little public pressure to strive for a permanent peace deal with the Palestinians, who are widely viewed as inadequate partners to such an arrangement. A partial list of examples of Israeli unilateral activity includes Israel's construction of the wall in the West Bank beginning in 2002, withdrawal of Israeli settlements and the military from the Gaza Strip in 2005 without coordinating with the PA, unrelenting expansion of settlements throughout the West Bank, and pursuit of the unilateral extension of sovereignty through the formal annexation of territory, including efforts to legitimize settlements on private land in Israeli law.

At least since Benjamin Netanyahu returned to power in Israel in 2009, non-solutionism has found backing at the highest echelons of Israeli politics. Netanyahu and other high-ranking officials, such as former foreign and defense minister Avigdor Lieberman, have argued publicly that negotiations are futile and that the conflict needs to be "managed" indefinitely. In place of a comprehensive agreement, Netanyahu at first promoted an "economic peace" with Palestinians that deliberately avoided the political dimension of the conflict, even while the administration of Barack Obama engaged in efforts to revive the peace process. At the same time, successive Netanyahu-led governments took decisive actions on the ground to enhance Israel's presence and grip over the occupied territories. The first post-Netanyahu government not only extended the "management" of the conflict through the rhetoric of "shrinking" but also explicitly adopted the economy-in-exchange-for-peace concept advanced by Netanyahu.[28]

Over time, a comprehensive peace has become progressively less of an imperative in Israeli discourse and in the public imagination.[29] Support for unilateralism across the political spectrum has legitimized it fully as a policy approach in Israeli discourse,[30] whether its intention is to create separation between Israeli and Palestinian communities while not precluding negotiations or to be a permanent measure devised to thwart negotiations, such as large-scale annexation.

In an example from March 2019, Israel's INSS released its "Strategic Framework for the Israeli-Palestinian Arena," which sought to "design an improved situation that will retain future options for the end of Israel's rule over the Palestinians in the West Bank, and ensure a solid Jewish majority in a democratic Israel." Significantly, the INSS did not see its objective as determining a way out of the current imbroglio or contributing to the development of an alternative framework that might anchor peace; rather, its aim was to consolidate Israel's current positions while preventing the country's "slide toward a one state reality" from reaching a point of no return.[31]

Although the INSS proposal claims to preserve Israeli options for peace, its support for unilateral measures actually limits the notion of a menu of options within a negotiation framework and normalizes the unilateral approach currently being used by Israel's right-wing leadership to preclude negotiations altogether. Broadly, there has been little public resistance to this unilateralist method of Israel's leaders, and until the convoluted annexation debate in the months prior to July 2020 raised concerns about unilateral annexation, few arguments against it were heard.

What Does Non-Solutionism Look like among Palestinians?

For Palestinians, the status quo does not represent a state of comfort or indifference as it seems to mean for Israelis. Rather, for Palestinians the status quo involves gradually deteriorating circumstances and a sense that the problem is intractable and the worsening environment inescapable. In a poll conducted by PSR in June 2020, 61 percent of West Bank respondents described the conditions of Palestinians in that territory as bad or very bad, whereas only 14 percent described conditions as good or very good. Among Gazans, 87 percent described the conditions of people in the territory as bad or very bad; less than 5 percent described them as good or very good. Over the past decade, residents of both territories have viewed living conditions with increasing distress: the trend is stark, showing perceptions of current conditions in increasingly negative terms (see figures 6 and 7).

In this environment, when Palestinians across the territories were asked by PSR in June 2020 which of four possibilities reflected their "views about what to do

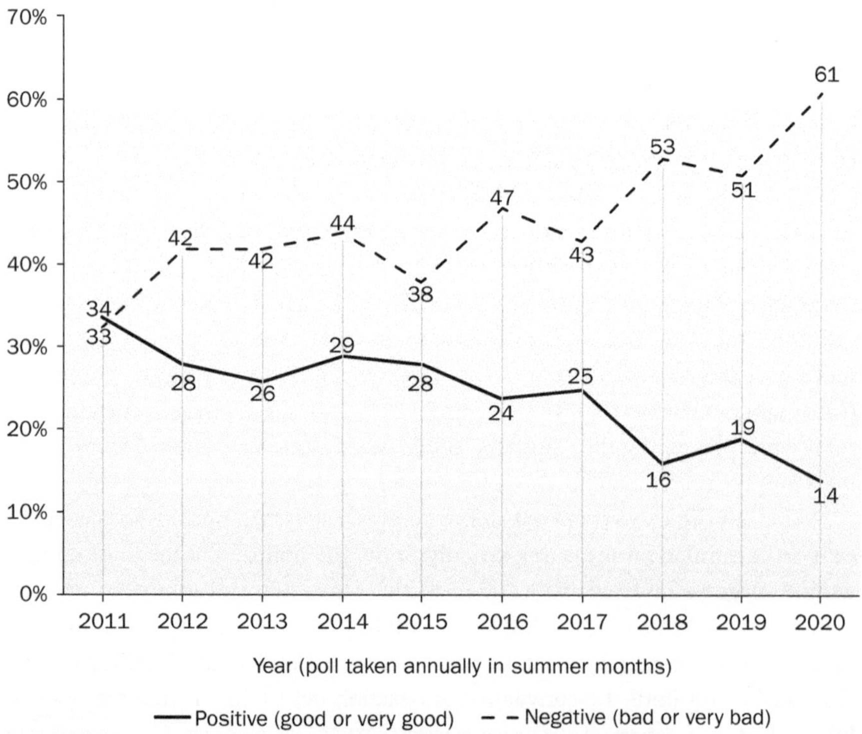

FIGURE 6. West Bankers' assessment of current conditions.

(Chart by authors; Data from PSR Index Polls, 2011–2020)

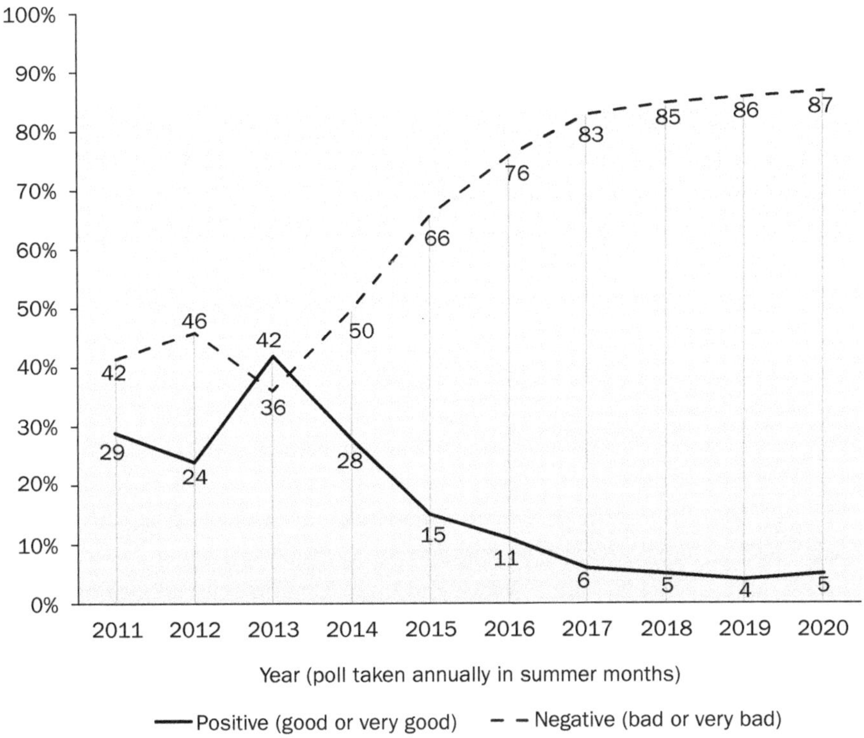

FIGURE 7. Gazans' assessment of current conditions.

(Chart by authors; Data from PSR Index Polls, 2011–2020)

with regard to Israeli-Palestinian relations," only 13 percent said maintaining the status quo. The rest were divided between waging armed struggle against the occupation (38%), waging unarmed struggle (15%), and reaching a peace agreement with Israel (28%).

Despite the overwhelming dissatisfaction with the present state of affairs, the Palestinian public has not mobilized against it in any concerted or meaningful way since the end of the Second Intifada in 2004–2005. There are likely several reasons for this, including the exceedingly complex lived reality that has developed as a result of the Oslo Accords framework and its breakdown[32]; the polarization and demobilization of the Palestinian public by authoritarian governments[33] and the general confusion of the public in the face of multilayered oppression by the PA in conjunction with Israeli military occupation[34]; the introduction of neoliberal economic policies,[35] the increased involvement of international organizations and donors in Palestinian civil and economic life,[36] and the attendant depoliticization and demobilization of civil society[37]; the failure of any strategy or method, from armed and unarmed resistance to bilateral negotiations, to advance Palestinian national goals and the exhaustion with decades of unproductive sacrifice; and the oppressive siege of the Gaza Strip.

It is unsurprising in this context to see that Palestinians in the occupied territories largely reject the status quo. Yet not having a unifying vision of the future appears to be a novel experience for the Palestinian national movement, which has largely maintained a unity of purpose even as the ultimate objective evolved over time. In the aftermath of the War of 1948, the consensus among Palestinians was to secure the total liberation of their homeland, primarily through armed struggle, with the implication that Zionists would be expelled. Over time the PLO objective came to be framed as a secular, democratic state that would include Jews as long as they rejected Zionism. Eventually, this gave way to majority support for two states living side by side and arrived at through bilateral negotiations. (This support held even with the rise of Islamist politics that rejected compromise and the two state solution.) Yet unlike in the past, many Palestinians are eschewing a focus on political solutions altogether in favor of grassroots organizing in pursuit of universal human rights—what Nathan J. Brown and Iman Elbanna refer to in chapter 6 as the "slow reorientation of the nationalist movement away from the centrality of any kind of statehood." This change appears to stem from pessimism over the failure of the international system to resolve the conflict through the peace process and frustration with the unsuccessful experience of state-building while under occupation.

Furthermore, some segments of Palestinian society have concluded that, given the fragmentation of Palestinian politics and the lack of basic legitimacy among PA institutions, it makes little sense to focus on a final political arrangement with Israel while internal politics require significant attention and reform. Indeed, the PA's continued adherence to the objective of two states through bilateral negotiations with Israel has led to a growing divergence between the public and the leadership.[38] A six-month policy study conducted between 2015–2016 by the PSR revealed deep dissatisfaction from the Palestinian public and intellectual elites with the status quo and a demand to adopt "a strategy of total political confrontation" with Israel, including organizing a movement of popular nonviolent resistance and fully embracing local and international boycott campaigns such as Boycott, Divestment, and Sanctions (BDS).[39]

It is worth noting that the BDS campaign is centered on three basic principles, none of which presuppose an overarching political framework or outcome. Rather, they are rights-based demands related to each of the three fundamental Palestinian communities: those under occupation in the West Bank and Gaza, refugees, and Palestinian citizens of Israel (see https://bdsmovement.net). Similarly, in June 2020, more than 120 Palestinian Americans in the academic, political, and civil society spheres published a statement of thirteen principles and policies, none of which identified a commitment to a comprehensive framework (see https://www.palestinianprinciples.com).

Thus, what might be described as the more dynamic parts of the Palestinian national movement today view the debate over whether to pursue one or two states as both an abstraction and a distraction, causing divisions between Palestinians at a time when unity is more important than ever and creating confusion in the public discourse over how to address the Palestinian question.[40]

Emerging Alternative: Scenarios, Strategies and Visions of the Future

In this section, we review public support for alternatives to two states, including a single democratic state and the hybrid system of a confederal approach to governance. The goal of the section is not only to explore whether one solution stands out as preferable to either or both publics; it also implicitly questions the notion that peace can emerge from a constitutional political framework at all, thereby raising questions about what advancing peace really means.

Broadly, we find indications that support for two state alternatives is increasing. But this level of support still does not rival that given to two states, even considering how much support for the old approach has declined. Further, shifts in public opinion are slow and incremental, and only partial data are available on new ideas, some of which, such as the notion of one democratic state, are actually old but have been revived in survey research with greater attention in recent years. For this reason, we have at points included indicators of underlying values and attitudes that imply support for one approach or the other to supplement the gaps in research, which is still in its incipient stages.

Before examining the alternatives, it is worth noting that the two state paradigm still enjoys strong reinforcement by institutional power structures inside Israel/Palestine and abroad, including the PLO-PA, the United Nations, the Quartet, and wider international community; although the Trump administration moved the United States away from this position, most other institutions in the country continued to espouse support for two states, and the Biden administration returned America to its prior stance in favor of two states. Moreover, decades of intellectual and practical study have been devoted to enhancing development and understanding of the two state paradigm, including through bilateral negotiations and a twenty-five-year-old Palestine state-building project; in contrast, one state, although far from a novel idea, is still in its infancy as an applied concept with no clear understanding of how to implement it in practice. As Ian Lustick notes in chapter 1, bringing into focus the "one state reality" may require a shift in thinking of an ontological magnitude, revisiting fundamental assumptions that view Palestinians in the West Bank and Gaza Strip as living outside Israel rather than inside it.

There are, however, civil society activists from a range of backgrounds who are advancing alternative approaches and modalities for resolving the conflict, including federal, confederal, democratic, and undemocratic single state models.

Over the years—indeed, even from the early years of Zionism—the primary competing political paradigm was a single democratic state in which all citizens are equal. The concept can refer either to a "binational" state, one founded on principles of civic national identity that downplay national identity altogether, or one that undergoes a process of denationalization as defined by Nadav Shelef in chapter 9, which may be required for peaceful coexistence in one state. The two are not necessarily exclusive: a single state may provide collective national rights while cultivating a metalevel civic identity.

For Palestinians, the idea of a single state also has a long history, beginning with the early articulation of national goals after establishment of the State of Israel when the major factions expressed the desire for a secular democratic state encompassing all of historic Palestine. Because systematic survey research began at the same time as the emergence of the two state solution, survey findings favored two states, as seen in the first section. However, JMCC polling tested a "single binational state" beginning in 2001 alongside two states. At that time, when the potential for achieving a two state solution appeared greater than ever, Palestinian support for two states outnumbered support for a single state by more than three to one (69% compared to just 18% for a single state).

However, the JMCC tracking found that Palestinian support for a single binational state grew during the difficult decade of the 2000s, while support for two states ebbed. By the last JMCC poll of the decade in 2010, support for a single binational state had nearly doubled from the 2001 level to 34 percent. Moreover, Palestinian supporters of a binational single state had closed the support gap significantly; support for two states by 2010 was just eleven points higher (45%).

In JMCC polls, this peak of 34 percent support for one state proved unstable, declining unevenly over the next five years and then rising somewhat from a low point in 2015 of just 16 percent. Over the next few years—overlapping with the leadership of Donald Trump—support rose again to a peak of 30 percent in 2018. Throughout those years, support for two states declined more steadily and dramatically—from 50 percent in 2017 at the end of Obama's second term to just 31 percent in 2020 (JMCC data provided to author).

Yet when the question was asked in different manner—not as a choice between two states and one, but rather support or opposition to one state—the findings show a similar range of support (see figure 8). In PSR and Tel Aviv University's

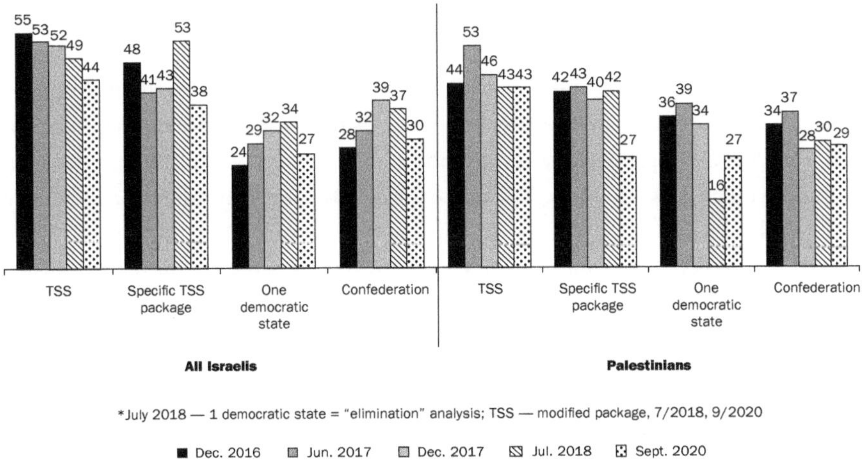

FIGURE 8. Frameworks over time: incremental erosion for two states but no clear successor. Levels of support for different frameworks for solving the conflict (%, All Israelis, Palestinians).

(PSR/Evens Program, TAU, Oct 2020 Press Conference).

Note: Palestinian citizens of Israel regularly show higher support for all forms of conflict resolutions than all other groups in the joint survey research. In the joint polling, over 80% generally support the two state solution.

joint polling of Palestinians and Israelis in 2016 and 2017, Palestinian support for one state ranged from 34 to 36 percent compared to 19–20 percent among Israelis. Support for one state was highest among Palestinian Arab citizens of Israel, at 52–56 percent.

Similarly, an earlier set of surveys among Palestinian Arab citizens of Israel by Sammy Smooha at Haifa University showed higher support for one equal state than among Jews, although in response to a different type of question.[41] Between 2008–2010, Smooha asked, "If I have to choose between the solution of two states, a Jewish state and a Palestinian state, or a single Jewish-Palestinian state from the Jordan River to the sea, I would choose a two state solution"—thereby setting up a pro-two state positioning and asking the respondents to state whether they agree or disagree. A majority of respondents agreed, but a large portion (between 38–44%) also disagreed (Data Israel J0033, J0034, J0035, J0037). This is far more than the Jewish population alone, of whom only 21 percent disagreed with the statement that they prefer a two state solution.

There are fewer available data regarding the Palestinian diaspora. However, there is ample evidence in the form of articles and statements that important voices among Palestinians outside the occupied territories support a single state outcome. This is not altogether surprising given that diaspora Palestinians may feel less attached to the state-building project in the occupied territories, are not directly tied to the Palestinian public sector established by the Oslo Accords, and mostly come from areas of historic Palestine that would not be part of a prospective Palestinian state. Indeed, a 2016 study of Palestinians that included a large sample in Lebanon found that 93 percent of those living in Lebanon consider Palestine to be "all of historic Palestine with all its borders and landmarks."[42]

Among Israelis, the concept of a binational state was tested routinely between 1999 and 2010 in the Peace Index. Like the JMCC polling, these surveys asked respondents to choose their preference between two states and one; throughout the entire decade, support among Jews (the only population for which tracking is available on this question) for one state ranged from just 6 percent to 22 percent compared to those who preferred a two state solution.[43] When the Peace Index offered a different and more detailed question in 2008—"In your opinion, is the idea of a binational state, that is, a single state in which Jews and Palestinians live together, with equal rights and equal representation in government, a better or worse idea than the solution of two states for two people?" (Data Israel P0803)—the portion of respondents who thought one state was better remained at 18 percent, within the same range as the tracking question.

It is important to recall that throughout the decades, the prospect of reaching an agreement to form one single state has remained manifestly unlikely. In 2010, a study from the University of Maryland asked about the likely outcome if the two state solution failed and found that just 4 percent of Jewish Israelis believed a one state outcome of any sort would be the result. Instead, the vast majority—84%—thought that either the status quo would continue or violent conflict would flare up (42% for each response).[44]

In the second decade of the 2000s, the PSR Joint Survey, then conducted with Hebrew University, also examined this issue. In 2013, when it asked about "one democratic state with equality between Arabs and Jews," one-third (32%) of Israelis supported it versus 63 percent who rejected the concept; this total included Arab and Jewish respondents (PSR/Hebrew University 2013). However, just three years later, support for one state among all Israelis in the joint poll project declined to under one-quarter (24%). Israeli support nevertheless rose again over the next two years—the phase during which the Trump administration became active and expectations of a two state solution declined dramatically at large—returning to about one-third (32%) among all Israeli respondents.[45]

Peace Index surveys from 2019 and 2021 indicate even lower overall support. Beginning in early 2019 the Index tested support or opposition to "the establishment of a binational state between the Jordan [River] and the [Mediterranean] sea with full equality of rights for Jews and Palestinians," finding significantly lower support through to 2021. The range of support during that time was 18–25 percent for all Israelis; among Jewish Israelis, support was as low as 10 percent, which is consistent with the low range of the Peace Index findings in the 2000s cited earlier.[46]

Therefore, the main observation is that, unlike the two state solution, there has never been a majority who support a single equal state, nor among each side separately, which precludes the question of a simultaneous majority. Further, it is difficult to discern a trend or direction of change, other than limited phases in which the appearance of an upward trend is either limited in time and later reversed, or data from different surveys show different patterns.

That being said, the two state approach gained legitimacy over time primarily because neither side was able to achieve its ideal or maximalist vision, rendering the two state compromise attractive by necessity, at least for a time. It is conceivable that the same process—adverse political realities at present or an inability to achieve the current version of both sides' preferred political solutions—could make a one state option more legitimate. Yet it is not a given that even such legitimization would guarantee an equal, binational version, rather than a version in which one side is dominant.

Given skepticism about both one state outcomes and the feasibility of two states alike, hybrid constitutional models of governance have gained prominence in discourse among academics and activists. These focus mainly on confederal or federal arrangements. Polls have not addressed these issues extensively or in depth; however, the joint Palestinian-Israeli polls (PSR/TAU) between December 2016 and June 2018, and then in July 2020, asked the two sides a single question describing the broad outlines of a confederation and using the term "confederation" as the solution (see figure 9).[47] In late 2016, support among all Israelis stood at just over one-quarter (28% in total), whereas 34 percent of Palestinians supported the idea. Over the next two years of semiannual surveys, Israeli Jewish support for confederation rose in a straight upward trend, from 20 to 33 percent, but then declined incrementally to 28 percent in July 2020. Palestinian support showed a less consistent trend, rising to a peak of 37 percent before falling again to 28 percent where support remained fairly constant (29% in the 2020 joint survey).

Once again Palestinian citizens of Israel supported a confederation idea at the highest rate, with support ranging from 61 to 74 percent in the same 2016–2017 period (without a consistent direction for the trend.) However, between 2018 and 2020, support for a confederation among Palestinian citizens of Israel declined sharply, falling to just 44 percent in 2020—a twenty-four-point decline from the previous survey in 2018 (PSR/Evens 2020); this is consistent with the overall decline in positive responses toward all proposals in the 2020 survey among Palestinian citizens of Israel.

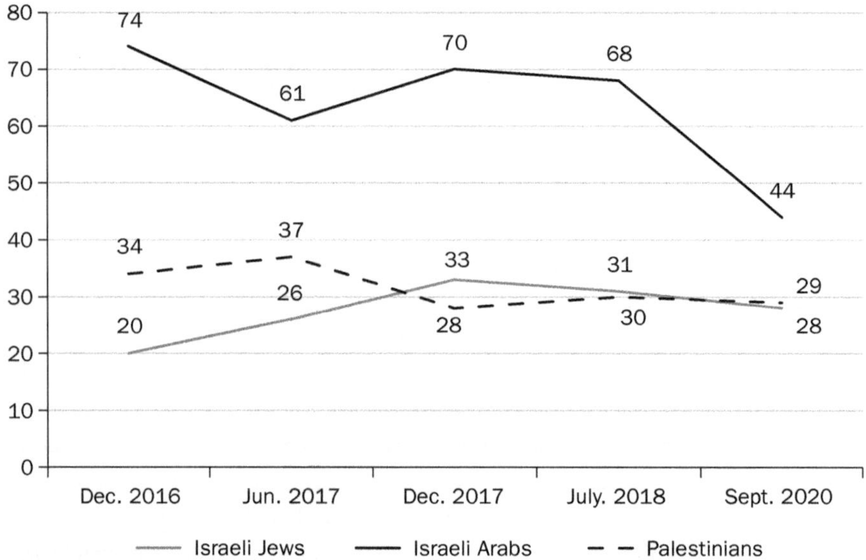

FIGURE 9. Alternatives: Confederation (without/with explanation). "Two states, Pal/Isrl, enter a confederation—citizens of one country allowed to live as permanent residents in territory of other, each national group votes only in its state for elections. Freedom of movements for all, Jerusalem is not divided, serves as the capital of two states. Isrl & Pal cooperate on security and economy." (% "support" *12/16, minimal explanation; 6/17—detail added).

(PSR/Evens Program/TAU October 2020 Press Conference)

The only known data examining a more detailed description of a confederation approach—without using the word "confederation"—preceded these general questions in 2016–2018. In late 2014, a survey commissioned by *+972 Magazine* and the Israeli-Palestine Creative Regional Initiatives considered several core ideas, testing the confederation in the same manner that polls generally test the details of a two state solution. The findings showed that between one-third and about 45 percent supported these core ideas: two states with open borders (42%), a shared but undivided Jerusalem (45%), allowing each side to live as residents but not citizens on the other side (33%), allowing refugees to return to their respective states with an option for residency on the other side (48%), and specific shared institutions for technical items such as water, roads. and electricity, including security cooperation "like today" (in 2014); Israelis showed the highest support at 60 percent for this last item.

After hearing all aspects, the respondents were asked whether they support the full package, and 56 percent said they did, which was within the range of support for a two state solution at the time. Consistent with other surveys, Palestinian Arab citizens showed far higher support, both for the specific items and for the overall package, than Jewish respondents: 80 percent and 51 percent, respectively, supported the full package describing a confederal arrangement after hearing its main details.

On the question of confederation, once again the idea was tested earlier among Palestinians than Israelis. During the early Oslo years (mid-1990s), The Center for Policy and Survey Research surveys asked at least once about an Israeli-Jordanian-Palestinian confederation without providing significant description about what it might mean.[48] But in 2001, after the Second Intifada had already begun, a CPSR survey asked specifically about support for joint institutions leading to an Israeli-Palestinian confederation. Support was low—just 25 percent. However, the survey also tested two aspects that are likely to be components of a confederal arrangement, producing significantly different results: 84 percent supported "open borders between Palestine and Israel," and 60 percent supported "joint Palestinian-Israeli economic institutions and ventures." These findings appeared at a time when the peace process was collapsing, but the basic idea of two states was still strong; perhaps the vision of a cooperative relationship within two states appeared visible on a future horizon.

In sum, alternatives exist, but public attitudes toward them remain an open question: at times there appears to be small incremental rising support for one state, but this support never crosses a fairly low ceiling. The idea of a two state confederation shows contrasting trends: openness among Palestinians at an earlier stage and a complex, still low, but perhaps more malleable basis of support on both sides at the present. At least in one source, the PSR/TSC Palestine Israel Pulse (in 2020, with the Evens program at TAU) shows Palestinian support for confederation and a single state within the same general range.

Here again, the polls reflect some confusion within the political environment. The most elaborate and systematic surveys are generally focused on the two state solution, with consistent tracking over time; some include a range of details reflecting negotiations of the previous decade and incentives oriented at future negotiations for the same approach. It is less common to find elaborate polling on the alternatives: polling on a serious program for one state, either a democratic or an unequal one state, and on a confederation solution is both minimal and sporadic. Even if Israel is taking a decidedly supremacist, conquest-oriented direction as per Gershon Shafir's argument in chapter 2, this has not been significantly tested either. It appears that the stagnation of the policy debate at elite levels about how to resolve the conflict is mirrored in public opinion studies, while activists on the ground have long moved beyond the type of questions being asked most widely in polls.

However, while public attitudes toward alternatives percolate, the Israeli right-wing leadership has advanced significantly on another front regarding public attitudes: legitimization of exclusive Jewish sovereignty over the entire territory of Israel/Palestine in the form of the Trump Plan and unilateral annexation. A review of public attitudes in Israel shows that already nearly half of Israelis—and a majority of the Jewish public—support this broad direction. If equitable alternative solutions are not found, it is likely that the one unequal state under Israeli control will become increasingly permanent.

Implications

The viability of a hard two state partition continues to erode in reality and in the public imagination. As a result, Israeli and Palestinian publics appear to have lost confidence that an overall comprehensive political framework exists that can resolve the conflict. At present, no such solution enjoys majority support on either side; although public support for a two state solution has declined, that approach has not been replaced by a more popular alternative in the public mind. This situation leaves an absence of bottom-up pressure to seek a comprehensive peace agreement based on a specific formula. Nonetheless, possibilities for both an alternative negotiated political framework or for a unilaterally imposed system of ethnoreligious domination are emerging from the periphery in the public imagination and gaining traction.

Conceivably, the Palestinian public—and small portions of the Israeli left-wing public—may become a driving force for change based on a rights- and equality-oriented struggle, without taking a clear position on the constitutional framework for those rights. Or the Israeli right-wing public, specifically settlers, may lead the drive for Israel to take permanent control of the whole territory (excluding Gaza) through unilateral action and unequal statehood.

However, as the Israeli government, the most powerful force in the region, promotes an annexationist agenda, it may well goad portions of the public to oppose the policy more actively, especially Palestinians. If there is sufficient common cause among portions of Israeli society, perhaps the public can take on a new activist role to advance the values of equality and democracy, even in the absence of clear constitutional frameworks. But if such a reconfiguration of the public role does not happen and the annexation agenda succeeds, the options for future solutions dwindle. Once a single state becomes permanent, there are only two left: equal or unequal.

Part 4

POLICY OPTIONS

The Possible and the Plausible

12

PALESTINIAN STATEHOOD IN AMERICAN POLICY

The Changing Roles of Values, Interests, and Domestic Politics

Kevin Huggard and Tamara Cofman Wittes

For more than forty years, since mediating the Camp David treaty between Egypt and Israel, the United States has played a central part in international efforts to resolve the Arab-Israeli dispute. American regional and geopolitical interests, as well as domestic politics, drove US leaders to take on that central role. Cold War competition with the Soviet Union spurred US engagement in Arab-Israeli peacemaking, as American leaders sought to prevent violent conflict and to resolve tensions between US partnerships with Israel, on the one hand, and pro-American, conservative Arab states like Saudi Arabia and Jordan, on the other. At the same time, domestic interest in the fate of the Holy Land and the emergence of a beleaguered Jewish state after the horrors of the Holocaust helped drive public support for US engagement in efforts to promote Israel's security and bring peace between Israel and its neighbors.

American leaders had the capacity to take on the role of mediator in successive efforts at Arab-Israeli peacemaking due to geopolitical conditions and the close US relationship with Israel. Especially after the 1973 war made clear both that Israel would not be defeated by conventional Arab militaries and that the United States was committed to supporting Israel's self-defense, it became both logical and necessary that Washington be a main sponsor for diplomatic efforts to achieve acceptance of Israel by its neighbors in the region. But from the 1970s until the onset of the 1990s, that US effort did not include meaningful engagement with the Palestinian national movement.

After Israel and the Palestine Liberation Organization (PLO) achieved their historic mutual recognition in 1993 and laid out a framework for resolving their dispute over the territories occupied in 1967, successive US administrations made immense investments in attempting to advance a conflict-ending agreement between Israel and the Palestinians. American presidents devoted significant personal time and attention to this conflict, driven in part by their understanding of the proximity to breakthrough and the tantalizing possibility of being the one to shepherd the century-long Israeli-Palestinian conflict to a final peace agreement.

In recent years, however, American interests and capabilities have both shifted. Especially since the breakdown of the last Oslo framework effort at US-brokered negotiations, led by Secretary of State John Kerry in 2013–2014, the American understanding of all these factors—proximity to a breakthrough, the conflict's relationship to regional stability, America's geopolitical interests, and the US–Israel relationship—has changed.

First, the conflict between Israel and the Palestinians is far from resolution. On both sides, political leaders facing domestic volatility are disinclined to risk their political capital in a bid for peace. Publics are losing faith that a negotiated two state outcome is possible or that the other side is interested in peaceful coexistence. In 2020, the Israeli move—now frozen—to annex West Bank territory and the months-long halting of PA cooperation with Israel suggested that the conflict was backsliding from one contained by a political framework for dispute resolution and functional cooperation to a new phase of uncoordinated unilateralism and more existential, mutually exclusive stances by the two parties. In any case, no conflict-ending agreement is imminent.

US geopolitical interests have also shifted in relation to peace diplomacy. In earlier eras, the United States sought to resolve the conflict out of a desire to reduce interstate Arab-Israeli war and resolve tensions within its coalition of regional partners, thereby stabilizing the regional order under American hegemony. Today, US policymakers do not understand the region's underlying stability problems primarily as a reflection of the Arab-Israeli conflict but of long-standing governance failings, sectarian tensions, and local power rivalries. Major regional actors view efforts to address the Israeli-Palestinian conflict as more of an irritant or impediment than an imperative (Jordan, Egypt, and the PLO excepted). Further, the era of unchallenged American global hegemony is ending, and new challenges in Asia and Europe, as well as domestic political and economic upheaval, pull US attention away from the Middle East.

Thus, American policymakers now see successful mediation of the conflict as highly unlikely, while Washington's own geopolitical interests in the conflict are declining and its leverage over the parties is likewise relatively more modest. Meanwhile, Israel's moves in 2020 toward unilateral annexation of territory in the West Bank threatened to erode, if not explode, the remaining minimal components of the Oslo-era political understandings and agreements it had in place with the PLO. Efforts or declared intentions by Israel's elected leaders to legislate permanent control over territories occupied in June 1967 could drive the conflict decisively away from a negotiated separation into two states and into a future in which Israel would exercise full control over the territory from the Jordan to the Mediterranean, while maintaining two distinct legal regimes and two distinct categories of population: citizens and subjects.

The Trump administration's proposal for "Peace to Prosperity" framed its plans for the conflict in terms of a nominal but practically inviable "Palestinian state" that was in fact dozens of isolated enclaves connected by roads over which Israel would retain de facto control. The cynicism of calling this plan a two state outcome placed a spotlight on the gap between that US government aspiration and the dynamics of power and control on the ground.[1] A future of two sovereign states is difficult, perhaps impossible, absent dramatic and determined steps to alter this reality. Given the asymmetry that exists today, those steps would primarily involve Israel yielding power and control over populations, territory, resources, and infrastructure. The debate over whether a negotiated two state outcome remains viable hinges on the depth, complexity, and likelihood of those steps.

Some scholars, including in this volume, describe that asymmetry and Israel's exercise of power and control on the ground as a "one state reality." In this chapter, we focus our analysis on the mainstream US policy approach to Israeli-Palestinian conflict resolution, which remains rooted tightly in a two state framework. Indeed, that approach and its domestic drivers continue to rest on an understanding by US policymakers of the present situation as interim and indeterminant.

The gap revealed by Trump's plan indicates that, for any future US policy approach to offer better prospects of success, it must confront these substantially altered circumstances and undertake a fundamental reevaluation of the American role in Israeli-Palestinian peacemaking—what Washington aims to achieve, why, and how. Chief among the questions that demand examination is why the United States has continued to embrace a two state paradigm for resolving the Israeli-Palestinian conflict even as many argue that it is no longer possible and even as behaviors by the two key actors trend against it. It is thus crucial to assess what might shape the American approach to conflict resolution in this case, should the possibility of a two state outcome no longer be understood as viable by US policymakers.

This chapter reviews the history of American foreign policy on the question of a two state outcome to the Israeli-Palestinian conflict, a narrative that is in essence the history of US engagement with the concept of Palestinian statehood and with the Palestine Liberation Organization. This record reveals that US policymakers have always perceived the prospect of Palestinian statehood as in tension with Israel's security, and thus their support for statehood has always been and remains conditional.

At the same time, US support for the establishment of a Palestinian state alongside Israel coheres strongly with deep-seated American attitudes about national self-determination, identity conflicts, and democracy. This helps explain why, even under present conditions, many US policymakers sincerely continue to see the establishment of a Palestinian state alongside Israel as likely the only way to end the bloodshed of the conflict.[2]

Finally, holding out the two state outcome as the objective of American policy—and allowing for flexibility in defining its parameters—has enabled US policymakers to minimize political conflict on both the domestic and the international fronts. At home, sustaining the goal of a two state solution has allowed for reconciling the American public's support for Israel as a democratic and Jewish state that is closely allied with Washington with the same public's affinity for human rights and self-determination. Diplomatically, so long as the two state solution remains the stated goal of both Israel and the United States, it provides Washington the ability to view Israeli actions under the occupation as temporary concerns, even when those actions have the effect of making a two state outcome considerably more challenging to achieve and implement.

Strong incentives, therefore, push American policymakers to retain their commitment to the two state solution, but they will be increasingly challenged to do so. As the Israeli occupation of the West Bank reaches its fifty-sixth year, as Israeli public opinion and policy preferences increasingly favor permanent control over at least some of the territories occupied in 1967, as the US relationship with Israel becomes increasingly politicized both in Washington and Jerusalem, and as America's wider interests in the Middle East recede relative to other global concerns, we are likely to see greater volatility in US policy toward the Israeli-Palestinian conflict. Domestic politics and political culture may play relatively greater roles in influencing US policy choices. The chapter concludes with some broad suggestions for how this altered environment might reshape American policy.

Why Does the United States Still Care about Israeli-Palestinian Peace?

Given the shift in regional and global geopolitics, it is not surprising that there is some inclination among American policy thinkers simply to leave the Israeli-Palestinian conflict alone. But despite the altered circumstances laid out earlier, it is important to recognize that the United States still has considerable interests in resolving this conflict. Many of those interests are in the category of downside risks. Left unmanaged and unresolved, the Israeli-Palestinian conflict continues to pose risks to regional stability, and especially to the security of Israel, Palestinians, Jordan, and Egypt. And even though the Israeli-Palestinian conflict has not been a primary driver of regional turmoil during the most recent decade, its backsliding could contribute significantly to the further deterioration of a highly disrupted regional order.

With the movement of Israeli political leaders in 2020 toward the ending of Israel's Oslo commitment to negotiating territory and borders, and instead to enact unilateral annexation, the conflict teetered on the precipice of a new phase. The prospect of Israeli annexation of West Bank territory further undermined the shaky authority and legitimacy of the Palestinian Authority, and the breakdown of relations between them began to unravel the intricate web of Israeli-Palestinian security, economic, and regulatory coordination in the West Bank. When annexation was put on hold in August 2020, and again when a new Israeli government took power in 2021 promising not to annex territory (while also promising not to negotiate the conflict with the Palestinians), some of that cooperation resumed. But the prospect of annexation, alongside continued settlement expansion and the forcible relocation of Palestinian families in East Jerusalem and communities in the West Bank, confronted the Palestinian Authority with new challenges in justifying its very existence, much less its cooperation with Israel, to the Palestinian public. As time goes on, and especially should annexation go forward, the Israel Defense Forces (IDF) may find itself enmeshed in direct occupation once again, while Palestinians may have no authoritative entity that can effectively represent them or their interests to Israeli authorities in negotiations or internationally. This will produce more suffering for Palestinians while likely generating more frequent and more significant tensions between Palestinians and Israelis.

Ending the Israeli-Palestinian conflict would not solve the turmoil of the recent decades in the Middle East, which is driven by other factors—but greater violence in the conflict would almost certainly produce further regional disorder. Any upheaval or military crackdown in the West Bank would affect Jordan both directly and indirectly. Roughly half of Jordan's population is of Palestinian descent, and Jordan's monarchy retains a unique, treaty-mandated role in the management of Muslim holy sites on the Haram al-Sharif in Jerusalem. Jordan's tourist economy is tightly linked to Israel's, and a breakdown in Israeli-Palestinian relations would inevitably harm tourism on both sides of the Jordan Valley. Further, severe violence in the West Bank could lead the Israeli military to redeploy into Palestinian cities, possibly sending Palestinians as refugees into Jordan, a country already hosting hundreds of thousands of displaced Syrians and Iraqis. Jordan's struggling economy and political system would come under severe pressure in such circumstances. Meanwhile, unrest there could create further spillover effects in neighboring countries with little capacity to absorb them.

Beyond Jordan, the humanitarian emergency in the Gaza Strip especially demands American and international attention.[3] Recurrent bouts of violence between Hamas and Israel continually degrade human development and threaten wider war. Although common security interests have enabled historic gains in Israeli-Arab relations in recent years, when the Israeli-Palestinian conflict is in crisis or generates violence, heightened public concern in surrounding countries puts pressure on Arab governments to distance themselves from Washington. The conflict also remains a *cause celebre* for terrorist actors in the region.

Underappreciated, but no less significant, is that the cooperative search for peace has been a major dimension of the bilateral US-Israel relationship since the 1970s during Israeli and American administrations that spanned the political spectrum. Interests aside, this relationship has roots in American political culture, which values peace in the Holy Land and between the monotheistic religions born there and values the bonds between Israel and America as two nations with a shared narrative of building democratic safe havens for those persecuted elsewhere.

The shared search for peace has been a driver (though not the only driver) of increased American commitments to Israel in the forms of economic assistance, military support, intelligence cooperation, diplomatic and trade coordination, and more. American public and elite opinion broadly support the relationship with Israel and view the country as a "strategic asset."[4] And yet, as one of us noted in 2015, "Israel expects American understanding as it takes steps it deems necessary to protect its citizens and ensure their future security. But American patience with Israel's control over the West Bank is predicated on that control being temporary."[5] Should Israel drift or dive into permanent control over the West Bank and its Palestinian inhabitants in a one country, two systems framework, its democracy would be irrevocably compromised—and this would pose a danger as well to the American public's ready support for Israel.

Conflict Asymmetry, US Mediation, and the Two State Solution

Even as the nature and scope of American *interests* in addressing the Israeli-Palestinian conflict are shifting, other developments directly challenge US *capabilities* to remain in the central role it has held in conflict resolution efforts since the 1970s. Its position at the center of Israeli-Palestinian mediation is a consequence of the conflict's fundamental asymmetry and of America's unique role as a security guarantor both for Israel and Arab states—giving it leverage to induce and reward compromise and also the capacity to mitigate the risks that compromise entails. Together, the collapse of the Oslo framework, the policy upheaval of the Trump administration, and the prospect Trump held out of US approval for Israeli unilateral annexation generated fundamental questions about the ability of the United States to use its leverage and risk-mitigation abilities to be an effective convenor and mediator for Israelis and Palestinians.

America has never been "evenhanded" in this conflict. In fact, its lopsided affinity with and commitments to Israel are precisely what made the United States a sought-after interlocutor for the PLO from the 1970s on and what ultimately led European powers and the USSR (later Russia) to cede peace diplomacy to Washington. In this asymmetric conflict, in which Israel but not the PLO is a recognized state with sovereign territory, and in which Israel has held all the territorial "cards," no negotiated agreement is possible without Israel's government feeling secure in and compensated for the concessions it would have to make to the PLO. Historically, only the United States has been able to offer the diplomatic ballast, security guarantees, assistance, and other benefits to encourage the Israeli government to "take risks for peace." While the conflict is still unresolved, only the US-Israel relationship is sufficiently developed to offer real leverage on Israeli policies toward settlement construction and expansion, especially in diplomatically sensitive areas in and around Jerusalem (although this leverage has had only a limited impact on Israeli behavior and only when the US administration in question was willing to put significant political capital at stake to press the issue). The PLO sought American recognition and welcomed mediation after the Oslo Agreement was reached because of its understanding that the United States' special relationship with Israel meant it could encourage and enforce Israeli concessions.

The US-Israel relationship, which provided the United States with unique capacities in the conflict and made its active role indispensable for both Arabs and Israelis, has over the past decade become entangled in polarizing domestic politics both inside Israel and inside the United States. The reduced ability of either Israelis or Palestinians to trust that American policy is motivated by more than parochial political interests, and thus reliable beyond the next election, compromises the parties' faith in the US ability to mediate their dispute effectively. As US-mediated talks stalled in the 2000s, Congress also stepped in with legislative mandates that imposed new constraints on US spending for an embassy outside Jerusalem, new conditions on US assistance to the Palestinian Authority, and other measures constraining the executive branch's flexibility to provide incentives and side payments. These limits, largely imposed on US policy to the Palestinians, also indirectly reduced American flexibility in interactions with Israeli leaders.[6]

More recently, the Trump administration's one-sided moves on issues like Jerusalem fractured the American relationship with the PLO and the Palestinian people in ways that created new obstacles to their trust in US mediation of the conflict. In principle, the unprecedented, unilateral US policy shifts in Israel's favor under President Trump might have brought the United States greater influence with Israel than ever, but Trump showed no willingness to use this standing to induce Israeli flexibility with the Palestinians. This, along with Trump's abandonment of even limited respect for Palestinian aspirations, reduced significantly the willingness of the Palestinian political leadership to look to Washington for mediation with Israel. In the meantime, Israel's economic ties with Europe, India, and China and its budding engagement with the Arab Gulf states reduced the unique value of its partnership with Washington, except in the security domain. The sources of "leverage" over Israeli policies in the West Bank and Gaza are, at least in theory, more diverse and diffuse today than in previous decades.

American Attitudes toward Palestinian Statehood

How should we understand the historical American relationship with the idea of Palestinian statehood? After all, formal US policy support for an independent Palestinian state came only in 2001–2002. The American reconciliation to Palestinian nationalism was enabled, first, by the Arab states' unified insistence on the idea; second, by the slow shift in the PLO leadership away from terrorism and toward diplomacy; and third, by the First Intifada's demonstration of Palestinians' demand for an end to Israeli occupation.

In the early decades of the twentieth century, the American conception of self-determination for the peoples that were formerly part of the Ottoman Empire was understood to apply in the context of Palestine to "Arabs," not to "Palestinians" per se. After World War II and the creation of the United Nations, the United States supported the UN Partition Plan of 1947. But the plan's rejection by Arab governments, growing domestic American support for the establishment of a Jewish state, and the unilateral declaration of statehood by the Jewish Yishuv in May 1948 left the Truman administration in the position of recognizing a Jewish state while having no mechanism by which to advance a separate Arab state.

This outcome did not seem to present a problem for the Truman administration; indeed, it was largely met with relief. The Jordanian occupation of the West

Bank in the 1948–1949 war allowed Washington to sidestep the issue of creating an Arab national homeland in Palestine by treating Jordan as a manifestation of Arab self-determination and focusing on the humanitarian issue of Palestinian refugees displaced by the war. Meanwhile, the US military was impressed by the performance of the Israeli military in the 1948–1949 war and wanted to keep Israel pro-American in its orientation (while the Soviets were also courting Israel).[7] Establishing a pattern evident in later years as well, the United States in the postwar years viewed Palestine mainly through the lens of geopolitical power politics, and this perspective made American policymakers more skeptical of the virtues of a Palestinian state.

In the 1960s and early 1970s, the United States developed a closer and more supportive relationship with Israel, and the Arab states split between pro-American monarchies and pro-Soviet authoritarian republics. US policymakers during this period considered whether Palestinian statehood could be compatible with Israeli security—but their observation of the politics and behavior of the Palestine Liberation Organization suggested that it could not. The PLO held to a maximalist mission of replacing Israel with a Palestinian state from the Jordan River to the Mediterranean Sea, pursuing that goal through cross-border raids into Israel that killed civilians, through an attempt to overthrow the Jordanian monarchy in 1970, and, increasingly, through international terrorism. The PLO's commitment to armed struggle, its anticolonial rhetoric, and its international associations also earned it American enmity, and inevitably, that meant enmity for Palestinian independence as well. As Khaled Elgindy notes, "In the increasingly polarized global order of the Cold War, the Palestinians fell squarely in the 'radical' camp, alongside Syria, Iraq, Algeria, and other Arab nationalist, pro-Soviet regimes."[8]

That said, there was an understanding among US officials that Palestinian identity and Palestinian demands would have to be accommodated in some manner. In 1970, President Nixon declared, "No lasting settlement can be achieved in the Middle East without addressing the legitimate aspirations of the Palestinian people."[9] But US policy was directed to finding some outlet for Palestinian aspirations other than independent statehood, ideally under the authority of Jordan. Asked in 1974 for his view regarding an independent Palestinian state in the West Bank, President Ford answered that "the US position has always been that any final settlement must take into account the legitimate interests of the Palestinians."[10] But reflecting the skepticism of the PLO noted earlier, he added, "As far as negotiations between the PLO and Israel, or so-called US recognition of the PLO," he said, "that issue is really academic since the PLO does not recognize Israel's right to exist."[11]

For its part, the PLO's leadership in the 1970s began to toy with moderating its stance on Israel's existence and its total rejection of UN Security Council

Resolution 242, passed after 1967, calling for recognition of the right of all regional states to live in peace within secure and recognized boundaries and for Israel to withdraw from territory in exchange for peace with the Arabs. Yassir Arafat sought, in private contacts with US officials in Beirut and through messages passed through third parties, to signal flexibility. But the tight constraints of factional politics within the PLO, complicated by its precarious position in Beirut amidst a civil war there, prevented any meaningful moderation of the organization's position. Ultimately, the United States committed to Israel that it "would not engage with the PLO unless it acknowledged Israeli's right to exist and accepted UN Security Council Resolutions 242 and 338."[12]

The escalation of international Palestinian terrorism in the 1970s, along with the launch of Egypt-Israel peace talks, doomed any effort at US-PLO rapprochement. When Fatah in 1978 perpetrated a horrific attack on Israel's coastline that killed more than thirty Israeli civilians, any prospect of serious US engagement with the national movement of the Palestinian people was closed off.[13] Meanwhile, in talks with Washington, Anwar Sadat made clear that he was unwilling to allow Israel's occupation of the West Bank to prevent his securing the return of the Sinai Peninsula through his own peace treaty with Israel. Thus, President Carter's mediation of the Camp David Accords failed to yield meaningful results on the question of Palestinian self-determination in part, according to Elgindy, because of "the absence of a strategic imperative."[14]

President Reagan entered office with no evident sympathy for the Palestinians and their national cause. Written during the campaign, his August 1979 article in the *Washington Post* titled "Recognizing the Israeli Asset" discussed the US relationship with Israel almost exclusively through a Cold War lens. It offered a novel analysis of the sources of conflict in the region: "The Carter administration has yet to grasp that in this region conflict and tension are endemic, a condition traceable largely to the fragmented sectarian nature of Middle Eastern society. For example, territorial disputes among states are persistent; ethnic and religious rivalries abound; conservative and radical regarding social change are continuously in conflict."[15] It mentioned the Palestinians only to criticize the Carter administration for potentially weakening Israel "through building the basis of a radical Palestinian state on her borders."[16] The view that a Palestinian state would inevitably be "radical" and a danger to Israel echoed the skepticism we outlined as evident in US policy thinking as early as the Truman administration. But as a talking point in the public debate over US policy, this view became an article of faith for many on the American Right during the Reagan administration and has been reinforced by subsequent events, leading Congress and the executive branch to layer on additional criteria for the character and behavior of acceptable Palestinian interlocutors, and later for the preconditions that the Oslo-created Palestinian Authority must meet to win US support.

Even as President Carter lost the 1980 election to Ronald Reagan, and the Camp David Treaty's autonomy talks slowly stalled, changes in the region were also reshaping the incentives facing American engagement with the conflict. The Islamic Revolution in Iran and the Iran-Iraq War shifted the interests of American partners in the Arab Gulf. As Itamar Rabinovich notes, "In the 1960s and 1970s, they [the Arab Gulf states] had been genuinely concerned about the Arab-Israeli conflict and its radicalizing effect on their own polities. By the 1980s, different dangers were emanating. . . . Concerns about Israel were dwarfed by existential threats posed by Iran and Iraq."[17] If Carter had no strategic imperative to engage the Palestinian question, Reagan had even less. The Iran-Iraq war, the Israeli invasion of Lebanon, and the series of crises for US policy and presence there kept the Reagan administration away from any serious engagement with the question of Palestine until late in the president's second term.

The Palestinian uprising that began in December 1987 marked a turning point in the conflict, in the politics of the Palestinian national movement, and consequently in American perceptions and attitudes toward Palestinian nationalism and Palestinian statehood. The images of young Palestinians throwing rocks and Molotov cocktails confronted by heavily armed Israeli soldiers underscored for American audiences the asymmetry of the conflict, the reality of Israeli occupation, and the moral weight of the cause of Palestinian self-determination.[18] Israel had sought through diplomacy to sidestep the question of Palestinian self-determination and engagement with the PLO by dealing only with Arab state governments. The homegrown uprising made the demand for Palestinian self-determination inescapable for Israelis.

For its part, the PLO, now displaced to Tunis, struggled to coopt the energy of the Intifada and make use of the international political capital it generated, while confronting a changing international environment that reduced the PLO's resources and weakened its friends in the Soviet bloc. In December 1988, after a long series of engagements with European governments and American nongovernmental actors, including prominent American Jews, Yassir Arafat made a verbal renunciation of terrorism and embraced UN Resolution 242, recognizing the right of all states in the region to live in peace and security and opening the door to a vision of Palestinian statehood rooted in territorial compromise that was, at least in principle, compatible with Israel's continued security and survival. That declaration became the basis for American willingness to engage with the PLO in a short-lived official dialogue and later to encourage inclusion of Palestinians from within the occupied territories, but with ties to the PLO, in the 1991 Madrid

Peace Conference; notably, however, even those Palestinians were, at Israel's insistence, officially part of the Jordanian delegation.

The First Intifada, Israel's forceful response, and the international spotlight these events placed on the conflict's asymmetry increased tensions between the George H. W. Bush administration and the Likud-led Israeli government, even as Israel participated in the 1991–1992 Madrid Peace Conference and subsequent bilateral talks in Washington. The official Israeli view was that Arafat's Geneva declaration changed nothing. As it turned out, those US-Israeli tensions became one factor in an election campaign that led to the rise of a new Labor-led government in Israel; this government chose to explore the PLO's new flexibility through backchannel talks, ultimately resulting in the 1993 Oslo Declaration of Principles. It is noteworthy that, having insisted on written US assurances on conditionality for engaging the PLO, the Israeli government chose in the end to pursue secret diplomacy with the PLO without American involvement. This suggests that, at least for Rabin and Peres in the early 1990s, the backstop of American support was not a necessary condition for effective Israel-PLO negotiations and compromise.

Historians and biographers note that Rabin did not intend the Oslo Declaration to open the way to independent statehood for the Palestinians. But the PLO certainly did, and US officials, when they learned of the deal, understood that statehood was now on the table between Israelis and Palestinians. In acknowledging the PLO as its inescapable interlocutor, the Israeli government recognized that it would have to negotiate the demands that the PLO stood for: statehood and sovereignty. As US negotiator Dennis Ross put it in his memoir, "An agreement would indicate mutual recognition and all that it entailed. For Israel, mutual recognition would mean an acceptance of the PLO agenda, including statehood. For the Palestinians, it means unequivocal acceptance of Israel and its right to exist. That meant a complete redefinition of the PLO and an acknowledgement of Israel's needs."[19]

Statehood was on the table when Bill Clinton convened the ill-fated Camp David Summit in July 2000 and was explicit in the parameters he laid out before leaving office in January 2001. So, when George W. Bush formally announced US support for two states in November 2001 and expanded on his support for Palestinian statehood in June 2002, it was not perceived at the time as a dramatic innovation in American policy. This was especially true because Bush's speech attached US support for statehood to an extensive list of conditions: that the Palestinian Authority have new leadership legitimated through democratic elections; undergo reforms of its finances, security services, and judiciary; and reach security arrangements with Jordan and Egypt as well as Israel.[20] The paradigm for American support of Palestinian statehood, then, was conditional on two interrelated criteria: the Palestinian Authority's successful "preparation for statehood" and the assurance that Palestinian statehood would be "safe" for Israel.

For the United States, meanwhile, other factors underscored to American policy the value of an independent Palestinian state in resolving the Israeli-Palestinian conflict. Ronald Reagan's invocation of fractious Middle Eastern sectarian groups making regional conflict endemic was not, in fact, a regionally or historically bound view for American officials.[21] Perhaps because of America's own "melting pot" narrative and civic-nationalist creed, US policymakers have often viewed identity conflicts like those in Israel/Palestine, Bosnia, Cyprus, Kosovo, East Timor, Iraq, or Syria as inscrutable, primordial, and impervious to efforts at resolution short of territorial separation. This primordial lens on ethnic conflict offers "a definitive explanatory thesis for all disputes among all peoples whose names we struggle to pronounce."[22]

As Denison and Mujanovic note, "For a generation of policymakers and analysts, the dissolution of Yugoslavia in 1991 and its subsequent wars of succession was a watershed moment. As violence unfolded across the region, thousands of diplomats and journalists cut their professional teeth trying to make sense of the havoc."[23] Under the influence of the Balkan wars of the 1990s, many policy analysts and policymakers embraced the notion that the best, and perhaps the only, solution to such conflicts was to separate the warring factions politically—if not into separate states, then into a federal system sharply defined along ethnic lines.[24]

The collapse of the Camp David Summit in 2000 was the beginning of a series of events that profoundly undermined Israeli and Palestinian faith in the possibility of negotiated coexistence. Beginning in September 2000, the violence of the second Palestinian uprising, including horrific suicide bombings, killed more than one thousand Israelis and traumatized the population. Israel's military reoccupied Palestinian cities, killing about three thousand Palestinians in the fighting, and nearly destroyed the Ramallah compound housing Palestinian Authority president and PLO chairman Yassir Arafat.[25]

After Arafat's death in November 2004 and Palestinian elections for a new PA president, Israeli prime minister Ariel Sharon decided to unilaterally pull Israeli forces and settlers out of the Gaza Strip, leaving the territory to PA control. The Palestinian Authority held parliamentary elections in early 2006, and divisions within the PLO's Fatah movement enabled the militant Hamas movement to win a plurality of the parliament. Facing intense international opposition to a Hamas-run PA, a shaky coalition government between Fatah and Hamas was formed but quickly broke down. Hamas forcibly took over Gaza, which it has used since as a base for infiltrations, kidnappings, rockets, and other attacks on Israeli soldiers and civilians.

This political and territorial division between the West Bank and Gaza became yet another major obstacle on the road to the emergence of a Palestinian state. The primary lesson Israelis drew from this period was to conclude that a Palestinian state would, like Gaza after Israel's withdrawal, almost certainly harbor extremist forces and continue to produce terrorist attacks against Israeli territory and civilians. This conclusion, argued to and internalized by American policymakers, linked back to the Reagan-era views cited earlier and raised the bar considerably for the United States in imagining policy solutions that would allow for a Palestinian state consistent with Israel's security.

Palestinian Statehood: US Conditionality

The preceding review reveals that American policymakers consistently took note of Palestinian demands for independent statehood but usually sought to avoid the issue, seeing it as irrelevant or even an impediment, to other foreign policy goals. Even those who considered the notion legitimate in principle found it inconvenient in practice and set it aside whenever possible. The competing imperatives were primarily the geopolitical competition with the Soviet Union, the desire to secure state-to-state agreements between Israel and its Arab neighbors and end the destabilizing era of Arab-Israeli wars that began in 1948, and the view of a Palestinian state as likely to be of a "radical" political orientation and thus a threat to Israeli security and US. regional interests.

From the time of Israel's establishment in 1948 and Truman's recognition of the Jewish state, American engagement with the idea of Palestinian statehood has been conditional on that state's being "moderate" and well governed, and not a threat to Israeli security and survival. This conditionality pervaded American constraints on engagement with the PLO, enshrined in Kissinger's assurances to Israel, although it did not prevent covert and indirect US dialogue with the PLO throughout the Nixon and Carter administrations. In preparing the Geneva and Madrid conferences, the United States acknowledged the PLO's relevance to the proceedings but sought to impose conditions on Palestinian participation in peace negotiations that were focused on Palestinian acceptance of Israel's right to exist.

In addition to the conditions placed on American engagement with the PLO and the negative US attitude toward the organization, American consideration of Palestinian statehood was conditional on its own terms. In his memoir of the Camp David summit preparations, Carter's secretary of state, Cyrus Vance, articulated a very similar attitude to Reagan's: "The president and I shared their [Israel's] concerns about a radicalized Palestinian state. We concluded that some form of transitional arrangement was needed so that the Palestinians could demonstrate whether they were prepared to govern themselves and live peacefully beside Israel."[26] These two criteria—adequate preparation for statehood and assurance of safety for Israel—mirror the conditions articulated by the George W. Bush administration thirty years later.

The fundamental skepticism about Palestinian statehood was only resolved temporarily, when the PLO and Israel decided, without American mediation, to recognize one another and embark on negotiations over the fate of the occupied territories. When Bill Clinton's new secretary of state, Warren Christopher, learned in August 1993 of a secret agreement between Israel and the PLO for mutual recognition and peace negotiations, his lead adviser on Middle East Peace described the impact as historic: "In effect, it would transform an existential conflict into a political conflict. In the Middle East, nothing could be more revolutionary."[27]

This dramatic description clarifies why American policymakers became so invested in Oslo. Understanding that Oslo transformed the conflict utterly, they were reluctant to recognize the flaws and failings of this framework. They especially overlooked how its gradualist and conditioned approach to Palestinian self-determination left room for developments on the ground, including violence and Israeli settlement expansion, to undermine the prospects for a negotiated settlement and establishment of an independent, viable Palestinian state. Despite the "revolutionary" transformation of the conflict wrought by mutual recognition and the advent of direct Israel-PLO negotiations, the product of those negotiations was a framework that imposed almost insurmountable obstacles to Palestinian statehood.

In so doing, the Oslo framework also institutionalized the fundamental asymmetry of the conflict. With its five-year interim stage marked by the creation of a Palestinian Authority that had only limited, conditional territorial control delegated by Israel, this framework was in theory a pathway to Palestinian independence. Yet, in practice it enshrined (with an added territorial dimension) the limited autonomy that Begin favored as a final outcome of the post–Camp David Treaty talks: a Palestinian governance structure that was wholly dependent on Israel's delegation of authority and daily sufferance, along with Israel's continued ability to unilaterally expand settlements and associated infrastructure and to implement security measures that constrained and overtook the real-world exercise of Palestinian autonomy and future prospects for independent, viable Palestinian statehood.[28] Ultimately, the framework established by the Oslo Accords cultivated a situation in the West Bank and Gaza that undermined the very possibility of Palestinian statehood that the process supposedly promised.

The conditional approach to Palestinian statehood embedded in the Oslo framework and in US policy has been one factor eroding Palestinians' faith in the possibility of a negotiated, two state outcome to their conflict with Israel. This loss of faith inevitably has led some Palestinians to question the wisdom of the fundamental choice in favor of coexistence with Israel that their leadership made in 1988 and again in 1993. A stark example is former Palestinian Authority prime minister Salam Fayyad, who wrote in an opinion article published in 2020, as Israeli annexation seemed imminent, that the PLO's 1988 declaration accepting Israel's right to exist has merely achieved "three decades of a 'peace process' that ended the first intifada and deflated the can-do spirit it inspired, while making it possible for Israel to progressively deepen its occupation. It made it impossible for Palestinians to get anything but self-rule in areas under Israel's dominion, and gave Israel an important counterargument against charges of apartheid." In light of this Pyrrhic victory, Fayyad asks, "Is it unreasonable for the Palestinian people to expect their sole legitimate representative to reconsider this gamble?"[29]

Why the United States Has Stuck with the Two State Solution

As the conflict moved from active negotiations alongside escalating terrorism in the mid-1990s to a failed summit and the intense violence of the Second Intifada in the early 2000s, and especially after the Israeli withdrawal from Gaza and the Hamas takeover there, the hopes for a negotiated peace dimmed along with the territorial prospects for two viable, independent states. The situation on the ground moved steadily away from presenting options for a two state outcome to de facto Israeli control over all the territory, under two distinct systems. Meanwhile, at the policy level, the United States maintained its focus on a peace process marching toward the horizon of a two state solution.

Why? In part, the US policy focus sought to prevent the widening of the conflict. An ongoing process formally directed toward a two state outcome served as a guardrail for the behavior of both parties in navigating tensions between them, as well as a signal to their publics of the compromises the parties would have to make to achieve that goal. Their formal commitment to two states and US sponsorship of the process on that basis, in principle, offered a way for American policymakers to bound the unilateral behavior of the two sides and for the two leaders to push back against their own more extreme political factions. This "golden handcuffs" effect helped avoid backsliding in the conflict by giving leaders an external imperative to refuse the demands of their own maximalists for destabilizing, unilateral actions and perhaps more violence. This could be seen, for example, in the stern opposition of the George W. Bush administration to Israeli construction in the "E1" area, which would have cut off options for linking a Palestinian state in the West Bank to a nominal capital in East Jerusalem.

But in seeking to head off backsliding in the diplomatic and political arenas, this theater sacrificed a blunt assessment of the backsliding already underway. As the disconnect between US policy and the reality on the ground grew, maintaining that a two state solution was "on the horizon" weakened the real possibility for achieving that solution. Ultimately, emptying the concept of a two state solution of meaningful content opened the door for the Trump administration to present its "Peace to Prosperity" plan in January 2020 as a proposal based on a "two state solution," with David Friedman, US ambassador to Israel, writing, "The two-state solution is not dead, it has just morphed from an unattainable illusion to a pragmatic and realistic plan to end a century-old conflict. President Trump's Vision for Peace proposes an achievable means for the Palestinians to self-govern within the bulk of Judea and Samaria without jeopardizing Israel's security."[30] Sapped of its conceptual force, the term "two state solution," along with the terms "peace," "state," and "self-govern," was expanded beyond recognition.

Was there an alternative path for American policy, in which officials frankly acknowledged the damage ongoing to the prospects for two viable states and opened the door to US policy approaches other than a two state solution? Might such an approach have had any impact on the dynamics described that undermined the prospects for two states? Counterfactual history is a dangerous game. But Secretary of State John Kerry, one of the last American policymakers to buy into and seek to advance the Oslo framework, may have begun to move in this direction by the end of his term. In December 2016, Kerry argued forcefully that the window for a two state solution was rapidly closing, outlining in detail the territorial and demographic changes that were undermining prospects for its realization.[31] A different kind of US administration might have moved from that stance to begin developing alternative approaches for American policy, for example by declaring that, whatever the parties may prefer, the United States would only accept and recognize outcomes that provide for democracy and equal rights for all those living between the Jordan River and the Mediterranean Sea. But by then, Obama was almost out of office, and the administration's last act on the issue was to abstain on a UN Security Council resolution criticizing Israeli settlement activity.

Instead, Kerry's thrown gauntlet was taken up by the policy entrepreneurs of the Trump administration, with President Trump carelessly remarking, "Two states, one state, whatever the parties want," thereby encouraging accelerated Israeli unilateralism. The administration ultimately released a proposal that proposed two states in name only, while effectively eliminating the prospect for a sovereign Palestinian entity. The combination of Kerry's failed mediation efforts and then Trump's reckless approach pushed the United States even farther away from considering alternative policy approaches to the two state paradigm. Kerry's belated warning that the two state outcome might be moving beyond reach remains to be integrated into a future administration's policy planning.

The Emerging Policy Environment

The 1990s saw US policy trying to reconcile Jewish nationalism and Palestinian nationalism within the framework of the Oslo process. This policy framework was intended as a roadmap for negotiated conflict resolution, but it also functioned in practice as a straitjacket on the realization of Palestinian self-determination. Today, the conflict may be on the cusp of a new phase, in which the currently reigning interpretation of Jewish nationalism on the Israeli Right devours not only the prospect of a negotiated compromise but perhaps also the Jewish democratic state itself. Meanwhile, having been denied statehood through territorial compromise, Palestinian nationalism could revert, as Fayyad suggested, to the absolutism and rejection of Israel that characterized the pre-1980s era.

From the Oslo Accords in 1993 until Obama and Netanyahu entered office in 2009, the perception that a two state solution was within reach created a strong middle ground for a bipartisan coalition of elites to agree on American policy, limiting the influence of voices that preferred other policy outcomes. After 2002, the shared commitment of Israel, the PLO, and the United States to two states as the negotiating objective meant that US diplomacy on the conflict could proceed without provoking a major confrontation with Israel that would carry domestic political costs for a US president. Over time, as American interests in peace diplomacy declined and US domestic politics became more polarized, as the Oslo process became increasingly unproductive, and as Israel's dominant political factions and its prime minister moved away from a commitment to the two state solution, this consensus has eroded.

As noted at the outset of this chapter, a combination of national interests and domestic politics drives US policy toward the Israeli-Palestinian conflict. The two overlap—domestic political concerns often shape how Americans perceive their national interests—while representing differing sources of American policy.

The primary interests that have drawn past American leaders to involve themselves in Israeli-Palestinian peacemaking are a broad interest in Middle Eastern stability, a commitment to Israel's security as a homeland and safe haven for the Jewish people, a humanitarian interest in resolving a conflict that inflicts pain on Israelis and Palestinians, a political interest of successive presidents to bolster their legacies by resolving the conflict, a diplomatic interest in addressing Arab states' demands regarding the Palestinians, and a geopolitical interest in sustaining the American preponderance of great-power influence in regional diplomacy.

Several of these interests have declined as American priorities over the last decade or two. The Middle East as a region figures less prominently in America's global priorities today than in the last several decades.[32] Israeli-Palestinian peace almost certainly sits out of reach for the next president's term in office. With little chance to deliver near-term political benefits or a legacy-defining achievement, peacemaking becomes a less useful investment of a president's most precious resource: time. Arab states, for their part, have seen domestic and regional crises consume their attention, compounded by the COVID pandemic. And most recently, key Arab states have chosen to prioritize strategic and economic cooperation with Israel over their fealty to the Palestinian national cause, opening formal diplomatic relations and encouraging people-to-people ties. Only one of these Arab governments used the prospect of diplomatic ties to induce an Israeli policy change on Palestine—the Emiratis won an Israeli agreement to postpone any decision on West Bank annexation in exchange for recognition and full diplomatic relations. Thus, most influential Arab governments seem content to live with the conflict's status quo while still seeking to avoid a crisis such as might be sparked by Israeli annexation. Together, these factors serve to diminish Israeli-Palestinian peacemaking as an American priority.

There are exceptions to this trend—most notably, that American policy remains committed to Israeli security and that US-Israel cooperation on a host of security and non-security issues brings significant benefits to both sides. But compared to the 1970s when Arab-Israeli diplomacy was a core arena for Cold War positioning, or to the 1990s when it was a central dimension of American global hegemony, the conflict today simply does not move the same mountains in US geopolitical strategy.

As declining interests and a decayed process have eroded the previous US domestic consensus in favor of a two state outcome and thus of Palestinian statehood, domestic political actors in Israel and the United States have exploited and widened the political fissures. Israeli prime minister Benjamin Netanyahu, in power continuously from March 2009 until the summer of 2021, coordinated with Republican officials and political activists (such as white Christian evangelicals) in support of his policy preferences, which clashed with those of President Obama on both the Palestinian issue and, notoriously, the Iranian nuclear issue. Conservatives demonized Obama as hostile to Israel, and Netanyahu circumvented his administration to lobby Congress, earning recriminations from other Democrats and giving force to those on the Left of the Democratic Party pushing for a harder-line policy toward the Israeli government.

After Donald Trump's election, Netanyahu used Trump's unconditional support to validate himself with the Israeli public. Trump, for his part, exploited Israel's emerging status as a polarizing issue within American politics to strengthen his populist coalition, using Netanyahu's praise of him as the most pro-Israel president ever to validate himself with Republican Christian evangelical voters, as well as with a portion of the American Jewish community.

The polarization and politicization around US-Israel relations, along with the rightward shift of Israeli policies toward the occupied territories, likewise accelerated criticism of Israeli policies among Democrats, especially among the party's younger, more progressive activists. Polling shows that younger, female, and Black Democrats tend to see the Israeli-Palestinian conflict through a human rights lens, making them particularly sensitive to Palestinian political aspirations, punitive Israeli policies like home demolitions, and the widespread suffering of Palestinians in Gaza, highlighted most recently during the conflict between Israel and Hamas in May 2021.[33] A new Israeli prime minister and American president have voiced a determination to blunt this polarization of the bilateral relationship. But many of the other factors fueling Democrats' criticisms of Israeli policy remain in place.

What do the relative decline of a national-interest imperative on Israel/Palestine and the fractured political consensus mean for American policy? Absent a clear conception of how the new paradigm of great-power competition in the US national security strategy applies to the Israeli-Palestinian conflict, US policy may well become even more a reflection of domestic politics. And absent an unforeseen change in the course of US politics, this will mean a policy environment informed by heightened levels of polarization. American policymakers and politicians might respond by attempting to maintain, revise, or abandon consensus in their approach to Israeli-Palestinian diplomacy, with several routes available for each choice.

One reason that the two state solution has survived for so long as a core component of American policy is because of its unique utility in that policy context: it allows the United States a path by which to address a desired end to the conflict without sacrificing any of its core priorities. For this reason, there are strong incentives to attempt to maintain the policy consensus for the two state solution for as long as possible, no matter the positioning of the two parties to the conflict or the material situation between them on the ground.

This maintenance could be attempted in two ways. First, the United States could continue to act as though progress toward a two state solution were ongoing, seeking to preserve any constraint this attitude still imposes on the parties. To the extent that the Israeli and Palestinian leaderships are willing to sustain their formal commitments to the two state objective, this would suggest that they might also be constrained from action that would frontally undermine or attack a two state outcome. Such constraints could allow the United States to mitigate confrontations with Israel by, for example, reserving confrontation over settlement expansion to settlements that are outside the so-called blocs previously discussed as part of the land swaps in a two state compromise. But without a change in day-to-day policies on the ground, this approach would mean de facto accepting the previously described slow erosion of the Israeli-Palestinian status quo, as structured by the Oslo agreements, and the likely escalation of other unilateral steps by the parties that take them farther from a mutually agreed outcome.

A second approach to sustaining the two state solution would see the United States pursue steps that keep alive the prospect of negotiated conflict resolution while recognizing that negotiations themselves are unlikely in the near term. Such an approach would likely include offering carrots and sticks to the two parties to deter them from counterproductive unilateralism and to encourage cooperation, as well as efforts to leverage regional actors and trends like Arab-Israel diplomatic openings to bolster the incentives for moderation and compromise. Thus far, this appears to be the approach taken by the Biden administration.

Given the shift in the drivers of American policy toward the conflict and the negative trends in the conflict itself, the two state solution may appear to be an increasingly flimsy reed as a basis for American policy; indeed, many authors in this volume see that outcome as already beyond reach. Recognizing this, US policy elites might choose to abandon the hope of a two state outcome and accept that the costs of that shift are no higher than the costs of sustaining fealty to a vision that no longer has adherents among the parties to the conflict. Instead, a future US administration might seek a new policy consensus domestically, one that could be rooted in principles instead of specific outcomes. For example, such a policy might involve making clear that the United States will only recognize and support outcomes in Israel/Palestine that guarantee full equality and rights for all people living between the Jordan and the Mediterranean, whether in two states, one, a confederation, or some other configuration. Interestingly, the Biden administration has embraced the rhetorical commitment to advancing "equal measures of security, dignity and prosperity for Israelis and Palestinians," adding that this is important for its own sake, as well as being an important pathway to a two state outcome.

A policy rooted in such principles could potentially place new guardrails on the behavior of the Israeli and Palestinian leaderships that would replace the eroded ones of the Oslo framework. For example, should Israel proceed with annexation in the West Bank, US policymakers who took this approach would have to consider whether Israel is permanently exercising effective control over Palestinians to whom it refuses to grant citizenship. In this instance, Israel might no longer be seen as meaningfully democratic in the eyes of many Americans. This would alter the domestic foundation for a strong US-Israel bilateral relationship and induce pressure for the United States to revise its relationship with Israel into a form more like ties with other autocratic allies. For example, President Obama enunciated to the Gulf Arab states at Camp David in 2015 a promise to help secure them against external threats but not from those they face internally through a failure to be responsive or accountable to their citizens.[34] Such a revision would dramatically constrain certain forms of cooperation between the United States and Israel, likely at a cost to other American interests.

Another scenario would see American policymakers attempt to forge a revised consensus around a minimalist approach to the Israeli-Palestinian conflict. As the Middle East and this conflict diminish relative to other concerns in US foreign and domestic policy, it is possible that US policymakers may face greater degrees of freedom in making choices about whether and how the United States engages in conflict resolution efforts here and what objectives it sets for that work.

Such a stance could pull Washington back from the role of active conflict manager or mediator into a more agnostic role that might better match its relative interests in the conflict for the present. This approach might even leave the two parties more space to find new modes of engagement unconstrained by American expectations or their own previously stated positions, as Israel and the PLO did with the Oslo channel. However, a hands-off approach would be difficult to sustain in the face of the domestic political trends described earlier: it would be feasible only if American policymakers can forge a new, minimalist consensus among political elites from the Left and Right.

It is also possible that the trends laid out in this chapter will lead a future US administration to remain highly engaged in diplomacy without replacing the two-state solution with any other policy premise that garners wider support among political elites. In this instance, we would expect to see American policy on this conflict enter a seesaw driven by domestic politics, with policy positions swinging dramatically depending on the party in power—akin to US policy on funding international development programs that include abortion. Moreover, those in power will have strong incentives to pursue policy moves that cannot easily be reversed in an attempt to make short-term gains that meet their domestic political needs and tie the hands of their successors.

Although his "Peace to Prosperity" plan presented itself as a two state solution, Donald Trump himself helped shift the US policy environment toward open partisanship. His moving the American embassy to Jerusalem and recognition of Israel's sovereignty in the Golan illustrate the trend of seeking to make difficult-to-reverse moves in a partisan policy environment. With the breakdown of Arab states' unified insistence on Palestinian statehood as a condition of relations with

Israel, and with the continued divide in Palestinian politics between Fatah and Hamas, the conditions that enabled American gradual reconciliation to Palestinian nationalism have faded. For the US political Right, segments of which have viewed Palestine as an inevitably radical state since the Reagan administration, the present state of affairs allows for a more open rejection of Palestinian statehood as a policy preference. For their part, although they remain marginal on foreign policy issues in the Democratic Party, progressives critical of the traditional US policy approach to the conflict might press for economic or diplomatic sanctions on Israel or an option such as American recognition of a Palestinian state outside the context of a negotiated solution.[35]

The last four years suggest another way in which domestic American polarization affects the calculations of regional actors: it leads them to try to grab what gains they can from the sitting US president to prevent or deter a future US president from enforcing unwelcome expectations on them. This seems to have been the driver of several regional states' policies during the Trump administration, including a major escalation of Israeli settlement activities, the Saudi break with Qatar in 2017, and the Moroccan normalization agreement with Israel in 2020. The prospect for that kind of short-termism provides a strong policy reason for American leaders to seek to build some degree of domestic consensus to sustain a policy trajectory across administrations despite polarization.

What might change that would compel US policymakers to abandon the two state paradigm? Two possibilities do not seem far-fetched: Israeli annexation of West Bank territory or a collapse of the Palestinian Authority. Annexation has significant support among the Israeli public and was the formal policy of Israel's 2020 coalition government that held seventy-two seats in the Knesset.[36] Israel's formal abandonment of its commitment to negotiate territorial dispensation with the Palestinians would be a fatal blow to the Oslo Accords. And the Palestinian Authority faces multiple crises, any one of which could provide fatal: an aging leader with no plan for succession, economic crisis, escalating popular protests, and escalating repression.[37] Should the Palestinian Authority prove incapable of maintaining order in the most populous areas of the West Bank or should its institutions begin to fail, the Israeli military could find itself again in full occupation of Palestinian cities, and Israel could lose its Palestinian partner for managing the conflict, much less for negotiating its resolution. With either outcome threatening to force Washington's hand, it is past time for US policymakers to start planning for alternate approaches.

13

BEYOND OSLO

Reimagining Israeli-Palestinian Futures

Khaled Elgindy

The Oslo process is dead and has been for some time, and the prospect of a negotiated two state solution, in both political and physical terms, appears to be headed for a similar fate. The Trump administration's policies, including the Trump Vision released in January 2020, have sought to radically rewrite the terms of an Israel-Palestinian settlement on the basis of permanent Israeli occupation and a consolidation of the current one state reality. The collapse of Oslo and the likely demise of a two state solution need not inspire despair, however, but rather can provide us with a clean slate by which to rethink old assumptions and explore new possibilities in terms of both process and substance. As the classic two state model based on territorial partition and demographic separation becomes increasingly unworkable, policymakers in the United States and abroad must begin looking at alternative solutions, including the possibility of one binational state and hybrid models such as confederation, as well as a new peace process and peacemaking architecture, regardless of whether the goal is two states or one.

Before looking at the range of possible approaches to an Israeli-Palestinian settlement, it is worth taking stock of where we are and how we got here.

How We Got Here

A Hierarchy of Rights

Today, only one state—Israel—rules over the entire territory between the Mediterranean Sea and the Jordan River, an area in which some fourteen million people live; this population is almost evenly split between Arabs and Jews.[1] Within this single territorial unit, however, are a variety of legal/political regimes that apply to different constituencies, including limited Palestinian self-rule in certain areas of the occupied territories, in what Harvard University's Yael Berda refers to as "a sophisticated, graded and racialized matrix of political membership in which one's political status, identity and territorial location determine their political rights, which laws will apply to them and, perhaps primarily, their possibilities for mobility."[2] There are five such categories in this hierarchy of rights.

At the top are Israeli Jews, who enjoy full citizenship rights, regardless of where they reside. This category includes the roughly 650,000 Israeli settlers living beyond the 1967 border, or Green Line, in the occupied West Bank and East Jerusalem. The Nation-State Law of 2018, which has the force of a constitutional provision, defines Israel as a state of and for the Jewish people, rather than as a state for all its citizens. It makes official what had been implicit since Israel's founding in 1948—that "the right to national self-determination in the State of Israel is unique to the Jewish People."[3]

The next group consists of roughly 1.9 million Palestinians who are citizens of Israel but who face institutional discrimination in a variety of spheres, making them effectively second-class citizens.[4] On the next lower rank are 375,000 Palestinians in occupied East Jerusalem; they are afforded residency in Israel, which is often conditional but does not confer formal citizenship rights, and their communities often lack basic services. The fourth category comprises Palestinians living in the West Bank; there the Palestinian Authority (PA) has limited autonomy over most of its 2.6 million Palestinian inhabitants while controlling just 18 percent of the territory. At the very bottom of this totem of rights are the nearly two million Palestinians of the Gaza Strip, which, despite being governed by Hamas, remains under Israel's effective control in the form of a blockade through which it controls the strip's air, land, and sea borders; imports and exports; and even the population registry, as well as movement in and out of the impoverished coastal enclave, which remains severely restricted.[5]

Collapsing Pillars

Adding to this gloomy picture, most pillars of a negotiated two state solution have collapsed or are collapsing. The Oslo framework, a five-year interim arrangement that has lasted more than twenty-eight years, has run its course. Numerous rounds of formal negotiations, along with an array of protocols, memoranda, commissions of inquiry, peace plans, and other initiatives, have failed to produce a conflict-ending agreement or even to manage the conflict or prevent periodic outbreaks in violence. The few conflict mitigation mechanisms that had existed, such as the Quartet's ill-fated Roadmap peace plan of 2003, have long since been abandoned, and US officials have shown little interest in reviving them or establishing new ones.

The demise of the Oslo process has paralleled that of its signature achievement: the Palestinian Authority (PA). Once seen as the embryo of a future Palestinian state, the PA is now facing its own inexorable decline thanks to a perfect storm of internal and external threats. A sharp drop in international donor aid, exacerbated by the sweeping aid cuts of the Trump era and the loss of tax transfers collected by Israel on the Palestinians' behalf, have put the PA on the brink of financial bankruptcy. Internally, the fourteen-year-old division between the Fatah-dominated West Bank and the Hamas-ruled Gaza Strip has paralyzed Palestinian institutional politics and eroded the legitimacy of the Palestinian leadership while helping fuel violence and instability, particularly in Gaza. The decision by President Abbas to cancel long-delayed national elections at the last minute in the spring of 2021, along with the crackdown on anti-PA protests after the murder of political dissident Nizar Banat by PA security forces later that summer, only highlighted the growing corruption and authoritarianism of the Palestinian leadership.

The failings of the peace process and the PA stand in stark contrast to the enormous success of Israel's ever-expanding settlement enterprise, which now dominates both the physical and political landscape of the West Bank. Since the start of the Oslo process, Israel's settler population has soared from roughly 250,000 in 1993 to well over 650,000 today. Although formal annexation has (for the moment at least) been taken off the agenda, de facto annexation in the form of ongoing settlement expansion and the continued fragmentation of Palestinian territory has continued in all parts of the West Bank, most notably in and around East Jerusalem.

Perhaps most decisively, the precarious consensus within Israeli, Palestinian, and American politics that has kept the two state solution afloat during the last two decades is now collapsing on all sides. This is particularly true in Israel, where right-wing parties opposed to Palestinian statehood have dominated the Knesset and successive governments for most of the last two decades and the traditional peace camp has all but disappeared. Like his long-serving predecessor Benjamin Netanyahu, Israel's prime minister from 2021–2022, Naftali Bennett of the hard-right Yamina Party, has ruled out the possibility of a Palestinian state or even a return to negotiations.[6]

Meanwhile, among Palestinians in the occupied territories, the constituency that historically has been the most supportive of an independent state in the West Bank and Gaza, support for a two state solution has dropped to less than 40 percent, the lowest level since the signing of the Oslo Accords in 1993.[7] Although the PA/PLO leadership remains firmly committed to the goal of two states, a growing number of Palestinians, particularly those who came of age during the Oslo years, are abandoning the increasingly unlikely goal of an independent state in favor of a struggle for equal rights in a single state.[8]

The same is true of the United States, where one of the two major political parties has formally abandoned the goal of two states. In 2016, the Republican Party officially removed references to a two state solution from its party platform while declaring that the party "reject[s] the false notion that Israel is an occupier."[9] The Trump administration translated this approach into policy. Trump's "Peace to Prosperity" plan released in January 2020, which called for a Palestinian "state" made up of disconnected fragments of territory surrounded and controlled by Israel, was more reminiscent of the Bantustans of apartheid South Africa than anything that might reasonably be called a sovereign state. The aim of the Trump vision was not to alter or challenge the inequities created by five decades of Israeli occupation but to consolidate them and make them permanent while simultaneously doing away with the basic principles undergirding the peace process, including UN Security Council Resolution 242 that called for ending Israel's occupation on the basis of "land for peace." In addition to recognizing Israeli sovereignty over all of Jerusalem and Syria's Golan Heights, the administration worked to erase the distinction between Israel and the territories it occupied by declaring that it would no longer consider Israeli settlements to be illegal and even requiring products originating in the settlements to be labeled as "Made in Israel."[10]

The election of Joe Biden has given proponents of a two state solution a renewed sense of hope. However, the Biden administration's deprioritization of and decidedly minimalist approach to the issue may yet leave them disappointed. Despite recentering the two state solution, the administration has shown that it does not intend to invest substantial political capital toward achieving that goal.[11] Administration officials have stressed their desire to avoid public disagreements with Israel over issues like Israeli settlement expansion. Moreover, apart from adopting a decidedly less hostile tone toward the Palestinians than his predecessor; reinstating assistance to the Palestinians, including to UNRWA, the UN agency responsible for Palestinian refugees, albeit at more modest levels than in previous years; and promising to reopen the US Consulate in Jerusalem and the PLO mission in Washington, both of which still face serious political and legal hurdles, much of the Trump legacy remains intact. President Biden and Secretary of State Antony Blinken have made clear that they do not intend to move the US Embassy back to Tel Aviv or reverse the previous administration's recognition of Jerusalem as Israel's capital.[12] Meanwhile, key elements of the Trump agenda, such as the reversal of long-standing State Department policy on the illegality of Israeli settlements and new "rules of origin" guidelines legitimizing Israeli settlements, remain in place. These policies, along with Secretary Blinken's statement that control over the Golan Heights "remains of real importance to Israel's security," raises real questions about the administration's commitment to Resolution 242.

Perhaps most tellingly, the unrest in Jerusalem in response to the pending expulsions of Palestinian families in Jerusalem and the subsequent outbreak of war in Gaza in May 2021 showed the limits of what the Biden administration was willing to do. During the eleven-day conflict, which left 243 Palestinians and 12 people in Israel dead, the administration repeatedly expressed unqualified support for Israel and its right to defend itself while repeatedly blocking attempts by the Security Council to call for an immediate ceasefire.

Therefore, far from being a full repudiation of the previous administration's legacy, the Biden administration's approach may be more akin to "Trump-plus." Yet even Trump's policies did not emerge in a vacuum and were less indicative of a new approach to Israeli-Palestinian peacemaking than they were the culmination of the *old* approach.[13] Although the failure of Oslo had many authors and multiple causes, three key structural deficiencies ultimately doomed the US-led peace process. Long before the Trump administration's legitimization of Israeli settlements or its formal jettisoning of UN Resolution 242, previous administrations had eroded the established ground rules of the peace process while acquiescing to Israeli-imposed "facts on the ground." Despite their rhetorical opposition to Israeli settlements as a hindrance to peace, successive US administrations from both parties found ways to accommodate Israeli settlement expansion by carving out exemptions for "natural growth," East Jerusalem, the large settlement blocs, and other loopholes—exemptions that amounted to de facto recognition of Israeli policies of de facto annexation.

Likewise, although previous administrations were never so brazen as to deny the existence of Israel's occupation, they effectively downplayed its centrality to the conflict by focusing on secondary issues such as security, economics, and institution-building, all of which were constrained by and ultimately derivative of Israel's occupation. This was partly a function of the vast power asymmetry between the two sides, but it was also "baked" into the process of Oslo itself, which focused as much—and often more—on transforming Palestinian politics and institutions as it did on altering the dysfunctional dynamics between Israelis and Palestinians. Perhaps the most prominent example was the Roadmap, the internationally backed peace plan put forward by the United States, the EU, the UN, and Russia in 2003. Although intended to be mutual and parallel, the Roadmap's implementation was ultimately subverted and effectively transformed into a tool of conditionality and a blueprint for "reforming" Palestinian politics.

This brings us to the third failing of the US-led peace process: the absence of mutual accountability. Although both the White House and Congress remained vigilant in holding Palestinian leaders accountable for various transgressions ranging from incitement to support for terrorism, US officials steadfastly avoided any means of accountability for Israeli violations—whether settlement expansion, the killing of civilians, or other problematic actions. It comes down to a basic rule-of-law issue: if the rules of the process are consistently ignored or are applied only to one side—the weaker side—the process loses credibility and ultimately cannot function.

Options and Scenarios

Before addressing the range of possible options and scenarios, some general observations and clarifications are in order.

Guiding Assumptions

The ensuing analysis is based on three basic assumptions.

1. *Outcomes vs. Solutions*: The first assumption is the crucial distinction between outcomes and solutions. That there is broad international consensus (excluding the Trump administration) on the need for a two state solution is of course no guarantee that such a solution will be achieved. Nor does it change the fact that Israelis and Palestinians currently live in a one state reality. Any solution, as such, would need to be equitable in nature; that is, it must satisfy the basic right of both Israelis and Palestinian to live in freedom, security, and dignity. In practical terms, an equitable solution is one that affords the right of self-determination to all people in the Holy Land, whether Jews or Arabs, regardless of the political, legal, or demographic configuration(s) that are in place. Any plan that involves the domination, subjugation, or expulsion of one group by another therefore cannot be considered a

viable solution. Similarly, plans or initiatives aimed at managing or tweaking current realities without fundamentally altering the status quo of indefinite Israeli control over the West Bank and Gaza Strip also do not meet this threshold and hence do not qualify as viable solutions. This latter category of *non-solution outcomes* includes partial or interim initiatives, such as calls for limited "disengagement" from parts of the West Bank, "economic peace," or the Trump Plan itself, all of which are designed to maintain effective Israeli control over both the people and the land while relieving Israel of its responsibilities as an occupying power.

2. *Power dynamics matter*—Israel clearly has the ability to shape or dictate outcomes in ways that Palestinians do not. How sustainable such unilaterally imposed outcomes may be is, of course, a different matter. The relationship between Israel and the Palestinians is not merely one of conflict; it is also an occupation in which Israel, which boasts a first-world economy and the most powerful military in the Middle East, rules over the lives and resources of some five million stateless Palestinians in the West Bank and Gaza Strip. Despite the tendency of US officials over the years to downplay its centrality—and, in the case of the Trump administration, to deny it altogether—Israel's occupation and all that it entails, including the settlement enterprise and its associated infrastructure and regime of control over West Bank land and resources, are an inescapable reality and a primary driver of the conflict. It is this enormous power asymmetry between Israelis and Palestinians that makes effective third-party mediation so crucial and essential to a successful peace process. Moreover, any solution—whether it is based on one state or two—will necessarily entail a loss in Israeli Jewish power and privilege.
3. *Politics matter (including Palestinian politics)*—Just as power dynamics can limit or enhance the options available to one party or the other, domestic politics also help animate or constrain each side's decision making and behavior both inside and outside the negotiating room. But whereas US officials typically have been highly attuned and quite deferential to the internal political priorities and preferences of Israelis leaders, they have had far less patience or appreciation for Palestinian political needs. Thus, successive administrations have variously opted to ignore, suppress, or, in some cases, even reengineer internal Palestinian politics to suit the perceived needs of peace process. These actions were enabled both by the Palestinians' distinct power disadvantage vis-à-vis both Israel and the United States and the highly intrusive nature of the Oslo process itself, which focused not only on transforming

Israeli-Palestinian relations but also on reorganizing and redefining Palestinian political and governing institutions. Thus, the debilitating schism between Hamas and Fatah, which has paralyzed Palestinian politics, fueled violence and instability in Gaza, and eroded the legitimacy of Mahmoud Abbas's leadership; although primarily self-inflicted, these challenges were nonetheless reinforced by the US-led peace process, in part because of American and Israeli opposition to Palestinian reconciliation efforts. In the end, a cohesive and unitary Palestinian leadership and polity that enjoys a modicum of domestic legitimacy is a requirement for a credible peace process.

The defining feature of any outcome or solution is sovereignty—in terms of which party exercises it and where, whether on a de facto or a de jure basis. Although there may be any number of non-solution outcomes, only three scenarios would satisfy, if only theoretically, the basic right of both groups to self-determination: partition (i.e., divided sovereignty), a one state solution (i.e., unitary sovereignty), or hybrid models such as confederation (i.e., mixed/blurred sovereignty). This is not to say that such solutions are in any way inevitable but only that the universe of possible solutions is limited to these three broad categories. Indeed, it is entirely possible—perhaps even likely—that the status quo as a non-solution outcome, could continue indefinitely. The feasibility of any solution will ultimately depend on the extent to which it is broadly acceptable to both sides of the conflict—that is, mutually agreed on—and sustainable over time (i.e., not likely to induce a desire by either side to overturn it later).

Lastly, because neither Israeli nor Palestinian societies are as yet postnationalist in orientation, any realistic solution should ideally allow (or at least not deny) both sides a measure of national self-expression. Any solution should be evaluated on whether it meets these three basic criteria—that is, whether it upholds the right of self-determination, is mutually acceptable, and allows some form of national self-expression for *both* Palestinians and Israelis.

Scenario 1: Salvaging a Two State Solution

Dividing the Holy Land into two sovereign states, which would satisfy both groups' desire for self-determination and national self-expression, remains the preferred option in the wider international community. It has also been the most elusive, dating back to the 1937 Peel Commission.[14] Despite a broad international consensus around the goal of creating two states based on the 1967 borders, repeated attempts to negotiate such an outcome—in 2000, 2001, 2007–2008, and 2013–2014—have consistently ended in failure. The only other basis for territorial division with any grounding in international law would be UN General Assembly Resolution 181—the 1947 Partition Plan—although neither side seems inclined to reopen this file at present.[15]

Despite past failures and the Trump administration's attempts to bury the two state framework once and for all, the classic two state model remains the guiding framework for the international community and for a large share of the Washington policy community and is still—at least theoretically—achievable. For such an effort to succeed, however, it would need to be conducted very differently than what we have seen in the past. A return to the status quo ante in any case may not even be possible. As discussed earlier, the Oslo framework is simply too outdated and disconnected from realities on the ground to serve as an effective basis for resolving or even containing the conflict: attempting to do so would be akin trying to run Windows 95 on today's computers. To the extent a two state solution is still achievable, it will require an entirely different "operating system," both in terms of the process and Washington's role in it. It is not enough simply to urge the parties to resume direct negotiations, which in any case are unlikely to succeed.

In short, the United States, in partnership with European, Arab, and other stakeholders, will need to build a new framework and peace process architecture that can help create the conditions for those negotiations to succeed, particularly given past failures. Any new process, first and foremost, should uphold and reaffirm international norms—namely UN Resolution 242, the unacceptability of acquiring land by force, the centrality of the 1967 lines, and the goal of ending Israeli occupation—with the same force and clarity that the Trump administration sought to do away with them. The sheer enormity of the power asymmetry between Israel and the Palestinians requires adopting an almost fundamentalist approach to these principles, with the understanding that realities on the grounds will likely deviate from them anyway. To that end, UN Resolution 2334, adopted in the waning weeks of the Obama administration, can be a major asset to US officials. In addition to reaffirming the "established consensus that settlements have no legal validity," it calls on member states "to distinguish, in their relevant dealings, between the territory of the State of Israel and the territories occupied since 1967"—precisely the opposite of what the Trump administration sought to achieve.

No less crucially, a credible diplomatic process would also need to focus on altering (if not reversing) the dynamics that drive the conflict and help fuel instability—namely, Israel's occupation and all that it entails and the Gaza blockade—as well as the ongoing Palestinian political division. Among other things, this would mean taking a firm stance against, and even working to roll back, Israeli settlements, land confiscations, home demolitions, expulsions, and other measures designed to deepen Israeli control over the West Bank and East

Jerusalem and working to create an environment conducive to Palestinian reconciliation. Likewise, a new diplomatic push for a two state solution would also require concrete mechanisms of implementation and accountability for noncompliance, both of which were absent from the Oslo Accords and US mediation. Just as compliance should generate political progress and other rewards, violations by either party ought to carry tangible consequences, whether political, diplomatic, or economic. Any new process will also need to address the massive chasm of mistrust and lack of goodwill that exists on both sides, ideally in a more holistic and balanced way than previous efforts.

Lastly, building a new peace process will require a rethinking of the US role. Although the United States can still play a leading and perhaps even a choreographic role in Israel/Palestine diplomacy, the US monopoly over the peace process is simply no longer feasible, given the constraints imposed by domestic US politics and the special relationship with Israel. Even though no other single actor can replace the United States as sole mediator, it is possible to imagine a new peace process architecture involving key European, Arab, and other stakeholders, in which key international actors like the European Union and the United Nations play a much more robust role, particularly on issues like Israeli settlements, human rights abuses and other issues deemed too sensitive for US officials.

To achieve these objectives, American officials must be prepared to use US leverage with both sides but particularly with Israel, the stronger of the two parties. Although third-party mediation typically involves positive and negative inducements for both sides, the US-Israel relationship is exceptional in that it is already saturated with positive inducements, including $3.8 billion of largely unconditional and unscrutinized military aid.[16] The greater challenge will be in creating incentives (or disincentives) for Israel to undertake the difficult and politically unpopular decisions needed for a two state solution, including the removal of tens of thousands of Jewish settlers (perhaps as many 200,000 or more), the transfer of biblically significant West Bank territory to Palestinian sovereignty, and, perhaps most difficult of all, dividing Jerusalem. Because Israeli leaders are unlikely to move on these on their own, the United States should be prepared to use its considerable leverage in the service of these objectives, including the possibility of linking US military aid and other aspects of the bilateral relationship to Israel's treatment of Palestinians. Although the notion of applying pressure, much less any type of sanction, on Israel remains anathema to large segments of the political and policy establishments, there is a growing political appetite for doing so, both within the American public and among policymakers, particularly Democrats.[17]

Rebuilding the collapsed pillars of a two state solution will undoubtedly be a heavy lift, requiring considerable effort, creativity, humility, and, above all, political capital on the part of US officials; it may not even be feasible in the near term given the domestic political realities in the United States, which only underscores limits on US mediation. Yet, there is no getting around the fact that any attempt to salvage whatever may be left of a two state solution will necessarily entail some form of pressure on Israel as the stronger party. The only question is whether a future US administration would be prepared to pay the potential political and other costs that are likely to accompany it.

Scenario 2: One State with Equal Rights

For many, the time for "two states for two peoples" has come and gone, if in fact it was ever possible. The demise of the Oslo process, along with the damage wrought by the Trump administration, has breathed new life into the old-new idea of a single state with equal citizenship rights for both Israeli Jews and Arab Palestinians. Proponents of a one state solution argue that more than a quarter-century of "peace processing" has done nothing to roll back more than fifty years of Israeli occupation and the one state reality that now exists between the Mediterranean and the Jordan. Instead of each side getting "half a loaf," critics of partition view it as more akin to negotiating over "half a baby."

As with the two states option, there are different iterations of a one state solution, the most prominent of which is binationalism. The idea of a binational state for Arabs and Jewish was first seriously broached by renowned Palestinian American intellectual, Edward Said, at the apex of the Oslo process, but it has steadily gained ground among diaspora Palestinians and, more recently, among younger Palestinians in the occupied territories.[18] Unlike the one state vision embraced by the PLO before 1988, which called for undoing the events of 1948, the contemporary binational vision imagines a more straightforward and egalitarian future based on existing demographic realities in the whole of Israel/Palestine.

As the successor to both Israel and the Palestinian Authority, such a state would require, first and foremost, a new constitution that upholds the rights of both Arabs and Jews on the basis of equality before the law and that acknowledges the historical ties and narratives of both groups in the whole of Israel/Palestine. To rectify past wrongs and allow both groups to move forward, one staters call for a South Africa-style truth and reconciliation process, while putting in place new safeguards to prevent illiberal majoritarianism or the domination of one group over the other.[19] In any event, it is argued, the vision of one binational state is no more naïve or impractical than the goal of "unscrambling the omelet that the Israeli occupation has created."[20] A variation of this model involves federalism, under which Israel/Palestine would be divided into territorially (and perhaps demographically) defined, semi-autonomous cantons or states, similar to the systems put in place by Spain or Canada to address Catalan and Québecois separatism, respectively.[21]

Moreover, binationalism in Israel/Palestine is less alien than many might imagine. In fact, the idea of a unitary, democratic state for Arabs and Jews had enjoyed wide currency in US policy circles in the 1930s and 1940s as an alternative to partition, which many imagined would become a source of perpetual conflict and violence.[22] Even the "Jewish state" originally envisioned in the UN Partition Plan of 1947—much like the envisioned state of Israel-Palestine—would have included nearly equal numbers of Arabs and Jews.[23] Although a majority of these Palestinians were forced to flee over the course of Israel's creation, the Zionist movement had at least in principle accepted a de facto binational state. Likewise, the military regime that governed Israel's Arab citizens from 1948 to 1966 provides a precedent for transitioning from military rule to the enfranchisement of Palestinians within its borders. Despite having the right to vote, Israel's Arab citizens, like their Palestinian brethren across the Green Line today, were subjected to movement restrictions, land confiscations, internal dislocation, and other abuses.

The appeal of "one person/one vote" is difficult to deny. A study by the University of Maryland's Shibley Telhami found that, although Americans were evenly split between support for a one state and a two state solution, nearly two-thirds favor one state with equal rights if a two state solution became impossible.[24] The main obstacles to the one state vision, however, are not moral but *political.* Proponents of a binational state generally have been long on ideals and short on practical details, particularly in light of the persistence of two competing (and often mutually exclusive) nationalist narratives on both sides and the vast power asymmetry between the two groups. Although a growing number of Palestinian intellectuals are embracing the idea of one state, only a handful of Israeli thinkers have done so.[25] The vast majority of Israeli Jews—which remains the dominant group on both sides of the Green Line—are steadfastly opposed to the integration and enfranchisement of millions of Palestinians, which they believe would effectively end the Jewish character of the state.[26]

Even on the Palestinian side, where a one state solution seems to be gaining the most traction, its most prominent advocates are typically found in the diaspora, an important political constituency that has long been neglected by both the Oslo process and the Palestinian leadership and that has had little, if any, stake in the two state model. Although growing numbers of Palestinians in the occupied territories, particularly among the youth, are embracing the idea as well, there is not yet an organized political movement, party, or actor pushing in that direction on the Palestinian scene. This may be a reflection of the current fragmentation and paralysis within Palestinian politics writ large and thus could very well change in the coming years. For the time being, however, even Hamas, which has a long history of violent opposition to the Oslo process and rejects any recognition of Israel, has steadily come to terms with a Palestinian state in the West Bank, East Jerusalem, and Gaza Strip.[27]

That said, it may only be a matter of time before the idea of one state with equal rights begins to take hold in Palestinian and perhaps even Israeli politics, particularly in the absence of any credible challenge to the "separate and unequal" one state reality that exists today. After all, it was not so long ago that the two state solution was itself dismissed as both unrealistic and unachievable. As Peter Beinart, a leading figure in the American Jewish Left and one-time proponent of two states, recently wrote, "The traditional two-state solution no longer offers a compelling alternative to Israel's current path. It risks becoming, instead, a way of camouflaging and enabling that path. It is time for liberal Zionists to abandon the goal of Jewish–Palestinian separation and embrace the goal of Jewish–Palestinian equality."[28] Unlike Palestinian activists and scholars whose support for one state is grounded in a rejection of Zionism, Beinart's embrace of one state, which is directed primarily at Jewish audiences, remains firmly anchored in a Zionist ideological framework. As such, it is reminiscent of a strand of Zionism promoted by the likes of Judah Magnes and others during the Mandate era that has since disappeared but could now be revived.[29]

Scenario 3: Hybrid Models/Confederation

There is another set of options that may offer a reasonably equitable solution to the conflict but that have largely been overlooked by American policymakers. Along the spectrum between the two state and one state models lies the idea of shared sovereignty, or confederation. These hybrid models offer a potential way around some of the most difficult challenges posed by either hard partition or strict binationalism. The basic idea behind confederation that it is possible to divide sovereignty in the Holy Land without physical or territorial separation. The key to such confederal models, such as the Israeli-Palestinian Creative Regional Initiative's (IPCRI) "Two States in One Space" proposal or the "Two States, One Homeland" project, hinges on establishing open borders between Israel and Palestine in which citizens of both states enjoy full freedom of movement, and even residency, in the whole of the land between the river and the sea.[30]

The primary advantage of a confederation approach lies in the recognition that both Israelis and Palestinians continue to maintain an attachment to both sides of the 1967 border. Confederation also opens up the possibility of new solutions to some of the most intractable issues of the conflict.[31] For one, Palestinian refugees wishing to return to their former homes or villages could live in Israel as legal residents while gaining citizenship in a Palestinian state in the West Bank and Gaza, thus fulfilling their dream of return without altering Israel's demographic balance. The prospect of open borders would also allow some settlers—for example, in highly disruptive settlements like Maale Adumim or Ariel—to reside in a Palestinian state while maintaining their citizenship in and access to Israel, thus reducing the political and financial costs associated with a large-scale evacuation by Israel while minimizing damage to the contiguity of the Palestinian state. The idea of open borders also helps avoid many of the practical problems arising from a territorial division of Jerusalem, particularly in the highly contentious Old City and its surroundings.

Once again, there are precedents from which to draw. For instance, the 1947 partition plan—the original two state solution—envisioned a territorial division "with economic union."[32] Similarly, during the Taba negotiations of 2001, the two sides discussed the option of an open city in Jerusalem, although they had different definitions of what that would mean.[33] Indeed, the status quo of a Palestinian Authority operating under indefinite Israeli occupation is itself a mixed model of sorts—albeit on a highly inequitable and unsustainable basis.

The challenges and shortcomings associated with confederal models, however, are significant. With many more moving parts to connect, a confederation would be considerably messier and more difficult to negotiate than either the traditional two state or one state models. In addition, this arrangement assumes a much greater level of trust and goodwill between the parties than presently exists. Indeed, the prospect of allowing Israeli settlers to remain in their present locations raises difficult challenges for both sides. Israelis would be reluctant to entrust the safety of their citizens to any Palestinian government; likewise, Palestinians would have a hard time legitimizing Israeli settlers and settlements, whose presence was established through coercive means and very often on confiscated Palestinian land. In the end, the question of how to manage security, which would require even more intensive cooperation than that conceived under the Oslo framework, particularly given the massive power asymmetry between the two sides, may pose the biggest challenge in finding a workable confederation model.

In the end, the real value of confederal models may be less as an alternative to the two state solution than in providing new ways of thinking *about* two states. Despite its many shortcomings, a confederation model can help expand the range of possible options and negotiating tools available to the two sides—particularly at a time when physical realities have all but foreclosed the classic two state model and political conditions do not yet allow for an egalitarian, one state option.

Reflections and Recommendations

Wherever one stands on the conflict or on how best to resolve it, there is little doubt that the old peace process is dead and that a credible two state solution is facing a similar fate—if it has not already expired. The Trump administration's policies accelerated the demise of two states, and the Biden administration's attempt to return to the status quo ante seems equally untenable. As we have seen, the Oslo framework is simply too outdated to serve as an effective framework for peacemaking or to challenge the highly inequitable one state reality that already exists. Any attempt to salvage a two state solution will likely require a new peace process architecture and a new approach by Washington. In addition to reinstating and upholding the internationally accepted parameters, including UN Resolution 242 and international humanitarian law, any renewed push toward a two state solution will need to focus on confronting and rolling back Israel's occupation, with clear mechanisms of accountability for both sides. This will require making difficult decisions and investing considerable political capital, costs the Biden administration may be unwilling to bear. It will also require a degree of humility on the part of Washington in recognizing that it can no longer continue to dominate an Israeli-Palestinian peace process and that it must be prepared to participate in a genuinely multilateral process involving a range of other stakeholders.

The collapse of Oslo and the likely demise of a two state solution require us to consider alternative solutions, including the possibility of a binational state with equal rights and hybrid scenarios like confederation, both of which would guarantee self-determination and a measure of national self-expression for both Jews and Arabs in the Holy Land. Despite the egalitarian appeal of the one state model, it will take time for it to ripen politically and, specifically, for a mobilized political constituency of Israelis and Palestinians that can champion it to emerge. Confederation, likewise, offers a way for both groups to share "the loaf" instead of dividing it, though it is difficult to imagine what incentive Israel would have to do so when it already possesses the full loaf. If nothing else, hybrid models offer a way to expand the toolkit of future diplomats and negotiators in achieving a more equitable two state solution. Indeed, the more the choice is framed as a binary—either territorial partition or a unitary state—especially in the context of a highly inequitable one state reality, the more appealing the egalitarian model will become—not only because partition has been tried and failed but also because egalitarian binationalism, for all its shortcomings, still holds a kind of idealistic moral appeal.

All these scenarios, whether binationalism, confederation, or the traditional two state model, would require a fundamental change to the power dynamics between Israelis and Palestinians: this remains the biggest single challenge to an equitable peace settlement. Simply put, there is no credible solution that does not entail Israel, and specifically Israeli Jews, giving up some degree of power and privilege. A viable peace process therefore must also have the right incentive structure in terms of the costs and consequences for maintaining the status quo versus the benefits for altering it. The question of which of the three scenarios is most feasible may therefore depend on which one involves the least cost for Israeli Jews, as the dominant group. But as long as the status quo remains less costly than any of these other scenarios, Israeli leaders will have no reason to make such a choice.

In the meantime, instead of focusing on restarting negotiations or attempting to revive an obsolete peace process, American officials should retrain their sights on the broader goal of reaching an equitable resolution to the conflict that is mutually acceptable and sustainable over time. To that end, there are four steps that US officials can and should take:

1. The first and most important step would be to engage in a full and frank debate on the Israel/Palestine issue, which is long overdue. To that end, the State Department should conduct a comprehensive review of US policy toward Israel/Palestine, similar to the one carried out in 1975. In parallel, Congress should convene a series of hearings into all aspects of the Israel/Palestine issue, including the reasons for past failures and the US role in them, the extent to which a two state solution is still viable, and the role of aid to both parties.
2. As part of these reassessments, US policymakers should explore the full range of possible solutions, including a binational state and confederal models, as well as post-Oslo visions of two states. Moreover, regardless of the feasibility or desirability of any of these scenarios, US officials should affirm their commitment to basic principles of equality, freedom, and self-determination for all people living between the river and the sea.
3. In the wake of Oslo's demise, the United States should work with its partners in the region (e.g., Egypt, Jordan, Saudi Arabia, UAE, and Turkey) as well as other international stakeholders (e.g., EU, UK, Norway, Russia, China, etc.) to devise a new peace process architecture and framework that (1) is consistent with and upholds international norms and standards, whether international humanitarian law (IHL) or human rights law (IHRL); (2) is genuinely multilateral; (3) is capable of putting forward a new peace plan and laying out benchmarks and timetables for ending the Israeli occupation; and (4) includes mechanisms of accountability.
4. As part of a holistic approach to peacemaking, whether the goal is two states, one state, or some sort of confederation, US officials and other international stakeholders, including the parties themselves, should look seriously at models of transitional or restorative justice—for example,

through the creation of a truth and reconciliation commission—as a way to address past grievances and promote genuine reconciliation in a conflict that is more than a century old. Such reconciliation efforts, along with people-to-people and other peacebuilding programs between Palestinians and Israelis, would necessarily be implemented in a postconflict setting as part of a final peace arrangement.

14

THE EUROPEANS AND THE ISRAELI-PALESTINIAN CONUNDRUM

Wedded to Mantras

Muriel Asseburg

Over the last decades, a one state reality with unequal rights has become entrenched in Israel/Palestine, a situation that has increasingly been described as conforming to the legal definition of apartheid by Israeli, Palestinian, and international human rights organizations.[1] In fact, in 2020, Israel's planned formal, unilateral annexation of up to 30 percent of West Bank territory, the ground for which had been prepared by the Trump administration's so-called Deal of the Century, unmasked beyond any doubt the failure of the Oslo approach to resolve the Israeli-Palestinian conflict and threatened to destroy its cooperative conflict management component. It also accentuated the dilemmas of Europe's approach to Israel/Palestine.

Over the last forty years, Europe has been seeking ways to help advance Israeli-Palestinian peace. The Israeli-Palestinian conflict has been one of the few policy areas where the European Union (EU) and its member states have had a well-defined, detailed, and consistent stance. As a matter of fact, the Europeans also played a key role in shaping international language on the conflict, not least with their 1980 Venice Declaration. At the same time, the Europeans have remained in the back seat when it comes to shaping dynamics on the ground. These dynamics—as other contributions in this volume outline in detail—have rendered not only a two state settlement but also any agreed settlement of the conflict ever more difficult to achieve. Yet, Europeans have clung to the mantra of a negotiated two state solution. After the intra-Palestinian division in 2007, they added another mantra to their repertoire—the one on intra-Palestinian reconciliation—while, at the same time, erecting hurdles to achieving that goal.

Consequently, the chasm between European rhetoric on conflict resolution and conflict realities on the ground has widened. Europeans have not only remained a payer rather than becoming a player when it comes to Israel/Palestine but developments have also negatively affected the credibility of European policies in the Middle East in general—calling into question European actorness and paving the road for further erosion of a rules-based international order.

This chapter analyzes European policy objectives and instruments relating to Israel/Palestine, explains why there is such a large gap between European rhetoric and actual policies and why Europeans remain unable to assume a more prominent and effective role in realizing their proclaimed objectives, and discusses prospects for European policymaking on Israel/Palestine.

Europe and the Two State Approach

Europe has been a champion of a two state settlement to the Israeli-Palestinian conflict for the last forty years.[2] With their 1980 Venice Declaration, the European Community (EC) and its member states acknowledged the Palestinian right to self-determination and the right of all countries (including Israel) to live in peace in secure and recognized borders; called for a comprehensive solution to the Arab-Israeli conflict; and emphasized Europe's obligation to play a special and concrete role in peacemaking, including with the Palestine Liberation Organization (PLO).[3] Henceforth, the EC (and, later, the EU) became the main supporter of a two state approach to resolving the Israeli-Palestinian conflict, successfully anchoring the paradigm and corresponding parameters in international resolutions and approaches to conflict resolution,[4] such as UN Security Council Resolution 2334 (2016).[5]

To achieve their objectives, the Europeans have stressed in their declaratory politics that there is no alternative to a two state approach for resolving the Israeli-Palestinian conflict. Based on that paradigm, they have engaged diplomatically and signaled their willingness for supporting conflict management and peacemaking by cooperating with the United States, the UN, and Russia in the now largely defunct Quartet for Middle East Peace, by endorsing the 2002 Arab Peace Initiative, and by appointing a series of Special Representatives for the Middle East Peace Process.[6] Since Oslo, and with the aim of state- and institution-building, the EU and its member states have by far been the biggest and most reliable donor to the Palestinians, giving considerable financial support to the Palestinian Authority (PA) and Palestinian civil society; to Israeli human rights, pro-peace, and pro-democracy groups; and to UNRWA.[7] In addition, they have deployed two civilian missions to the Palestinian territories: one to support the Palestinian police and rule of law (EUPOL COPPS) and one to provide a third-party presence at the Rafah Crossing Point (EUBAM Rafah), the latter being on standby since 2007. These missions aimed at institution-building and conflict management, respectively. During the Trump years, the Europeans increased their support to the Palestinians and to UNRWA and devised quick-impact projects in the Gaza Strip to compensate, at least partially, for US funding cuts.

Scaled-Down Ambitions, Inconsistent Implementation

Yet, the EU and its member states were not able to prevent a two state settlement from being ever more undermined by Israel's settlement, occupation, and annexation policies in the territories occupied in 1967. The feasibility of a two state approach was moreover put in question by the intra-Palestinian split that followed the January 2006 elections and the short-lived national unity government that broke down in June 2007. And, although the EU and its member states continue to rhetorically adhere to a two state arrangement "as the only realistic solution to the Middle East conflict," this commitment has long since degenerated into an empty formula—or rather one that has maintained the illusion of the occupation being temporary, rather than serving as a guideline that would provide direction for European policy.[8] In practice, and in particular since the US-mediated Israeli-Palestinian negotiations broke down in April 2014, the Europeans have scaled down their ambitions from contributing to a two state settlement to merely maintaining the option on the table.[9] In practice they have not been able to prevent the fast erosion of its feasibility and the subsequent entrenchment of a one state reality with unequal rights. At no point over the last fifteen years have the EU and member states seriously considered using their potential leverage—as the biggest trading partner of Israel and the largest donor to the Palestinians—to affect the cost-benefit calculations of the conflicting parties. Rather, the European approach has become ever more inconsistent.

Such inconsistencies have yielded ambiguous European signals. On the one hand, Europeans have criticized Israeli settlement and annexation policies and the PA's increasingly authoritarian governance. On the other hand, such criticism has not been linked to tangible costs that would have affected any of the two actors' calculations and thus policies. For example, the Europeans suspended a formal upgrade of EU-Israel relations in 2008 and halted the meetings of the EU-Israel Association Council after July 2012 to signal their dissatisfaction with Israeli policies, in particular the excessive use of violence in Gaza. Yet, at the same time, cooperation between Israel and the EU, and between Israel and individual EU member states, has deepened considerably—for example, in the framework of

Horizon 2020 and other EU programs that Israel has profited from—thus muddying the message.[10] This expanded cooperation has also diminished the appeal of a formal upgrade of relations. Accordingly, Israeli (as well as Palestinian) policy circles hardly took note of the EU's December 2013 offer for a Special Privileged Partnership.[11]

Similarly, despite dissatisfaction with an ever more authoritarian Palestinian leadership, the EU has not scaled back its aid to the PA significantly. Instead, and in contradiction to its self-proclaimed "more for more" principle, aid to the Palestinians has remained detached from performance in the fields of governance and human rights. Even the dismantling of checks and balances by the Palestinian president—above all, the dissolution of parliament, systematic interference with the judiciary, and curtailing of freedom of expression—has not prompted a review of funding. Ultimately, Europe has allowed the PA to develop a sense of entitlement to its support, rather than demanding from it a clear commitment to democratic, transparent, and accountable governance. Indeed, European support for the PA seems to have been given, first and foremost, to maintain the Oslo regime of joint conflict management, rather than to build a democratic system of governance and effective state institutions.[12]

In their 1999 Berlin Declaration, EU member states announced that they looked forward to the early fulfillment of the Palestinians' right to self-determination, that the right must not be subject to any veto, and that they would recognize a Palestinian state "in due course."[13] Yet, although they have repeatedly debated state recognition, to date, only Sweden has done so, the rest arguing that a Palestinian state would have to emerge from bilateral negotiations with Israel.[14] In doing so, the member states granted Israel an effective right of veto on the realization of the Palestinian right to self-determination and missed an opportunity to reaffirm the 1967 borders. Similarly, the differentiation policies adopted by the Europeans since 2012, which oblige Europeans to differentiate between their dealings with Israel and with Israeli entities in the occupied territories, continue to be implemented inconsistently by the member states.[15] For example, member states have not correctly and consistently indicated the origin of settlement products and have not prevented European businesses from continued cooperation with Israeli entities in the settlements.[16]

In view of the EU's normative self-perception as a community of law and values and a champion of the international rules-based order, it is particularly irritating that the EU and its member states have not been more consistent on the issue of accountability for suspected war crimes and crimes against humanity committed by parties to the conflict. Indeed, some member states have pressured the Palestinian leadership not to seek legal recourse for the denial of rights and violations of international humanitarian law; for example, EU member states exerted pressure on the PA not to join the International Criminal Court (ICC). What is more, in their 2020 "amicus curiae" letters to the ICC, Austria, the Czech Republic, Germany, and Hungary argued that it should not have jurisdiction to investigate war crimes in the Palestinian territories because Palestine was not a state.[17] Although Israeli governments have accused Europeans of supporting a "singling out of Israel" in UN bodies, the track record of European voting on UN Commissions of Inquiry tells a different story: Israel/Palestine has been the exception when it comes to Europeans supporting investigations into and accountability for crimes committed.[18]

Last but not least, Europe has applied different standards to the parties to the conflict. For example, since the Hamas victory in the 2006 parliamentary elections, European contacts and cooperation with Palestinian officials have been conditioned on their commitment to the so-called Quartet criteria: recognition of Israel, commitment to previous agreements signed by Israel and the PLO, and renunciation of violence.[19] By contrast, contacts and cooperation with Israeli officials have been largely independent of their position on recognition of the PLO, their stance on violence, and their commitment to the Oslo Accords or to a negotiated conflict settlement. In particular, the EU and its member states have never conditioned cooperation with the Government of Israel on its committing to the pursuit of a two state outcome.[20]

Why the Inconsistencies?

Three main factors have been the source of these inconsistencies or have impeded the Europeans from being more effective in realizing their positions.[21]

The United States as Main Mediator

First, the EU and its member states have refrained from challenging the US administration's position as the chief mediator or facilitator in the conflict. As a rule, Europeans held back as long as US initiatives were in the making—even if they did not look promising. For example, the delay in publication of Donald Trump's long-announced peace plan seemed to serve as an excuse for inaction. After France tried to push for an alternative approach to the Israeli-Palestinian conflict with its January 2017 peace conference, which remained without tangible impact, Europeans refrained from engaging in further efforts at peacemaking. And even though the Trump administration departed far from international law and the international consensus on conflict resolution, abandoned the claim of previous US administrations of being an honest broker between the two sides, condoned Israeli breaches of international law (for example, when Washington recognized Jerusalem as the capital of Israel in 2017 and Israel's sovereignty over the Syrian Golan Heights in 2018), and seriously undermined the PA, Europeans refrained from putting forward an alternative approach—limiting themselves to statements and to compensating for parts of the funding that the United States withdrew from UNRWA, the PA, and Palestinian civil society.[22] And again, after Joe Biden assumed the US presidency and announced that he would deprioritize engagement in conflict resolution, Europeans did not step forward to try to shape dynamics instead. There are plausible reasons for the EU to cede the role of main facilitator to the US administration: both Israel and the United States have made it clear that they would not accept Europe in the driving seat.[23] But in practice that has meant that the EU and its member states have shown little ambition to play an active role in shaping the course of developments, largely resigning themselves to being a taker of policies. It has also meant that policies on Israel/Palestine have remained hostage to US election cycles.

Hiding behind the EU

Second, EU member states have hidden behind the EU rather than being active proponents of EU stances, valuing their bilateral relations with Israel more than sending unambiguous signals about European positions on the conflict and its resolution. That trend has become even stronger in view of campaigns by the Government of Israel to delegitimize any criticism of its policies and attacks on the EU, for example by deliberately confusing between differentiation and boycott.[24] In that context, the Israeli government has also pushed EU member states to adopt the May 2016 International Holocaust Remembrance Alliance's (IHRA) working definition of antisemitism: this vague definition—complemented by illustrative examples, among others, of Israel-related antisemitism—has been used to delegitimize criticism of Israeli politics as antisemitic and to establish a network of antisemitism coordinators throughout Europe on the EU, member state, and substate levels.[25] These coordinators have not only engaged in (much needed) work against antisemitism but have also come to play an important role in delegitimizing criticism of Israel, as well as Palestinian organizations, aspirations and narratives.[26] These efforts have been accompanied by a powerful campaign by the Government of Israel (the Ministry of Strategic Affairs under Gilad Erdan, in particular) and international and Israeli NGOs, such as NGO Monitor, aimed at delegitimizing Palestinian actors and their international supporters.[27] In this context, the EU and its member states have been massively criticized.[28] For example, in 2015, the Simon Wiesenthal Center ranked as the third worst antisemitic act of that year the EU's decision to label products made in Israeli settlements as such, rather than as produced in Israel.[29]

As a consequence, EU member states' representatives have not proactively propagated EU stances—for example, on differentiation—and have shied away from public diplomacy. They have mostly left it to the High Representative to explain EU policies and defend them against slander. They also did not take diplomatic action against the Netanyahu government's sidelining of the High Representative Federica Mogherini (2014–2019), nor have they pushed back strongly against Israel's EU bashing.[30] As a result, although EU-Israel relations have actually been thriving in terms of trade, Israeli participation in EU-funded programs such as Horizon 2020, and deeper cooperation in a growing number of areas, such allegations have created an ever more toxic atmosphere around the Israeli-Palestinian conflict in Europe: it has disabled constructive dialogue on visions for Israel/Palestine and European policy options. In Israel, they have also fed the perception of the EU as an unfriendly, irresponsible actor that should not assume a more prominent role in conflict resolution.[31]

Europe Divided

Third, and most importantly, although at least in principle consensus on the parameters of conflict resolution has been maintained among the EU and its member states, there is no consensus on how to move forward to advance conflict resolution or at least to effectively maintain the option of conflict resolution on the table. Consensus has also been lacking on the weight that the Israeli-Palestinian conflict should have in European foreign policies and with regard to relations with Israel. This lack of agreement among member states—stemming from different historical experiences, self-understandings, political cultures, and closeness to the United States, among other factors—has markedly increased over the last few years against the backdrop of the rise of right-wing politics in Europe, the 2015 "refugee crisis," and the Trump administration's approach to the conflict. The Israeli government has also exploited disagreements among member states on other foreign and domestic policy issues, as well as grievances of some member states with EU policymaking, to forge alliances with individual heads of state and government and of subregional groups, thereby further dividing the EU and reducing the influence of Brussels and member states critical of the occupation.[32] As a consequence, EU member states have split unevenly into three major blocs: the states most critical of Israel's policies, the states most closely aligned with it, and the states that see themselves mainly in the role of balancing the divergent European positions and achieving consensus.[33]

However, the lack of consensus predates these recent divisions. For example, there has been persistent disagreement among close partners, such as Germany and France, over what kind of diplomacy should push the peace process forward, with Germany favoring bilateral negotiations versus France advocating for an international conference. Another issue has been how to nudge the parties to engage in constructive politics, whether through incentives or pressure/disincentives, including tools such as sanctions, recognition of a Palestinian state, negotiations on a full-fledged Association Agreement with the Palestinians in preparation for statehood, the convening of an Association Council with Israel, and so on. An additional unresolved issue has been how to deal with the situation on the ground; for example, which approach to take toward the occupation authorities in Area C of the West Bank with regard to master plan processes or claiming compensation for EU-funded projects destroyed by the Israeli army.[34]

As a result of these divisions, there has been a marked absence of proactive European policies, particularly over the last five years. There have been no substantial EU Council Conclusions on the Middle East peace process since June 2016, because they would have required unanimity of the EU-28 (after Brexit, EU-27).[35] In addition, there have been split European votes in the UN General Assembly, such as in the vote on the US Embassy move to Jerusalem. The EU-28/-27 has also not been able to agree on joint statements on important developments, such as US recognition of Jerusalem as Israel's capital, the US Embassy move, the planned eviction of the Bedouin village of Khan al-Ahmar, or a call for an immediate ceasefire in the violent escalation in May 2021. Consequently, it has increasingly relied on statements by the High Representative or coalitions of member states, which, have had even less of an impact than statements that would have signaled European unity.[36]

The EU-27 did not even manage to agree on a strong common stance on Israel's announced plan to annex large swaths of the West Bank.[37] Although every member state agreed that the acquisition of territory by force was inadmissible under international law, they were not able to find a common position on the rejection of the annexation nor on potential measures to take in response, thereby highlighting tensions between a European commitment to international law and values, on the one hand, and to the State of Israel, on the other.[38] An options paper that would have detailed the range of measures Europe could take to prevent and react to the annexation was apparently prepared by the European External Action Service but not completed and shared, despite it having been demanded by a sizable number of member states.[39] Neither was a legal assessment commissioned of the impact of the annexation on EU-Israel and EU-PLO/PA relations. Instead, member states such as Germany, while stressing their concern about the annexation, rejected any measures that could be conceived by Israel as punitive or unfriendly, including recognition of the state of Palestine.[40] Thus, even in a dramatic situation that threatened to forestall a two state settlement and put at risk the continuation of the conflict management approach agreed in Oslo, EU member states resorted to a flurry of activities and statements, but were unable to speak with one voice and throw their combined weight into the balance to prevent the annexation. That failure only confirmed the attitude of many Israeli policymakers that joint European action was effectively blocked by veto actors allied with Israel (such as Hungary) and that, even though the annexation would arouse strong European condemnation, it would not incur major costs for Israel, at least with regard to relations with Europe. In the end, therefore, Europe played only a minor role in suspension of the formal annexation. Rather, it was the US-mediated September 2020 Abraham Accords between Israel and the UAE/Bahrain that provided Prime Minister Benjamin Netanyahu with the opportunity to put off formal annexation and thus revert to his preferred "no solutionism" approach to the Israeli-Palestinian conflict.

The Way Forward

In November 2020, Joe Biden's victory in the US presidential election augured a return of the United States to a two state approach. Yet, the Biden administration emphasized from the start that it would not make Israeli-Palestinian peacemaking a foreign policy priority. It also had to spend considerable political capital on at least partially reversing the utterly one-sided policies of Trump's Middle East team, rather than being able to invest from the outset in forward-looking politics. Although such an approach is in line with the Bennett government's approach of "shrinking the conflict," might address the self-interest of the PA elite, and might lead to an improvement in the socioeconomic situation for some Palestinians, at least in the short term, it risks further deepening the one state reality with unequal rights.[41]

It has also led to a situation in which the EU and its member states, rather than seeing the emperor-without-clothes moment of the previous government's annexation plan as an opportunity to review and fundamentally adapt their approach to the post-Oslo setting, have once more contented themselves with lending support to a US administration perceived as friendly, open to transatlantic cooperation, and in line with European values—and thus also sticking to an increasingly meaningless two state paradigm.

Toward a Binational State?

Thus, the US return to a two state approach has contributed to forestalling a much-needed debate in Europe about approaches better geared to dealing with the one state with unequal rights reality that has been consolidating in Israel/ Palestine. Contrary to the European mantra, there are alternatives to a two state arrangement that would allow both for the expression of national identities and the realization of individual and collective rights. The EU and its member states would therefore do well to explore the creative and constructive dimensions of alternative models that could contribute to conflict resolution.[42] An open and inclusive debate that embraces the younger generation of Israelis and Palestinians (including those in the diaspora) and is exploring alternative futures for Israel/ Palestine and paths to get there is urgently needed—and should not be suppressed by taboos and delegitimization campaigns.

One counterargument often heard is that, although a two state arrangement hardly seems a realistic option any longer, other formats are no more promising. For example, a confederation would be based on divided sovereignty just as much as a two state settlement, and a binational state would depend on both peoples renouncing their right to self-determination in their own independent state—a concession that a majority in neither society is ready to make today and that is rejected outright by a majority of Jewish Israelis because it is incompatible with political Zionism. Yet, popular support is not set in stone but rather contingent. For example, majority support for a two state approach only developed once that became a realistic approach—and waned over the last few years in response to its decreasing probability and feasibility. Interestingly, during the annexation debate, the idea of a one state arrangement gained increasing support not only among Palestinians: polls suggest that support for one state is rising among Israelis as well, even though that might reflect different understandings of a one state arrangement.[43]

Yet, a European move to abandon the two state mantra in favor of a demand for equal rights in a binational state faces major hurdles and is unlikely for two main reasons.[44] First, it would bring Europe in direct contradiction with Israel's self-definition as a Jewish and democratic state and an exclusive safe haven for Jews. Against the backdrop of twentieth-century European history, including the Balfour Declaration and the prosecution and genocide of European Jewry, such a step is unlikely unless it has significant Jewish Israeli support. The hurdle is particularly high in Germany, given the country's Nazi past, the dominant interpretation of its historical responsibility, and the role Germany's political elite has allowed Israel to play as an arbiter of Germany's rehabilitation as a civilized nation.

Second, abandoning the two state paradigm would entail a complete overhaul of the European approach toward Israel/Palestine that has become well entrenched over the last forty years and would necessitate a rethinking of objectives, values, strategies, and policy instruments. This is not only a major challenge because of path dependency. It is also extremely unlikely that such a major revision would be successful at a time when member states differ fundamentally on the relevance that the conflict should have for their relations with Israel, on the instruments that they should employ to pressure for the realization of Palestinian rights, and even whether they should do so at all. The risk of losing what is usually called the European "acquis" on Israel/Palestine has thus prevented—and is likely to continue to prevent—any substantial move toward support for equal rights in a binational state (or in any other format) or a substantial revision of the European approach.

More Consistent Engagement for a Two State Outcome?

Are the EU and its member states likely to focus their energy instead on reversing trends on the ground and push for the realization of a two state settlement? Three lines of action—on occupation/de facto annexation, Palestinian state-building, and conflict resolution—would be key to making progress in that endeavor. First, there should be a consistent differentiation between Israel and the occupied Palestinian territories by inserting respective territorial clauses into all agreements with Israel, correctly indicating the origin of goods, reporting regularly on the implementation of differentiation measures on the basis of UN Security Council Resolution 2334, supporting a regular update of the UN Human Rights Council's database on entities doing business in the settlements, and so on.[45] Given that Europeans consider Israeli settlements in the occupied territories a violation of international law, they would actually have to enact an import ban for settlement products.[46] At the same time, Europeans would have to better explain and defend differentiation policies to their own—and to the Israeli—publics and adamantly reject the equation of differentiation measures with antisemitism or boycott. European recognition of a Palestinian state on the 1967 lines would, of course, be the clearest signal of where the Europeans see the future borders, without foreclosing the possibility for limited land swaps.

Second, Europeans should rethink their stance toward and support for the Palestinians. In particular, Europeans will have to find out how support can be provided in the Palestinian territories to more sustainably improve living conditions and prevent forced displacement from strategic areas, without at the same time cooperating with the occupation authorities in a way that legitimizes prolonged occupation, annexation, or both. In this context, Europeans would need to conduct a legal and political review of their contractual relations with Israel, as well as with the PLO/PA, to ensure that they do not legitimize annexation and behavior contrary to international law. This approach would also demand that Europe contribute effectively to overcoming internal Palestinian divisions and support a democratic renewal of Palestinian representative institutions. This will force Europeans to examine where they themselves stand in the way of achieving progress; for example, with their "no contact policy" toward Hamas, their support for Mahmud Abbas's "West Bank first" approach, and their restraint when it comes to exercising pressure on the PA in view of its increasingly authoritarian governance. The last point is even timelier after Abbas, in April 2021, postponed indefinitely the legislative elections that had been scheduled for May, a prominent PA critic was killed when taken into custody by PA security forces in June, and repression of demonstrations and criticism increased markedly in the aftermath.

Europeans have routinely called for Palestinian Legislative Council (PLC) and presidential elections to be held; the EU also provided election assistance and monitoring of Palestinian elections in 1996 and 2006 and offered its support for the then-aborted 2021 elections. Indeed, the EU could play an active role in the renewal of Palestinian institutions. In addition to assisting with the process, Europeans should contribute their share by clearly stating their readiness to work with whatever government is formed through fair elections, provided it commits to nonviolence. They should also work (in cooperation with the United States) to secure Israel's consent for voting to take place in East Jerusalem in one way or the other and for guaranteeing the freedom of movement between the West Bank and Gaza Strip and within the West Bank that is necessary for voting.

Last but not least, the EU and its member states will need to upgrade their role in promoting a settlement of the conflict based on the right of self-determination of both peoples, which guarantees individual human rights and the security of all; it also resolves the refugee question by taking into account both the individual right of Palestinian refugees to return and the interests of current and potential host states, including Israel. Although Europe will not be in a position to replace the United States as the main mediator, it could still play a much more active role in a multilateral approach to Israel/Palestine. Based on lessons learned from earlier mediation efforts, it should start working toward an appropriate multilateral framework for talks. This would include reasserting the parameters for a settlement, offering robust and impartial mediation, chaperoning the implementation of an agreement through an independent monitoring and conflict-resolution mechanism, and providing substantial security guarantees. Even more crucial than establishing the negotiations framework, however, will be devising a strategy for nudging the parties to engage in negotiations in good faith and to be ready for genuine compromise. That is unlikely to succeed without spelling out concretely the costs of noncooperation and continued breaches of international law. In line with a rights-based and rights-centered approach, Europeans would also need to support, rather than trying to prevent, international investigations and court proceedings; for example by the International Criminal Court. If the EU and its member states want to be taken seriously in their commitment to a rules-based international order, they should not give the impression that they are giving Israel and armed Palestinian groups a free ride regarding the violation of international law.

Alas, for the reasons outlined earlier—Europeans being divided, on the defensive, torn between allegiance to international law and a commitment to Israel as a safe haven for Jews, and resigned to a supportive rather than a formative role—it is highly unlikely that consensus will be achieved among the EU-27 on aligning their policies with their values and stated objectives. Neither should it be expected that a coalition of member states with sufficient weight would form and take assertive steps and thus induce change. After all, the Israeli-Palestinian conflict has been downgraded in European foreign policy priorities. As a consequence, Europe is likely to remain wedded to the two state mantra and seek ways to support the Biden administration's approach to Israel/Palestine. But that also means that it will remain a payer that funds a game that cannot be reconciled with European values and interests.

Conclusion

RECOGNIZING A ONE STATE REALITY

Marc Lynch

"Israel is reporting that they've vaccinated half of their population, and I'm gonna guess it's the Jewish half," joked *Saturday Night Live*'s Michael Che on a February 20, 2021, broadcast. Che's one-liner sparked an avalanche of criticism, perhaps because it offered an unlikely point of entry into a debate that many Israelis would prefer to avoid: What exactly is Israel today? Are Jews only half of its population? What obligations does it owe to Palestinians who live west of the Jordan River? If Israel is only a sovereign state within its pre-1967 borders that is temporarily occupying the West Bank and Gaza, then Che might still be correct about its international legal obligations under the Fourth Geneva Convention to vaccinate Palestinians living under occupation.[1]

But if, as this volume explores, there already exists a de facto one state reality west of the Jordan River, then his quip was frighteningly accurate.[2] Jews make up roughly half the population within that territory, with the identity and location of individuals demarcating extreme inequalities of access and rights. At the time of the broadcast, only 27 percent of residents of Arab East Jerusalem had received the first dose of the vaccine, compared to 57 percent of the city as a whole.[3] Israel had given only two thousand doses of the vaccine to the Palestinian Authority and promised three thousand more for some five million Palestinians living in the West Bank and Gaza.[4] The international scrutiny had Israel simultaneously arguing that the International Criminal Court had no standing because Palestine was not a sovereign state and that it had no obligations to vaccinate Palestinians because the Palestinian Authority held sovereign responsibility.[5] This volume set out to explore these realities, their conceptual foundations, and the difference they make for analysis and policy.

Decades ago, another comedian, Steve Martin, began his shows by declaring, "I like to start the show by doing one impossible thing. Now watch me suck this piano through a straw." This volume may not successfully suck a piano through a straw, but it has achieved something almost as impossible: engaging thoughtfully, rigorously, and deliberately with the implications of the de facto existence of a one state reality for Israelis and Palestinians. Such dispassionate engagement is not the rule, to put it mildly. The ferocity and volume of the public discourse surrounding the Boycott, Divestment, and Sanctions (BDS) movement and the comparison of Israel's control of the Palestinians to apartheid, including efforts to criminalize such discussions in many US jurisdictions, may be taken as a signal of its importance. It also makes it almost an ethical obligation for political scientists and policy experts to engage in reasoned discourse on the subject. In the absence of an accurate understanding of the reality of the situation, policy will continue to fail, conflict will continue, and millions will continue to suffer domination and the denial of their identity and their aspirations.

As Michael Barnett, Nathan Brown, and Shibley Telhami posit in the introduction to this volume, the one state reality is simultaneously obvious and inscrutable, existing in a deeply unsettling space of ontological uncertainty. Israel clearly controls all the territory and the people who live there, exercising its power at will to shape the life conditions of every Israeli citizen and noncitizen in the area. Its withdrawal to the borders of Gaza and its reliance on the semi-functional Palestinian Authority to govern the West Bank offer it a degree of plausible deniability for this reality, even as it exerts effective sovereign control over the entire territory and its population. The formal and informal systems of identity-based exclusion invite comparisons to apartheid South Africa that have generated, to this point, more heat than light.

Ontological uncertainty and policy stalemate have kept diplomacy locked within the two state solution framework, even though it has been many years since such an outcome looked plausible to even its most fervent advocates. The disconnect between policy formulations and realities, along with shifting political realities and new forms of activism, has opened considerable space for new ideas outside the formal policy realm. But such suggestions, whether of a binational democratic state based on equal rights or of formal annexation of the West Bank under Israeli sovereignty, are unsettling in their own way. Any policy response to a one state reality seems to challenge core ethical and identity commitments on all sides of the conflict, threatening both those committed to a Jewish state and those committed to a state for the Palestinians. But squaring the circle through a one state reality that realizes the national aspirations of both Israelis and Palestinians appears as implausible as a two state solution. Can this circle be broken?

This volume sought to sidestep the rhetorical and political obstacles to rigorous analysis of the nature of a one state reality by focusing not on what could be or what should be but on what is. Not every contributor agrees that Israel and Palestine today are already a single state, but all worked within, around, or through the premise. The introduction captures the intellectual stakes: to assess clearly and dispassionately what Israel and Palestine actually are today across multiple domains so we can realistically assess how we got here and where we might go. As the chapters demonstrate, the prospects for a two state solution have become vanishingly small. Israelis and Palestinians today exist in an unacknowledged one state reality defined by systematic structures of domination and control imposed by one identity group over another in varying degrees based on location and legal status. These systems of control have deeply shaped every institution within both Israel and the Palestinian territories in ways that defy any possibility of easy partition. But recognition of that reality has been stymied by the inability to formulate any workable alternative political formula. And so the wheels have spun, even as Israel relentlessly expands its settlements and builds the infrastructure of exclusion and control.

The moment is right for such an engagement. The last several years have seen a greater openness toward questioning foundational ideas about the nature of the conflict than there has been for decades.[6] Academic and policy discussions have increasingly turned in this direction as well. My own interest in the topic crystallized around a Project on Middle East Political Science (POMEPS) workshop organized with the other editors of this volume that brought together almost two dozen scholars to discuss the one state reality concept.[7] As several contributions to this volume note, both Palestinians and Israelis have increasingly reoriented their political horizons around different lodestars than two states for two peoples. Concepts such as settler colonialism and the racialization of Palestinians under Israeli rule have gained considerable traction in the academic literature, while many Israeli academics and politicians have equated the BDS campaign with not only anti-Semitism but also actual terrorism.

The international policy community has been slower to respond. But, in its own way, Donald Trump's 2020 "Vision for Peace" shows movement here as well.[8] Trump's plan had little to do with Israeli-Palestinian peace as it has been defined for decades. It had no realistic vision for a two state solution. It involved no direct diplomacy between Israelis and Palestinians and made no reference to their long record of negotiations or to long-standing interpretations of international law. Nor did it offer any plausible path toward a stable political alternative to the status quo.

But it did have the virtue of tacitly acknowledging the one state reality that much of the Israeli-Palestinian policy community would prefer to ignore. Former Israeli prime minister Benjamin Netanyahu may have temporarily backed away from his push for annexation of parts of the West Bank following the decision by the United Arab Emirates to normalize relations with Israel several months later, despite the absence of any progress toward a Palestinian state. But this represented only a pause in the move toward some unknown future. His replacement, Naftali Bennett, speaks of "shrinking the conflict," avoiding negotiations while seeking to manage conditions to avoid eruptions of turbulence that complicate the status quo.[9]

Palestinians, in turn, have increasingly pointedly noted the failures of the Oslo solution as the institutions of the Palestinian Authority relentlessly subordinated momentum toward statehood in favor of enforcement of Israeli security demands, which Diana Greenwald lays out in her chapter. The energy in Palestinian politics today is behind the BDS campaign, an active and remarkably successful effort to harness international norms as a form of power outside formal institutions that Nathan Brown and Iman Elbanna document. As I discuss later, it is telling and significant that this effort has been met with such intense pushback from the Israeli government. I take up the question of whether BDS can survive today's global resurgence of populism and xenophobic dismissal of all forms of international norms—a resurgence to which Israel has contributed and with which its current political realities are closely aligned.

In this concluding chapter, I reflect on the contributions to this volume, which are analytical, descriptive, normative, and prescriptive. What shines through in the contributions by this experienced and thoughtful group of authors is a powerful sense of an old reality that has long since died but that continues to shamble on. The two state zombie is propped up not by an alien virus or a laboratory experiment gone wrong but by the institutional and ideational legacies of decades of lived experience. It has taken on elements of structure that defy the agency of those attempting to transcend it from all directions, whether Israeli annexationists or Palestinian one state advocates. Breaking free of such entrenched structures is never easy. There are profound limits to agency in the face of the myriad forces working to keep the status quo in place. But, as Ian Lustick argues, these structures often appear immutable and eternal right up until the moment they suddenly collapse.

In this conclusion, I take up the challenge posed by the volume's contributors. I do not seek to impose an artificial consensus. Nor do I simply repeat what the chapters have already said. Instead, I offer my thoughts on four major themes that cut across the volume: how to conceptualize the institutional arrangements of the one state reality, the possibilities of ideational and policy change, the policy implications of adopting the one state reality frame, and the ethical demands of engaged analysis.

Observing the One State Reality

What is a "one state reality"? The term runs through the volume beginning with the introduction and then weaving through the chapters. But what exactly does it mean? Even those who roughly agree with the idea struggle to articulate exactly what it implies. Ian Lustick's chapter 1 captures the ontological uncertainty surrounding the definition of the situation: "the stark discrepancy between perceiving West Bank and Gaza Arabs as if they are living outside of the State of Israel and the actuality of their status as living within it." It remains difficult, I suspect, even for those who believe that the two state solution is dead to conceptualize Palestinians in the West Bank and Gaza in this way—in some imagined future perhaps but already actually living within Israel.

The chapters leave little possibility of avoiding the conclusion that those Palestinians currently live under conditions of domination by Israel in which they lack a state of their own to provide governance, protection, or meaningful representation. But even there, many will blanch at the idea of their inclusion in the State of Israel. But what else can a one state reality mean, other that all the territories or people are functionally part of the same state? Consider again, the COVID-19 vaccinations. Legal entry into Gaza remains completely controlled by Israel and Egypt, leaving the Hamas-led government entirely dependent on them for acquiring vaccines; as a result, the Gazan population was for a time completely unvaccinated.[10] In the West Bank, settlers connected by their own roads and protected by Israeli security forces received vaccinations in line with the rest of Israel's population while Palestinians living close by did not. Differential treatment under a single sovereign seems quite an accurate description of this reality.

Perhaps the issue is simply that Israel's relationship to the Palestinian territories and populations is not well captured by the concept of "state." One option for preserving our ontological maps of "states and not states" is to focus on infrastructures of power. We can track changing physical geography and checkpoints, trace the flows of trade and resources and exchange, and contemplate the mechanisms of surveillance and control without committing to a move from "not state to state." Here, Diana Greenwald's conception of the Palestinian Authority in chapter 5 helps make sense of its limited but real coercive capacity as something clearly "not state," despite having some trappings of "state." From the vantage point of "delegated domination," the PA is better understood as an agent of the Israeli state than as an agent of the Palestinian people or as a negotiating partner toward a two state solution.

If we remain ontologically committed to "not state," then surely there must be some other viable description. But the difficulty of finding a common framework for even describing Israel and Palestine that is not a "de facto one state reality" is itself one of the most striking features of the situation. Can an occupation that has now lasted more than fifty years truly be still ontologically classified as temporary, a passing phase on the path toward something else? Is it best captured, as Youssef Munayyer suggests in chapter 3, by an ongoing campaign of settler colonialism? Is it the creation of a caste-like system defined by Jewish supremacy, as Gershon Shafir suggests in the second chapter? Whatever language is used, Palestinians living in today's West Bank have no chance to avoid living in a one state reality, a reality that structures every aspect of their lives and their political horizons and even identities. But as Nathan Brown and Iman Elbanna argue in chapter 6, the search for state (as Yezid Sayigh once called it) has diminishing purchase on the Palestinian imagination. Political praxis has moved on. And, as Mohanad Mustafa and As'ad Ghanem point out in chapter 7, that praxis increasingly includes Palestinian citizens of Israel who were completely excluded from the logic of the Oslo peace process.

How does one observe a one state reality outside formal rules? Lustick focuses on property rights as the key mechanism. No Palestinian property, he observes, anywhere between "the river and the sea," can be protected from an Israeli government demolition of seizure of order. From the lens of property rights, then, Palestinians live under the state authority of Israel. Yael Berda, in chapter 4, connects these property rights to a mobility regime defined by an unequal relationship to citizenship rights. Tareq Baconi extends this mode of analysis to tracing Israeli strategies of land consolidation over history.[11] Munayyer too points to the "structured inequality" that defines the existence of all living in this territory as the historically determined outcome of an ongoing settler colonialism project defined to replace, not coexist, what came before. For Munayyer, settler colonialism is not something from the distant past: it is the best description for the current process by which Israel progressively claims, reshapes, and replaces ever more of the West Bank. Negotiations toward two states were never sincere in this analysis, but merely a cover for an ongoing process of colonization.

Gaza is often glaring in its absence from these discussions. Since Israel's 2005 withdrawal from the Gaza Strip, and particularly since Hamas seized power, there has been a general inclination to shift Gaza to a side category of its own.[12] But Hamas governance does not change the reality of ongoing occupation. Israel controls all points of entry, alone or in coordination with Egypt, allowing for occupation by proxy. It bombs this densely populated area with impunity while maintaining a rigorous blockade and aggressively searching and destroying tunnels built to find exits. But Gaza is as much a part of the Palestinian story as is the West Bank and is similarly defined by differential rights and similarly controlled by an Israeli proxy, no matter how reluctant a proxy it might be.

Perhaps the focus on the territory and its control to determine "state or not state" is itself the mistake. Several chapters tentatively invoke the concept of "caste" to describe the relationship between different types of human beings occupying the land in question. This, along with the kin concept of "racialization" of Palestinians, seems worth pursuing.[13] The naturalization of a system in which individuals embody essentially different degrees of rights captures an aspect of Palestinian reality not explained by simply military occupation and physical control. Thus, as the introduction notes, Jewish Israelis remain full citizens with rights inherently superior to all others in the one state reality. In chapter 13, Khaled Elgindy lays out five such levels in the hierarchy of political rights for individuals in this one state reality. Arab citizens of Israel may enjoy more rights than those in the West Bank or Gaza, but within clear legal and ideational limits. Gershon Shafir, in chapter 2, provocatively labels this a realm of Judaic supremacy. Such a caste-like system shows the dangers posed to the project by the universalized aspiration for a single state in which all enjoy equal citizenship rights articulated by Munayyer and more broadly by the architects of the BDS campaign. The move to thinking about the one state reality in racial or caste terms strikes me as a progressive step toward a more satisfying ontology—but one that offers no obvious policy prescription under the current structural conditions.

Is this caste-like system of control comparable to apartheid? Contributions to this volume circle this question but at key moments evade it: Does the analogy of apartheid South Africa usefully illuminate today's one state reality? The analogy is central to the BDS campaign and has recently been invoked by both Human Rights Watch and Amnesty International.[14] Its invocation is routinely met with loud accusations of antisemitism or with strained efforts at concept parsing designed to drown the political critique within academic pedantry. For all the rhetorical fire against former President Jimmy Carter's "peace or apartheid" framing, what was once controversial has now been broadly accepted.[15] On the face of it, the analogy seems painfully obvious. The one state reality today dominated by the State of Israel is clearly and uncontestably structured by the explicit and aspirationally permanent subordination of one national group by the other, with legally enforced gradations of belonging, manifestly unequal access to citizenship resources, and brutally enforced geographic internal divides. No analogy is needed to recognize the injustice of this political order.

The Prospects for Ideational and Material Change

The 2020 Abraham Accords brokered by the Trump administration raise the question about the limits and dynamics of change from a different perspective. For many decades, the formal Arab boycott of Israel and the political taboo against open relations until the creation of an independent Palestinian state may have been honored primarily in the breach. But here, the combination of the Trump administration's decision to make normalizing Arab relations with Israel a top priority and the changing calculation of national interest in key states such as the United Arab Emirates succeeded in bringing about real change. But how deep is that change? Is Palestine still an Arab/Muslim/global commitment around which publics might mobilize or which states might prioritize in their diplomacy? What does the acceptance of normal relations with Israel by the United Arab Emirates really mean? Here, we confront competing Israeli visions for regional normative change. The Oslo peace process was predicated on the belief that only a Palestinian state would unlock the doors to the Arab and Muslim worlds. The Abraham Accords facilitated by the Trump Administration in 2020 manifest Benjamin Netanyahu's long-stated vision of "peace for peace," in which Palestine is at most one of many factors that might be of interest to the various parties and is no obstacle to strategic cooperation. The UAE has seized the opportunity to redefine regional norms and make warm cooperation with Israel a positive rather than a negative; thus far, this bid has achieved little public resonance. Although this has been seen as a victory for Israel, it is worth considering this question: If this dimension of the long-stagnant status quo can change so quickly and decisively, what else might?

For the purposes of this volume, the critical question is what might trigger a change in the direction of recognizing and acting on a one state reality. Inherent in the intensity of the controversy over the term "apartheid" is the conceit that naming Israel's regime of control in that way would somehow cause it to change. As Nathan Brown has argued, however, "The fact that Israeli Apartheid, to the extent that it exists, is undeclared has actually been part of its essential nature."[16] The release, in close proximity, of major reports by the Israeli NGO B'Tselem and Human Rights Watch, followed by another major report by Amnesty International less than a year later, arguing that the occupation of the West Bank and Gaza met the legal definition of apartheid brought the issue powerfully to the forefront of public discourse.[17] But there is still little evidence to support the belief that naming Israel's reality would necessarily force it to change. It is incumbent on those battling over words to specify a theory of change: What is the plausible, causal mechanism by which imposing a label—and the narrative frame that it encompasses—leads to political change?

There are three primary answers. First, naming Israel's system as "apartheid" might trigger such revulsion at home that it leads to a domestic demand for change. This seems highly unlikely, given the rightward trend in Israeli politics. Second, it could trigger some form of international response by states or international organizations. Again, despite important European legal initiatives directed toward Israeli products produced in the occupied territories discussed by Muriel Asseburg in chapter 14, there is little in the current international system to suggest that any formal sanction would be forthcoming. Although the International Criminal Court's decision to consider the Palestinian case against Israel suggests some movement, the US imposition of sanctions shows again the limits of legal strategies in the face of state power, as has been argued by Noura Erakat.[18] If anything, as Michael Barnett and Lara Friedman show in chapter 8, Israeli offensive efforts at "lawfare" have succeeded in criminalizing criticism or boycott of Israel across a wide range of jurisdictions. Third, naming Israel's system as "apartheid" could trigger global normative action at the societal and individual, rather than at the state, level. This effort to link the apartheid label to the production of a global cultural boycott comparable to that faced by South Africa is both the most plausible theory of change and the primary objective of the BDS movement.

The BDS movement stands as a critical and deeply fascinating example of normative entrepreneurship in international relations.[19] It has largely been excluded from the IR literature on normative change, likely because of its controversial status.[20] But the rapid spread through the international community of the calls to boycott, divest, and sanction Israel as forms of peaceful protest and principled objection to Israel's occupation of Palestine shows the power of ideas.[21] Launched in 2005 by Palestinian intellectuals, BDS has manifestly shifted the terms of the debate about Israel and Palestine, in part through the effective invocation of norms against colonialism and analogies to the cultural boycott of apartheid South Africa. Within a decade and a half, the BDS campaign could be plausibly described as "one of the most widespread instances of solidarity politics in the world."[22] Israel has, from the start, treated BDS as an "existential threat," in ways that make little sense from the vantage point of material power and realpolitik.[23]

The rhetorical battles over BDS are themselves a case study in the role of argumentation, framing, and symbolic power in international affairs.[24] Israeli elites and their supporters moved early and aggressively to define BDS as essentially a form of antisemitism and a rhetorical justification for terrorism.[25] In contrast, Palestinian advocates for BDS presented it as a quintessential form of nonviolent activism, invoking universal norms of equality, fairness, and democracy in ways well captured by the "boomerang model" of norm development.[26] Critically, as Ilana Feldman argues, the BDS framing explicitly seeks to set aside the alleged exceptionalism of Israel and Palestine to allow for meaningful comparative analysis and to disarm routinely deployed rhetorical gambits.[27] Such a reframing, not coincidentally, would tend to neuter the strongest claims on the Israeli side and empower those on the Palestinian.

It is intriguing that, as Omar Rahman and Dahlia Scheindlin note in chapter 11, the core calls of BDS are not dependent on any particular political institution or solution: "state or not state," so central to the earlier discussion, is of only marginal relevance here. The BDS campaign had to navigate the one state reality from an early stage as differences emerged over whether BDS should apply only to Israeli settlements in the West Bank or to all of Israel as an essentially settler colonial enterprise (see Munayyer, chapter 3). Whereas BDS supporters sought to win victories in academia and in the economic realm, BDS opponents increasingly turned to the political and legal spheres, pushing state legislatures in the United States to criminalize BDS and to impose restrictive definitions of antisemitism (see Barnett and Friedman, chapter 8). Although it is difficult to identify clear winners or losers, of course, it seems that the battlefield in these rhetorical wars is considerably more balanced than in their military or geopolitical counterparts.[28]

Israeli attacks against Gaza in 2009, 2012, and 2014 played an important role in shifting the terms of this debate.[29] It is worth exploring how and why this is the case. In military terms, Israel's overwhelming advantage allowed it to bomb the densely populated strip at will, while missile defenses increasingly offered protection against what counterstrikes could be offered.

But whatever their military effects, the repeated wars produced indelible images of a captive population subjected to relentless bombardment. This reminded the world that Gaza remained occupied by Israel despite disappearing from the "peace process" discourse following Israel's 2005 withdrawal to beyond the perimeter fence. Its sudden reappearance, in such cataclysmic and violent forms, offered something of an epistemic shock, as Lustick might put it, forcing a recalibration of basic understandings of the world. The scale of human suffering in Gaza raised the issue's profile. So did the timing, particularly the 2009 attacks during the transition to the incoming Obama administration. The fierce battles over the Goldstone Report in turn shone a spotlight on Israel's impunity from international legal scrutiny, prompting efforts to find other venues—including the turn to the International Criminal Court discussed later.

Public attitudes may also be more open to a sudden and rapid shift. Rahman and Scheindlin (chapter 11) show how dramatically Israeli and Palestinian views have changed on questions related to the possibility and forms of peace. They show that support for the two state solution is far more recent than we tend to believe and that the rapid opening of that window in the 1990s—in their metaphor—should offer perspective when we confront seemingly immutable political realities. The changing views of American Jews, as documented by Barnett and Friedman (chapter 8), and of the American public at large (Telhami, chapter 10), offer convincing evidence of the possibilities and limits of change. During the years of the peace process, the Israeli-centric motivation was typically framed as two states being the only way to resolve the tension between being Jewish and democratic. Over the last fifteen years, Israel as a state has rather decisively chosen in favor of its Jewishness over its democracy. American Jews, by contrast, remain far more invested in democratic values. This has brought out "a profound and growing dissonance between Jewish Americans and Jewish Israelis regarding the values and interests that define their identities."

Nadav Shelef's discussion in chapter 9 of how nationalisms evolve foregrounds the need for robust theoretical accounts of ideational change (see also Lustick, chapter 1). National movements can, and do, change their referent and their focus: scaling up to become part of a larger project, scaling down to accept lesser territoriality, and replacing it with some other identity commitment. The aspiration for Palestine could contract from all the land west of the Jordan to a state located in the West Bank and Gaza. It could incorporate only Palestinians living in that territory, or it could expand to include the Palestinian diaspora and Palestinian citizens of Israel. The same is true for the Zionist movement, which has over the course of history shifted its territorial referent and adopted different perspectives on how to include the Jewish diaspora. For both, the concept of a binational one state reality is less unthinkable than it is simply highly unlikely. But if politics changes without ideational change, it could produce even greater conflict.

Of course, there are more direct ways that things could change suddenly and unexpectedly. The Palestinian Authority could finally collapse, forcing Israel to resume direct control over the areas of the West Bank that had been nominally under the PA's governance. Another Palestinian Intifada could trigger a violent Israeli reoccupation—or a renewed Israeli recognition of the need for two states. An Israeli government could decide to move to formal annexation. Such scenarios have been proposed for so long without them coming to pass that they are often relegated to the background or effectively ruled out. But were one of them to happen, it would likely be viewed in retrospect as virtually inevitable.

Policy Stagnation despite Rapid Conceptual Change

In his February 2021 phone call with Israel's foreign minister Gabi Ashkenazi, Biden's newly appointed secretary of state Anthony Blinken affirmed the United States' continued belief that "the two-state solution is the best way to ensure Israel's future as a Jewish and democratic state, living in peace alongside a viable and democratic Palestinian state."[30] Policy, at least, seemingly remains trapped outside the one state reality. Nor does this volume provide nearly as wide a horizon for transformed policy engagement as it does on the analytical and conceptual fronts.

The stagnation of the policy debate may lie not in a failure of imaginative horizons or in an empirical awareness but, as ably explored by Tamara Wittes and Kevin Huggard in chapter 12, in the recognition of the forces locking the current status quo into place and the restraining force the two state aspiration still exerts on actors on the ground. We tend to assume, rather than prove, that the current situation is unsustainable. Israeli occupation has been sustained for more than fifty years, however, with Israelis showing a remarkable lack of difficulty reconciling this occupation with their identity, however defined, and the international community seeing little need or ability to force change.[31]

In chapter 13, Elgindy warns of the difference between outcomes and solutions, with the latter requiring a degree of justice that could satisfy the essential needs of both sides of the conflict. Although an outcome that does not involve "the domination, subjugation or expulsion of one group by another" seems difficult to conceive, Elgindy argues that only such an outcome could truly offer a "solution" as opposed to a temporary waystation. But why would we expect any major international conflict—much less the Israeli-Palestinian conflict—to ever be truly "solved"? In the world of policy, outcomes are often far more plausible than solutions. As Shelef puts it, "A one state reality . . . will not necessarily produce the denationalization required for peaceful coexistence." The most likely outcome even from recognizing a one state reality may look very little like anyone's preferred solution.

Policy toward Israel and Palestine is locked in by a wide range of familiar structural factors. There is simple path dependence, with generations of policy actors and analysts, legislation, institutions, and policy focal points deeply shaped by the legacy of decades. This path dependence is reinforced by the realities of power. The current status quo, of a fruitless search for two states while Israel steadily consolidates and expands, reflects a constellation of power and interests. American unipolar global status ensured that its preferences would be broadly reflected in the regional outcome, whereas Israel's dominant position within US politics ensured that those preferences would be aligned with its own. That dominant position, in turn, is reinforced by pro-Israeli lobbying and by the constant shaping of public narratives and media.

The decline of US regional and global unipolarity could perhaps change this situation, because rising powers such as China and a more independent Europe perhaps have less interest than America in ensuring that the status quo be sustained. American politics changes more slowly but does evolve, as Barnett and Friedman's chapter articulates. A right-wing ethnonationalist Israeli one state reality still receives support from Washington—but only when Republicans control the White House. The rush to lock in changes as the Trump administration came to its chaotic end reflects a recognition that Israel's external support has in some ways faded to one-half of one major power.

These would not necessarily change the ontological barriers to change highlighted by Lustick in chapter 1, however. It is difficult to miss the enormous disconnect between most policy discussions from the perspectives of most academics, observers on the ground, and people living through the unacknowledged one state reality. To the extent that the Biden administration has engaged at all, its efforts have revolved around creative paths back toward a two state solution, while embracing the Abraham Accords brokered by the Trump administration.[32] This may reflect a recognition of the realm of plausibility. A successful policy advocacy requires at least some expectation of success and some constellation of powerful interests that would benefit from its success. There is no shortage of alternative policy proposals, including creative ideas advanced by contributors to this volume. But what has been missing is a plausible path toward policy change.

One way to respond to the policy debate remaining largely locked within the two state solution discourse is to expand the conceptualization of policy. Things look far less stagnant if we shift our gaze from official policy to other levels of analysis, as described masterfully in the chapters by Wittes and Huggard and by Asseburg. Vocal members of Congress have pushed the bounds of acceptable discourse and opened the door to meaningful official discussion of Palestinian rights. And rapid shifts on the grassroots Left show the possibility of change from below, which could sooner than expected force politicians to adapt to new public preferences.

Ethical Engagement

A decade ago, Charli Carpenter began her evocative essay on ethical engagement in conflict studies with a comment she received on her own work: "You write of terrible things in such a matter-of-fact way."[33] This volume too, no doubt, will trigger such responses. The choice to privilege empirical and theoretical analysis is itself a normative stance and one taken intentionally. This volume began from the premise that there is real ethical and normative value to the effort to sidestep heated political arguments and hopeful normative aspirations alike. But the way we frame research questions is never neutral. While we parse the meaning of apartheid in the context of Israel and Palestine, millions of Palestinians suffer enormously from the reality of capricious domination, expropriation, and dispossession. How does one sustain a focus on the effects of Israeli military action in Gaza on global narratives while watching Israeli snipers mow down unarmed Palestinians at the border fence? What do we give up by adopting the cool, rational analysis of power and interests against the raw passions of dispossessed Palestinians or Israelis who fear the delegitimization of their own identity?

The choice between ethical and empirical analysis is a false one. Every stage of political science research, from the framing of questions to the analytical process to the presentation of findings, should be informed by an ethical sensibility. The urgent needs of the people affected by unjust realities should be centered in those research choices. But the political scientist can add little to the efforts of activists, the wordplay of pundits, or the cultivated outrage that too often dominates public discourse. Moral posturing can be satisfying and can be useful in rallying support for a political course of action, but it will be a dead end if the proposed policy does not fit the realities of the conflict. The contribution that we can make to an ethical engagement on Israel and Palestine is to get the analysis right, so that activists can craft their strategies appropriately to those realities. Any truly ethical course of action needs to be one with a plausible prospect of successfully achieving its goals.[34]

The failure of the two state solution exemplifies this conception of ethics. For decades, many well-meaning scholars and analysts—and here, I would include myself and the other editors of this volume—have passionately worked and argued on behalf of a two state solution as the only viable way to meet the existential needs of Israelis and Palestinians. Our research and argumentation were informed by an ethical commitment and a deeply held belief that no other outcome could work. But decades of support for a two state solution only provided diplomatic cover for the ongoing expansion of Israeli regimes of control and the continued subordination of Palestinians to various forms of occupation, abuse, and dispossession. At some point, recognition of the unintended consequences of an ethically grounded commitment to the two state solution demands at least an openness to rethinking that stand.

There is no guarantee that demonstrating the empirical or conceptual value of a one state reality will result in a better world. As Nadav Shelef (chapter 9) reminds us, its effects could manifest in very different ways that defy our ethical aspirations. The chapters in this volume show in graphic detail the deeply entrenched regimes of control, ideational underpinnings, and imbalances of power that would shape the politics of such a single state. Although a one state reality could, in principle, open the door for the democratic state based on equality and citizenship rights to which advocates aspire, it could also more deeply and formally entrench apartheid-like regimes of control.[35] Its consolidation could invite more extreme forms of state violence or dispossession. But effectively conceptualizing those realities would be the first step toward allowing activists and political entrepreneurs to act effectively in pursuit of their normative goals.[36] Ignoring them would guarantee the perpetuation of unjust outcomes. This volume, then, makes an ethical statement by demanding an honest recognition of Israel and Palestine as it actually exists. It falls on the political actors to make of that reality what they will.

Notes

INTRODUCTION

1. The authors are listed alphabetically, as is the case with the coeditors of this volume.

2. See, for instance, Nathan Thrall, *The Only Language They Understand: Forcing Compromise in Israel and Palestine* (New York: Metropolitan Books, 2017); Edward P. Djerejian, Marwan Muasher, Nathan J. Brown, Samih Al-Abid, Tariq Dana, Dahlia Scheindlin, Gilead Sher, and Khalil Shikaki, "Two States or One? Reappraising the Israeli-Palestinian Impasse," Carnegie Endowment for International Peace, September 18, 2018, https://carnegieendowment.org/2018/09/18/two-states-or-one-reappraising-israeli-palestinian-impasse-pub-77269; Ian Lustick, *Paradigm Lost: From Two-State Solution to One-State Reality* (Philadelphia: University of Pennsylvania Press, 2019); Yousef Munayyer, "There Will Be a One-State Solution: But What Kind of State Will It Be?" *Foreign Affairs* (November/December 2019), https://www.foreignaffairs.com/articles/israel/2019-10-15/there-will-be-one-state-solution; B'TSELEM—The Israeli Information Center for Human Rights in the Occupied Territories, "A Regime of Jewish Supremacy from the Jordan River to the Mediterranean Sea: This Is Apartheid," *B'TSELEM,* January 12, 2021, https://www.btselem.org/publications/fulltext/202101_this_is_apartheid; Paul Pillar, "The One-State Reality and the Plight of the Palestinians," *The National Interest*, February 1, 2021, https://nationalinterest.org/blog/paul-pillar/one-state-reality-and-plight-palestinians-177407; "New RAND Research Evaluates Opinions on Alternative Solutions for the Israeli-Palestinian Conflict," Royal Institute for International Affairs (Egmont Institute), February 11, 2021, https://www.egmontinstitute.be/events/new-rand-research-evaluates-opinions-on-alternative-solutions-for-the-israeli-palestinian-conflict/.

3. The history offered here is not intended to be comprehensive but only to illustrate the ways in which the focus was often on what Palestine/Israel should be, distracting from the embedded nature of seemingly interim arrangements. Those interested in a comprehensive history may wish to consult one of the several attempts by scholars to give a general overview: Mark Tessler, *A History of the Arab-Israeli Conflict* (Bloomington: Indiana University Press, 2009); Charles D. Smith, *Palestine and the Arab-Israeli Conflict* (New York: St. Martins, 2016); Martin Bunton, *The Palestinian-Israeli Conflict: A Very Short Introduction* (Oxford: Oxford University Press, 2013); and David W, Lesch, *The Arab-Israeli Conflict: A History* (Oxford: Oxford University Press, 2008). Each of those books contains sources for further reading.

4. Parenthetically, the claim that there is a one state reality overlaps with an alternative approach to the history of the Palestinian-Israeli conflict—that of settler colonialism. This framework has become increasingly popular in some fields (literature, history) but not so much in political science. Yousef Munayyer's chapter forwards this view with an eye to engaging political scientists.

5. The text of the Mandate can be viewed at "The Palestinian Mandate." Avalon Project, Yale Law School, accessed August 30, 2021. https://avalon.law.yale.edu/20th_century/palmanda.asp.

6. Max Weber, *Politics as a Vocation* (New York: Oxford University Press, 1946), 4.

7. For an exploration of the concepts in the Middle East, see James N. Sater and Zahra R. Babar, eds., *Routledge Handbook of Citizenship in the Middle East and North Africa* (New York: Taylor & Francis, 2020).

8. Hans Kohn, *The Idea of Nationalism: A Study in Its Origins and Background* (New York: Macmillan, 2005). See, also, George Mosse, *Nationalism and Sexuality: Respectability and Abnormal Sexuality in Modern Europe* (New York: Howard Fertig, 1997); and Yael Tamir, *Why Nationalism* (Princeton: Princeton University Press, 2019).

9. Michael Ignatieff, *Blood and Belonging: Journeys into the New Nationalism* (New York: Farrar, Straus and Giroux, 1995), 3–5.

10. Ignatieff, *Blood and Belonging.*

11. Shibley Telhami and Marc Lynch, *Middle East Scholar Barometer*, University of Maryland Critical Issues Poll and the Project on Middle East Political Science at George Washington University, February 8–15 2021, https://criticalissues.umd.edu/sites/criticalissues.umd.edu/files/Middle%20East%20Scholar%20Barometer%20Questionnaire%20September%202021%20Final.pdf.

12. Shibley Telhami, "Stop Calling Israel a Jewish Democracy," *Foreign Policy*, June 8, 2020, https://foreignpolicy.com/2020/06/08/netanyahu-annexation-palestinians-stop-calling-israel-a-jewish-democracy/.

13. David M. Halbfinger and Isabel Kershner, "Israeli Law Declares the Country the 'Nation-State of the Jewish People,'" *New York Times*, July 19, 2018, https://www.nytimes.com/2018/07/19/world/middleeast/israel-law-jews-arabic.html.

14. *The Nation State of the Jewish People*. Basic Law: Knesset, 2018, https://main.knesset.gov.il/EN/activity/Documents/BasicLawsPDF/BasicLawNationState.pdf.

15. "Israel's Religiously Divided Society," Pew Research Center, March 8, 2016, https://www.pewforum.org/2016/03/08/israels-religiously-divided-society/.

16. B'TSELEM, "A Regime of Jewish Supremacy"; "The Occupation of the West Bank and the Crime of Apartheid," *Yesh Din*, September 7, 2020, https://www.yesh-din.org/en/the-occupation-of-the-west-bank-and-the-crime-of-apartheid-legal-opinion/.

17. Telhami and Lynch, *Middle East Scholar Barometer*, August 26–September 15, 2021, https://criticalissues.umd.edu/sites/criticalissues.umd.edu/files/Middle%20East%20Scholar%20Barometer%20Questionnaire%20September%202021%20Final.pdf.

1. WHAT AND WHERE IS ISRAEL?

1. For the larger argument from which is derived this analysis of the fate of the two state solution paradigm and the status of an approach anchored by the "one state reality," see Ian S. Lustick, *Paradigm Lost: From Two-State Solution to One-State Reality* (Philadelphia: University of Pennsylvania Press, 2019).

2. George A. Reisch, *The Politics of Paradigms: Thomas S. Kuhn, James B. Conant, and the Cold War "Struggle for Men's Minds"* (Albany: SUNY Press, 2017), 62. Reisch reports (p. 109) that initially Kuhn considered using the word "ideology" in the title of the book that became known as *The Structure of Scientific Revolutions.*

3. "The crisis consists precisely in the fact that the old is dying and the new cannot be born; in this interregnum a great variety of morbid symptoms appear." Antonio Gramsci, *Selections from the Prison Notebooks*, edited by Quintin Hoare and Geoffrey Nowell Smith (New York: International Publishers, 1971), 276.

4. In its colloquial usage and in my treatment the terms "research program" and "paradigm" can be treated as interchangeable. I use the Lakatosian vocabulary associated with research programs to analyze the crisis encountered by the TSS paradigm because it is both richer and more precise than the language used by Thomas Kuhn in his discussion of the rise and decline of paradigms. See Imre Lakatos, "Falsification and the Methodology

of Scientific Research Programmes," in *Criticism and the Growth of Knowledge*, ed. Imre Lakatos and Alan Musgrave (Cambridge: Cambridge University Press, 1970), 91–196.

5. Lakatos, "Falsification and the Methodology," 132–133.

6. Lakatos, "Falsification and the Methodology," 118–119.

7. Lakatos, "Falsification and the Methodology," 134.

8. Lakatos, "Falsification and the Methodology," 154.

9. Phlogiston chemistry formed the basis of a thriving metallurgy industry in eighteenth-century Germany. For a discussion of how typical it is that scientists operating in new paradigms can offer exhilarating new perspectives, but yet not solve standard problems as well as those using the established ideas they will eventually displace, see Thomas S. Kuhn, *The Structure of Scientific Revolutions*, 2nd ed. (Chicago: University of Chicago Press, 1970), 152–159.

10. Ian S. Lustick, "The Danger of Two-State Messianism," *Daily Beast*, October 20, 2013, https://www.thedailybeast.com/the-danger-of-two-state-messianism.

11. Shlomo Hasson and Rami Nasrallah, eds., *2050 Strategic Plan: Between the Mediterranean Sea and the Jordan River* (Jerusalem: Sasha Center for Strategic Studies, Hebrew University of Jerusalem and International Peace and Cooperation Center, 2017), 2.

12. Hasson and Nasrallah, *2050 Strategic Plan*, 4 (emphasis in original).

13. Hasson and Nasrallah, *2050 Strategic Plan*, 3.

14. Lustick, *Paradigm Lost*, 111–112.

15. "How Feasible Is the Two-State Solution Today?" Geneva Initiative, June 2020, https://index.genevainitiative.org/.

16. Omri Boehm, "After Liberal Zionism, the One Hope for a Democratic Israel," *New York Review*, June 9, 2020.

17. "About Us," Standing Together, https://www.standing-together.org/about-us.

18. *Judgment of the Supreme Court of Israel, Sitting as the High Court of Justice*, HCJ 1308/17; HCJ 2055/17 (Hebrew).

2. FROM JEWISH PRIVILEGE TO JUDAIC SUPREMACY

1. I wish to thank Ishay Rosen-Zvi, David N. Myers, and Barbara Rose Stone for their invaluable comments and suggestions.

2. Ian S. Lustick, *Paradigm Lost: From Two-State Solution to One-State Reality* (Philadelphia: University of Pennsylvania Press, 2019), 140–149 and his chapter 1 in this volume.

3. Eric Hobsbawm, "Introduction: Inventing Traditions," in *The Invention of Tradition*, ed. Eric Hobsbawm and Terence Ranger (New York: Cambridge University Press, 1983), 1.

4. James Clifford, *Returns: Becoming Indigenous in the Twenty-First Century* (Cambridge, MA: Harvard University Press, 2013).

5. James Clifford, *The Predicament of the Century: Twentieth-Century Ethnography, Literature, and Art* (Cambridge, MA: Harvard University Press, 1988), 15.

6. Tim McDaniel, "Islam: Historical Legacies and Modern Dilemmas." Unpublished manuscript, 2009.

7. Max Weber, *The Methodology of the Social Sciences*, trans. and edited by Edward A. Sills and Henry A. Finch (Glencoe: Free Press, 1949).

8. McDaniel, *Islam*, chap. 2, p. 9.

9. McDaniel, *Islam*, chap. 5, p. 3.

10. McDaniel, *Islam*, chap. 5, pp. 2, 5; chap. 3, p. 8.

11. Michel Foucault, *Security Territory, and Population* (New York: St. Martin's Press, 1978) 123–130.

12. Alexander Kaye, *The Invention of Jewish Theocracy: The Struggle for Legal Authority in Modern Israel* (New York: Oxford University Press, 2020), 10–11.

13. Kaye, *Invention*, 1, 14.

14. Kaye, *Invention*, 16.

15. Menachem Friedman, "The State of Israel as a Theological Dilemma," in *The Israeli State and Society: Boundaries and Frontiers*, ed. Baruch Kimmerling (Albany: State University of New York Press), 167–168.

16. Friedman, "State of Israel," 208.

17. Yehuda Brandes, "Modern Mamlachti Halakhic Rulings (Psika Mamlachtit Modernit)," in Stern and Sheleg, 33; Yedidiya Stern and Yair Sheleg, *Zionist Hakalha* [Halakha Tziyonit] (Jerusalem, The Israel Institute for Democracy, 2017).

18. Michael Walzer, Menachem Lorberbaum, and Noam J. Zohar, eds., *The Jewish Political Tradition* (New Haven, CT: Yale University Press, 2000), 447.

19. Walzer et al., *Jewish Political Tradition*, 445–446.

20. Adi Ophir and Ishay Rosen-Zvi, *Goy* (Oxford: Oxford University Press, 2018), 28–30.

21. Ophir and Rosen-Zvi, *Goy*, 39–45.

22. Ophir and Rosen-Zvi, *Goy*, 31–22.

23. Ophir and Rosen-Zvi, *Goy*, 180–193.

24. Walzer et al., *Jewish Political Tradition*, 447.

25. Eliezer Hadad, "Zionist Halakhic Rulings and Non-Jews in the State of Israel (Hapsika hatsiyonit benoge'a lenokhrim bemedinat yisrael)," in Stern and Sheleg, 321.

26. George R. Wilkes, "Religious Wars in the Works of Maimonides: An Idea and Its Transit across the Medieval Mediterranean," in *Just Wars, Holy Wars, and Jihad: Christian, Jewish, and Muslim Encounters and Exchanges*, ed. Sohail H. Hashmi (Oxford: Oxford University Press, 2012), 156. See also Menachem Lorberbaum, "Medieval Jewish Political Thought," in *The Cambridge Companion to Medieval Jewish Philosophy*, ed. Daniel H. Frank and Oliver Leaman (Cambridge: Cambridge University Press, 2003), 176–200.

27. Wilkes, "Religious Wars," 147, 151, 152, 160.

28. Avi Sagi, "Zionist Halakha and the Challenge of Liberalism (Hahalakha hatsiyonit ve'etgar haliberalism)," in Stern and Sheleg, 86–87; Chaim Burgansky, "Zionist Halakha in the Rulings of Rabbi Herzog (Halakha tsiyonit bepsikato shel harav herzog)," in Stern and Sheleg, 641–643; Hadad, "Zionist Halakhic Rulings," 314–317.

29. Sagi, "Zionist Halakha," 84–86.

30. Yosef Achituv, "Zionist Halakha and the Issue of War Booty (Halakha tsiyonit besugiyat shalal milchama)," in Stern and Sheleg, 451–452.

31. Sagi, "Zionist Halakha," 76–78, 84–86; Hadad, "Zionist Halakhic Rulings," 74.

32. Shira Robinson, *Citizen Strangers: Palestinians and the Birth of Israel's Liberal Settler State* (Stanford: Stanford University Press, 2013), 75, 37.

33. Hadad, "Zionist Halakhic Rulings," 336–343.

34. Janet O'Dea, "Gush Emunim: Roots and Ambiguities," *Forum on the Jewish People, Zionism, and Israel* 25 (1976): 40–41.

35. Moshe Hellinger and Isaac Hershkowitz, *Obedience and Disobedience in Religious Zionism: From Gush Emunim to the Price Tag Attacks* [Tsiyut vei'tsiyut betsiyonut hadatit: megush emunim ve'ad tag mechir] (Jerusalem: Israel Democracy Institute, 2015), 55–56.

36. Hellinger and Hershkowitz, *Obedience and Civic Disobedience*, 126–127.

37. Hellinger and Hershkowitz, *Obedience and Civic Disobedience*, 129–130.

38. Hadad, "Zionist Halakhic Rulings," 322–323.

39. Hellinger and Hershkowitz, *Obedience and Civic Disobedience*, 116–117.

40. Ariel Picard, "The Status of the Alien in the Rulings of the Religious-Zionist Rabbis (Ma'amad hanokhri be'ertz yisrael bepsikat rabbaney hatsiyonut hadatit)," *Reshit* 1 (2009): 187–208, https://reshit.hartman.org.il/Article_View_Heb.asp?Article_Id=8#65.

41. See also Picard, "Status of the Alien."

42. Elisha Aviner, "The Status of the Ishmaelites in the State of Israel according to the Halakha (Ma'amad hayishma'elim bemedinat yisrael lefi hahalakha)," *Tchumin* 8 (1987): 351, http://www.ybm.org.il/Admin/uploaddata/LessonsFiles/Pdf/4162.pdf.

43. Raanan Mallek, "Historical Developments of the Term Ger Toshav and the Halakhic Implications Therein for Relating to Non-Jews," in *Jews in Dialogue: Jewish Responses to the Challenges of Multicultural Contemporaneity*, ed. Magdalena Dziaczkowska and Adele Valeria (Leiden: Brill, 2020), 43–48.

44. Meir Kahane, "The Special Status of the 'Palestinians," in *Beyond Words: Selected Writings of Rabbi Meir Kahane*, vol. 7, 2nd ed., trans. David Fein (Jerusalem: Institute for the Publication of the Writings of Rabbi Meir Kahane, 2010), 299–302.

45. Kahane, "Special Status," 306.

46. Meir Kahane, "The Non-Jew in Eretz Yisrael," in *Or Hara'ayon: The Jewish Idea*, vol. 2, trans. Raphael Blumberg (Jerusalem: Institute for the Publication of the Writings of Rabbi Meir Kahane, 1998), 597.

47. Kahane, "The Non-Jew," 610; Aviner, "The Status," 356.

48. See Shaul Magid, "Kahana Won," *Tablet*, March 15, 2019, https://www.tabletmag.com/sections/israel-middle-east/articles/kahane-won.

49. Bentzi Gopstein, "Unless We Expel the Gentiles We Will Not See the Redemption of Our Land (Bli gerush hagoyim lo nizke legeaulat ha'aretz)," Actualic.co.il, March 10, 2016, http://actualic.co.il (accessed July 18, 2020); "Baruch Marzel to the Rav Aviner: 'It's a Done Deal: Rabbi Kahane Was Right (Lo ya'azor klum—harav kahana tzdak)," *Srugim*, August 2, 2016, https://www.srugim.co.il/158150.

50. Bezalel Smotrich, "Israel's Decisive Plan," *Hashiloach*, https://hashiloach.org.il/israels-decisive-plan/.

51. Quoted in Aviner, "The Status," 356.

52. Orlando Patterson, *Slavery and Social Death* (Cambridge, MA: Harvard University Press, 2018).

53. "Hundreds of Rabbis: The Plan of the Century Is Dangerous, Annexation Is Not Worth the Risk," *Chabad*, https://chabad.info/news/575975/; Elisha Ben Kimon, "Attachment Alert: Yesha Council Launches Campaign against 'Plan of the Century,'" *Ynet*, June 10, 2020, https://www.ynet.co.il/articles/0,7340,L-5745675,00.html; Elisha Ben Kimon, "Struggling against Annexation: 'We Will Stop the Trump Plan with Our Feet,'" *Ynet*, June 4, 2020, https://www.ynet.co.il/articles/0,7340,L-5741953,00.html.

54. Ravit Hecht, "The Heads of the Yesha Council: "Trump's Plan Is a Scam, Netanyahu Knew and Worked on Our Eyes," *Haaretz*, June 17, 2020, https://www.haaretz.co.il/misc/article-print-page/.premium-MAGAZINE-1.8924362.

55. Ophir and Rosen-Zvi, *Goy*, 265.

56. See chapter 9 in this volume.

57. See chapter 3 in this volume.

3. ISRAEL/PALESTINE

1. Jennifer Pitts, "Political Theory of Empire and Imperialism," *Annual Review of Political Science* 13, no. 1 (2010): 211–235, https://doi.org/10.1146/annurev.polisci.051508.214538.

2. Paul Keal, *European Conquest and the Rights of Indigenous Peoples: The Moral Backwardness of International Society* (Cambridge: Cambridge University Press, 2003), https://doi.org/10.1017/CBO9780511491467.

3. Aziz Rana and Associate Professor of Law Aziz Rana, *The Two Faces of American Freedom* (Cambridge: Harvard University Press, 2010).

4. Duncan Ivison, Paul Patton, and Will Sanders, *Political Theory and the Rights of Indigenous Peoples* (Cambridge University Press, 2000).

5. Hannah Arendt, *The Origins Of Totalitarianism* (New York: HarperCollins, 1973).

6. United States Congress, *Congressional Record: Proceedings and Debates of the . . . Congress.* (U.S. Government Printing Office, 2011).

7. Theodor Herzl, *The Complete Diaries of Theodor Herzl*, ed. Raphael Patai, trans. by Harry Zohn (New York: Herzl Press, 1960).

8. Lorenzo Veracini, "Introducing." *Settler Colonial Studies* 1 (2011): 1–12. https://doi.org/10.1080/2201473X.2011.10648799.

9. Patrick Wolfe, "Settler Colonialism and the Elimination of the Native." *Journal of Genocide Research* 8, no. 4 (2006): 387–409, https://doi.org/10.1080/14623520601056240.

10. Zionist movement goals outlined in Basel Program: "1. The promotion of the settlement of Jewish agriculturists, artisans, and tradesmen in Palestine. 2. The federation of all Jews into local or general groups, according to the laws of the various countries. 3. The strengthening of the Jewish feeling and consciousness. 4. Preparatory steps for the attainment of those governmental grants which are necessary to the achievement of the zionist purpose."

11. Shafir argues that it was during this period that the Zionist Movement developed a socioeconomic model of settlement that sought to be both autonomous and homogeneous while excluding and not relying on indigenous labor or economy. Gershon Shafir, *Land, Labor and the Origins of the Israeli-Palestinian Conflict, 1882–1914* (Berkley: University of California Press, 1996).

12. Polkehn notes that this is a reference to the British South Africa Company, founded by Cecil Rhodes, which was instrumental in the colonization of Africa south of the Zambezi River. Klaus Polkehn, "Zionism and Kaiser Wilhelm," *Journal of Palestine Studies* 4, no. 2 (1975): 76–90. For a description of Herzl's efforts to create a government-chartered Jewish land company, see Walid Khalidi, "The Jewish-Ottoman Land Company: Herzl's Blueprint for the Colonization of Palestine" *Journal of Palestine Studies* 22, no. 2 (1993): 30–47. https://doi.org/10.2307/2537267.

13. Walid Khalidi, *From Haven to Conquest: Readings in Zionism and the Palestine Problem until 1948* (Institute for Palestine Studies, 1971).

14. Gershon Shafir, "Israeli Decolonization and Critical Sociology" *Journal of Palestine Studies* 25, no. 3 (1996): 23–35, https://doi.org/10.2307/2538256.

15. Kenneth W. Stein, *The Land Question in Palestine, 1917–1939* (Chapel Hill: University of North Carolina Press, 1984).

16. John Hope Simpson, "PALESTINE Report on Immigration, Land Settlement and Development" (His Majesty's Stationery Office, 1930), https://unispal.un.org/DPA/DPR/unispal.nsf/0/E3ED8720F8707C9385256D19004F057C.

17. Charles Anderson, "The British Mandate and the Crisis of Palestinian Landlessness, 1929–1936." *Middle Eastern Studies* 54, no. 2 (2018): 171–215. https://doi.org/10.1080/00263206.2017.1372427.

18. Anglo-American Committee of Inquiry on Jewish Problems in Palestine and Europe and United Nations General Assembly Special Committee on Palestine, *A Survey of Palestine* (Institute for Palestine Studies, 1991).

19. Geremy Forman and Alexandre (Sandy) Kedar, "From Arab Land to 'Israel Lands': The Legal Dispossession of the Palestinians Displaced by Israel in the Wake of 1948" *Environment and Planning D: Society and Space.* July 2016, https://doi.org/10.1068/d402.

20. Forman and Kedar "From Arab land to 'Israel Lands.'"

21. Shira N. Robinson, *Citizen Strangers: Palestinians and the Birth of Israel's Liberal Settler State* (Stanford, CA: Stanford University Press, 2013).

22. For an expanded treatment of settler-colonial aspects to citizenship in Israel, see Nadim N. Rouhana and Areej Sabbagh-Khoury, "Settler-Colonial Citizenship: Conceptualizing the Relationship between Israel and Its Palestinian Citizens" *Settler Colonial Studies* 5, no. 3 (2015): 205–225, https://doi.org/10.1080/2201473X.2014.947671.

23. Nur Masalha, "Settler-Colonialism, Memoricide and Indigenous Toponymic Memory: The Appropriation of Palestinian Place Names by the Israeli State" *Journal of Holy Land and Palestine Studies* 14, no. 1 (2015): 3–57, https://doi.org/10.3366/hlps.2015.0103.

24. Ismael Abu-Saad, "State-Controlled Education and Identity Formation Among the Palestinian Arab Minority in Israel" *American Behavioral Scientist* 49 (August 2006): 1085–1100, https://doi.org/10.1177/0002764205284720.

25. State Education Law, 5713-1953

26. See https://main.knesset.gov.il/EN/about/history/documents/kns2_education_eng.pdf.

27. Abu-Saad, "State-Controlled Education."

28. Tarif Khalidi, "Palestinian Historiography: 1900–1948" *Journal of Palestine Studies* 10, no. 3 (1981): 59–76, https://doi.org/10.2307/2536460.

29. Amal Jamal, *The Arab Public Sphere in Israel: Media Space and Cultural Resistance* (Bloomington: Indiana University Press, 2009).

30. Matthew Hughes, *Britain's Pacification of Palestine: The British Army, the Colonial State, and the Arab Revolt, 1936–1939* (Cambridge: Cambridge University Press, 2019), https://doi.org/10.1017/9781316216026.

31. Robinson, *Citizen Strangers.*

32. Robinson, *Citizen Strangers.*

33. "Secret 1970 Document Confirms First West Bank Settlements Built on a Lie," n.d. Haaretz.Com, https://www.haaretz.com/israel-news/.premium-document-confirms-first-settlements-built-on-a-lie-1.5416937.

34. George Bisharat, "Land, Law, and Legitimacy in Israel and the Occupied Territories" *American University Law Review* 43 (January 1994): 467; "Land Grab." n.d. B'Tselem. https://www.btselem.org/publications/summaries/200205_land_grab.

35. See Jean du Plessis, "Land Restitution in South Africa: Overview and Lessons Learned" (Working Paper No. 6, BADIL Resource Center, December 2004); Paul Prettitore, "The Right to Housing and Property Restitution in Bosnia and Herzegovina" (Working Paper No. 1, BADIL Resource Center, April 2003).

36. Heinrich Böll Stiftung, "The Impact of the 1948 Desaster: The Ways That the Nakba Has Influenced Palestinian History | Heinrich Böll Stiftung," n.d, https://www.boell.de/en/2010/03/04/impact-1948-desaster-ways-nakba-has-influenced-palestinian-history.

37. Michael R. Fischbach, "The Impact of the 1948 Desaster: The Ways that the Nakba has Influenced Palestinian History," March 4, 2010; "The Transformation of Palestine: Palestine and the Palestinians 60 Years after the 'Nakba,'" Conference Paper for the International Symposium. See http://pubdocs.worldbank.org/en/169601538076901007/mpo-am18-palestinian-territories-pse-ks-9-13-fin.pdf.

38. Cyanne E. Loyle and Christian Davenport, "Transitional Injustice: Subverting Justice in Transition and Postconflict Societies" *Journal of Human Rights* 15, no. 1 (2016): 126–49, https://doi.org/10.1080/14754835.2015.1052897.

39. The most recent poll by the Palestinian Center for Policy and Survey Research that asked this question found that 83 percent of respondents backed the movement; https://www.pcpsr.org/en/node/775.

40. Ari Shavit, "Survival of the Fittest," Haaretz.Com, July 1, 2004. https://www.haaretz.com/1.5262454.

41. Tony Judt, "Israel: The Alternative," October 23, 2003, https://www.nybooks.com/articles/2003/10/23/israel-the-alternative/.

4. CITIZENSHIP AS A MOBILITY REGIME

1. Hagar Kotef, *Movement and the Ordering of Freedom* (London: Duke University Press, 2015).

2. Radhika Mongia, *Indian Migration and Empire* (London: Duke University Press, 2018); Jane Caplan and John Torpey, "Introduction," in *Documenting Individual Identity: The Development of State Practices in the Modern World*, ed. Jane Caplan and John Torpey (Oxford: Princeton University Press, 2001), 1–12.

3. For the role of mobility regimes in the making of European citizenship, see John Torpey, "Coming and Going: On the State Monopolization of the Legitimate 'Means of Movement,'" *Sociological Theory* 16, no. 3 (1998): 239–259. For the role of mobility regimes in the making of postcolonial citizenship, see Vazira Fazila-Yacoobali Zamindar, *The Long Partition and the Making of Modern South Asia: Refugees, Boundaries, Histories* (New York: Columbia University Press, 2007).

4. Yael Berda, *Living Emergency: Israel's Permit Regime in the Occupied West Bank* (Stanford: Stanford University Press, 2017).

5. Nur-eldeen Masalha, *The Palestine Nakba: Decolonizing History, Narrating the Subaltern, Reclaiming Memory* (London: Zed Books, 2012).

6. Adriana Kemp, "'Dangerous Populations': State Territoriality and the Constitution of National Minorities," in *Boundaries and Belonging: States and Societies in the Struggle to Shape Identities and Local Practices*, ed. Joel S. Migdal (Cambridge: Cambridge University Press, 2009), 73–98. Shira Robinson, *Citizen Strangers: Palestinians and the Birth of Israel's Liberal Settler State* (Stanford: Stanford University Press, 2013).

7. Catriona Drew, "Self-determination, Population Transfer and the Middle East Peace Accords," in *Human Rights, Self-Determination and Political Change in the Palestinian Occupied Territories*, ed. Stephen Bowen (The Hague: Kluwer Law, 1997), 119–168.

8. Elia Zureik, "Colonialism, Surveillance, and Population Control," in *Surveillance and Control in Israel/Palestine: Population, Territory, and Power*, ed. Elia Zureik, David Lyon, and Yasmeen Abu-Laban (London: Routledge, 2010), 3–45; Ilan Saban, "Theorizing and Tracing the Legal Dimensions of a Control Framework: Law and the Arab-Palestinian Minority in Israel's First Three Decades (1948–1978)," *Emory International Law Review* 25 (2011): 299; Robinson, *Citizen Strangers*; Nadim N. Rouhan and Areej Sabbagh-Khoury, "Settler-Colonial Citizenship: Conceptualizing the Relationship between Israel and Its Palestinian Citizens," *Settler Colonial Studies* 5, no. 3 (2015): 205–225.

9. Lana Tatour, "Citizenship as Domination: Settler Colonialism and the Making of Palestinian Citizenship in Israel," *Arab Studies Journal* 27, no. 2 (2019): 8–39.

10. Ann Laura Stoler, Carole McGranahan, and Peter Perdue, eds., *Imperial Formations* (Santa Fe: SAR Press, 2007).

11. Laleh Khalili, "The Location of Palestine in Global Counterinsurgencies," *International Journal of Middle East Studies* 42, no. 3 (2010): 413–433; Laleh Khalili, "Counterterrorism and Counterinsurgency in the Neoliberal Age," in *The Oxford Handbook of Contemporary Middle Eastern and North African History*, ed. Amal N. Ghazal and Jens Hanssen (Oxford: Oxford University Press, 2015), 1–23, DOI: 10.1093/oxfordhb/9780199672530.013.16.

12. Christopher Tomlins, "Framing the Fragments—Police: Genealogies, Discourses, Locales, Principles," in *The New Police Science: The Police Power in Domestic and Inter-*

national Governance, ed. Markus D. Dubber and Mariana Valverde (Stanford: Stanford University Press, 2006), 249.

13. Ann Swidler, "Culture in Action: Symbols and Strategies," *American Sociological Review* 51, no. 2 (1986): 273.

14. The binary distinction between friend or foe is the classic perception of the use of emergency laws, stemming from Carl Schmitt's definition of sovereignty as the ability to suspend the law in times of crisis. For a helpful summary, see Gopal Balakrishnan, *The Enemy: An Intellectual Portrait of Carl Schmitt* (London: Verso, 2000); and Yael Berda, "Managing 'Dangerous Populations': How Colonial Emergency Laws Shape Citizenship," *Security Dialogue* (2020): 0967010620901908.

15. Ann Laura Stoler, *Duress: Imperial Durabilities in Our Times* (Durham, NC: Duke University Press, 2016), 63.

16. Ranabir Samaddar, "Law and Terror in the Age of Colonial Constitution Making," *Diogenes* 53, no. 4 (2006): 18–33.

17. Berda, "Managing 'Dangerous Populations.'"

18. This understanding was based on two historical moments: the first was the partition of Bengal in 1906 to separate Hindu and Muslim Bengalis, introduced by Lord Curzon. The second was the Treaty of Lausanne that viewed population transfer to achieve ethnic homogeneity as compatible and at times necessary for achieving national self-determination.

19. Catriona Drew, "Remembering 1948: Who's Afraid of International Law in the Israeli-Palestinian Conflict?" in *Who's Afraid of International Law?*, ed. Raimond Gaita and Gerry Simpson (Melbourne: Monash University Publishing, 2017), 214; See also Umut Özsu, *Formalizing Displacement: International Law and Population Transfers* (Oxford: Oxford University Press, 2015); and Victor Kattan, "The Empire Departs: The Partitions of British India, Mandate Palestine, and the Dawn of Self-Determination in the Third World," *Asian Journal of Middle Eastern and Islamic Studies* 12, no. 3 (2018): 304–327.

20. See Drew, "Remembering 1948," 119, note 3.

21. See Drew, "Remembering 1948," 119, note 3.

22. Laurent Dubois, *Avengers of the New World: The Story of the Haitian Revolution* (Cambridge: Harvard University Press, 2005); Julian Go, "Relational Sociology and Postcolonial Theory: Sketches of a 'Postcolonial Relationalism'" (Pelgrave Handbook of Relational Sociology, 2018), 357–373

23. See Zamindar, *The Long Partition*.

24. Alina Korn, "From Refugees to Infiltrators: Constructing Political Crime in Israel in the 1950s." *International Journal of the Sociology of Law* 31, no. 1 (2003): 1–22.

25. Nasser Hussain, *The Jurisprudence of Emergency: Colonialism and the Rule of Law* (Ann Arbor: University of Michigan Press, 2009), 19.

26. Home Member Srinivas, quoted in Ujjwal Kumar Singh, *The State, Democracy and Anti-Terror Laws in India* (New Delhi: SAGE Publications India, 2007), 56.

27. John Reynolds, "The Political Economy of States of Emergency," *Oregon Review of International Law* 14 (2012): 85.

28. The state of emergency is central to colonial states in which the colonial power rules without sovereignty. I am referring here to declarations of states of emergency by officials, which formed the legal and administrative environment for innovation of surveillance and monitoring practices, peaking between the two world wars.

29. Radhika Singha, "Settle, Mobilize, and Verify: Identification Practices in Colonial India," *Studies in History* 16, no. 2 (2000): 151–198.

30. British imperial officials used the term "race" fluidly and frequently, lumping together an array of population characteristics. Classifications according to nationality

emerge later, even in colonies marked by intercommunal conflict in which classification according to nationality emerges closer to partition/independence. See Anthony J. Christopher, "Race and the Census in the Commonwealth," *Population, Space and Place* 11, no. 2 (2005): 103–118. On the fluidity of the term "race," see also Paul Gilroy, *Postcolonial Melancholia* (New York: Columbia University Press, 2005).

31. Ann Laura Stoler, "A Deadly Embrace: Of Colony and Camp," in *Duress: Imperial Durabilities in Our Times* (Durham, NC: Duke University Press, 2016), 68–120, 116.

32. Uditi Sen, *Citizen Refugee: Forging the Indian Nation after Partition* (Cambridge: Cambridge University Press, 2018); Walid Khalidi, "Why Did the Palestinians Leave, Revisited," *Journal of Palestine Studies* 34, no. 2 (2005): 42–54; Nur Masalha, "A Critique of Benny Morris," *Journal of Palestine Studies* 21, no. 1 (1991): 90–97.

33. Hillel Cohen, "The Two Wars of 1948," *Hazman Haze*, October 16, 2018, https://www.haaretz.co.il/hazmanhazeh/MAGAZINE-1.6071227.

34. Robinson, *Citizen Strangers*. For a critique of Robinson's framework, see Arnon Yehuda Degani, "The Decline and Fall of the Israeli Military Government, 1948–1966: A Case of Settler-Colonial Consolidation?" *Settler Colonial Studies* 5, no. 1 (2015): 84–99.

35. Elia Zureik, *The Palestinians in Israel: A Study in Internal Colonialism* (London: Routledge, 1979); Ahmad H. Sa'di, "The Incorporation of the Palestinian Minority by the Israeli State, 1948–1970: On the Nature, Transformation, and Constraints of Collaboration," *Social Text* 21, no. 2 (2003): 75–94; and *Thorough Surveillance: The Genesis of Israeli Policies of Population Management, Surveillance and Political Control towards the Palestinian Minority* (Manchester: University of Manchester Press, 2016), 150–182; Alina Korn, "Military Government, Political Control and Crime: The Case of Israeli Arabs," *Crime, Law and Social Change* 34, no. 2 (2000): 159–182.

36. Sharri Plonski, *Palestinian Citizens of Israel: Power, Resistance and the Struggle for Space* (London: Bloomsbury, 2017); Oren Yiftachel, "Ghetto Citizenship: Palestinian Arabs in Israel," in *Israel and the Palestinians–Key Terms* (Haifa: Mada Center for Applied Research, 2009); Nadim N. Rouhana, *Palestinian Citizens in an Ethnic Jewish State: Identities in Conflict* (New Haven: Yale University Press, 1997); Robert Blecher, "Citizens without Sovereignty: Transfer and Ethnic Cleansing in Israel," *Comparative Studies in Society and History* 47, no. 4 (2005): 725–754.

37. Benni Nurieli, "Foreigners in National Space: Jews and Arabs in the Lod Ghetto, 1950–1959," *Theory and Criticism* 26 (2005): 13–42.

38. See "Legal Dimensions of a Control Framework," note 9.

39. Magid Shihade, "Settler Colonialism and Conflict: The Israeli State and Its Palestinian Subjects." *Settler Colonial Studies* 2, no. 1 (2012): 108–123; Rasem Khamaisi, "Territorial Dispossession and Population Control of the Palestinians," in *Surveillance and Control in Israel/Palestine: Population, Territory, and Power*, ed. Elia Zureik, David Lyon, and Yasmeen Abu-Laban (London: Routledge, 2010), 359–376; Degani, "The Decline and Fall of the Israeli Military Government," 84–99.

40. Irit Ballas, "Boundaries, Obligations and Belonging: The Reconfiguration of Citizenship in Emergency Criminal Regimes," *Theoretical Criminology* 16, no. 4 (2021):417–434.

41. Hannah Arendt, "We Refugees." *Menorah Journal* 31, no. 1 (1943): 69–77.

42. Ariella Azoulay and Adi Ophir, *The One-State Condition: Occupation and Democracy in Israel/Palestine* (Stanford: Stanford University Press, 2012), 13–14.

43. Julia Peteet, *Space and Mobility in Palestine* (Indianapolis: Indiana University Press, 2017).

44. Tobias Kelly, "In a Treacherous State: The Fear of Collaboration among West Bank Palestinians," in *Traitors Suspicion, Intimacy, and the Ethics of State-Building*, eds. Sharika Thiranagama and Tobias Kelly (Philadelphia: University of Pennsylvania Press, 2011), 169–187.

45. See Walid Habbas, "The West Bank-Israel Economic Integration: Palestinian Interaction with the Israeli Border and Permit Regimes," in *Political Economy of Palestine*, eds. Alaa Tartir, Tariq Dana, Timothy Seidel (Cham, Switzerland: Palgrave Macmillan, 2021), 111–134.

46. The exception was emergency decrees curbing protest during "the disengagement" from Gaza in 2005.

47. Yoav Peled, "Citizenship Betrayed: Israel's Emerging Immigration and Citizenship Regime," *Theoretical Inquiries in Law* 8, no. 2 (2007): 603–628.

48. Tobias Kelly, *Law, Violence and Sovereignty among West Bank Palestinians* (Cambridge: Cambridge University Press, 2006).

49. Nufar Avni, "Between Exclusionary Nationalism and Urban Citizenship in East Jerusalem/al-Quds," *Political Geography* 86 (2020): 102314, https://doi.org/10.1016/j.polgeo.2020.102314.

50. Lana Tatour, "Citizenship as Domination: Settler Colonialism and the Making of Palestinian Citizenship in Israel," *Arab Studies Journal* 27, no. 2 (2019): 8–39.

51. Mansour Nasasra, "The Politics of Exclusion of Palestinians in Israel since Oslo," in *From the River to the Sea: Palestine and Israel in the Shadow of "Peace,"* ed. Mandy Turner (Lanham, MD: Lexington Books, 2019), 125.

52. Aeyal Gross, *The Writing on the Wall: Rethinking the International Law of Occupation* (Cambridge: Cambridge University Press, 2017), esp. chap. 2 on the "indeterminacy of occupation."

5. DELEGATING DOMINATION

1. James C. Scott, *Seeing like a State: How Certain Schemes to Improve the Human Condition Have Failed* (New Haven: Yale University Press, 1998), 7.

2. Population estimates for Palestinians in the West Bank and Gaza Strip come from the Palestinian Central Bureau of Statistics, excluding the population of Israeli-occupied East Jerusalem. Population estimates for the Jewish and Palestinian populations in Israel, within its 1949 armistice lines, in East Jerusalem, and in the Jewish settlements of the West Bank come from the Israel Central Bureau of Statistics.

3. Limiting one's attention to the West Bank risks reifying the geographic fragmentation of Israel/Palestine that serves certain ideological programs more than others. The reader should rest assured this is a conceptual, not normative, choice. Although the realities described in this chapter may echo patterns observed in other parts of Israel/Palestine at different periods in time, I focus on the contemporary West Bank because, on the surface, it represents a "likely case" for observing the institutional features of indirect rule. This relatively restricted empirical scope illuminates areas of conceptual fit and, by contrast, areas of tension that can inform inferences and predictions about future political outcomes.

4. Data on settler population from Peace Now, 2021.

5. Alexei Abrahams, "Not Dark Yet: The Israel-PA Principal-Agent Relationship, 1993–2017," in *Proxy Wars: Suppressing Violence through Local Agents*, ed. Eli Berman and David A. Lake (Ithaca, NY: Cornell University Press, 2019): 185–209; Dana El Kurd, *Polarized and Demobilized: Legacies of Authoritarianism in Palestine* (London: Hurst & Co., 2019); Alaa Tartir, "Securitised Development and Palestinian Authoritarianism under Fayyadism," *Conflict, Security & Development* 15, no. 5 (2015): 479–502; Jeremy Wildeman, and Alaa Tartir, "Political Economy of Foreign Aid in the Occupied Palestinian Territories: A Conceptual Framing," in *Political Economy of Palestine: Critical, Interdisciplinary, and Decolonial Perspectives*, ed. Alaa Tartir, Tariq Dana, and Timothy Seidel (Cham, Switzerland: Palgrave Macmillan, 2021): 223–247; Andy Clarno, *Neoliberal Apartheid: Palestine/Israel*

and South Africa after 1994 (London: University of Chicago Press, 2017); Diana Buttu. "Why the Palestinian Authority Should Be Shuttered," *New York Times,* May 26, 2017, https://www.nytimes.com/2017/05/26/opinion/palestinian-authority-mahmoud-abbas .html.

6. Joel Perlmann, "The 1967 Census of the West Bank and Gaza Strip: A Digitized Version," Levy Economics Institute of Bard College, 2012, http://www.levyinstitute .org/palestinian-census/.

7. Neve Gordon and Yinon Cohen, "Western Interests, Israeli Unilateralism, and the Two-State Solution," *Journal of Palestine Studies* 41, no. 3 (2012): 10.

8. Brynjar Lia, *A Police Force without a State: A History of the Palestinian Security Forces in the West Bank and Gaza* (Reading, PA: Ithaca Press, 2006): 135–139, 191–212.

9. Clarno, *Neoliberal Apartheid*; Yezid Sayigh, *Policing the People, Building the State: Authoritarian Transformation in the West Bank and Gaza* (Washington, DC: Carnegie Endowment for International Peace, February 2011).

10. John Gerring et al. "An Institutional Theory of Direct and Indirect Rule," *World Politics* 63, no. 3 (2011): 377–433; Mahmood Mamdani, *Citizen and Subject: Contemporary Africa and the Legacy of Late Colonialism* (Princeton: Princeton University Press, 1996).

11. Max Weber, "Politics as a Vocation," in *The Vocation Lectures*, ed. David Owen and Tracy B. Strong, (Indianapolis: Hackett Publishing, 1919); Adnan Naseemullah and Paul Staniland, "Indirect Rule and Varieties of Governance," *Governance* 29, no. 1 (2016): 14.

12. Mamdani, *Citizen and Subject.*

13. Mamdani, *Citizen and Subject*; Michael Hechter, *Containing Nationalism* (Oxford: Oxford University Press, 2001), 37.

14. Gerring et al. "An Institutional Theory," 378.

15. Naseemullah and Staniland, "Indirect Rule and Varieties of Governance."

16. Further, it may be empirically difficult to separate institutions of indirect rule from the ideological regime in question. In discussing the example of South Africa's apartheid regime, Brown notes that ideological content did not entirely precede the construction of state institutions: "'Apartheid' as an ideology was as much a product of 'apartheid' in practice as it produced those practices. For reasons partly having to do with politics among South African whites, the National Party . . . asserted a need to deepen, systematize, and name prevailing arrangements that were already based on profound racial discrimination. And it sketched out a future path. There was a racialized system before 1948 that might be termed apartheid in effect and in mentality; after 1948, apartheid was a formal system that was *always in the process of becoming* until those building the system saw the need to sue for peace in the late 1980s" (40, emphasis added). Nathan J. Brown, "The Powerful Strategic Logic of a Hazy Mentality with Hard Edges," *Project on Middle East Political Science,* July 2020, https://pomeps.org/pomeps-studies-41-israel-palestine-exploring-a-one-state -reality.

17. Mamdani, *Citizen and Subject*, 145.

18. Eli Berman et al. "Introduction: Principals, Agents, and Indirect Foreign Policies," in *Proxy Wars: Suppressing Violence through Local Agents,* ed. Eli Berman and David A. Lake (Ithaca, NY: Cornell University Press, 2019), 1–27.

19. El Kurd, *Polarized and Demobilized*; Manal A. Jamal, *Promoting Democracy: The Force of Political Settlements in Uncertain Times* (New York: New York University Press, 2019).

20. Abrahams, "Not Dark Yet."

21. Abrahams, "Not Dark Yet," 186.

22. Abrahams, "Not Dark Yet," 196.

23. El Kurd, *Polarized and Demobilized.*

24. El Kurd, *Polarized and Demobilized.*

25. Tariq Dana, "Crony Capitalism in the Palestinian Authority: A Deal among Friends," *Third World Quarterly* 41, no. 2 (2007): 247–263.

26. Polls were carried out in March, June, September and December 2021. Each poll was conducted with a sample of 1,200–1,270 Palestinians designed to be representative of the adult Palestinian population in the West Bank, excluding occupied East Jerusalem and the Gaza Strip. For more information, see www.pcpsr.org.

27. Isabel Kershner and Adam Rasgon, "Critic's Death Puts Focus on Palestinian Authority's Authoritarianism," *New York Times*, July 7, 2021, https://www.nytimes.com/2021/07/07/world/middleeast/Palestinian-Authority-protestors.html.

28. Adam Rasgon, "Palestinian Authority Indicts 14 Security Force Members in Activist's Death," *New York Times*, September 6, 2021, https://www.nytimes.com/2021/09/06/world/middleeast/palestinian-authority-officers-indicted-nizar-banat.html.

29. Qassam Muaddi, "Family of killed Palestinian activist Nizar Banat turn to international court for justice after suspects released," *The New Arab*, May 19, 2022, https://english.alaraby.co.uk/news/nizar-banat-family-look-justice-international-courts.

30. Clarno, *Neoliberal Apartheid*, 159.

31. Abrahams, "Not Dark Yet."

32. Lia, *A Police Force without a State*, 135–139.

33. Clarno, *Neoliberal Apartheid*, 188.

34. Anas Iqtait, "The Palestinian Authority Political Economy: The Architecture of Fiscal Control," in *Political Economy of Palestine: Critical, Interdisciplinary, and Decolonial Perspectives*, ed. Alaa Tartir, Tariq Dana, and Timothy Seidel (Cham: Palgrave Macmillan, 2021), 249–270.

35. Clarno, *Neoliberal Apartheid*; Leila Farsakh, "Palestinian Economic Development: Paradigm Shifts since the First Intifada," *Journal of Palestine Studies* 45, no. 2 (2016): 55–71.

36. Fadi Quran, "The Russian-Doll Carceral State," *Jadaliyya*, March 24, 2022, www.jadaliyya.com/Details/43978/The-Russian-Doll-Carceral-State.

37. Mamdani, *Citizen and Subject*, 50–51.

38. Stockholm International Peace Research Institute, "SIPRI Military Expenditure Database," 2021, https://www.sipri.org/databases/milex.

39. Mamdani, *Citizen and Subject.*

40. As a caveat, some would argue that Israeli policies toward Arab Druze and Bedouin populations, for example, have reinforced "tribal" divisions between these communities and those Arab citizens of Israel who self-identify as Palestinian. For more on identity construction among Israel's Druze population, see: Laila Parsons, *The Druze between Palestine and Israel, 1947–49* (London: Palgrave MacMillan, 2000); Ilana Kaufman, "Ethnic Affirmation or Ethnic Manipulation: The Case of the Druze in Israel," *Nationalism and Ethnic Politics* 9, no. 4 (2004): 53–82; and Rabah Halabi, "Invention of a Nation: The Druze in Israel," *Journal of Asian and African Studies* 49, no. 3 (2014): 267–281. On Bedouin identity, see: Longina Jakubowska, "Resisting 'Ethnicity': The Israeli State and Bedouin Identity," in *The Paths to Domination, Resistance, and Terror*, ed. Carolyn Nordstrom and Joann Martin, (Berkeley: University of California, 1992), 85–105; Seth J. Frantzman, Havatzelet Yahel, and Ruth Kark, "Contested Indigeneity: The Development of an Indigenous Discourse on the Bedouin of the Negev, Israel," *Israel Studies* 17, no. 1 (2012): 78–104; and Mansour Nasasra, Sophie Richter-Devroe, Sarab Abu-Rabia-Queder, and Richard Ratcliffe, eds., *The Naqab Bedouin and Colonialism: New perspectives* (New York: Routledge, 2015).

41. Mamdani, *Citizen and Subject*, 24.

42. Lakshmi Iyer, "Direct versus Indirect Colonial Rule in India: Long-Term Consequences," *Review of Economics and Statistics* 92, no. 4 (2010): 693–713; Alexander Lee,

"Land, State Capacity, and Colonialism: Evidence from India," *Comparative Political Studies* 52, no. 3 (2019): 412–444; Shivaji Mukherjee, "Colonial Origins of Maoist Insurgency in India: Historical Institutions and Civil War," *Journal of Conflict Resolution* 62, no. 10 (2018): 2232–2274.

43. Matthew Lange, *Lineages of Despostism and Development: British Colonialism and State Power* (Chicago: University of Chicago Press, 2009).

44. "The Military Courts," *B'Tselem*, November 11, 2017, https://www.btselem.org/military_courts.

45. Lange, *Lineages of Despostism and Development*, 6.

46. Natalie Wenzell Letsa and Martha Wilfahrt, "The Mechanisms of Direct and Indirect Rule: Colonialism and Economic Development in Africa," *Quarterly Journal of Political Science* 15, no. 4 (2020): 539–577.

47. Daron Acemoglu et al., *Indirect Rule and State Weakness in Africa: Sierra Leone in Comparative Perspective* (Cambridge, MA: National Bureau of Economic Research, 2016), 4.

48. Hechter, *Containing Nationalism*.

49. Noura Erakat, *Justice for Some: Law and the Question of Palestine*. (Stanford: Stanford University Press, 2019).

6. THE THOROUGH INSINUATION OF THE ONE STATE REALITY INTO PALESTINIAN POLITICAL LIFE

1. See the text of Abbas's speech as reported by the Palestinian News and Information Agency (WAFA) 2020.

2. Voter turnout data are provided by the Israel Democracy Institute, classified as "Arab" voter turnout. Karin Tamar Schafferman, "Participation, Abstention and Boycott: Trends in Arab Voter Turnout in Israeli Elections," *Israel Democracy Institute*, April 21, 2009, https://en.idi.org.il/articles/7116.

3. Arik Rudnitzky, "The Arab Israeli Vote in the 23rd Knesset Elections," *Israel Democracy Institute*, March 10, 2020, https://en.idi.org.il/articles/30961.

4. Renee Lewis, "Abbas Meeting with Israeli Joint List Blurs Green Line," *Al Jazeera America*, March 25, 2015, http://america.aljazeera.com/articles/2015/3/25/Abbas-Joint-Arab-List-Ramallah.html.

5. Hana Levi Julian, "Ra'am Party Chairman Mansour Abbas: 'The Time Has Come to Listen To Each Other,'" *Jewish Press*, April 1, 2021, https://www.jewishpress.com/news/israel/israeli-arabs/raam-party-chairman-mansour-abbas-the-time-has-come-to-listen-to-each-other/2021/04/01/.

6. Ofer Kenig, "Voting Patterns in Knesset Elections 2021 vs. 2020," *Israel Democracy Institute*, April 21, 2021, https://en.idi.org.il/articles/34367.

7. "Launch of 'The National Economic Week' in Palestine from the River to the Sea," *Arabi21*, June 5, 2021, https://tinyurl.com/25e89hzp.

8. PalEcoWeek1948, "Unified Palestinian Culture Week | July 1–7." *Facebook*, June 24, 2021, https://www.facebook.com/PalEcoWeek1948/posts/117109470589188.

9. "Decade-Long High in Israelis' 'Sense of Belonging,'" *Israel Democracy Institute*, April 27, 2020, https://en.idi.org.il/articles/31437.

10. Akiva Eldar, "Should Palestinians Keep Boycotting Jerusalem Elections?" *Al-Monitor*, March 29, 2018, https://www.al-monitor.com/pulse/originals/2018/03/israel-east-jerusalem-palestinians-municipal-elections-mayor.html.

11. Rasha Abou Jalal, "Arab Bloc Could Get out Palestinian Vote in Jerusalem Municipal Elections," *Al-Monitor*, August 13, 2018, https://www.al-monitor.com/pulse/originals/2018/08/palestinian-bloc-jerusalem-elections-boycott-israel.html#ixzz6dGFZifQw.

12. Yara Hawari, "The Israeli Legal System: No Place for Justice," *Al Jazeera*, August 5, 2021. https://www.aljazeera.com/opinions/2021/8/5/the-israeli-legal-system-no-place-for-justice.

13. Cheryl A. Rubenberg, "The Civilian Infrastructure of the Palestine Liberation Organization: An Analysis of the PLO in Lebanon until June 1982," *Journal of Palestine Studies* 12, no. 3 (1983): 55–72.

14. Palestine National Council. "The Final Statement Issued by the Palestinian National Council, 23rd Session," May 5, 2018, https://www.palestinepnc.org/news/item/505-2018-05-05-04-49-46.

15. Palestinian Civil Society. "Palestinian Civil Socicty Call for BDS," July 9, 2005, https://www.bdsmovement.net/call.

7. PALESTINIANS IN ISRAEL AND THE ONE STATE REALITY

1. We use the term as it was coined by Ian Lustick in *Paradigm Lost: From Two-State Solution to One-State Reality* (Philadelphia: University of Pennsylvania Press, 2019).

2. The relevant literature refers to this population with different terms: "Palestinians in Israel," "Arabs in Israel," "Arab citizens of Israel," "the Palestinian minority," and "Palestinians inside 1948 borders." "Central Bureau of Statistics Estimates," media release, December 30, 2020. https://www.cbs.gov.il/en/mediarelease/Pages/2020/Population-of-Israel-on-the-Eve-of-2021.aspx.

3. Aziz Haidar, *The Arab Society in Israel Yearbook* (Jerusalem: Van Leer Institution, 2005), [Hebrew], 30.

4. Jewish Virtual Library, *Vital Statistics: Latest Population Statistics for Israel*, 2020, https://www.jewishvirtuallibrary.org/latest-population-statistics-for-israel.

5. Myers JDC-Brooklyn, *The Arab Population in Israel: Facts & Figures 2018*, https://brookdale.jdc.org.il/wp-content/uploads/2018/03/MJB_Facts_and_Figures_on_the_Arab_Population_in_Israel_2018-English.pdf.

6. As'ad Ghanem and Mohanad Mustafa, *Palestinians in Israel: The Politics of Indigenous Minorities in the Ethnic State* (Ramallah: Palestinian Center for Israeli Studies, 2009) [Arabic].

7. Central Bureau of Statistics, "Localities (excluding Bedouin Tribes) and Population, by Type of Locality and Population Group," 2021, https://www.cbs.gov.il/he/publications/doclib/2021/2.shnatonpopulation/st02_21x.pdf.

8. Haidar, *Arab Society in Israel Yearbook*, 28.

9. Arik Rudnitzky, *Demographic, Socio-Economic and Political Factors* (Tel Aviv: Tel Aviv University, 2018).

10. Ian Lustick, *Arabs in the Jewish State: Israel's Control of a National Minority* (Austin: University of Texas Press, 1980).

11. Lustick, *Arabs in the Jewish State*; Yair Bauml, *A Blue and White Shadow: The Israeli Establishment's Policy and Actions for Its Arab Citizens, The Formative Years, 1985–1968* (Haifa: Pardes Press, 2007) [Hebrew].

12. Elia Zureik, *The Palestinians in Israel: A Study in Internal Colonialism* (London: Routledge, 1979).

13. Majid Al-Haj, *The Arabs' Educational System in Israel: Issues and Trends* (Jerusalem: Floersheimer Institute for Policy Studies, 1993).

14. Nadim Rouhana and As'ad Ghanem, "The Crisis of Minorities in Ethnic States: The Case of the Palestinian Citizens in Israel," *International Journal of Middle East Studies* 30, no. 3 (1998): 321–346.

15. As'ad Ghanem and Ibrahim Khatib, "The Nationalisation of the Israeli Ethnocratic Regime and the Palestinian Minority's Shrinking Citizenship," *Citizenship Studies* 21 no. 8 (2017): 889–902.

16. As'ad Ghanem and Mohanad Mustafa, *Palestinians in Israel: The Politics of Faith after Oslo* (Cambridge: Cambridge University Press, 2018).

17. Ayman K. Agbaria and Muhanad Mustafa, "Two States for Three Peoples: The 'Palestinian-Israeli' in the Future Vision Documents of the Palestinians in Israel," *Ethnic and Racial Studies* 35, no. 4 (2012): 718–736; As'ad Ghanem and Mohanad Mustafa, "Coping with the Nakba: The Palestinians in Israel and the 'Future Vision as a Collective Agenda," *Israel Studies Forum* 24 no. 2 (2009): 52–66.

18. Nabil Saleh, Nadim, Rouhana, and N. Sultani. *Voting without a Voice: The Palestinian. Minority in Israel's 2003 Elections* (Haifa: Mada al Carmel Center, 2004) [Arabic].

19. Ghanem and Mustafa, *Palestinians in Israel.*

20. Ghanem and Mustafa, "Coping with the Nakba."

21. Ghanem and Mustafa, "Coping with the Nakba."

22. "The Palestinians in Israel: Attitudes between Covid-19 and the Popular Uprising, May 2021," in *The Palestinians in Israel: Political and Social Perspectives between Covid-19 and Current Intifada*, ed. Mohanad Mustafa (Haifa: Mada al-Carmel Center, 2021), 9–21 [Arabic].

23. For more information on this topic see Ghanem, and Khatib, "The Nationalisation of the Israeli Ethnocratic Regime."

24. Yossri Khaizran, "Arab Society in Israel and the 'Arab Spring,'" *Journal of Muslim Minority Affairs* 40, no. 2 (2020).

25. Ghanem and Mustafa, "Coping with the Nakba."

26. Mohanad Mustafa, ed., *70 Years of Nakba* (Haifa: Mada al-Carmel Center, 2019).

27. As'ad Ghanem, "Settler Colonialism, Apartheid and Rising Violence among Palestinians in Israel," AARDi, July 25, 2021, https://aardi.org/2021/07/25/settler-colonialism-apartheid-and-rising-violence-among-palestinians-in-israel-by-prof-asad-ghanem/; As'ad Ghanem, "The Political Institutions of the Palestinian Minority in Israel," in *The Oxford Handbook of Israeli Politics and Society*, ed. Reuven Hazan, Menachem Hofnung, Gideon Rahat, and Alan Dowty (Oxford: Oxford University Press, 2021), 3959–21409.

28. As'ad Ghanem and Mohanad Mustafa, "The Palestinians in Israel: The Challenge of the Indigenous Group Politics in the 'Jewish State,'" *Journal of Muslim Minority Affairs* 31, no. 2 (2011): 177–196.

29. "Attitudes between Covid-19 and the Popular Uprising, May 2021."

30. "Attitudes between Covid-19 and the Popular Uprising, May 2021."

8. AMERICAN JEWRY AND THE ONE STATE REALITY

1. Robert Eisen, *The Chosen People in America: A Study in Religious Jewish Theology* (Bloomington: Indiana University Press, 1983); Irving Kristol, "The Liberal Tradition of American Jews," in *American Pluralism and the Jewish Community*, ed. Seymour Martin Lipset (New Brunswick, NJ: Transaction Books, 1990), 109–116; Daniel Greene, "A Chosen People in a Pluralist Nation: Horace Kallen and the Jewish-American Experience," *Religion and American Culture* 16, no. 2 (2006): 161–193.

2. Jessica Martinez and Gregory A. Smith, "How the Faithful Voted: A Preliminary 2016 Analysis," *Pew Research Center*, November 9, 2016, https://www.pewresearch.org/fact-tank/2016/11/09/how-the-faithful-voted-a-preliminary-2016-analysis

3. For a sampling of the extensive literature on Jewish Americans and Israel, see Melvin Urofsky, *American Zionism: From Herzl to the Holocaust* (Lincoln: University of Nebraska Press, 1975); Naomi Cohen, *American Jews and the Zionist Idea* (New York: Ktav Publishing House, 1975); Arnold Eisen, "Israel at 50: An American Jewish Perspective," *American Jewish Year Book* (1998): 47–71; Theodore Sasson, "Mass Mobilization to Direct Engagement: American Jews' Changing Relationship to Israel," *Israel Studies* 15, no. 2 (2010): 173–195.

4. Eisen, *The Chosen People in America*.

5. Irving Howe, *World of Our Fathers* (New York: New York University Press, 2005).

6. For a selection of the rich literature on the anti-Zionism of American Jews, and especially those of the liberal and reform persuasions, see Walter Laquer, "Zionism and Its Liberal Critics 1896–1948," *Contemporary History* 6, no. 4 (1971): 161–182; Naomi Cohen, "The Reaction of Reform Judaism in America to Political Zionism (1897–1922)," *American Jewish Historical Society*, September 1950.

7. Benjamin Balint, *Running Commentary: The Contentious Magazine that Transformed the Jewish Left into the Neoconservative Right* (New York: Public Affairs, 2010), 33.

8. Ben Halprin, *An American Jew: A Zionist Analysis* (New York: Schocken Books, 1956).

9. Henry Feingold, *Jewish Power in America: Myth and Reality* (New Brunswick, NJ: Transaction Books, 2011).

10. "East Jerusalem," *B'Tselem*, January 27, 2019, www.btselem.org/jerusalem.

11. Nir Hasson, "All the Ways East Jerusalem Palestinians Get Rejected in Bid to Become Israelis," *Haaretz*, January 15, 2019, https://www.haaretz.com/israel-news/.premium-east-jerusalem-palestinians-face-uphill-battle-in-bid-for-israeli-citizenship-1.6844543.

12. See www.latimes.com/archives/la-xpm-1990-06-22-mn-431-story.html.

13. Interview with Yitzhak Rabin, *McNeil-Lehrer Newshour*, Monday September 13, 1993. Also see Ben Lynfield, "Rabin Tries to Make Less of 'Greater Israel,'" *Christian Science Monitor*, January 25, 1994, p. 22.

14. "President Bush Calls for New Palestinian Leadership," *The White House*, June 24, 2002, https://georgewbush-whitehouse.archives.gov/news/releases/2002/06/20020624-3.html.

15. Atalia Omer, *Days of Awe: Reimagining Jewishness in Solidarity with Palestinians* (Chicago: University of Chicago Press, 2019).

16. This analysis draws heavily from Michael Barnett, *The Star and the Stripes* (Princeton: Princeton University Press, 2016).

17. Theodore Sasson, Benjamin Phillips, Charles Kadushin, and Leonard Saxe, "Still Connected? American Jewish Attitudes about Israel" and Uzi Rebhun Nadia Beider, and Chaim I. Waxman, "Jews in the United States and Israel: A Comparative Look upon Israel's 70th Anniversary," *American Jewish Year Book* (2019): 3–37.

18. Stephen Cohen and Ari Kelman, *Beyond Distancing: Young Adult American Jews and their Alienation from Israel* (New York: Berman Jewish Policy Archive, 2007); Alain Dieckhoff, "The Jewish Diaspora and Israel: Belonging at Distance?" *Nations and Nationalism* 23, no. 2 (2017): 271–288.

19. Reut Institute, "21st Century Tikkun Olam: Improving the Lives of a Quarter Billion People in a Decade," in *A Global Engagement Strategy for the State of Israel and the Jewish People* (Jerusalem: Reut Institute, 2012), 121–131.

20. Jonathan Weisman, "American Jews and Israeli Jews are Headed for a Messy Breakup," January 4, 2019, *New York Times*, https://www.nytimes.com/2019/01/04/opinion/sunday/israeli-jews-american-jews-divide.html.

21. Chemi Shalev, "To Save Their Troubled Marriage, Israel and American Jews Should Consider a Trial Separation," *Haaretz*, November 26, 2018, https://www.haaretz.com/opinion/.premium-to-save-their-marriage-israel-and-american-jews-should-consider-a-trial-separation-1.6687067.

22. Peter Beinart, "Yavne: A Jewish Case for Equality in Israel-Palestine," *Jewish Currents*, July 7, 2020.

23. Daniel Gordis, "The American Zionist Assault on Israel," *Times of Israel*, January 8, 2019, https://blogs.timesofisrael.com/the-american-zionist-assault-on-israel/. Also see Daniel Gordis, *We Stand Divided: The Rift Between American Jews and Israel* (New York: Ecco Press, 2019).

24. Lahav Harkov, Jeremy Sharon, and Omri Nahmias, "Netanyahu: 'Trump Deal is a Once-in-histroy opportunity,'" *Jerusalem Post*, https://www.jpost.com/breaking-news/netanyahu-trump-deal-is-a-once-in-history-opportunity-615348.

25. Shibley Telhami, "*What Americans (Especially Evangelicals) Think about Israel and the Middle East* (Washington, DC: Brookings Institution, 2015); Samuel Goldman, *God's Country: Christian Zionism in America* (Philadelphia: University of Pennsylvania Press, 2018).

26. Daniel Estrin, "Israel's Netanyahu Faces Criticism For Delayed Reaction to Charlottesville Rally," National Public Radio, August 16, 2017, https://www.npr.org/sections/parallels/2017/08/16/543913980/israels-netanyahu-faces-criticism-for-delayed-reaction-to-charlottesville-rally.

27. Mairav Zonsztein, "After the Pittsburg Shooting, Israeli Politicians Sound Even More Like Trump," *Washington Post*, October 30, 2018, https://www.washingtonpost.com/outlook/2018/10/30/after-pittsburgh-shooting-israeli-politicians-sound-even-more-like-trump.

28. Danielle Ziri, "Trump: Some U.S. Jews 'Don't Love Israel Enough'," *Haaretz*, December 8, 2019, https://www.haaretz.com/us-news/.premium-trump-set-to-speak-before-thousands-of-jews-israelis-at-adelson-backed-conference-1.8229882.

29. Mairiv Zonstein, "Netanyahu's Silence on Trump and antisemitism," *+972 Magazine*, February 2, 2017.

30. Lara Friedman, "Changing the Conversation on Boycott, Divestment, and Sanctions," *Heinrich Boll Stiftung*, November 5, 2015, https://us.boell.org/en/2015/11/05/changing-conversation-boycott-divestment-and-sanctions; Brian Mast, Twitter post, June 25, 2020, 1:30 pm, https://twitter.com/RepBrianMast/status/1276206020730257412; Jackie Walorski, Twitter post, June 25, 2021, 2:15 pm, https://twitter.com/RepWalorski/status/1276217414909394944.

31. "The Right to Stand for Justice Is under Attack," *Palestinan Legal*, October 15, 2021, https://palestinelegal.org/righttoboycott.

32. "Special Report The ties between NGOs promoting BDS and Terror Organizations," Prime Minister's Office, https://www.gov.il/en/Departments/General/terrorists_in_suits.

33. Khaled Elgindy and Lara Friedman, "The End of Oslo Is an Opportunity," *Foreign Policy*, April 3, 2019, https://foreignpolicy.com/2019/04/03/israel-palestine-settlements-peace/. Also see Lara Friedman, "BDS Is a Trap for Democrats," *Forward*, January 28, 2019, https://forward.com/opinion/418265/bds-is-a-trap-for-democrats/; Joshua Leifer, "Jamaal Bowman Reminds Progressives They Can Win," *Jewish Currents*, June 25, 2020, https://jewishcurrents.org/jamaal-bowman-reminds-progressives-they-can-win/; Sahil Handa, "Rashida Tlaib, Ilhan Omar, Miftah, and the Problem of Anti-Semitism within the Movement for Palestinians' Right to Self-Determination," *Business Insider*, August 25, 2019, https://www.businessinsider.com/rashida-tlaib-ilhan-omar-miftah-anti-semitism-israel-palestine-bds-2019-8.

34. For example, see Daniel Schwammenthal, "BDS Is Antisemitic," *AJC Global Jewish Advocacy*, September 23, 2019, https://www.ajc.org/news/bds-is-antisemitic.

35. Allan Brownfeld, "Israel's War on BDS Increasingly Alienating Jewish Americans," *Washington Report on Middle Eastern Affairs* 36, no. 4 (2017): 42–44.

36. Kenneth Stern, *The Conflict over the Conflict: The Israel/Palestine Campus Debate* (Toronto: New Jewish Press, 2020), chap. 7.

37. Hillel Halkin, "The Persistence of the Oldest Hatred," *New York Times*, September 10, 2019, https://www.nytimes.com/2019/09/10/books/review/how-to-fight-anti-semitism-bari-weiss.html; "'The New Antisemites': New Report Uncovers the Dangerous Connection Between BDS and Antisemitism," *Stop AntiSemitism.org*, December 16, 2019, https://www.stopantisemitism.org/new-anti-semites-report.

38. Mairav Zonszein, "How the Right Has Tried to Rebrand Antisemitism," *New York Review of Books*, September 4, 2019, https://www.nybooks.com/daily/2019/09/04/how-the-right-has-tried-to-rebrand-antisemitism/.

39. For this transnational field of governance over race, see Esther Romeyn, "(Anti) 'New Antisemitism' as a Transnational Field of Racial Governance," *Patterns of Prejudice* 54, nos. 1–2 (2020): 199–214.

40. Amos Goldberg and Raz Segal, "Distorting the Definition of Antisemitism to Shield Israel from All Criticism," *972 Magazine*, August 5, 2019, https://www.972mag.com/antisemitism-israel-jews-ihra/.

41. Manifestations might include the targeting of the state of Israel, conceived as a Jewish collectivity.

42. "Executive Order on Combating Anti-Semitism," *The White House*, December 11, 2019, https://trumpwhitehouse.archives.gov/presidential-actions/executive-order-combating-anti-semitism/.

43. Lara Friedman, "States are Moving to Class Criticism of Israel as Antisemitism," *Jewish Currents*, February 20, 2020, https://jewishcurrents.org/states-are-moving-to-class-criticism-of-israel-as-antisemitism/.

44. "Simone Zimmerman—The Enemy Within," *Stop AntiSemitism.Org*, March 7, 2020, https://www.stopantisemitism.org/antisemite-of-the-week-2/antisemite-of-the-week-simone-zimmerman-the-enemy-within.

45. "Understanding Campus Antisemitism," *Amcha Initiative*, July 2020, https://amchainitiative.org/wp-content/uploads/2020/07/Antisemitism-Report-2019.pdf.

46. Daniel Blatman, "Maybe, When It Comes to anti-Semitism, No 'Different Germany' Exists?" *Haaretz*, July 3, 2019, https://www.haaretz.com/opinion/.premium-maybe-when-it-comes-to-anti-semitism-no-different-germany-exists-1.7434793; Yehuda Bauer, "Daniel Blattman's Anti-Semitic Attack," *Haaretz*, August 1, 2019, https://www.haaretz.com/world-news/europe/.premium-daniel-blatman-s-anti-semitic-attack-1.7613216.

47. "Lawfare: Targeting US Academia—Tracking the Cases," *Foundation for Middle East Peace*, November 30, 2021, https://fmep.org/resource/lawfare-targeting-us-academia-tracking-the-cases/.

48. Melissa Weiss, "GW University under Fire for Appointing BDS Activist to Head International Affairs School," *Jewish Insider*, May 20, 2020, https://jewishinsider.com/2020/05/gw-university-under-fire-for-appointing-bds-activist-to-head-international-affairs-school/. She also won the prestigious "antisemite of the week" award: "Ilana Feldman—The Self Hating Jewish Professor," *Stop AntiSemitism.Org*, May 23, 2020, https://www.stopantisemitism.org/antisemite-of-the-week-2/antisemite-of-the-week-ilana-feldman-the-self-hating-jewish-professor.

49. "Informational Materials," https://efile.fara.gov/docs/6676-Informational-Materials-20200526-2.pdf.

50. Canary Mission, https://canarymission.org.

51. Michael Barnett, "The Trouble with Israel's Enemy Lists," *Lawfare*, November 14, 2018, https://www.lawfareblog.com/trouble-israels-enemy-lists.

52. "The Jerusalem Declaration on Antisemitism," *Jerusalem Declaration*, https://jerusalemdeclaration.org/; "The Nexus Document," *Israel and Antisemitism*, https://israelandantisemitism.com/the-nexus-document/.

53. "House Members Send Letter to Secretary Blinken on Antisemitism Definitions," *Americans for Peace Now*, May 27, 2021, https://peacenow.org/entry.php?id=38181.

54. Ben Samuels, "U.S. State Dept. Doubles Down on Embrace of IHRA Antisemitism Definition," *Haaretz*, June 25, 2021, https://www.haaretz.com/us-news/.premium-u-s-state-dept-doubles-down-on-embrace-of-ihra-antisemitism-definition-1.9940759?lts=1624637655663.

55. David Bernstein, "The ACLU's Shameful Role in Promoting Antisemitism," *Reason*, March 11, 2019.

56. Marc Dollinger, *Black Power, Jewish Politics: Reinventing the Alliance in the 1960s* (Waltham, MA: Brandeis University Press 2018).

57. Hasia Diner, *In the Almost Promised Land: Jewish Americans and Blacks, 1915–1935* (Baltimore, Johns Hopkins University Press, 1995), xiv.

58. Jonathan Sarna, *American Judaism: A History* (New Haven: Yale University Press, 2004), p. 48.

59. Stuart Svonkin, *Jews against Prejudice* (New York: Columbia University Press, 1999).

60. "Zionist Logic—Malcom X on Zionism," *Malcom-X*, https://www.malcolm-x.org/docs/gen_zion.htm; "Stokely Carmichael Contends Palestinian Arabs in Just Struggle Against Israel," Archive, *Jewish Telegraphic Agency*, April 10, 1970, https://www.jta.org/1970/04/10/archive/stokely-carmichael-contends-palestinian-arabs-in-just-struggle-against-israel; William Claiborne, "Jesse Jackson Warns Israel of Black Influence, *Washington Post*, September 25, 2019, https://www.washingtonpost.com/archive/politics/1979/09/25/jesse-jackson-warns-israel-of-black-influence/935fcf1b-29da-4d75-8bd4-f75c68dc8bda/; Fay S. Joyce, "Jackson Admits Saying 'Hymie' and Apologizes at a Synagogue," *New York Times*, February 27, 1984, https://www.nytimes.com/1984/02/27/us/jackson-admits-saying-hymie-and-apologizes-at-a-synagogue.html.

61. Mazin Sidahmed, "Critics Denounce Black Lives Matter platform accusing Israel of 'genocide,'" *The Guardian*, August 11, 2016, https://www.theguardian.com/us-news/2016/aug/11/black-lives-matters-movement-palestine-platform-israel-critics.

62. Yair Rosenberg, "From Left to Right, Jewish Groups Condemn 'Repellent' Black Lives Matter Claim of Israeli 'Genocide'," *Tablet*, August 5, 2016, https://www.tabletmag.com/sections/news/articles/from-left-to-right-jewish-groups-condemn-repellent-black-lives-matter-claim-of-israeli-genocide; Caroline B. Glick, "The Silent American Jews," *Israel Hayom*, June 26, 2020, https://www.israelhayom.com/2020/06/26/the-silent-american-jews/; "Jewish Groups Condemn Black Lives Matter Platform for Accusing 'Apartheid' Israel of 'Genocide,'" *Haaretz*, April 10, 2018, https://www.haaretz.com/israel-news/jewish-allies-condemn-black-lives-matters-apartheid-platform-1.5421194.

63. Mari Cohen, "Jewish Groups Embrace BLM, With Conditions," *Jewish Current*, June 23, 2020, https://jewishcurrents.org/jewish-groups-embrace-blm-with-conditions/.

64. "Zachor Legal Asks DOJ to Investigate BLM for Terror Connections and Other Criminal Activity," https://www.wfmj.com/story/42349169/zachor-legal-asks-doj-to-investigate-blm-for-terror-connections-and-other-criminal-activity.

65. Dan Diker, "The Alignment of BDS and Black Lives Matter: Implications for Israel and Diaspora Jewry," *Jerusalem Center for Public Affairs*, July 16, 2020, https://jcpa.org/the-alignment-of-bds-and-black-lives-matter-implications-for-israel-and-diaspora-jewry/.

66. "The Occupation of the West Bank and the Crime of Apartheid: Legal Opinion," *Yesh Din*, July 9, 2020, https://www.yesh-din.org/en/the-occupation-of-the-west-bank-and-the-crime-of-apartheid-legal-opinion/; "A regime of Jewish supremacy from the Jordan River to the Mediterranean Sea: This Is Apartheid," *B'Tselem*, January 12, 2021, https://www.btselem.org/publications/fulltext/202101_this_is_apartheid; Letter from member of Congress to President Joe Biden, May 26, 2021, https://gottheimer.house.gov/uploadedfiles/may_2021_letter_to_potus_re_antisemitism.pdf; Ron Kampeas, "Calling Israel 'Apartheid' and 'Terrorist' Is antismetic, says 4 Jewish Democrats Targeting Party Colleagues," *Jewish Telegraphic Agency*, May 26, 2021, https://www.jta.org/quick-reads/calling-israel-apartheid-and-terrorist-is-antisemitic-say-4-jewish-democrats-targeting-party-colleagues.

67. Rom Kampeas, "Is pro-Israel advocacy in crisis? How the Gaza Conflict Exposed Political Fault Lines," *Jewish Telegraphic Agency*, June 3, 2021, https://www.jta

.org/2021/06/03/politics/is-pro-israel-advocacy-in-crisis-a-war-exposes-fault-lines; David Harris, "15 Israel-related whoppers," *The Times of Israel*, May 22, 2021, https://blogs.timesofisrael.com/15-memorable-anti-israel-whoppers/; Arno Rosenfeld, "For Jews on the right and left, Reps. Omar and Tlaib Are Centerstage," *Forward*, May 19, 2021, https://forward.com/news/469906/ilhan-omar-rashida-tlaib-israel-gaza/.

68. Eva McKend, Twitter Post, June 15, 2021, 10:15 a.m., https://twitter.com/evamckend/status/1404813942904561679.

69. See http://cufi.convio.net/site/PageServer?pagename=media_Support_Pastor_Hagee. "Liberal Democrat Alan Dershowitz Defends Bannon," *Zionist Organization of America*, November 15, 2016, https://zoa.org/2016/11/10342459-liberal-democrat-alan-dershowitz-defends-bannon/; Jonathan Swan, "Zionist Group Defends Trump Officials Accused Of Nazi Ties," *Axios*, March 17, 2017, https://www.axios.com/zionist-group-defends-trump-official-accused-of-nazi-ties-2318365606.html; Stephen Lurie, "The Dismal Failure of Jewish Groups to Confront Trump," *The New Republic*, October 24, 2017, https://newrepublic.com/article/145482/dismal-failure-jewish-groups-confront-trump. Goldberg and Segal.

70. Jonathan S. Tobin, "Will the Democrats' generational Shift Turn the Tide against Israel?" *Jewish News Syndicate*, July 22, 2020, https://www.jns.org/opinion/will-the-democrats-generational-shift-turn-the-tide-against-israel/.

71. Lara Friedman, "U.S. Politicians Are Backing a Free Speech Exception for Israel & Creating a Template for Broader Assault on the First Amendment," *Medium*, March 19, 2018, https://medium.com/@LFriedman_FMEP/u-s-politicians-are-backing-a-free-speech-exception-for-israel-creating-a-template-for-broader-ebe406fdf3b7.

72. Peter Beinart "I No Longer Believe in a Jewish State," *New York Times*, July 8, 2020, https://www.nytimes.com/2020/07/08/opinion/israel-annexation-two-state-solution.html; Peter Beinart, "Yavne: A Jewish Case for Equality in Israel-Palestine," *Jewish Currents*, July 7, 2020, https://jewishcurrents.org/yavne-a-jewish-case-for-equality-in-israel-palestine/.

73. Beinart, "I No Longer Believe in a Jewish State,"; Benjamin Wallace-Wells, "A Liberal Zionist's Move to the left on the Israel-Palestinian Conflict," *The New Yorker*, May 23, 2021, https://www.newyorker.com/news/annals-of-populism/a-liberal-zionists-move-to-the-left-on-the-israeli-palestinian-conflict.

9. LESSONS FROM HOW NATIONALISMS EVOLVE FOR A ONE STATE REALITY

1. Palestine Royal Commission, *Report* (London: His Majesty's Stationery Office, 1937).

2. Peter L. Berger and Thomas Luckmann, *The Social Construction of Reality: A Treatise in the Sociology of Knowledge* (London: Penguin, 1991), 89; Umut Özkirimli, *Theories of Nationalism: A Critical Introduction* (London: Macmillan, 2017); Ronald Grigor Suny, "Constructing Primordialism: Old Histories for New Nations," *Journal of Modern History* 73, no. 4 (2001): 862–896.

3. Rawi Abdelal, Yoshiko M. Herrera, Alastair Iain Johnston, and Rose McDermott, "Identity as a Variable," *Perspectives on Politics* 4, no. 4 (2006): 695–711.

4. Nadav G. Shelef, *Evolving Nationalism: Homeland, Identity and Religion in Israel 1925–2005* (Ithaca, NY: Cornell University Press, 2010); and *Homelands: Shifting Borders and Territorial Disputes* (Ithaca, NY: Cornell University Press, 2020).

5. See, for example, Loren D. Lybarger, *Identity and Religion in Palestine: The Struggle between Islamism and Secularism in the Occupied Territories* (Princeton: Princeton University Press, 2007); Sarah E. Parkinson, "Practical Ideology in Militant Organizations," *World Politics* 73, no. 1 (2021): 52–81.

6. Tatjana Lichtenstein, "Racializing Jewishness: Zionist Reponses to National Indifference in Interwar Czechoslovakia," *Austrian History Yearbook* 43 (2012): 85.

7. Pavel Kladiwa, "National Classification in the Politics of the State Census: The Bohemian Lands 1880–1930," *Bohemia* 55, no. 1 (2015): 80.

8. Tara Zahra, *Kidnapped Souls: National Indifference and the Battle for Children in the Bohemian Lands* (Ithaca, NY: Cornell University Press, 2008); Faith Hillis, *Children of Rus': Right-Bank Ukraine and the Invention of a Russian Nation* (Ithaca, NY: Cornell University Press, 2013).

9. On nominal and activated identities, see Kanchan Chandra, ed., *Constructivist Theories of Ethnic Politics* (Oxford: Oxford University Press, 2012).

10. See, respectively, Rogers M. Smith, *Civic Ideals: Conflicting Visions of Citizenship in U.S. History* (New Haven: Yale University Press, 1999); and Ashutosh Varshney, "Contested Meanings: India's National Identity, Hindu Nationalism, and the Politics of Anxiety," *Daedalus* 122, no. 3 (1993): 227–261.

11. Jacqueline Urla, "Cultural Politics in an Age of Statistics: Numbers, Nations, and the Making of Basque Identity." *American Ethnologist* 20, no. 4 (1993): 818–843; David I. Kertzer and Dominique Arel, eds., *Census and Identity: The Politics of Race, Ethnicity, and Language in National Censuses* (Cambridge: Cambridge University Press, 2002); Eugen Weber, *Peasants into Frenchmen: The Modernization of Rural France 1870–1914* (Palo Alto: Stanford University Press, 1976); Rogers Brubaker, *Nationalism Reframed: Nationhood and the National Question in the New Europe* (Cambridge: Cambridge University Press, 1996).

12. Shelef, *Evolving Nationalism*; Stacie E. Goddard, *Indivisible Territory and the Politics of Legitimacy: Jerusalem and Northern Ireland* (Cambridge: Cambridge University Press, 2010); Shelef, *Homelands.*

13. Henri Tajfel, ed. *Social Identity and Intergroup Relations* (Cambridge: Cambridge University Press, 1982); David D. Laitin, *Nations, States, and Violence* (Oxford: Oxford University Press, 2007); John Boli, "Contemporary Developments in World Culture," *International Journal of Comparative Sociology* 46, nos. 5–6 (2005): 383–404; Min Zhou, "Social and Individual Sources of Self-Identification as Global Citizens," *Sociological Perspectives* 59, no. 1 (2015): 153–176; Brandon Gorman and Charles Seguin, "World Citizens on the Periphery: Threat and Identification with Global Society," *American Journal of Sociology* 124, no. 3 (2018): 705–761.

14. Laitin, *Nations, States, and Violence.*

15. David D. Laitin, *Identity in Formation: The Russian-Speaking Populations in the Near Abroad* (Cambridge: Cambridge University Press, 1998).

16. Shelef, *Evolving Nationalism*; Shelef, *Homelands.*

17. Benedict Anderson, *Imagined Communities: Reflections on the Origin and Spread of Nationalism* (New York: Verso, 1991), 6.

18. Nadav G. Shelef, "Denationalization in the Israeli-Palestinian Context," in *Continuity and Change in Political Culture: Israel and Beyond,* ed. Yael S. Aronoff, Ilan Peleg, and Saliba Sarsar (Lanham, MD: Lexington Books, 2020), 63–84.

19. Brubaker, *Nationalism Reframed*; Lars-Erik Cederman, *Emergent Actors in World Politics: How States and Nations Develop and Dissolve* (Princeton: Princeton University Press, 1997).

20. Samuel P. Huntington, "Dead Souls: The Denationalization of the American Elite," *The National Interest* 75 (Spring 2004): 5–18; Jean-Marie Guéhenno, *End of the Nation-State* (Minneapolis: University of Minnesota Press, 2000); Zhou, "Social and Individual Sources"; Steve Fenton, "Indifference towards National Identity: What Young Adults Think about Being English and British," *Nations and Nationalism* 13, no. 2 (2007): 321–339.

21. For this distinction between nations and ethnic groups, see, for example, Walker Connor, "A Nation Is a Nation, Is a State, Is an Ethnic Group is A . . ." *Ethnic and Racial Studies* 1, no. 4 (1978): 377–400.

22. Shelef, *Evolving Nationalism.*

23. Shelef, *Evolving Nationalism.*

24. Shelef, *Evolving Nationalism.*

25. See, for example, Israel Labor Party. 2019. "Political Platform 2019," https://www.havoda.org.il/wp-content/uploads/2019/03/%D7%9E%D7%A6%D7%A2-2019.pdf.

26. "Israel's Religiously Divided Society," *Pew Research Center*, https://www.pewforum.org/2016/03/08/israels-religiously-divided-society/; Rosella Tercatin, "Half of Israelis Think Diaspora Jews Should Be Taken Into Account In Policy Decisions," *The Jerusalem Post*, November 12, 2019, https://www.jpost.com/israel-news/half-of-israelis-think-diaspora-jews-should-be-taken-into-account-in-policy-decisions-607426.

27. Muhammad Muslih, "The Rise of Local Nationalism in the Arab East," in *The Origins of Arab Nationalism*, ed. Rashid Khalidi, Lisa Anderson, Muhammad Muslih, and Reeva S. Simon (New York: Columbia University Press, 1991), 167–185; Baruch Kimmerling, "The Formation of Palestinian Collective Identities: The Ottoman and Mandatory Periods," *Middle Eastern Studies* 36, no. 2 (April 2000): 48–81; Helga Baumgarten, "The Three Faces/Phases of Palestinian Nationalism 1948–2005," *Journal of Palestine Studies* 34, no. 4 (2005): 25–48; Weldon C. Matthews, *Confronting an Empire, Constructing a Nation: Arab Nationalists and Popular Politics in Mandate Palestine* (New York: I. B. Tauris, 2006); Lybarger, *Identity and Religion.*

28. Walid W. Kazziha, *Revolutionary Transformation in the Arab World: Habash and His Comrades from Nationalism to Marxism* (London: Charles Knight, 1975), 55–56; Baumgarten, "Three Faces/Phases of Palestinian Nationalism"; Matthews, *Confronting an Empire*; As'ad AbuKhalil, "George Habash and the Movement of Arab Nationalists: Neither Unity nor Liberation," *Journal of Palestine Studies* 28, no. 4 (1999): 99–101.

29. Alain Gresh, *The PLO: The Struggle Within: Towards an Independent Palestinian State* (London: Zed Books, 1985); Yezid Sayigh, *Armed Struggle and the Search for State: The Palestinian National Movement 1949–1993* (Oxford: Clarendon Press, 1997); Helena Lindholm Schulz, *The Reconstruction of Palestinian Nationalism: Between Revolution and Statehood* (Manchester: Manchester University Press, 1999); Baumgarten, "Three Faces/Phases of Palestinian Nationalism"; Shelef, *Homelands.*

30. Muslih, "The Rise of Local Nationalism"; As'ad Ghanem, "Palestinian Nationalism: An Overview," *Israel Studies* 18, no. 2 (2013): 11–29.

31. Matthews, *Confronting an Empire*; Nels Johnson, *Islam and the Politics of Meaning in Palestinian Nationalism* (London: Kegan Paul, 1982); Musa Budeiri, "The Palestinians: Tensions between Nationalist and Religious Identities," in *Rethinking Nationalism in the Arab Middle East*, ed., James Jankowski and Israel Gershoni (New York: Columbia University Press, 1997), 198.

32. Manuel Hassassian, "Historical Dynamics Shaping Palestinian National Identity," *Palestine—Israel Journal of Politics, Economics, and Culture* 8, no. 4 (2002); Baumgarten, "Three Faces/Phases of Palestinian Nationalism."

33. Sayigh, *Armed Struggle and the Search for State*, 158; Baumgarten, "The Three Faces/Phases of Palestinian Nationalism"; Kazziha, *Revolutionary Transformation*, 85.

34. Asʿad AbuKhalil, "Internal Contradictions in the PFLP: Decision Making and Policy Orientation," *Middle East Journal* 41, no. 3 (1987): 365.

35. AbuKhalil, "Internal Contradictions," 365; AbuKhalil, "George Habash."

36. The adoption of this perspective itself represented a dramatic ideological transformation since the ANM initially saw communism as "a dangerous ideological threat to the

concept of Arab nationalism" (Kazziha, *Revolutionary Transformation*, 22). The adoption of a Marxist diagnosis was deeply contested within the movement and was itself a product of the fight between the ANM's right and left wings and an attempt to broaden the movement's public appeal; Kazziha, *Revolutionary Transformation*, 104; William B. Quandt, Fuad Jabber, and Ann Mosely Lesch, *The Politics of Palestinian Nationalism* (Berkeley: University of California Press, 1973), 86; Sayigh, *Armed Struggle and the Search for State*, 232; Francesco Saverio Leopardi, "The Popular Front for the Liberation of Palestine in Decline (1982–2007): Political Agency and Marginalisation" (PhD diss., University of Edinburgh, 2017).

37. Kazziha, *Revolutionary Transformation*, 103; Michael Bröning, *Political Parties in Palestine: Leadership and Thought* (New York: Palgrave Macmillan, 2013), 116.

38. Quandt, Jabber, and Lesch, *Politics of Palestinian Nationalism*, 86; Sayigh, *Armed Struggle and the Search for State*, 232.

39. Sayigh, *Armed Struggle and the Search for State*, 158–160; Lybarger, *Identity and Religion*, 23, 33.

40. Schulz, *Reconstruction of Palestinian Nationalism*; Helena Cobban, *The Palestinian Liberation Organisation: People, Power and Politics* (Cambridge: Cambridge University Press, 1984); Ann Mosely Lesch, *Political Perceptions of the Palestinians on the West Bank and the Gaza Strip* (Middle East Institute, 1980).

41. AbuKhalil, "George Habash," 99.

42. Shelef, *Evolving Nationalism*.

43. Shelef, *Evolving Nationalism*, 155.

44. See, for example, Yishai Porat, "'All Israelis Have Equal Rights,' Rivlin Says in Apparent Rebuke to Netanyahu," Ynet.com, March 11, 2019, https://www.ynetnews.com/articles/0,7340,L-5476970,00.html.

45. The Israeli Communist Party, for example, never received more than 4.5% of the vote. Meretz and its forerunners peaked at 7.7% of the vote in 1999.

46. Sayigh, *Armed Struggle and the Search for State*, 87. For discussions of this exclusion in particular movements see, Kazziha, *Revolutionary Transformation*, 50–53; AbuKhalil, "George Habash," 94, 97; AbuKhalil, "Internal Contradictions," 364; Budeiri, "The Palestinians," 205.

47. Khaled Hroub, "A Newer Hamas? The Revised Charter," *Journal of Palestine Studies* 46, no. 4 (2017): 100–111.

48. See, for example, Bröning, *Political Parties in Palestine*, 41.

49. Budeiri, "The Palestinians"; Michael Vicente Pèrez, "Between Religion and Nationalism in the Palestinian Diaspora," *Nations and Nationalism* 20, no. 4 (2014): 801–820.

50. Pèrez, "Between Religion and Nationalism," 815–816.

51. Hroub, "A Newer Hamas?"

52. Lybarger, *Identity and Religion*, 113.

53. Lybarger, *Identity and Religion*, 1; Muslih, "The Rise of Local Nationalism"; Matthews, *Confronting an Empire*.

54. See, for example, Bröning, *Political Parties in Palestine*, 109, 119.

55. Between October 1993 and June 2020, support for the PFLP and DFLP combined averaged less than 5%; see PSR polls, 1993–2020.

56. PFLP, "Palestine: Towards a Democratic Solution," PFLP Information Department, 1970); Yehoshafat Harkabi, "The Meaning of 'A Democratic Palestinian State,'" *Wiener Library Bulletin* 24, no. 2 (1970):1–6; Ghanem, "Palestinian Nationalism," 21.

57. Budeiri, "The Palestinians," 201; Johnson, *Islam and the Politics of Meaning*; Frode Løvlie, "Questioning the Secular-Religious Cleavage in Palestinian Politics: Comparing Fatah and Hamas," *Politics and Religion* 7 (2014): 100–121; Lybarger, *Identity and Religion*, 53.

58. Johnson, *Islam and the Politics of Meaning*, 76.

59. See Arafat's speech to the UN General Assembly in 1988 in United Nations Archive, AM/3 A/43/PV.78, 8–10; Bröning, *Political Parties in Palestine*, 80, 85.

60. See, for example, Noah Browning, "Abbas Wants 'Not a Single Israeli' in Future Palestinian State," *Reuters.com*, July 29, 2013, https://www.reuters.com/article/us-palestinians-israel-abbas/abbas-wants-not-a-single-israeli-in-future-palestinian-state-idUSBRE96T00920130730.

61. Saeb Erekat, "Annexation: The Palestinian Leadership's Perspective," recorded May 22, 2000, at Americans for Peace Now, https://peacenow.org/entry.php?id=34717; Mohammad Shtayyeh, "The Way Forward for Palestine: A Conversation with Prime Minister Mohammad Shtayyeh." Carnegie Endowment for International Peace, recorded on July 1, 2020, https://carnegieendowment.org/2020/07/01/way-forward-for-palestine-conversation-with-prime-minister-mohammad-shtayyeh-event-7377.

62. Ian S. Lustick, *Paradigm Lost: From Two-State Solution to One-State Reality* (Philadelphia: University of Pennsylvania Press, 2019).

63. See, for example, Tami Steinmetz Center for Peace Research (TSC) and Palestinian Center for Policy and Survey Research (PSR), "Palestinian-Israeli Pulse: A Joint Poll," August 13, 2018. http://pcpsr.org/en/node/731; PSR Survey Research Unit, "Report on Poll no. 72," 2019. http://pcpsr.org/en/node/761.

64. PSR, "Report on Poll no. 72."

65. On the sacred value of nationalism see Jeremy Ginges et al., "Sacred Bounds on the Rational Resolution of Violent Political Conflict," *Proceedings of the National Academy of Sciences* 104, no. 18 (2007): 7357–7360. On the possibility of trade-offs of sacred values, see Alan Page Fiske and Philip E. Tetlock, "Taboo Trade-Offs: Reactions to Transactions that Transgress the Spheres of Justice," *Political Psychology* 18, no. 2 (1997): 255–297; A. Peter McGraw, Philip E. Tetlock, and Orie V. Kristel, "The Limits of Fungibility: Relational Schemata and the Value of Things," *Journal of Consumer Research* 30, no. 2 (2003): 219–229; A. Peter McGraw and Philip Tetlock, "Taboo Trade-offs, Relational Framing, and the Acceptability of Exchanges," *Journal of Consumer Psychology* 15, no. 12 (2005): 2–15; Philip E. Tetlock, "Thinking the Unthinkable: Sacred Values and Taboo Cognitions," *Trends in Cognitive Sciences* 7, no. 7 (2003): 320–324; Philip E. Tetlock et al., "The Psychology of the Unthinkable: Taboo Trade-offs, Forbidden Base Rates, and Heretical Counterfactuals." *Journal of Personality and Social Psychology* 78, no. 5 (2000): 853–870.

66. Anderson, *Imagined Communities*; Laitin, *Identity in Formation*; Michael Hechter, *Containing Nationalism* (Oxford: Oxford University Press, 2000).

67. See the series of surveys conducted by Sammy Smooha (https://dataisrael.idi.org.il/). Data courtesy of the Guttman Center for Public Opinion and Policy Research at the Israel Democracy Institute.

68. See, for example, Lior Kodner, interview with Mansour Abbas, *Haaretz*, podcast audio, July 27, 2021, https://www.haaretz.co.il/digital/podcast/weekly/.premium-PODCAST-1.10035188.

69. Hudson Meadwell, "The Politics of Nationalism in Quebec," *World Politics* 45, no. 2 (1993): 203–241; Albert Balcells, *Catalan Nationalism: Past and Present* (New York: St. Martin's Press, 1996); Arjun Chowdhury and Ronald R. Krebs, "Making and Mobilizing Moderates: Rhetorical Strategy, Political Networks, and Counterterrorism," *Security Studies* 18, no. 3 (2009): 371–399.

70. Susan Lee Hattis, *The Bi-National Idea in Palestine during Mandatory Times* (Haifa: Shikmona, 1970); Dimitry Shumsky, *Beyond the Nation-State: The Zionist Political Imagination from Pinsker to Ben-Gurion* (New Haven: Yale University Press, 2018).

71. Kathleen Gallagher Cunningham, *Inside the Politics of Self-Determination* (Oxford: Oxford University Press, 2014); Nicholas Sambanis, Micha Germann, and Andreas

Schädel, "SDM: A New Data Set on Self-Determination Movements with an Application to the Reputational Theory of Conflict," *Journal of Conflict Resolution* 62, no. 3 (2018): 656–686. Cunningham's data show that downshifting took place at least in one year in 13% of groups examined between 1960 and 2008. The data of Sambanis and coauthors show that such downshifting took place in 17% of movements for self-determination between 1960 and 2005 and 21% between 1945 and 2012.

72. Ian S. Lustick, Dan Miodownik, and Roy J. Eidelson, "Secessionism in Multicultural States: Does Sharing Power Prevent or Encourage It?" *American Political Science Review* 98, no. 2 (2004): 209–229.

73. David S. Siroky and John Cuffe, "Lost Autonomy, Nationalism and Separatism," *Comparative Political Studies* 48, no. 1 (2014): 3–34.

10. ARAB AND AMERICAN DIMENSIONS OF THE ISRAEL/PALESTINE ISSUE

1. Shibley Telhami, *The World through Arab Eyes: Arab Public Opinion and the Reshaping of the Middle East* (New York: Basic Books, 2013).

2. I noted earlier, "What is a little more puzzling, however, is the low ranking among Saudis of identification with country, both in comparison with other Arab states—Saudis give it the lowest ranking—and in comparison with Muslim and Arab identities, especially after the 2006 Lebanon war (Figure 1.4). Most likely this is the consequence of the government's failure to cultivate a deep sense of national identity, something that the royal family itself appears to have recognized. In 2010, for the first time, the kingdom's rulers began to emphasize and celebrate Saudi National Day, and in 2012 they decided to give public employees an extra day off to mark the occasion"; Telhami, *The World through Arab Eyes*, 30.

3. Telhami, "The Arab Prism of Pain," in *The World through Arab Eyes* (New York: Basic Books, 2013), 84.

4. Telhami, "Arab Prism of Pain."

5. It is notable that in a poll of Middle East scholars (members of APSA and MESA) that Marc Lynch and I carried out in August–September 2021, we found similar attitudes: 57% said the two state solution had become impossible; only 2% said the absence of two states would lead to a one state with equality, compared to 80% who said it would lead to a one state reality akin to apartheid. Shibley Telhami and Marc Lynch, Middle East Scholar Barometer, University of Maryland Critical Issues Poll, August 26–September 9, 2021, https://criticalissues.umd.edu/sites/criticalissues.umd.edu/files/Middle%20East%20Scholar%20Barometer%20Questionnaire%20September%202021%20Final.pdf).

6. "After the outbreak of the Arab Spring, Arab states felt the need to control even more the online activities of their citizens. Instead of protecting free speech against government censorship efforts, social media platforms suspended and removed thousands of accounts of political dissidents in Tunisia, Palestine, Egypt, Syria and elsewhere. They have also arbitrarily taken down content that advocated for free speech, justice, and basic human rights and have offered no explanation for doing so." Haythem Guesmi, "The Social Media Myth about the Arab Spring," *Al Jazeera*, January 27, 2021, https://www.aljazeera.com/opinions/2021/1/27/the-social-media-mythabout-the-arab-spring. "Egyptian President Abdel Fattah al-Sisi *ratified the law*, officially called the Anti-Cyber and Information Technology Crimes Law, on August 18. The law, which ostensibly aims to combat extremism and terrorism, allows authorities to block websites that are considered 'a threat to national security' or to the 'national economy.'" Elissa Miller, "Egypt Leads the Pack in Internet Censorship across the Middle East," Atlantic Council, August 28, 2018, https://www.atlanticcouncil.org/blogs/menasource/egypt-leads-the-pack-in-internet-censorship-across-themiddle-east/.

7. "Spyware sold by an Israeli private intelligence firm was allegedly used to hack the phones of dozens of Al Jazeera journalists in an unprecedented cyberattack that is likely to have been ordered by Saudi Arabia and the United Arab Emirates, according to leading researchers." Stephanie Kirchgaessner and Michael Safi, "Dozens of Al Jazeera Journalists Allegedly Hacked Using Israeli Firm's Spyware," *The Guardian*, December 20, 2020, https://www.theguardian.com/media/2020/dec/20/citizen-lab-nso-dozens-of-aljazeera-journalists-allegedlyhacked-using-israeli-firm-spyware; David D. Kirkpatrick, "Israeli Software Helped Saudis Spy on Khashoggi, Lawsuit Says," *New York Times*, December 2, 2018, https://www.nytimes.com/2018/12/02/world/middleeast/saudi-khashoggi-spyware-israel.html; Susan Quitaz, "Pegasus: The Israeli Spyware that Helped Saudi Arabia Spy on Khashoggi," *The New Arab*, October 3, 2019, https://english.alaraby.co.uk/english/indepth/2019/10/3/this-israeli-spyware-helped-saudi-arabia-spy-onkhashoggi.

8. Katie Benner, Mark Mazzetti, Ben Hubbard, and Mike Isaac, "Saudis' Image Makers: A Troll Army and a Twitter Insider," *New York Times*, October 20, 2018, https://www.nytimes.com/2018/10/20/us/politics/saudi-imagecampaign-twitter.html. "According to its creators, the film, *The Dissident*, saw as many as 500 low audience scores of just 2,400 flood the popular film-rating website Rotten Tomatoes, which they believe came from trolls operating on behalf of the Saudi government to create a false sense of popular dissatisfaction. The movie's approval rating soon plummeted from above 95% to just 68%." Steven Zeitchik, "An Alleged Saudi Troll Campaign Is Targeting a Movie about the Murder of Jamal Khashoggi," *Washington Post*, January 21, 2021. https://www.washingtonpost.com/business/2021/01/21/an-alleged-saudi-troll-campaign-appears-be-targeting dissident/.

9. "Arab States Issue 13 Demands to End Qatar-Gulf Crisis," *Al Jazeera*, July 12, 2017, https://www.aljazeera.com/news/2017/7/12/arab-states-issue-13-demands-to-end-qatar-gulf-crisis; Colin Dwyer, "Neighboring Arab Nations Slap Qatar with 13-Point List of Demands," NPR, June 23, 2017, https://www.npr.org/sections/thetwo-way/2017/06/23/534079045/neighboring-arab-nations-slap-qatar-with-13point-list-of-demands.

10. "The new sense of nationalism advocates a break not only from past religious conservatism, but also from any commitment to Arab and Muslim causes—particularly, the Palestinian issue, including the status of the holy city of Jerusalem." Ahmed Rashed Said, "Saudi Propaganda Is Demonising Islam and the Palestinian Cause," *Middle East Eye*, May 29, 2020. https://www.middleeasteye.net/opinion/saudi-propaganda-regime-shooting-itself-foot.

11. "Under fire for its military operations in Yemen and its lack of support to the Palestinian cause, Saudi Arabia has tried to portray itself as one of the world's leading supporters of global humanitarian aid and development, especially to the Palestinians. But despite this generous assistance, the Saudi leadership is conducting an ambivalent strategy towards the Israel-Palestine conflict, reflecting the dichotomy at the head of the Saudi State. While the King is seeking to preserve the traditional pro-Palestinian stance of the Kingdom, the Crown Prince is promoting a more pragmatic and reformist vision. Between the legitimist stance of the father and the hazardous ambitions of the son, Saudi Arabia is playing a risky and ambiguous game with the Palestinians." "Saudi Arabia and the Israel-Palestine Conflict: Between a Rock and a Hard Place," *The Conversation*, June 24, 2018, https://theconversation.com/saudi-arabia-and-the-israel-palestine-conflict-between-a-rock-and-a-hard-place98129. "Riyadh, which once drew much of its regional clout from defending the Palestinians, was mute as the hour drew near. So too, Abu Dhabi, which shares its larger neighbor's focus on Iran and the Muslim Brotherhood, and rails at the latter's links to the Palestinian group Hamas. In Cairo, a bedrock of the earlier years of Palestinian struggles, there was little talk of a plan set to shred the scope of deals put to earlier leaders."

Martin Chulov, "Where Once There Was Fury, Palestinian Issue Now Stirs up Apathy," *The Guardian*, January 28, 2020, https://www.theguardian.com/world/2020/jan/28/where-once-there-was-fury-palestinian-issue-now-stirs-upapathy-in-region. "A senior United Arab Emirates official on Tuesday shot back at the Palestinian ambassador to France, who had attacked Abu Dhabi over its establishment of formal relations with Israel." Raphael Ahren, "Top UAE official Laments PA's Ingratitude after Abbas Envoy Rants on Israel Ties," *Times of Israel*, October 13, 2020, https://www.timesofisrael.com/top-uae-official-laments-pas-ingratitude-after-envoys-rant-on-israel-ties/. "This dramatic break with the old pan-Arab *consensus*—which predicated any normalization of relations on a final peace settlement between Israel and the Palestinians—reflects a sea change in the Gulf states' approach to the Palestinian issue. No longer is the Palestinian cause at the center of Arab countries' politics, as was reflected in the Arab League's *refusal* of a demand by the Palestinian Authority to condemn the UAE-Israeli deal. Despite continued concern for the Palestinians, some Gulf states seem to have tired of the Palestinian Authority's obstinacy and rejectionism in its dealings with Israel, and now they're opting to flip the old equation: Normalization with Israel is seen as the first step to secure Palestinian rights." Varsha Koduvayur and David Daoud, "Welcome to a Brand-New Middle East," *Foreign Policy*, September 30, 2020, https://foreignpolicy.com/2020/09/30/israel-uae-bahrain-palestinians-peace/.

12. Martin Chulov and Michael Safi, "Ramadan TV Dramas Signal Shift in Arab-Israeli Relations," *The Guardian*, April 28, 2020, https://www.theguardian.com/world/2020/apr/28/ramadan-tv-dramas-signal-shift-in-arab-israelirelations. Khaled Abu Toameh, "The Final Nail in Palestinian-Arab Relations?" *Jerusalem Post*, October 8, 2020, https://www.jpost.com/israel-news/the-final-nail-in-palestinian-arab-relations-645070.

13. Tovah Lazaroff, "Israel-UAE Deal Nullifies Arab Peace Initiative, Yadlin Says," *Jerusalem* Post, August 17, 2020, https://www.jpost.com/arab-israeli-conflict/israel-uae-deal-nullifies-arab-peace-initiative-yadlin-says-639001; AFP and TOI Staff, "FM Ashkenazi: Normalization with UAE, Bahrain an 'Opportunity' for Palestinians," *Times of Israel*, December 6, 2020, https://www.timesofisrael.com/fm-ashkenazi-normalization-with-uae-bahrain-anopportunity-for-palestinians/.

14. TOI Staff, "UAE Massively Cut Aid to Palestinians after Normalization with Israel," *Times of Israel*, February 5, 2021, https://www.timesofisrael.com/uae-massively-cut-aid-to-palestinians-after-normalization-with-israel; "Apologise for Slamming the UAE over Israel Ties, the GCC Tells Palestinians," *TRT World*, September 8, 2020, https://www.trtworld.com/magazine/apologise-for-slamming-the-uae-over-israel-ties-the-gcc-tells-palestinians39581; Rami Ayyub and Lisa Barrington, "Land of Wine and Honey? Israeli Settlers Export to UAE, to Palestinians' Chagrin," *Reuters*, January 14, 2021, https://www.reuters.com/article/us-israel-emirates-settlementspalestini/land-of-wine-and-honey-israeli-settlers-export-to-uae-to-palestinian-chagrin-idUSKBN29J1DR; Raphael Ahren, "No Labels: Israel's New Gulf Partners Seem Happy to Do Business with Settlements," *Times of Israel*, December 9, 2020, https://www.timesofisrael.com/no-labels-israels-new-gulf-partners-seem-happy-to-dobusiness-with-settlements/; "Israeli Settler Delegation Visits Dubai following UAE Accord," *AP News*, November 11, 2020, https://apnews.com/article/israel-jerusalem-west-bank-dubai-united-arab-emiratesc93b75d6c575a7ccf6e0d8bccce53f9c.

15. "The 2019–2020 Arab Opinion Index: Main Results in Brief," Arab Center, http://arabcenterdc.org/wp-content/uploads/2020/11/Arab-Opinion-Index-2019-2020-Summary-Final.pdf; 24/Annexation+Update+v1.pdf.

16. "The Annexation Debate: Attitudes in Israel and Key Arab States," Zogby Research Services, July 2020, https://static1.squarespace.com/static/52750dd3e4b08c252c723404/t/5f7dbd0f49f01a0aa9ccec15/16020759227.

17. Mohamed Zain, "Saad Eddin Ibrahim under Fire for Visiting Tel Aviv," *Egypt Today*, January 4, 2018, https://www.egypttoday.com/Article/1/39247/Saad-Eddin-Ibrahim-under-fire-for-visiting-Tel-Aviv.

18. David D. Kirkpatrick, "Tapes Reveal Egyptian Leaders' Tacit Acceptance of Jerusalem Move," *New York Times*, January 6, 2018, https://www.nytimes.com/2018/01/06/world/middleeast/egypt-jerusalem-talk-shows.html.

19. In June 2019, Graham was quoted as saying: "I don't want to get in the way of Jared, but I can't envision a one-state solution. It won't work. I mean, you'd have to disenfranchise the Palestinians, that won't work. If you let them vote, as one state, they'll overwhelm the Israelis. That won't work. So if you want to have a Democratic, secure Jewish state, I think you have to have two states to make that work," www.mcclatchydc.com/news/politics-government/white-house/article231413548.html. Shibley Telhami, "What Americans Think about the Looming Israeli Annexation and Trump's Middle East Plan," *Order from Chaos*, June 29, 2020, https://www.brookings.edu/blog/order-from-chaos/2020/06/29/what-americans-think-about-the-looming-israeli-annexation-and-trumps-middle-east-plan/?preview_id=873908.

20. "A Threshold Crossed," Human Rights Watch, April 27, 2021, https://www.hrw.org/report/2021/04/27/threshold-crossed/israeli-authorities-and-crimes-apartheid-and-persecution#.

21. U.S. Congress, Senate, Foreign Relations Committee, Nominations Hearing, 117th Cong., 2021, https://www.foreign.senate.gov/hearings/watch?hearingid=9A40CA80-5056-A066-609E-CE28710D4B2A.

22. "Occupied Thoughts: Former Deputy National Security Advisor Ben Rhodes with Peter Beinart," Foundation for Middle East Peace, February 10, 2021, https://fmep.org/resource/occupied-thoughts-former-deputy-nationalsecurity-advisor-ben-rhodes-with-peter-beinart/.

23. Daniel C. Kurtzer, Scott B. Lasensky, William B. Quandt, Steven L. Spiegel, and Shibley Z. Telhami, *The Peace Puzzle: America's Quest for Arab-Israeli Peace, 1989–2011* (Ithaca, NY: Cornell University Press, 2012).

24. Kurtzer et al., *The Peace Puzzle*.

25. Shibley Telhami, "Trump's Middle East Plan: What Does America Stand For?" *Order from Chaos*, February 4, 2020, https://www.brookings.edu/blog/order-from-chaos/2020/02/04/trumps-middle-eastplan-what-does-america-stand-for/.

26. Shibley Telhami, "Stop Calling Israel a Jewish Democracy," *Foreign Policy*, June 8, 2020, https://foreignpolicy.com/2020/06/08/netanyahu-annexation-palestinians-stop-calling-israel-a-jewish-democracy/.

27. Shibley Telhami and Stella Rouse, University of Maryland Critical Issues Poll (September 12–October 9, 2018). https://criticalissues.umd.edu/sites/criticalissues.umd.edu/files/UMCIP%20Questionnaire%20Sep%20to%20Oct%2 02018.pdf.

28. Shibley Telhami, "Most Americans, including half of young Democrats, disapprove of Biden's handling of recent Gaza crisis," *Brookings Institution Order from Chaos*, July 29, 2021, https://www.brookings.edu/blog/order-from-chaos/2021/07/29/most-americans-including-half-of-young-democrats-disapprove-of-bidens-handling-of-recent-gaza-crisis/.

29. Shibley Telhami and Katayoun Kishi, "Widening Democratic Party Divisions on the Israeli-Palestinian issue," *Washington Post Monkey Cage*, December 15, 2014, https://www.washingtonpost.com/news/monkeycage/wp/2014/12/15/widening-democratic-party-divisions-on-the-israeli-palestinian-issue/?arc404=true.

30. For example, in October 2019, 76% of Republicans compared to only 31% of Democrats wanted the United States to do nothing or to limit opposition to words; in contrast, 66% of Democrats and only 23% of Republicans said that they wanted the United States to

impose some economic sanctions or take more serious action. Shibley Telhami and Stella Rouse, University of Maryland Critical Issues Poll (September 3–20, 2019), https://criticalissues.umd.edu/sites/criticalissues.umd.edu/files/UMCIP%20Middle%20East%20Questionnaire.pdf.

31. View the full survey methodology of the University of Maryland Critical Issues Poll here: Telhami and Rouse, University of Maryland Critical Issues Poll (September 3–20, 2019). https://criticalissues.umd.edu/sites/criticalissues.umd.edu/files/UMCIP%20Middle%20East%20Questionnaire.pdf.

32. Given that those who said they had heard "a little" about BDS are likely less informed about the movement than those who said they had heard "a good amount" or "a great deal," we probed the better-informed respondents. We found that a majority of the 16% of Democrats who said they had heard "a good amount" or "a great deal" about BDS supported it (66%), compared with 37% among those who said they heard just "a little." More in-depth probing of the issue confirmed the results and showed even deeper polarization along party lines.

33. Majorities of Democrats (80%), Republicans (62%), and independents (76%) indicated opposition to laws penalizing people who boycott Israel, principally because these laws infringe on the constitutional right to free speech and peaceful protest.

34. Shibley Telhami, "Changing American Public Attitudes on Israel/Palestine: Does It Matter For Politics?," Project on Middle East Political Science Studies 41—Israel/Palestine: Exploring A One-State Reality, July 2020.

35. Telhami and Rouse, University of Maryland Critical Issues Poll (November 1–6, 2017), https://sadat.umd.edu/sites/sadat.umd.edu/files/Nov%202017%20UMCIP%20Questionnaire%20FINAL%20VERSIO N%20V2.pdf.

36. View the full survey methodology here: Telhami and Rouse, University of Maryland Critical Issues Poll (March 12–20, 2020), https://criticalissues.umd.edu/sites/criticalissues.umd.edu/files/UMCIP%20March%202020%20Questionnaire.pdf.

37. Shibley Telhami, "Americans Are Increasingly Critical of Israel," *Foreign Policy*, December 11, 2018, https://foreignpolicy.com/2018/12/11/americans-are-increasingly-critical-of-israel/

38. Telhami and Rouse, University of Maryland Critical Issues Poll (March 12–20, 2020).

39. Shibley Telhami, "Changing American Public Attitudes on Israel/Palestine: Does It Matter for Politics?" *Project on Middle East Political Science Studies 41*, Israel/Palestine: Exploring a One-State Reality, July 2020, https://pomeps.org/changing-american-public-attitudes-on-israel-palestine-does-it-matter-for-politics.

40. Jon Krosnick and Shibley Telhami, "Public Attitudes toward Israel: A Study of the Attentive and Issue Publics," *International Studies Quarterly* 39, no. 4 (December 1995): 535–554.

41. Telhami and Rouse, University of Maryland Critical Issues Poll (September 3–20, 2019). https://criticalissues.umd.edu/sites/criticalissues.umd.edu/files/UMCIP%20Middle%20East%20Questionnaire.pdf.

42. Telhami and Rouse, University of Maryland Critical Issues Poll (March 12–20, 2020).

43. Shibley Telhami, "Israel Is about to Reveal Its West Bank Annexation Plans: How Will Congress Respond?" *Washington Post Monkey Cage*, June 22, 2020, https://www.washingtonpost.com/politics/2020/06/22/israel-isabout-reveal-its-west-bank-annexation-plans-how-will-congress-respond/.

44. Ron Kampeas, "Bernie Sanders: I'm Pro-Israel, but We Must Treat Palestinians with Dignity," *Jerusalem Post*, November 21, 2019, https://www.jpost.com/American-Politics/Bernie-Sanders-Im-pro-Israel-but-we-must-treatPalestinians-with-dignity

-608540; Alissa Wise, "The Democrats Are Changing their Talk on Israel: Will They Walk the Walk?" *Newsweek*, November 2019, https://www.newsweek.com/israel-democrats-military-aid-debate-human-rights-1473712.

45. AP, "Biden Says Cutting Israel Aid 'Bizarre,' Accuses PA of Fomenting Conflict," *Times of Israel*, December 8, 2019, https://www.timesofisrael.com/biden-says-cutting-israel-aid-bizarre-accuses-pa-of-fomenting-conflict/.

46. "Sanders Calls Netanyahu a 'Racist,' Biden Slams PM's 'Outrageous' Behavior," *Times of Israel*, December 20, 2019, https://www.timesofisrael.com/sanders-netanyahu-is-racist-us-must-also-be-propalestinian/.

47. This dynamic may have been at play in the Democratic primary in the 16th Congressional District of New York in June 2020, in which the challenger Jamaal Bowman defeated long-time incumbent Eliot Engel, a top pro-Israel voice in Congress. What was telling in that primary was that the issue of criticizing Israeli policy played a central role, with Bowman highlighting his opponent's unwillingness to defend Palestinian rights and Engel receiving substantial campaign contributions from pro-Israel groups. Still, Bowman appears to have won by a wide margin.

48. Chris Van Hollen, "Van Hollen, Democratic Senators Reject Trump Plan, Urge Administration to Commit to a Viable Two-State Solution," press release, January 28, 2020, https://www.vanhollen.senate.gov/news/press-releases/van-hollen-democratic-senators-reject-trump-plan-urgeadministration-to-commit-to-a-viable-two-state-solution.

49. Noa Landau and Reuters, "UN Chief Warns Israel West Bank Annexation Would Be 'Most Serious Violation of International Law,'" *Haaretz*, June 24, 2020, https://www.haaretz.com/israel-news/un-chief-mideast-envoy-urgeisrael-to-drop-west-bank-annexation-plan-1.8945045; Ron Kampeas, "Chuck Schumer, 2 Other Key Pro-Israel Democrats Warn Israel against Annexation," *Times of Israel*, June 19, 2020, https://www.timesofisrael.com/chuck-schumer-2-other-key-pro-israel-democrats-warnisrael-against-annexation; Ron Kampeas, "AIPAC Tells US Lawmakers It Won't Push Back if They Criticize Annexation," *Times of Israel*, June 11, 2020, https://www.timesofisrael.com/in-first-aipac-gives-us-lawmakers-green-light-to-criticize-israel-onannexation/.

50. "Van Hollen, Murphy, Kaine, Senate Democrats Caution Israel against Unilateral Annexation of West Bank Territory," press release, https://www.vanhollen.senate.gov/news/press-releases/van-hollen-murphy-kaine-senate-democrats-cautionisrael-against-unilateral-annexation-of-west-bank-territory.

51. Shibley Telhami, "As Israel Increasingly Relies on US Evangelicals for Support, Younger Ones Are Walking Away: What Polls Show," *Order from Chaos*, May 26, 2021, https://www.brookings.edu/blog/order-from-chaos/2021/05/26/as-israel-increasingly-relies-on-us-evangelicals-for-support-younger-ones-are-walking-away-what-polls-show/.

11. ISRAELI-PALESTINIAN CONFLICT RESOLUTION AND PUBLIC OPINION

1. Ali Abunimah, *One Country: A Bold Proposal to End the Israeli Palestinian Impasse* (New York: Metropolitan Books, 2006); Padraig O'Malley, *The Two-State Delusion: Israel and Palestine—A Tale of Two Narratives* (New York: Penguin Books, 2015); Avrum Burg, "Now It's Your Turn," *Haaretz*, December 23, 2011.

2. Peter F. Trumbore, "Public Opinion as a Domestic Constraint in International Negotiations: Two-Level Games in the Anglo-Irish Peace Process," *International Studies Quarterly* 42, no. 3 (1998): 545–565; J. Shamir and K. Shikaki, *Palestinian and Israeli Public Opinion: The Public Imperative in the Second Intifada* (Bloomington: Indiana University Press, 2010).

3. Richard Sobel, *Public Opinion and US Foreign Policy* (Oxford: Oxford University Press, 2001).

4. Benjamin I. Page and Robert Y. Shapiro, “Effects of Public Opinion on Policy,” *American Political Science Review* 77 no 1 (1983): 175–190.

5. Andrew Flores, *National Trends in Public Opinion on LGBT Rights in the United States*, Williams Institute, University of California, 2001, https://escholarship.org/uc/item/72t8q7pg.

6. The rapid shift of public attitudes in Israel is rarely tracked, but various sources show high resistance to territorial withdrawal after 1967; Data Israel has archived regular questions on this issue. News reports show that during negotiations, only one-third of Israeli Jews supported withdrawal from most of all of Sinai, yet support for the accords reached a strong majority after they were signed. January 24, 1978. “Majority of Israelis Opposed to Withdrawal from Occupied Territories,” *Jewish Telegraphic Agency*, January 24, 1978, https://www.jta.org/1978/01/24/archive/majority-of-israelis-opposed-to-withdrawal-from-occupied-territories; Yadin Kaufmann, “Israel’s Flexible Voters,” *Foreign Policy* no. 61 (1985): 209–124.

7. United Nations Security Council, 2002. “Resolution 1397,” https://undocs.org/S/RES/1397%20(2002); Office of the Spokesperson, “A Performance-Based Roadmap to a Permanent Two-State Solution to the Israeli-Palestinian Conflict,” US Department of State, April 30, 2003, https://mfa.gov.il/mfa/foreignpolicy/peace/guide/pages/a%20performance-based%20roadmap%20to%20a%20permanent%20two-sta.aspx.

8. Expressions of support for a Palestinian state in the West Bank and Gaza Strip within the PLO date back to the early 1970s, but were sporadic, tentative, and exploratory in nature. The adoption of two states as a national goal by the PLO was an incremental process that took decades and culminated with the formal declaration of statehood in 1988.

9. Data Israel is the archive of the Guttman Institute for Policy and Public Opinion at the Israel Democracy Institute: it houses several series of historic survey research including the Guttman Institute surveys, the Israel Election Surveys, the Israel Democracy Index, the Peace Index, and others. The archive is available for public use and is referenced here as “Data Israel,” with the survey code and year cited in the text when referring to specific survey data. These surveys are available through a searchable database at https://dataisrael.idi.org.il/.

10. Surveys available on Data Israel website.

11. Rashid Khalidi, *Palestinian Nationalism: The Construction of Modern National Consciousness* (New York: Columbia University Press, 1997).

12. Helena Cobban, *The Palestinian Liberation Organisation: People, Power and Politics* (Cambridge: Cambridge University Press, 1984), 24, 60.

13. Yaacov Bar-Siman-Tov, “Israel and the Intifada: Adaptation and Learning,” *Davis Occasional Papers* 78 (Jerusalem: Hebrew University, 2000).

14. Although separation conceptually underpinned the Oslo process from the Israeli side, functionally the accords included many spheres of cooperation and the establishment of joint committees.

15. Mohammed Shadid and Rick Seltzer, “Political Attitudes of Palestinians in the West Bank and Gaza Strip,” *Middle East Journal* 42, no. 1 (Winter 1988): 16–32.

16. Khalil Shikaki, “The Peace Process, National Reconstruction, and the Transition to Democracy in Palestine,” *Journal of Palestine Studies* 25, no. 2 (Winter 1996): 5–20; Mohammed Samhouri, “Oslo Process and the Palestinian Economy: Promises vs. Reality,” *Palestine-Israel Journal* 23, no. 2 (2018).

17. Ella Heller, “Public Opinion in Israel and the Peace Process with the Palestinians,” *Da’at—Polls and Current Affairs* (Jerusalem: Guttman Center, Israel Democracy Institute, 2012) (Hebrew), 12.

18. Charmaine Seitz, “Tracking Palestinian Public Support over 20 Years of the Oslo Agreements,” Jerusalem Media and Communications Center, December 11, 2013, https://www.jmcc.org/Documentsandmaps.aspx?id=864.

19. Heller, "Public Opinion in Israel."

20. Yehuda Ben Meir and Olena Bagno-Moldavsky, *Vox Populi: Trends in Israeli Public Opinion on National Security 2004–2009* (Tel Aviv: Tel Aviv University/Institute for National Security Studies, 2010), 76.

21. Heller, "Public Opinion in Israel."

22. Tzipi Israeli, *National Security Index 2018–2019* (Tel Aviv: Institute for National Security Studies, 2019).

23. Throughout this chapter, we use the term "Palestinian population" as measured in public opinion surveys to refer to surveys conducted in the West Bank, Gaza, and East Jerusalem. We refer to Palestinians in Israel as "Palestinian Arab citizens of Israel," and we specify when we are referring to those in the diaspora.

24. The initials "PSR" and "PCPSR" refer to the same organization. The Palestinian Center for Policy and Survey Research is the current name; in earlier years it was called Policy and Survey Research.

25. K. Shikaki and Dahlia Scheindlin, "Role of Public Opinion in the Resilience/Resolution of the Palestinian-Israeli Conflict," *Palestinian-Israeli Pulse: A Joint Poll (2016–2018)—Final Report* (Ramallah: PSR, and Tel Aviv: Tel Aviv University Tami Steinmetz Center for Peace Research, 2018).

26. Evens Program in Conflict Mediation, "Peace Index," Tel Aviv University, 2019–2020. All files are available at https://social-sciences.tau.ac.il/peace-index-file.

27. Jacob Magid, "A PM Bennett Won't Fix Tensions with Dems, but Ties with Biden Should Endure," *Times of Israel*, June 5, 2021, https://www.timesofisrael.com/a-pm-bennett-wont-fix-tensions-with-dems-but-ties-with-biden-should-endure/; Jonathan Lis, "'No Diplomatic Process with the Palestinians,' Source Close to Bennett Says after Gantz Meets Abbas," *Haaretz*, August 30, 2021, https://www.haaretz.com/israel-news/.premium-gantz-meets-with-abbas-in-ramallah-to-discuss-security-economy-1.10163773.

28. Dahlia Scheindlin, "President Biden: Don't Fall for the Israeli-Palestinian Economic Peace Fallacy," *Newsweek*, August 30, 2021, https://www.newsweek.com/president-biden-dont-fall-israeli-palestinian-economic-peace-fallacy-opinion-1624228.

29. Surveys from the last twenty years show a clear drop in priority given to peace efforts after the Second Intifada, with erratic patterns at points since then: "peace" as a national priority is either the first or second priority, with a net loss from 2000 to 2006 (Shamir and Shikaki, *Palestinian and Israeli Public Opinion*, 99) or second and third priority as per Heller's "Public Opinion in Israel " review of Peace Index and other data from 1969 onward); in the author's data in surveys commissioned for B'Tselem from 2016 to 2018, the issue ranged from third to fourth place (D. Scheindlin, "What the Candidates in Israel's Elections Say about the Conflict" 972 Magazine, March 14, 2019, https://www.972mag.com/israeli-election-campaign-two-state-conflict/.) In the *Palestinian-Israeli Pulse*, peace appears in first or second place, but the range of Israeli respondents who choose peace as a priority is consistent with the B'Tselem surveys; between 22% to 29%. The variations reflect wide differences in how this question is asked. Furthermore, the issue of peace is low on the level of public discourse, as seen in electoral campaigns in Israel throughout 2019 (see again Scheindlin 2019).

30. This is not to ignore broad critical discussions of the unilateral pullout of Lebanon in July 2000 or debates about the wisdom of withdrawing from Gaza, which are part of the discourse. But those debates tend to mix criticism of the unilateral aspect with the policy of withdrawing itself. Unilateralism is rarely criticized when it comes to *expanding* Israel's control, nor do plans such as the INSS concepts meet resistance for this reason.

31. Amos Yadlin, Udi Dekel, and Kim Lavi, "A Strategic Framework for the Israeli-Palestinian Arena," *Institute for National Security Studies (INSS)*, Tel Aviv University Special Publication, March 2019, https://www.inss.org.il/publication/strategic-framework

-israeli-palestinian-arena/?offset=5&posts=54&subject=255&from_date=08-02-2018&to_date=23-05-2019.

32. Omar Rahman, "From Confusion to Clarity: Three Pillars for Revitalizing the Palestinian National Movement," Brookings Doha Center Policy Briefing, December 2019, https://www.brookings.edu/wp-content/uploads/2019/12/From-confusion-to-clarity-English.pdf.

33. Dana El Kurd, *Polarized and Demobilized: Legacies of Authoritarianism in Palestine* (London: Hurst, 2019).

34. Rahman, "From Confusion to Clarity."

35. R. Khalidi and S. Samour, "Neoliberalism as Liberation: The Statehood Program and the Remaking of the Palestinian National Movement," *Journal of Palestine Studies* 40, no. 1 (Winter 2011): 6–25.

36. Jeremy Wildenman and Alaa Tartir, "Can Oslo's Failed Aid Model Be Laid to Rest?" *Al-Shabaka*, September 18, 2013, https://al-shabaka.org/briefs/can-oslos-failed-aid-model-be-laid-rest/; Tariq Dana, "Palestinian Civil Society: What Went Wrong?" *Al-Shabaka*, 2013, https://al-shabaka.org/briefs/palestinian-civil-society-what-went-wrong/.

37. Omar Shweiki, "Palestinian Civil Society and the Question of Representation," *Council for British Research in the Levant* 7, no. 1 (2012).

38. El Kurd, *Polarized and Demobilized.*

39. K. Shikaki, "Changing the Status Quo: What Directions for Palestinians?" Final Report: Executive Summary, *Palestinian Center for Policy and Survey Research*, May 2016, 1.

40. Perry Cammack, Nathan J. Brown, and Marwan Muasher, "Revitalizing Palestinian Nationalism: Options versus Realities," *Carnegie Endowment for International Peace*, 2017, https://carnegieendowment.org/2017/06/28/revitalizing-palestinian-nationalism-options-versus-realities-pub-71364.

41. Palestinian citizens of Israel regularly show higher support for all forms of conflict resolution than all other groups in the joint survey research. In the joint polling, more than 80% generally support the two state solution.

42. Jamil Hilal, ed., *Palestinian Youth: Studies in Identity, Space & Community Participation* (Birzeit: Birzeit University Centre for Development Studies and American Friends Service Committee, 2017).

43. Heller, "Public Opinion in Israel."

44. Shibley Telhami, "Israeli Jewish Public Opinion Survey," Saban Center for Middle East Policy, University of Maryland and Dahaf Institute, 2010, https://www.brookings.edu/wp-content/uploads/2016/06/israeli_jewish_powerpoint.pdf.

45. Policy and Survey Research (PSR) and Tami Steinmetz Center for Peace Research, Tel Aviv University, Palestine-Israel Pulse (2016–2018) material available at http://pcpsr.org/en/node/680 (Jan 2018 Press Conference material: http://www.pcpsr.org/en/node/717).

46. Evens Program in Conflict Mediation, "Peace Index," Tel Aviv University, 2019–2020. All files available at https://social-sciences.tau.ac.il/peace-index-file.

47. All material cited as PSR/TAU Palestine-Israel Pulse or the "joint polls" from the years 2016–2018 can be found at http://pcpsr.org/en/node/680.

48. CPSR is the earlier name of the organization referred to as PCPSR.

12. PALESTINIAN STATEHOOD IN AMERICAN POLICY

1. "Peace to Prosperity," Trump White House, https://trumpwhitehouse.archives.gov/peacetoprosperity/.

2. To be transparent, at least one of the authors of this chapter agrees with the assessment that a two state outcome remains the most likely prospect for peaceful resolution of

this conflict. See Ilan Goldenberg, Michael Koplow, and Tamara Cofman Wittes, *A New U.S. Strategy For the Iasraeli-Palestinian Conflict* (Washington, DC: Center for a New American Security, 2020), https://s3.amazonaws.com/files.cnas.org/CNAS+Report-Israel-Palestine-final+for+release.pdf. The other, who is agnostic as to the two state solution's superiority to other visions of conflict resolution that respect the rights of the parties, believes that a singular focus on a two state solution pursued through the Oslo Process hamstrings US policy.

3. For overview of US interests at stake in Gaza, see Hady Amr, Ilan Goldenberg, Kevin Huggard, and Natan Sachs, *Ending Gaza's Perpetual Crisis: A New U.S. Approach* (Washington, DC: Brookings and the Center for a New American Security, December 2018).

4. In a 2016 poll of Americans, 76% of respondents said that Israel was a "strategic asset" to the United States. Shibley Telhami, "American Attitudes to the Israeli-Palestinian Conflict," October 2016, https://www.brookings.edu/wp-content/uploads/2016/12/cmep_20161202_poll_key_findings_v2.pdf.

5. Tamara Cofman Wittes, "Israel's Inertia on Palestinian Conflict Has a Price: American Support," *Haaretz English Edition*, December 3, 2015, https://www.haaretz.com/opinion/israel-s-inertia-on-palestinians-has-a-price-u-s-support-1.5430350.

6. Patricia Zengerle, "Measure to Limit Palestinian Aid over 'Martyr Payments' due to Pass U.S. Congress," *Reuters*, March 21, 2018, https://www.reuters.com/article/idUSKBN1GY070.

7. Khaled Elgindy, *Blind Spot: America and the Palestinians, from Balfour to Trump* (Washington, DC: Brookings Institution Press, 2019), 56.

8. Elgindy, *Blind Spot*, 82.

9. Nixon's address to the United Nations General Assembly on October 23,1970, quoted in Elgindy, *Blind Spot*, 83.

10. Box 124, folder "Palestine Liberation Organization," of the Ron Nessen Papers at the Gerald R. Ford Presidential Library.

11. Box 124, folder "Palestine Liberation Organization."

12. Seth Anziska, *Preventing Palestine: A Political History from Camp David to the Oslo Accords* (Princeton: Princeton University Press, 2018), 11.

13. Anziska, *Preventing Palestine*, 117.

14. Elgindy, *Blind Spot*, 96.

15. Ronald Reagan, "Recognizing the Israeli Asset," *Washington Post*, August 15, 1979.

16. Reagan, "Recognizing the Israeli Asset."

17. Itamar Rabinovich, *The Lingering Conflict: Israel, the Arabs, and the Middle East, 1948–2011*, (Washington, DC: Brookings Institution Press, 2011), 21.

18. For example, see Amos Permutter writing in 1989: "The uprising has succeeded in gaining the sympathies of ever wider circles in the West. Moralism and emotion have served the Palestinians well, as they did the Zionists after World War II. Small boys with rocks have achieved what Yasir Arafat and his oil-rich supporters in the Arab world long failed to provoke: a genuine revolt in the land of Palestine." Amos Permutter, "Israel's Dilemma," *Foreign Affairs* 68, no. 5 (Winter 1989): 119–132.

19. Dennis Ross, *A Missing Peace: The Inside Story of the Fight for Middle East Peace* (New York: Farrar, Straus and Giroux, 2005), 115.

20. "Full Text of George Bush's Speech on Israel and a Palestinian State," *The Guardian*, June 25, 2002, https://www.theguardian.com/world/2002/jun/25/israel.usa.

21. President Clinton, speaking on Kosovo in 1999, said the United States was in a battle between "globalism and tribalism," in which the Yugoslav wars presented "the dark marriage of modern weapons and ancient ethnic, racial and religious hatred." President Bill Clinton speech to the American Society of Newspaper Editors, April 15, 1999,

https://www.washingtonpost.com/wp-srv/inatl/longterm/balkans/stories/excerpts041699.htm. Decades later, President Barack Obama similarly cited "ancient sectarian differences" to explain the civil war in Syria; https://www.npr.org/2013/08/31/217610904/transcript-president-obama-turns-to-congress-on-syria.

22. Benjamin Denison and Jasmin Mujanovic, "Syria Isn't Bosnia. And No, the Problem Isn't 'Ancient Hatreds.'" *Washington Post Monkey Cage,* November 15, 2015, https://www.washingtonpost.com/news/monkey-cage/wp/2015/11/17/syria-isnt-bosnia-and-no-the-problem-isnt-ancient-hatreds/.

23. Denison and Mujanovic, "Syria Isn't Bosnia."

24. A paradigmatic example of this view is Leslie H. Gelb and Joseph R. Biden, Jr., "Unity through Autonomy in Iraq," *New York Times*, May 1, 2006, https://www.nytimes.com/2006/05/01/opinion/unity-through-autonomy-in-iraq.html, accessed on August 5, 2020.

25. "Intifada Death Toll 2000–2005," *BBC*, February 8, 2005, http://news.bbc.co.uk/2/hi/middle_east/3694350.stm.

26. As quoted in Anziska, *Preventing Palestine*, 105.

27. Ross, *A Missing Peace*, 115.

28. "Israel's Self-Rule Plan—December 28, 1977," *Israeli-Palestinian Conflict: An Interactive Database*, Economic Cooperation Foundation, https://ecf.org.il/media_items/545.

29. Salam Fayyad, "How Palestinians Can Reunite under a New Agenda to Counter Israel's Annexation," *Time*, June 30, 2020, https://time.com/5861739/israel-annexation-west-bank-palestinians-plo/.

30. David Friedman, "Israel Will Always Be a Jewish State," *Jerusalem Post*, July 13, 2020, https://www.jpost.com/opinion/israel-will-always-be-a-jewish-state-634935.

31. "Secretary Kerry in a Conversation at the 2016 Saban Forum," US Department of State, December 4, 2016, https://www.youtube.com/watch?v=piZrH8dwt-s.

32. Mara Karlin and Tamara Cofman Wittes, "America's Middle East Purgatory," *Foreign Affairs*, January/February 2019, https://www.foreignaffairs.com/articles/middle-east/2018-12-11/americas-middle-east-purgatory.

33. Shibley Telhami, "Most Americans, Including Half of Young Democrats, Disapprove of Biden's Handling of Recent Gaza Crisis," *Order from Chaos*, July 29, 2021, https://www.brookings.edu/blog/order-from-chaos/2021/07/29/most-americans-including-half-of-young-democrats-disapprove-of-bidens-handling-of-recent-gaza-crisis/; Shibley Telhami and Katayoun Kishi, "Widening Democratic Party Division on the Israeli-Palestinian Issue," *Washington Post*, December 15, 2014, https://www.washingtonpost.com/news/monkey-cage/wp/2014/12/15/widening-democratic-party-divisions-on-the-israeli-palestinian-issue/?arc404=true.

34. The White House, "U.S.-Gulf Cooperation Council Camp David Joint Statement," May 14, 2015, https://obamawhitehouse.archives.gov/the-press-office/2015/05/14/us-gulf-cooperation-council-camp-david-joint-statement.

35. Ilan Goldenberg, "Recognizing the State of Palestine Is the Only Appropriate Response to Annexation," *Washington Post,* July 2, 2020, https://www.washingtonpost.com/opinions/2020/07/02/recognizing-state-palestine-is-only-appropriate-response-israeli-annexation/.

36. TOI Staff, "Rotation, Annexation et al: Key Elements of the Netanyahu-Gantz Coalition Deal," *Times of Israel*, April 20, 2020, https://www.timesofisrael.com/annexation-rotation-et-al-key-elements-of-the-netanyahu-gantz-coalition-deal/.

37. "While almost all Palestinians followed the news about the Gilboa prison break on daily basis, viewing it as inspiring to popular resistance, the killing of the opposition activist Nizar Banat and the PA behavior in its aftermath damage the standing of the PA as almost 80% of the public demand the resignation of President Abbas." "Press Release:

Public Opinion Poll No (81)," *Palestinian Center for Policy and Survey Research*, September 21, 2021, http://pcpsr.org/sites/default/files/Poll%2081%20English%20press%20release%20Sept2021.pdf.

13. BEYOND OSLO

1. According to official Israeli and Palestinian figures for 2019, Arabs slightly outnumbered Jews 6,957,900 to 6,773,200. See Israeli Central Bureau of Statistics, "Population, by Population Group," Table 2.1, https://www.cbs.gov.il/he/publications/doclib/2020/2.shnatonpopulation/st02 01.pdf; and Palestinian Central Bureau of Statistics, "Palestine in Figures 2019," https://www.pcbs.gov.ps/Downloads/book2513.pdf. See also "Figures Presented by Army Show More Arabs than Jews Live in Israel, West Bank and Gaza," *Haaretz*, March 26, 2018, https://www.haaretz.com/israel-news/armypresents-figures-showing-arab-majority-in-israel-territories-1.5940676.

2. Yael Berda, "Citizenship as a Mobility Regime," in *Israel/Palestine: Exploring a One-State Reality, POMEPS Studies 41*, George Washington University, July 2020, https://pomeps.org/citizenship-as-a-mobility-regime.

3. "Basic Law: Israel—The Nation State of the Jewish People," https://knesset.gov.il/laws/special/eng/BasicLawNationState.pdf.

4. See "Arab Minority Rights," Association for Civil Rights in Israel, https://www.acri.org.il/en/category/arab-citizens-of-israel/arab-minority-rights/.

5. See "UN: We Still Consider Gaza 'Occupied,'" January 19, 2012, video, https://www.youtube.com/watch?v=KYEjDR6Xpqo.

6. "Bennett Says He Won't Meet Mahmoud Abbas, Palestinian State a 'Terrible Mistake,'" *Times of Israel*, September 14, 2021, https://www.timesofisrael.com/bennett-says-he-wont-meet-mahmoud-abbas-palestinian-state-a-terrible-mistake/. See also Tovah Lazaroff, "Netanyahu: A Palestinian State Won't Be Created," *Jerusalem Post*, April 8, 2019, https://www.jpost.com/arab-israeli-conflict/netanyahu-a-palestinian-state-wont-be-created-586017.

7. *Public Opinion Poll No-75* (Ramallah, West Bank: Palestinian Center for Policy and Survey Research, February 2020), http://pcpsr.org/en/node/799.

8. See Jodi Rudoren, "A Divide among Palestinians on a Two-State Solution," *New York Times*, March 18, 2014, https://www.nytimes.com/2014/03/19/world/middleeast/a-divide-among-palestinians-on-a-two-state-solution.html.

9. Republican Party, "Republican Platform 2016," https://prod-cdn-static.gop.com/media/documents/DRAFT_12_FINAL%5b1%5d-ben_1468872234.pdf.

10. See US Department of State, "Secretary Michael R. Pompeo Remarks to the Press," November 18, 2019, https://2017-2021.state.gov/secretary-michael-r-pompeo-remarks-to-the-press/index.html; and Michael R. Pompeo, Secretary of State, "Marking of Country of Origin," November 19, 2020, https://www.state.gov/marking-of-country-of-origin/.

11. See Michael Crowley, "Violence in Israel Challenges Biden's 'Stand Back' Approach," *New York Times*, May 11, 2021 (updated May 19, 2021), https://www.nytimes.com/2021/05/11/us/politics/biden-israel-palestinians.html; Nahal Toosi, "Joe Biden Is Not Planning to Solve the Israeli-Palestinian Conflict," *Politico*, April 6, 2021, https://www.politico.com/news/2021/04/06/joe-biden-israel-palestine-conflict-479405.

12. Niels Lesniewski, "White House Confirms Biden Will Keep Embassy in Jerusalem," *Roll Call*, February 9, 2021, https://www.rollcall.com/2021/02/09/white-house-confirms-biden-will-keep-embassy-in-jerusalem/.

13. For a more detailed discussion, see Khaled Elgindy, "How the Peace Process (Probably) Killed the Two-State Solution," *The National Interest*, April 4, 2018, https://nationalinterest.org/feature/how-the-peace-process-probably-killed-the-two-state-solution-25219.

14. See League of Nations, Report of the Palestine Royal Commission (Peel Commission), C.495.M.336.1937.VI., (November 30, 1937), https://unispal.un.org/DPA/DPR/unispal.nsf/561c6ee353d740fb8525607d00581829/08e38a718201458b052565700072b358?OpenDocument.

15. See "The Plan of Partition and End of the British Mandate," in *The Question of Palestine: Brochure DPI/2517/Rev.1* (Geneva: UN Department of Public Information, March 2003), 9–15, https://www.un.org/Depts/dpi/palestine/ch2.pdf.

16. See Salih Booker, "How U.S. Taxpayers Are Invested in the Palestine-Israel Conflict," *American Prospect*, May 19, 2021, https://prospect.org/world/us-taxpayers-invested-in-palestine-israel-conflict-military-aid/.

17. Shibley Telhami, "Most Americans, Including Half of Young Democrats, Disapprove of Biden's Handling of Recent Gaza Crisis," *Order from Chaos*, July 29, 2021, https://www.brookings.edu/blog/order-from-chaos/2021/07/29/most-americans-including-half-of-young-democrats-disapprove-of-bidens-handling-of-recent-gaza-crisis/; Lydia Saad, "Americans Still Favor Israel while Warming to Palestinians," Gallup, March 19, 2021, https://news.gallup.com/poll/340331/americans-favor-israel-warming-palestinians.aspx?utm_source=twitterbutton&utm_medium=twitter&utm_campaign=sharing. See also "Prohibition on Use of Funds to Deploy Defense Articles, Services, or Training to Certain Annexed Territories in the West Bank or to Facilitate Annexation of Such Territories," U.S. Senate, S. 4049, 116th Cong. (2020). https://www.vanhollen.senate.gov/imo/media/doc/NDAA%20Annexation%20Amendment%20.pdf; Brooke Anderson, "US Lawmakers Try to Halt Weapons Deliveries to Israel," *The New Arab*, September 16, 2021, https://english.alaraby.co.uk/news/us-lawmakers-try-halt-weapons-deliveries-israel.

18. See Edward Said, "The One-State Solution," *New York Times Magazine*, January 10, 1999, https://www.nytimes.com/1999/01/10/magazine/the-one-state-solution.html.

19. See, for example, Ali Abunimah, *One Country: A Bold Proposal for Ending the Israeli-Palestinian Impasse* (New York: Metropolitan Books, 2007). See also Yousef Munayyer, "There Will Be a One-State Solution but What Kind of State Will It Be?" *Foreign Affairs* (November/December 2019): 30–36.

20. Munayyer, "There Will Be a One-State Solution," 30–36, 36.

21. See, for example, Arieh Hess and Emanuel Shahaf, "A Proposal for a Federal Republic of Israel," *Fathom*, Autumn 2017, https://fathomjournal.org/a-proposal-for-a-federal-republic-of-israel/; and Benjamin Wittes, "Imagining a Federalist Israel: Notes toward a Disruptive Fantasy," *Lawfare*, August 14, 2018, https://www.lawfareblog.com/imagining-federalist-israel-notes-toward-disruptive-fantasy.

22. See, for example, "Memorandum by President Roosevelt to the Secretary of State," May 17, 1939, FRUS, 1939, vol. 4, doc. 812, 757; "Memorandum Prepared in the Department of State," April 2, 1948, FRUS, 1948, vol. 5 part 2, doc. 133, 778–796; "Draft Diary Entry for April 4, 1948, by the Secretary of Defense (Forrestal)," April 4, 1948, FRUS, 1948, vol. 5 part 2, doc. 134, 797–98.

23. United Nations Conciliation Commission for Palestine, "Historical Survey of Efforts of the United Nations Conciliation Commission for Palestine to Secure the Implementation of Paragraph 11 of General Assembly Resolution 194 (III)," A/AC.25/W/81/Rev.2, (October 2, 1961), https://unispal.un.org/DPA/DPR/unispal.nsf/0/3E61557F8DE6781A052565910073E819.

24. Shibley Telhami, "What Americans Think about the Looming Israeli Annexation and Trump's Middle East Plan," *Order from Chaos*, June 29, 2020, https://www.brookings.edu/blog/order-from-chaos/2020/06/29/what-americans-think-about-the-looming-israeli-annexation-and-trumps-middle-east-plan/?preview_id=873908.

25. See, for example, One Democratic State Campaign, "Manifesto," https://onestatecampaign.org/all/en-manifesto/.

26. Gil Hoffman, "'Huge Majority Opposes One-State Solution between Israel, Palestinians,'" *Jerusalem Post*, February 16, 2017, https://www.jpost.com/Arab-Israeli-Conflict/Huge-majority-opposes-one-state-solution-481801.

27. See, for instance, "Hamas Accepts Palestinian State with 1967 Borders," *Al Jazeera*, May 2, 2017, https://www.aljazeera.com/news/2017/05/hamas-accepts-palestinian-state-1967-borders-170501114309725.html; Eyder Peralta, "Hamas Foreign Minister: We Accept Two-State Solution with '67 Borders," *NPR*, May 17, 2011, https://www.npr.org/sections/thetwo-way/2011/05/24/136403918/hamas-foreign-minister-we-accept-two-state-solution-with-67-borders.

28. Peter Beinart, "Yavne: A Jewish Case for Equality in Israel-Palestine," *Jewish Currents*, July 7, 2020, https://onestatecampaign.org/all/he-manifesto/.

29. Writing in 1943, Magnes argued, "Palestine as a Jewish state would mean Jewish rule over the Arabs; Palestine as an Arab state would mean Arab rule over the Jews. Palestine as a bi-national state must provide constitutionally for equal political rights and duties for both the Jewish and the Arab nations, regardless of which is the majority and which the minority. In this way neither people will dominate the other." Judah L. Magnes, "Toward Peace in Palestine," *Foreign Affairs* 21, no. 2 (January/February 1943).

30. *Two States in One Space: A New Proposed Framework for Resolving the Israeli-Palestinian Conflict* (Jerusalem: Israel Palestine Creative Regional Initiatives, November 2014), https://issuu.com/ipcri/docs/two_states_in_one_space; "Two States One Homeland, Together and Separate: One Land, Two States New Horizons for peace between Israelis and Palestinians," A Land for All, https://www.alandforall.org/en.

31. See, for example, Omar M. Dajani, "Divorce without Separation? Reimagining the Two-State Solution," *Ethnopolitics* 15, no. 4 (2016): 366–379; Dahlia Scheindlin and Dov Waxman, "Confederalism: A Third Way for Israel–Palestine," *Washington Quarterly* (Spring 2016): 84–94.

32. U.N. General Assembly, Resolution 181 (II), Future Government of Palestine, A/RES/181(II), (November 28, 1947), https://unispal.un.org/DPA/DPR/unispal.nsf/0/7F0AF2BD897689B785256C330061D253.

33. "The Taba Negotiations (January 2001)," *Journal of Palestine Studies* 31, no. 3 (Spring 2002): 79–89.

14. THE EUROPEANS AND THE ISRAELI-PALESTINIAN CONUNDRUM

1. See, for example, "A Regime of Jewish Supremacy from the Jordan River to the Mediterranean Sea. This is Apartheid," *B'Tselem*, January 12, 2021, https://www.btselem.org/apartheid; "A Threshold Crossed: Israeli Authorities and the Crimes of Apartheid and Persecution," *Human Rights Watch* (HRW), April 27, 2021, https://www.hrw.org/report/2021/04/27/threshold-crossed/israeli-authorities-and-crimes-apartheid-and-persecution.

2. This is not to discount earlier European concern with the Israeli-Palestinian conflict, but it has only been since 1980 that Europeans started to develop a shared approach and publicize common positions on the conflict. This effort has been closely linked to the overall development of a common European foreign policy. From 1970 onward, European Community (EC) member states aimed at coordinating their foreign policy in the framework of the European Political Cooperation (EPC). With the 1992 Maastricht Treaty the European Union (EU) was established; it included a formalized yet intergovernmental European Common Foreign and Security Policy (CFSP). The 1997 Amsterdam Treaty established the office of a High Representative for Common and Security Policy. Last but not least, the 2007 Lisbon Treaty created the European External Action Service (EEAS) and the office of the High Representative of the Union for Foreign Affairs and Security

Policy, thus moving toward a European foreign policy structure while maintaining member states' sovereign decision-making power on most foreign policy issues.

3. "Venice Declaration," European Community, June 13, 1980, http://eeas.europa.eu/archives/docs/mepp/docs/venice_declaration_1980_en.pdf. Of course, the notion of a two state settlement was not invented in 1980, but draws on earlier attempts at conflict resolution, particularly the 1937 Peel Commission's plan and the 1947 UNGA partition resolution.

4. The normative power of the EU was particularly relevant in legitimizing the Palestinians and the Palestine Liberation Organization (PLO) as an actor that would need to be included in negotiations (in the 1970s and 1980s) and in paving the way for a two state approach. Later, the EU's positions were crucial in shaping the Quartet's 2003 Roadmap, international language on parameters for conflict resolution, and the differentiation between Israel and Israeli settlements in the occupied Palestinian territories (OPT). Anders Persson, *EU Diplomacy and the Israeli-Arab Conflict, 1967–2019* (Edinburgh: Edinburgh University Press, 2020), 126, 170.

5. The resolution reaffirms the vision of a two state settlement and condemns Israeli settlement policy as a flagrant violation of international law and calls on all states to distinguish in their relevant dealings between the territory of the State of Israel and the territories occupied in 1967. "Resolution 2334," UN Security Council, December 23, 2016, https://www.un.org/depts/german/sr/sr_16/sr2334.pdf.

6. Persson, *EU Diplomacy and the Israeli-Arab Conflict.*

7. Anne Le More, *International Assistance to the Palestinians after Oslo: Political Guilt, Wasted Money* (Abingdon: Routledge, 2008); "PASSIA Fact Sheet: Economy," PASSIA (2019): 21, 25–27, http://passia.org/media/filer_public/b8/f4/b8f44cbe-0906-4050-8475-f6d52bc7e163/factsheet_economy_2019.pdf.

8. "Declaration by the High Representative Josep Borrell on Behalf of the EU on the Middle East Peace Process," Delegation of the European Union to Israel, January 28, 2020, https://bit.ly/2Ypw4mc.

9. In addition, although for decades the Europeans considered a resolution of the Arab-Israeli conflict key to successfully addressing other challenges in the region, this is no longer the case since the so-called Arab Spring in 2010–2011. The 2016 EU's Global Strategy is telling in this regard: it gives the conflict much less attention than did the 2003 EU Security Strategy, and its resolution is no longer defined as a strategic priority for Europe or even relevant for addressing the region's other challenges. Persson, *EU Diplomacy and the Israeli-Arab Conflict,* 121, 144, 171.

10. For European sticks and carrots and an alternative interpretation as to why they have not been successful, see Alfred Tovias, "EU Foreign Policy on the Israeli–Palestinian Conflict: A Reevaluation," *Israel Journal of Foreign Affairs* (September 2021), https://doi.org/10.1080/23739770.2021.1964900.

11. "Council Conclusions on the Middle East Peace Process," Council of the European Union, December 16, 2013, https://www.consilium.europa.eu/uedocs/cms_data/docs/pressdata/EN/foraff/140097.pdf. Although some observers hold that the main reasons for its lack of impact are the vagueness of the offer, the bureaucratic language in which it was presented, and the lack of public diplomacy accompanying it, two other reasons seem to be crucial. First, Israel sees its presence in the West Bank and East Jerusalem as a question of security, survival, and identity, not as a "normal" policy issue. Second, Israel witnessed ever closer relations with the EU and its member states in many areas of cooperation even without fulfilling the condition postulated in the EU offer: it thus did not have to "pay the price" of a peace agreement with the Palestinians. Bruno Oliveira Martins, "Interpreting EU–Israel relations: A Contextual Analysis of the EU's Special Privileged Partnership Proposal," *Cambridge Review of International Affairs* 29,

no. 1 (January 2016): 151–170. For ideas on how to make the Special Privileged Partnership relevant, see Krassimir Y. Nikolov, "Partnership after Peace? An Optimist's View on the EU's Future Special and Privileged Relations with the States of Israel and Palestine," *Journal of the Bulgarian Diplomatic Institute* 19 (2017): 228–267.

12. Muriel Asseburg, "The Palestinian Authority and the Hamas Government: Accessories to the Occupation," in *Actors in the Israeli-Palestinian Conflict: Interests, Narratives and the Reciprocal Effects of the Occupation*, ed. Peter Lintl (Berlin: Stiftung Wissenschaft und Politik, 2018), 21–31.

13. "Presidency Conclusions: Middle East Peace Process," Berlin European Council, March 24–25, 1999, https://www.un.org/unispal/document/auto-insert-205180/.

14. Eastern European countries (Bulgaria, Czechoslovakia, Hungary, Poland, and Romania), as well as Cyprus and Malta, recognized the 1988 Palestinian Declaration of Independence without establishing full-fledged state-to-state relations with the PLO at the time. Sweden recognized the State of Palestine in October 2014.

15. "Council Conclusions on the Middle East Peace Process," Council of the European Union, December 10, 2012, https://www.consilium.europa.eu/uedocs/cms_data/docs/pressdata/EN/foraff/134140.pdf; Operationalized by "Interpretative Notice on Indication of Origin of Goods from the Territories Occupied by Israel since June 1967," European Commission, November 11, 2015, https://www.eeas.europa.eu/archives/delegations/israel/documents/news/20151111_interpretative_notice_indication_of_origin_of_goods_en.pdf. See also the EU Court of Justice ruling, "Food products from territories occupied by the State of Israel must be labelled with their area of origin and, if they come from an Israeli settlement in that area, additionally with this origin," Press Release no. 140/19, Court of Justice of the European Union, November 12, 2019, https://bit.ly/3hPitwr.

16. On the status of the implementation of differentiation measures, see Hugh Lovatt, "Differentiation Tracker," European Council on Foreign Relations, https://www.ecfr.eu/specials/differentiation-tracker. For financial dealings of European businesses and financial institutions with settlements, see "Exposing the Financial Flows into Illegal Israeli Settlements," *Don't Buy into Occupation (DBIO)*, October 2021, https://dontbuyintooccupation.org/wp-content/uploads/2021/10/DBIO-report-DEF_aangepast.pdf.

17. By way of example, see "Situation in the State of Palestine: Observation by the Federal Republic of Germany," International Criminal Court, March 16, 2020, https://www.icc-cpi.int/CourtRecords/CR2020_01075.PDF.

18. At the UN Human Rights Council, since 2009 EU states unanimously voted for all resolutions establishing investigations into violent conflict situations, except for those on Israel/Palestine, where they mostly abstained. "EU Support for UN Investigations at the Human Rights Council: The Israel/Palestine Exception," European Middle East Project (EuMEP), May 26, 2021, https://eumep.org/wp-content/uploads/EuMEP-EU-voting-on-UNHRC-investigations-Israel-Palestine-exception-21-05.pdf.

19. "Quartet Statement," Middle East Quartet, May 9, 2006, https://www.un.org/depts/german/sr/sr_sonst/quartet-9may06.pdf. Although based on these criteria, the EU and its member states, as well as the United States, have applied a no-contact policy toward Hamas, the other members of the Quartet—the UN and Russia—have not.

20. None of the governments that Israeli Prime Minister Benjamin Netanyahu headed between 2009 and June 2021 committed itself formally to a two state settlement. Nor has the successor government of Naftali Bennett done so to date.

21. Muriel Asseburg, "Political Paralysis: The Impact of Divisions among EU Member States on the European Role in the Israeli-Palestinian Conflict," in *Divided and Divisive: Europeans, Israel and Israeli-Palestinian Peace-Making*, ed\. Muriel Asseburg and Nimrod Goren (Jerusalem: Mitvim, 2019), 36–51, https://bit.ly/3fJRAIr.

22. For example, a December 2018 statement by the incoming and outgoing European Security Council Members reiterated the European stance on the conflict by emphasizing principles with which any peace initiative would have to conform to be successful. "EU8 Statement for the Press Stakeout on MEPP," Permanent Representation of the Federal Republic of Germany at the UN, December 18, 2018, https://new-york-un.diplo.de/un-de/e8-mepp/2172242. In the summer of 2020, Germany and France engaged with Jordan and Egypt to issue joint statements against Israeli annexation plans but were not able to create momentum around an alternative approach. Noa Landau, "Jordan, Germany, France, Egypt Say Won't Recognize Unilateral Changes to 1967 Borders," *Haaretz*, July 7, 2020, https://www.haaretz.com/israel-news/.premium-egypt-germany-france-jordan-say-won-t-recognize-any-changes-to-1967-borders-1.8976889.

23. For the United States as the key mediator because of its unique role as a security guarantor for Israel, as well as the Arab states, and the leverage that that position has provided it to induce and reward compromise and mitigate risks, see the contribution by Tamara Cofman Wittes and Kevin Huggard in chapter 12.

24. "PM Netanyahu's Response to EU Decision Regarding Product Labeling," Israel Ministry of Foreign Affairs (MFA), November 11, 2015, https://mfa.gov.il/MFA/PressRoom/2015/Pages/PM-Netanyahu-responds-to-EU-decision-regarding-product-labeling-11-November-2015.aspx; "Behind the Headlines: EU Labeling Guidelines," Israel MFA, November 10, 2015, https://mfa.gov.il/MFA/ForeignPolicy/Issues/Pages/EU-labeling-guidelines-10-Nov-2015.aspx.

25. "Working Definition of Antisemitism," International Holocaust Remembrance Alliance (IHRA), May 26, 2016, https://www.holocaustremembrance.com/working-definition-antisemitism. In November 2018, the EU became a permanent international partner with the IHRA. "Response to Antisemitism and a Survey Showing Antisemitism Is on the Rise in the EU," EU Commission, December 10, 2018, https://ec.europa.eu/commission/presscorner/detail/en/IP_18_6724. For a critical analysis, see Peter Ullrich, "Expert Opinion on the 'Working Definition of Antisemitism' of the International Holocaust Remembrance Alliance," Rosa-Luxemburg-Stiftung, March 2019, https://www.rosalux.de/fileadmin/rls_uploads/pdfs/rls_papers/Papers_3-2019_Antisemitism.pdf. For critical statements, see "Israelis Warn against Equating Anti-Zionism with Anti-Semitism," Jewish Voice for Labour, November 21, 2018, https://www.jewishvoiceforlabour.org.uk/article/israelis-warn-against-equating-anti-zionism-with-anti-semitism; and "Palestinian Rights and the IHRA Definition of Antisemitism," *The Guardian*, November 29, 2020, https://www.theguardian.com/news/2020/nov/29/palestinian-rights-and-the-ihra-definition-of-antisemitism.

26. See, for example, the controversy around the German coordinator Felix Klein in the context of the antisemitism accusations of Achille Mbembe because of his alleged support for the Boycott, Divestment. and Sanctions (BDS) movement. Gadi Algazi et al., "Call to Replace Felix Klein as the Federal Government Commissioner for the Fight against Antisemitism," April 30, 2020, https://www.ipk-bonn.de/downloads/Call-on-German-Minister-Seehofer.pdf.

27. These campaigns can be seen as a reaction to the Palestinian leadership's attempts to realize Palestinian rights through international mechanisms (UN bodies, ICC, etc.) and to the Palestinian-initiated, international grassroots campaign BDS. They have also served to distract the international community from Israel's reinforced settlement and annexation policies.

28. See, for example, "The Money Trail: The Millions Given by EU Institutions to NGOs with Ties to Terror and Boycotts against Israel," Israeli Ministry of Strategic Affairs and Public Diplomacy, May 27, 2018, https://www.jewishvirtuallibrary.org/jsource/images/bdsmoneytrail.pdf; "The Money Trail: European Union Financing of Organ-

izations Promoting Boycotts against the State of Israel," Israeli Ministry for Strategic Affairs and Public Diplomacy, 2nd edition, January 2019, 2020, https://bit.ly/36yXCK4; Andrew Rettman, "Israeli Propaganda Attacks EU Funds for NGOs," *EU Observer*, May 28, 2018, https://euobserver.com/foreign/141915.

29. "Top Ten Worst Global Anti-Semitic Anti/Israel-Incidents 2015," Simon Wiesenthal Center, https://www.wiesenthal.com/about/news/top-10/top-ten-2015-pdf.pdf.

30. Noa Landau, "As Netanyahu Prepares to Visit Brussels, Tensions with EU's Mogherini Worsen," *Haaretz*, December 7, 2017, https://www.haaretz.com/israel-news/.premium-as-netanyahu-gears-to-visit-brussels-tensions-with-mogherini-worsen-1.5628105; Herb Keinon, "PM Can't Find Time for Mogherini; EU Foreign Policy Chief Cancels Trip," *Jerusalem Post*, June 10, 2018, https://www.jpost.com/Israel-News/PM-cant-find-time-for-Mogherini-EU-foreign-policy-chief-cancels-trip-559585.

31. A recent poll found that "45% of Israelis think that the EU is currently more of a foe to Israel than a friend. 29% see the EU as more of a friend." "The 2020 Israeli Foreign Policy Index," Mitvim, October 2020, https://mitvim.org.il/wp-content/uploads/English-Report-2020-Israeli-Foreign-Policy-Index-of-the-Mitvim-Institute.pdf.

32. For details, see Eyal Ronen and Nimrod Goren, "Divisive Policies: Israel's Foreign Policy towards the EU and Its Member States," in *Divided and Divisive: Europeans, Israel and Israeli-Palestinian Peacemaking*, eds. Muriel Asseburg and Nimrod Goren (Jerusalem: Mitvim: 2019), 21–35.

33. For an illustration, see Asseburg, "Political Paralysis," 42f. Yet, there are remarkable differences even within the three blocks. EU Member States have also shown different levels of activity toward the Israeli-Palestinian conflict.

34. For demolitions of EU funded structures, see, for example, "Six-Month Report on Demolitions and Seizures in the West Bank, including East Jerusalem: Reporting Period 1 January–30 June 2020," Office of the European Representative, November 18, 2020, https://eeas.europa.eu/sites/eeas/files/20201112_six-month_report_on_demolitions_jan-jun_2020.pdf.

35. The June 2016 Council Conclusions reiterated the EU's support for a two state approach, endorsed French peace efforts, and reaffirmed the European offer of December 2013 of "an unprecedented package of political, economic and security support to be offered to and developed with both parties in the context of a final status agreement." "Council Conclusions on the Middle East Peace Process," Council of the European Union, June 20, 2016, https://www.consilium.europa.eu/en/press/press-releases/2016/06/20/fac-conclusions-mepp.

36. Still, a statement by the EU, as well as incoming and outgoing European Security Council members, on Khan al-Ahmar apparently contributed to the Government of Israel's decision to suspend the displacement. The statement is available at "EU Members Press Stakeout on Khan al-Ahmar," Permanent Representation of the Federal Republic of Germany at the UN, September 20, 2018, https://new-york-un.diplo.de/un-de/20180920-joint-stmnt-khan-al-amar/2139144.

37. Muriel Asseburg and Peter Lintl, "Annexations in the West Bank: Europeans Need to Punch their Weight," *Stiftung Wissenschaft und Politik*, May 20, 2020, bit.ly/SWP-20PoV0520. Hugh Lovatt, "Israel's West Bank Annexation: Preparing EU Policy for the Day after," European Council on Foreign Relations, May 14, 2020, https://bit.ly/37RDNN6. Jamie Pleydell-Bouverie, "Israel's Threat to Annex West Bank Territory: A Moment of Reckoning for Europe," European Institute of Peace, June 26, 2020, https://www.eip.org/israels-threat-to-annex-west-bank-territory-a-moment-of-reckoning-for-europe.

38. Austria and Hungary objected to a joint statement referring to timing issues at the May 2020 Foreign Affairs Council. The EU's High Representative for Foreign and Security Policy, Josep Borrell, put out a statement urging the new Israeli government to refrain

from annexation but was not able to do so in the name of the EU-27. "Israel: Statement by the High Representative Josep Borrell on the Formation of a New Government," Office of the European Union Representative, May 18, 2020, https://eeas.europa.eu/delegations/palestine-occupied-palestinian-territory-west-bank-and-gaza-strip/79576/israel-statement-high-representative-josep-borrell-formation-new-government_en.

39. Noa Landau, "11 European Foreign Ministers Urge EU to List Options to 'Deter' Israeli Annexation," *Haaretz*, July 14, 2020, https://www.haaretz.com/israel-news/.premium-eleven-foreign-ministers-urge-eu-to-list-options-to-deter-israeli-annexation-1.8992346.

40. Noa Landau, "German FM Warned Israel: Some Nations May Impose Sanctions over Annexation, Recognize Palestine," *Haaretz*, June 10, 2020, https://www.haaretz.com/israel-news/.premium-german-foreign-minister-lands-in-israel-expected-to-warn-netanyahu-against-annexation-1.8910253.

41. Neri Zilber, "Israel's New Plan Is to 'Shrink,' Not Solve, the Palestinian Conflict: Here's What That Looks Like," *CNN*, September 16, 2021, https://edition.cnn.com/2021/09/16/middleeast/israel-palestinian-conflict-cmd-intl/index.html.

42. For alternative options of conflict resolution, see in detail Muriel Asseburg and Jan Busse, "The End of a Two-State Settlement? Alternatives and Priorities for Settling the Israeli-Palestinian Conflict," *Stiftung Wissenschaft und Politik*, April 2016, https://www.swp-berlin.org/fileadmin/contents/products/comments/2016C24_ass_Busse.pdf. See also chapter 13 by Khaled Elgindy.

43. In a *Haaretz* survey conducted in Israel in June 2020, 19% of respondents said that this was their preferred solution to the Israeli-Palestinian conflict. It remained unclear, however, whether Palestinians should be granted equal rights. See Dina Kraft, "Haaretz Poll: 42% of Israelis Back West Bank Annexation, including Two-state Supporters," *Haaretz*, March 25, 2019, https://bit.ly/2YoesY4. For long-time Zionist two state supporters turning toward a binational state, see Gershon Baskin, "Encountering Peace: Beyond Two States: The Vision for the Future," *Jerusalem Post*, May 27, 2020, https://bit.ly/3fPIwS6; Peter Beinart, "Yavne: A Jewish Case for Equality in Israel-Palestine," *Jewish Currents*, July 7, 2020, https://bit.ly/2JFqpns. For a detailed poll of Israelis and Palestinians on different solutions, see "Palestinian-Israeli Pulse: A Joint Poll," Palestinian Center for Policy and Survey Research, October 26, 2020, https://www.pcpsr.org/sites/default/files/Summary%20Report_%20English_Joint%20Poll%20Oct%202020.pdf.

44. For the longevity of paradigms in general and the two state paradigm in particular, as well as the distorting effect the paradigm has when using it as a heuristic devise for assessing and navigating the reality, see Ian Lustick's chapter 1.

45. Cf. Hugh Lovatt, "EU Differentiation and the Push for Peace in Israel-Palestine," European Council on Foreign Relations, October 31, 2016, https://ecfr.eu/publication/eu_differentiation_and_the_push_for_peace_in_israel_palestine7163/.

46. In September 2021, the European Commission recognized that it has the authority to make a proposal to ban trade with illegal settlements as an EU trade measure, rather than considering it as a sanction that would have to be initiated by the European Council. Cf. "Commission Implementing Decision (EU) 2021/1484," *Official Journal of the European Union*, September 8, 2021, https://eur-lex.europa.eu/legal-content/EN/TXT/HTML/?uri=CELEX:32021D1484&from=EN.

CONCLUSION

1. "Israel: Provide Vaccines to Occupied Palestinians," *Human Rights Watch*, January 17, 2021, https://www.hrw.org/news/2021/01/17/israel-provide-vaccines-occupied-palestinians.

2. Adam Rasgon, "Israel's Vaccine Success Unleashes a Debate on Palestinian Inequalities," *New York Times*, February 23, 2021, https://www.nytimes.com/2021/02/04/world/middleeast/israel-palestinians-vaccine.html.

3. "Israel Opens Vaccination Center at Checkpoint to Reach Palestinian East Jerusalem Residents," *Haaretz*, February 23, 2021, https://www.haaretz.com/israel-news/israel-opens-vaccination-center-at-checkpoint- in-bid-to-reach-e-jerusalem-residents-1.9563857.

4. Patrick Kingsley, "Israel Gives Vaccine to Far-Off Allies, as Palestinians Wait," *New York Times*, February 23, 2021, https://www.nytimes.com/2021/02/23/world/middleeast/israel-palestinians-vaccine-diplomacy.html.

5. Oliver Holmes and Hazem Balousha, "Palestinians Excluded from Israeli COVID Vaccine Rollout as Jabs Go to Settlers," *The Guardian*, January 3, 2021, https://www.theguardian.com/world/2021/jan/03/palestinians-excluded-from-israeli-covid-vaccine-rollout-as-jabs-go-to-settlers.

6. Leila Farsakh, "The One State Solution and the Israeli-Palestinian Conflict: Palestinian Challenges and Prospects." *Middle East Journal* 65, no.1 (2011): 55–71.

7. Fifteen of the memos prepared for the workshop were collected in POMEPS STUDIES 41 *Israel/Palestine: Towards a One State Reality*, edited by Marc Lynch (June 2020).

8. Vision for Peace, Prosperity, and a Brighter Future for Israel and the Palestinian People.

9. Patrick Kingsley, "'Shrinking the Conflict': What Does Israel's New Mantra Really Mean?" *New York Times*, September 30, 2021, https://www.nytimes.com/2021/09/30/world/middleeast/israel-bennett-palestinians-shrinking.html.

10. Rami Ayyub and Nidal al-Mughrabi, "Palestinians Accuse Israel of Preventing COVID-19 Vaccine Transfer to Gaza," *Reuters*, February 15, 2021, https://www.reuters.com/article/us-health-coronavirus-israel-palestinian/palestinians-accuse-israel-of-preventing-covid-19-vaccine-transfer-to-gaza-idUKKBN2AF1UG.

11. Tareq Baconi, "Land Consolidation and the One State Reality," in POMEPS STUDIES 41 *Israel/Palestine: Exploring a One State Reality* (2020): 20–24.

12. Sondeep Sen, *Decolonizing Palestine* (Ithaca, NY: Cornell University Press); Tareq Baconi, "Gaza and the One State Reality," *Journal of Palestine Studies* (2020), https://doi.org/10.1080/0377919X.2020.1842002).

13. Yasmeen Abu-Laban and Abigail B. Bakan, *Israel, Palestine, and the Politics of Race: Exploring Identity and Power in a Global Context* (London: I.B. Tauris/Bloomsbury, 2020).

14. "A Threshold Crossed," *Human Rights Watch*, April 27, 2021, https://www.hrw.org/report/2021/04/27/threshold-crossed/israeli-authorities-and-crimes-apartheid-and-persecution; "Israel's Apartheid Against Palestinians," Amnesty International, February 1, 2022, https://www.amnesty.org/en/documents/mde15/5141/2022/en/.

15. Jimmy Carter, *Israel: Peace, Not Apartheid* (New York: Simon & Schuster, 2006).

16. Nathan Brown, "The Powerful Strategic Logic of a Hazy Mentality with Sharp Edges," in POMEPS STUDIES 41 *Israel/Palestine: Exploring a One State Reality* (2020): 37–42.

17. "A regime of Jewish supremacy from the Jordan River to the Mediterranean Sea: This Is Apartheid," *B'Tselem*, January 12, 2021, https://www.btselem.org/publications/fulltext/202101_this_is_apartheid.

18. Noura Erakat, *Justice for Some: Law and the Question of Palestine* (Palo Alto, CA: Stanford University Press, 2019).

19. Ilana Feldman, "Reframing Palestine: BDS against Fragmentation and Exceptionalism," *Radical History Review* 134 (2019): 193–202.

20. For one exception, see Ronnie Olesker, "The Securitisation Dilemma: Legitimacy in Securitisation Studies," *Critical Studies on Security* 6, no.2 (2018): 312–329.

21. Sean McMahon, "The Boycott, Divestment, Sanctions Campaign: Contradictions and Challenges." *Race and Class* 55 (2014): 55–80.

22. William Clare Roberts and C. Heike Schotten, eds., "Critical Exchange: Boycott, Divestment and Sanctions (BDS) and Political Theory," *Contemporary Political Theory* 18 (2019): 448–476.

23. Joshua Freedman, "The Recognition Dilemma: Negotiating Identity in the Israeli-Palestinian Conflict," *International Studies Quarterly* (2021): 1–14; for an example, see Lev Topor, "The Covert War: From BDS to De-legitimization to Anti-Semitism," *Israel Affairs* 27, no.1 (2021): 166–180.

24. Michael Barnett, *Dialogues in Arab Politics: Negotiations in Regional Order*, New York: Columbia University Press, 1998.

25. Jonathan Rynhold, "Winning the BDS Battle," BESA Center Perspectives Paper No. 231, January 2014.

26. Amro Sadeldeen, "The Emergence of the BDS Movement through an Israeli Mirror," *Radical History Review* 134 (2019): 203–219.

27. Feldman, "Reframing Palestine."

28. Amit Efrati, "Who's Afraid of BDS? Economic and Academic Boycotts and the Threat to Israel," *Strategic Assessment* 19, no.4 (2017): 43–56.

29. Abigail B. Bakan and Yasmeen Abu Laban, "Palestinian Resistance and International Solidarity: The BDS Campaign," *Race and Class* 51 (2009): 29–54; Marc Lynch, "Political Science after Gaza," *Washington Post Monkey Cage*, July 29, 2014, https://www.washingtonpost.com/news/monkey- cage/wp/2014/07/29/political-science-after-gaza/.

30. Susie Gelman and David A. Halperin, "Can Biden Resolve the Israeli and Palestinian Conflict," *Times of Israel*, February 24, 2021, https://www.timesofisrael.com/can-biden-resolve-the-israeli-and-palestinian-conflict/.

31. Martin Kramer, "Israel and the Post-American Middle East: Why the Status Quo Is Sustainable" *Foreign Affairs* 95, no. (2016): 51–56.

32. Ilan Goldenberg, Michael Koplow and Tamara Wittes. A *New U.S. Strategy for the Israeli-Palestinian Conflict* (Washington, DC: Center for a New American Security, December 2019), https://www.cnas.org/publications/reports/a-new-u-s-strategy-for-the-israeli-palestinian-conflict.

33. Charli Carpenter, "'You Talk of Terrible Things So Matter-of-Factly in the Language of Science': Constructing Human Rights in the Academy," *Perspectives on Politics* 10, no. 2 (2012): 363–383.

34. Richard M Price, ed., *Moral Limit and Possibility in International Relations* (New York: Cambridge University Press, 2008).

35. For example, the Middle East Scholar Barometer poll conducted in February 2021, which is led by Marc Lynch and Shibley Telhami, showed that 77% of scholars concluded that if a two state outcome is no longer possible, the outcome would be a one state reality akin to apartheid; only 1% said that it would be a single state with equality. Shibley Telhami and Marc Lynch, Middle East Scholar Barometer (February 8–15, 2021), https://criticalissues.umd.edu/sites/criticalissues.umd.edu/files/Middle%20East%20Scholar%20Barometer%20Questionnaire.pdf.

36. For a good example of such work, see Joseph E Yi and Joe Phillips, "The BDS Campaign against Israel: Lessons from South Africa," *PS: Political Science and Politics* 48, no. 2 (2015): 306–310.

Contributors

Muriel Asseburg is Senior Fellow in the Africa and Middle East division at Stiftung Wissenshaft und Politik German Institute for International and Security Affairs. Her focus is on the Arab-Israeli conflict and European and US policies toward the region.

Michael Barnett is the University Professor of International Affairs and Political Science at George Washington University. His research is focused on the Middle East, humanitarianism, global governance, global ethics, and the United Nation. He is author of numerous books, including *Empire of Humanity: A History of Humanitarianism.*

Yael Berda is Assistant Professor of Sociology and Anthropology at the Hebrew University of Jerusalem, where her research is focused on the intersections of law, race, bureaucracy and the state, within a colonial and imperial context. Her most recent book is *Living Emergency: Israel's Permit Regime in the Occupied West Bank.*

Nathan Brown is Professor of Political Science and International Affairs at George Washington University where his research is focused on constitutionalism, comparative judicial politics, and Middle Eastern politics; specifically, religion and politics, authoritarianism. His most recent book is *Arguing Islam after the Revival of Arab Politics.*

Tamara Cofman Wittes is currently on leave from her position as Senior Fellow in the Center for Middle East Policy at Brookings Institution to serve a role in the Biden administration. Her work focuses on US policy in the Middle East, and she is the author of *Freedom's Unsteady March: America's Role in Building Arab Democracy.* Note: The views expressed in this article do not necessarily represent the views of the United States government.

Iman Elbanna is a manager of intelligence and analysis with Emergent Risk International. She recently completed her master's degree at George Washington University.

Khaled Elgindy is Senior Fellow at the Middle East Institute where he directs the Program on Palestine and Israeli-Palestinian Affairs. He is the author of *Blind Spot: America and the Palestinians, from Balfour to Trump.*

Lara Friedman is the president of the Foundation for Middle East Peace and a leading authority on US foreign policy in the Middle East, focusing on the Israeli-Arab conflict, Israeli settlements, Jerusalem, and the role of the US Congress. She is also a contributing writer at *Jewish Currents.*

As'ad Ghanem is a Senior Lecturer at the School of Political Science of the University of Haifa. His research focuses on the legal, institutional, and political conditions in ethnic states, where he has covered issues such as the Palestinian political orientation, the establishment and political structure of the Palestinian Authority, and majority-minority politics in a comparative perspective. He coauthored *Israel in the Post Oslo Era: Prospects for Conflict and Reconciliation with the Palestinians.*

Diana B. Greenwald is Assistant Professor in the Department of Political Science at the City College of New York where she researches Middle East politics, nationalism, conflict, and state-building. Her current book project researches how the Israeli West Bank annexation shapes Palestinian local politics.

Kevin Huggard is a senior research assistant with the Center for Middle East Policy at the Brookings Institution in Washington, DC, where he focuses on Israel and the Middle East.

Ian Lustick is Professor of Political Science and the Bess W. Heyman Chair and Professor of the University of Pennsylvania, where he researches Middle Eastern politics, comparative politics, and computer modeling. His most recent book is *Paradigm Lost: From Two-State Solution to One-State Reality.*

Marc Lynch is Professor of Political Science and International Affairs and Director of the Project on Middle East Political Science (POMEPS). His research is focused on Middle East politics, Arab media and public opinion, Islamist movements, and public diplomacy. His most recent book is *The New Arab Wars: Uprisings and Anarchy in the Middle East.*

Yousef Munayyer is Non-resident Senior Fellow at the Arab Center in Washington, DC, where he writes on the Arab-Israeli conflict. He serves as a member of the editorial committee of the *Journal of Palestine Studies* and is the former executive director of the US Campaign for Palestinian Rights.

Mohanad Mustafa is the Director of Research Programs at the Arab Center for Applied Social Studies in Haifa. His research is focused on Palestinian and Israeli politics, Islamic political thoughts, democratic transformation, and Arab political systems. He coauthored *Israel in the Post Oslo Era: Prospects for Conflict and Reconciliation with the Palestinians.*

Omar H. Rahman is a writer and analyst. He was formerly a visiting fellow at the Brookings Institution in Washington, DC, where he focused on the Middle East and US foreign policy.

Dahlia Scheindlin is a fellow at Century International in Tel Aviv where she researches Israeli politics. She also conducts public opinion and policy research on the Israeli-Palestinian conflict and peace process.

Gershon Shafir is Distinguished Professor in the Department of Sociology at the University of California, San Diego, where he researches comparative and historical sociology, focusing on nationalism, ethnicity, citizenship, and human rights. He is the coauthor of *Being Israeli: The Dynamics of Multiple Citizenships.*

Nadav G. Shelef is Professor of Political Science and the Harvey M. Meyerhoff Professor of Modern Israel Studies at the University of Wisconsin-Madison, where his research is focused on nationalism, territorial conflict, religion and politics, and Israeli politics and society. His most recent book is *Homelands: Shifting Borders and Territorial Disputes.*

Shibley Telhami is the Anwar Sadat Professor for Peace and Development, Distinguished Scholar-Teacher, and the Director of the University of Maryland Critical Issues Poll. His research is focused on Political Identity, US and Arab Public Opinion, and Middle East politics. His most recent book is *The World Through Arab Eyes: Arab Public Opinion and the Reshaping of the Middle East.*

Index

Note: Surnames starting with "al-" are alphabetized by remaining portion of name. Figures and notes are indicated by *f* and n following the page number.

Ingram Content Group UK Ltd.
Milton Keynes UK
UKHW041819190323
418703UK00003BA/99

9 781501 768392